RELIGIOUS AND SECULAR FORCES
IN LATE TSARIST RUSSIA

Religious and Secular Forces in Late Tsarist Russia

Essays in Honor of Donald W. Treadgold

Edited by Charles E. Timberlake

UNIVERSITY OF WASHINGTON PRESS

Seattle and London

Library of Congress Cataloging-in-Publication Data

    Religious and secular forces in late Tsarist Russia / edited by Charles
    E. Timberlake
    p. cm.
    Includes bibliographical references and index.
    ISBN 0-295-97198-3 (alk. paper)
    1. Church and state--Soviet Union--History. 2. Soviet Union--Church
history. 3. Secularism--Soviet Union--History. I. Timberlake, Charles E.
BR935.5.R45 1992
322'.1'094709034--dc20   91-44276
                                                            CIP

To Donald W. Treadgold

An earlier version of this collection was presented to
Don Treadgold on his sixty-fifth birthday in November
1987. To him as honored teacher, esteemed colleague, and
trusted friend, this book is respectfully dedicated.

CONTENTS

Contents   viii

ACKNOWLEDGMENTS

The editor wishes to recognize several persons and institutions that have contributed in major ways to giving this volume whatever praiseworthy qualities it has.

At the University of Missouri, the University Research Council was as generous as its limited resources would allow to provide the clerical and technical personnel who helped prepare this volume. The History Department made available its equipment and, on occasion, clerical assistance. I express gratitude to Marie Sloan for making those arrangements, to Patty Eggleston for the word processing, and to Marilyn Keil for assistance in solving a barrage of technical problems involved in merging various word-processing systems and diskettes of various sizes into one machine-readable form.

At the University of Manchester, where I taught for one of the years during this volume's preparation, Julie Hutton and John Urbansky of the University Computer Center's Microprocessor Unit and Terry Hewitt, Director of the Computer Center's Computer Graphics Unit, assisted me in teaching American and British computers, printers, and software how to speak the same form of English. I am extremely grateful for their help.

In assisting me with final printing of this volume to produce camera-ready copy, Marla Germann, of the University of Missouri's Campus Computing, proved to be super demystifyer of all things related to Word Perfect and laser printers. I am not only grateful to her; I am awed.

Naomi Pascal and Leila Charbonneau of the University of Washington Press have patiently rendered valuable advice on the format and other features of the volume. It has been especially gratifying, poetic justice personified, to have Leila Charbonneau serve as copyeditor of this volume dedicated to Don Treadgold, for she and he had an excellent working relationship as editor and associate editor of the *Slavic Review* when many of the contributors to this volume knew them both in Seattle in the 1960s and 1970s.

I profited much and often by advice from my fellow contributors to this volume, and I express my appreciation to them for their tolerance of my tampering with their manuscripts, especially to William James and Thomas

Sorenson for allowing me to cut, paste, and rework various sections of their dissertations to form them into essays. Robert Nichols and Nicholas Riasanovsky saved me from several silly mistakes by their careful reading of my introduction, but they should not be held responsible for ones that remain.

Daniel Schlafly, Jr., of St. Louis University, and my colleague Russell Zguta at the University of Missouri in Columbia also steered me in the right direction several times when I had veered off course.

I owe such a deep debt of gratitude to Ralph Fisher, Jr., of the University of Illinois, for help he has given me with this volume and with so much else that I cannot begin to write it all down. I am comforted in my inability to express it in writing only by the knowledge that he is aware of my deep respect and gratitude. At my request, he shared most generously his records and recollections of the early days of Slavic studies in the United States that helped me edit this volume in ways impossible without his kindness. He was my frequent consultant, and made numerous excellent suggestions that helped me give the very difficult introductory essay whatever strengths it has.

Along with all of the late Joe Schiebel's friends, I am indebted to Gary Ulmen for the pains he took to render so accurately and clearly the argumentation that Joe, our former fellow University of Washington classmate, developed in his dissertation.

To my patient wife and partner, Pat, who often found two or more of these essays surprise traveling companions, on British Rail, in ski condos, and even at intermissions at the theater in London, I once again--inadequately--attempt to express my respect and gratitude.

Charles Timberlake
Columbia, Missouri
May 18, 1992

RELIGIOUS AND SECULAR FORCES
IN LATE TSARIST RUSSIA

CHAPTER 1

INTRODUCTION:
RELIGIOUS PLURALISM,
THE SPREAD OF REVOLUTIONARY IDEAS,
AND THE CHURCH-STATE RELATIONSHIP IN TSARIST RUSSIA

Charles E. Timberlake

The fourth conference of Russian Orthodox missionaries held in Kiev in 1908 tried to comprehend the success of socialism in Holy Russia, and to devise measures to combat it. Missionary Ioann Vostorgov attributed socialism's popularity to "the failure of Christianity to make its presence felt in our mutual relationships" and to the "imperfections of our social life as exemplified by pauperism and the more extreme forms of capitalism." What action should be taken to combat socialism? The missionaries, like religious and civil bureaucrats before them, immediately assumed that the educational institutions could solve the problem. Into the curriculum of the four Russian Orthodox ecclesiastical academies and the fifty-five seminaries, the Russian Orthodox Church's national governing body, the Holy Synod, introduced a special course, "The History and Unmasking of Socialism." The course analyzed the writings of West European socialist writers, but did not mention Russian writers or the Russian Social Democrats.[1]

Throughout the nineteenth century, the tsarist government accepted the contention that ideas are disseminated, and combated, most efficaciously by educational institutions. Knowing that the Russian Empire must have modern universities to develop science and a material culture to make Russia competitive with the other major nations of Europe and Asia, Alexander I (1801-25) created a school system in 1802 that added three new universities and, as gradually implemented with modification during the nineteenth century, created gymnasiums and lower schools in each educational district. In the western borderlands acquired in the eighteenth century, and to which he added Finland (1809) and Poland (1815), he also promoted school systems from elementary level through universities.

3

While Alexander I's successors understood the necessity of an educational system to create and disseminate scientific and technical knowledge, they discovered that educational networks could also serve as conduits for religious and secular values that might threaten the time-honored bulwark of Russian society: the twin monopolies on politics and religion held by the autocracy and the Russian Orthodox Church. In annexed areas with non-Orthodox populations, schools served as custodians and disseminators of Roman Catholic, Protestant, and Muslim values within the Russian Empire. The insurrections in Poland and Lithuania in 1830 and 1863 combined Catholicism, local control over educational institutions, and autonomy for ethnic minorities as an evil brew in the minds of St. Petersburg bureaucrats, and they began serious efforts to subject all three to greater control by the tsarist central government and the Russian Orthodox Church. Having devised the policy (discussed later in this essay) for the Catholic portion of the empire, the government and church bureaucracies applied it as well to the Protestants in the Baltic provinces of Estonia and Latvia. Later they would devise a special policy for the Muslim areas.

Just as educational institutions in Poland and Lithuania served as centers for opposition to autocracy and Russian Orthodoxy, so did the educational institutions created in the Great Russian territorial core of the empire. Beginning in the 1840s, when graduate students trained at Russian government expense in German and French universities returned to Russia to become professors in Russian universities, their heads and notebooks filled with the ideas of Western thinkers, Russian universities became vehicles that transformed the lives of many teachers and students. Especially in the 1860s and 1870s, when the government used the university medical schools to increase the corps of doctors, young students from the villages, educated in the Orthodox seminaries or by tutors at home, came to the university to study medicine. Having discovered philosophy, many ceased attending medical classes and became full-time proselytizers for their newly found secular, often atheist, causes.[2] Thus the Catholic and Protestant challenge from the non-Orthodox western borderlands had a secular counterpart inside Great Russia itself. Educational institutions were the organizing centers for the opposition in both instances.

The essays that form this volume focus on the challenges that religious pluralism and secular and revolutionary ideas presented for the twin monopolies of autocracy and Russian Orthodoxy. These essays also illuminate the centrality of educational institutions in those challenges, and explain the way church and state bureaucracies responded in the nineteenth and early twentieth centuries. The essay by David Goldfrank, although it analyzes events two centuries before the period that is the focus of this book, uses the inquisitions of medieval Russia to illustrate the nature of the church-state alliance at its apex in the mid-sixteenth century. The state, as God's "secular arm" on earth, used its police powers to punish all, inside or outside the Russian Orthodox Church, who opposed interpretations issued by the chief church hierarchs. In return, the church branded the tsar's political critics as religious heretics.

Professor Goldfrank's essay also reveals quite poignantly the possibilities for one faction, during a struggle among church officials, to invoke state authority against its opponents. Conversely, during a struggle among political officials, one faction could sometimes invoke church authority as a foil against the opposing political faction.

In the eighteenth century, the state's power increased dramatically at the expense of the church's. During his reign (1682-1725) Peter I abolished the position of Patriarch of the Russian Orthodox Church, and in 1722 placed the Russian Orthodox Church under control of an appointed committee of laymen (the Holy Synod) that was to manage all its affairs. It made decisions on such critical matters as content of required courses on Russian Orthodox religious doctrine, and it approved all textbooks to be used in such courses. The Holy Synod was chaired by a layman, the "over-procurator," who was to serve as the sovereign's "eyes" in the synod. Perhaps it would be too extreme to say that Peter I was antireligious, but he certainly seems to have been anticlerical. He ridiculed the clergy by creating "The Most Drunken Synod of Fools and Jesters," whose elaborate rituals were presided over by a mock pope that Peter appointed. The activities of this group consisted primarily of long, ribald drunken parties.[3]

Later in the century, Catherine II's secularization of church landholdings was a further blow to the wealth and power of the Russian Orthodox Church. In the nineteenth century, the state increasingly used the office of over-procurator to gain control of the Holy Synod and, through it, utilize the Russian Orthodox Church as an instrument for achieving its own political objectives, often at the expense of the interests of the Church itself.[4]

Despite the increasing imbalance of power and influence in favor of the state, both parties in the church-state alliance still adhered to the basic tenet of the alliance in 1800: each would protect the other's monopoly against outside challengers. The church would defend autocracy and rail against other political systems; the autocracy would finance the Russian Orthodox Church and use its powers to prevent the rise of any serious competitor in the spiritual realm.

Two major changes perpetrated by the government in the eighteenth and nineteenth centuries introduced secular and religious forces that would eventually play significant roles in abolishing the traditional political and religious monopolies. The first was the extensive territorial expansion that occurred especially rapidly in the late eighteenth century under Catherine the Great (1762-96) and during the first eight decades of the nineteenth century.

The second was the creation of higher educational institutions that served as magnets attracting provincial youth to Russia's major cities, where they encountered foreign ideas that challenged the fundamental values of the political-religious culture that had nurtured them. When the government decided to stimulate rapid industrialization in the mid-1880s, it opened new higher special institutes and expanded enrollments at existing institutes and universities to train the specialists that industrialization required. As new schools opened in the borderlands, or existing schools were reorganized in the last half of the century, the Russian-dominated central government contested with ethnic leaders on the periphery of the empire for control of the curriculum to determine the religious and political values the schools would transmit while teaching technical skills. In the interior of Great Russia, the tsarist government contested with liberal humanists and revolutionary agnostics or atheists for control of schools to ensure that Russian Orthodox explanations would prevail. In the heavy-handed manner that it imposed itself on the ethnic minorities, the government made Protestant and Catholic believers into opponents of autocracy, and in the same heavy-handed approach it took toward the zemstvos, city dumas, and other nongovernment founders of schools, the tsarist government made opponents of autocracy into opponents of the privileged, but politically subservient, position of the Russian Orthodox Church.

By 1880 the thousands of square miles of territory the Russians conquered and annexed in the eighteenth and nineteenth centuries, containing a conglomeration of non-Russian peoples, constituted a broad territorial band attached by various glues and devices to the original core territorial home of the Great Russians. While the heartland of Great Russia was never ethnically homogeneous, its expanded version as the Russian Empire was an enormously heterogeneous array of ethnic groups speaking more than a hundred languages, embodying scores of cultures, and having various religious faiths. A church that strove to embrace all inhabitants of the state, in the sense of the sixteenth-century church that Professor Goldfrank's essay illuminates, was impossible. Even though the state could retain a *protected* and *privileged* church, it could not preserve a *monopoly* church in such diverse conditions. To attempt it would provoke rebellion among recently conquered peoples and provide a pretext for Russia's rivals to intervene in defense of repressed co-religionists.

In the sixteenth century, the conquest and annexation of Siberia added millions of pagans and a small number of Muslims to the empire, but they did not constitute a spiritual or political challenge to autocracy or Orthodoxy. The first major groups of non-Russian-Orthodox believers annexed to the Russian Empire, who posed a threat to the Russian church-state relationship, were Lutherans (when Latvia and Estonia were acquired by the Treaty of Nystad in 1721), Jews, and Catholics (Roman Catholics and Uniat Catholics) when Russia acquired Lithuania (including Belorussia) during the third partition of Poland in 1795.[5] Among the Catholics of Belorussia was a group of Jesuits operating various colleges and an academy at Polotsk.[6] Roman Catholics and Lutherans were also present in considerable numbers among the German colonists who migrated from Germany to southern European Russia at the end of the eighteenth century. The numbers of Lutherans in the empire increased dramatically in 1809 when Finland was incorporated into the Russian Empire as a Grand

Principality (or Grand Duchy), with the Russian emperor taking the title Grand Prince of Finland and promising to protect the religion of his Lutheran subjects. The number of Roman Catholics in the empire increased in 1815 when various sections of Poland were consolidated under Russian rule as the Kingdom of Poland, with the tsar taking the title King of Poland. Tsar Alexander I assured religious autonomy to the Catholics of Poland in the constitution he granted them in 1815, but he was mute on such promises for his Catholic subjects in Lithuania.

Annexation of Armenia in the first half of the nineteenth century added Christians of still another rite: the adherents of the Armenian Apostolic Church. Annexation of the Crimean Peninsula (1778-83) and vast stretches of the central Asian deserts in the 1860s and 1870s, with their oases governed by independent spiritual-political khans, added hundreds of thousands of Muslims to the Russian emperor's subjects.[7]

Traditionally, soon after acquisition of new territory the tsar informed his new subjects about their status in the empire. Since religious values and practices were a part of the ethnic and national identity of his newly acquired subjects, the tsar's religious policy was tightly bound, though not completely identical, to his nationality policy. Essentially, the tsarist government's religious policy perceived the empire's inhabitants as two groups--Orthodox believers, including a sizable Ukrainian population in addition to the Great Russians, and all others, or non-Orthodox. This concept was, in many ways, the religious parallel of the political-ethnic concept that guided the tsarist government's nationality policy: the empire was composed of two basic groups: Russians (Great Russians, Ukrainians ["Little Russians," as the tsarist government persisted in calling them], and Belorussians), virtually all of whom were Orthodox. The second group were "outsiders," or non-Russians who lived on the periphery of the core territory. Virtually all of them were non-Orthodox. The tsarist government began to perceive acute cultural and ethnic differentiation among Russians, Ukrainians, and Belorussians only at the end of the nineteenth century.

The general category of outsiders was subdivided into several geopolitical-ethnic units such as Poland, Finland, Estonia, and Georgia, depending on the position the tsar had assigned to that subgroup after it was annexed to the empire. In addition to such specific subdivisions as Poles or

Finns, the tsarist government also classified some residents of the empire as "members of other tribes" (*inorodtsy*), which scholars usually translate simply as "others." Initially, the term meant "all tribes other than Slavs." As time passed and other ethnic groups were given specific statuses within the empire, the term came to describe a miscellaneous category of ethnic groups, including nomadic tribesmen, Gypsies, and Jews given no other specific legal status.[8] The difference between religious and nationality policy was that a Pole or Finn remained ethnically a Pole or Finn, and never became a Great Russian; but a Roman Catholic Pole or Lutheran Finn could abandon the outsider religious category by converting to Russian Orthodoxy. A person having done so was forbidden by law to reconvert to the original religion.

Where the tsarist government gave the administrator of the Russian Orthodox Church (the over-procurator of the Holy Synod) ministerial status and allowed him to participate in meetings of the Committee of Ministers, it administered all other faiths through a Directorate of Foreign Confessions. This agency functioned as a separate government agency from 1824 to 1832, at which time it became an agency within the Ministry of the Interior. As ethnic groups constituted separate units for purposes of nationality policy, so each religious faith practiced by one or more ethnic minorities (Catholic, Muslim, etc.) was assigned to a subgroup within the Directorate of Foreign Confessions.[9] This arrangement allowed the emperor (king, grand prince) to maintain two separate systems to provide for the spiritual and material welfare of his subjects. As Russian emperor, he would continue to be defender of the privileged position of the Russian Orthodox faith, the official religion of the empire. As sovereign over non-Russian "others" (those who were not Russian Orthodox believers), he would provide for his subjects' spiritual needs, including creating educational institutions to train clergy to perform their religious services. But he did not feel compelled to grant them *all* the privileges he granted the Russian Orthodox Church.

To the very end of tsardom, the Russian Orthodox Church enjoyed greater legal privileges than any non-Orthodox religious group.[10] According to the Fundamental Laws of the Russian Empire, the Russian Orthodox Church was "the foremost and dominant faith in the Russian

Empire." It alone had the right to proselytize within the empire, and no person converted to Orthodoxy was allowed to reconvert. Any non-Orthodox clergyman performing Communion for a former member of his flock who attempted to reconvert, or for any other person of Orthodox faith or born into an Orthodox family, was committing a "crime against Orthodoxy" punishable by confiscation of property, imprisonment, or even exile to Siberia.[11]

Furthermore, the state established the course, "The Law of God" (*Zakon Bozhii*), which was controlled by the Holy Synod, as a requirement in every student's program of studies for every year in school, from elementary school through university, with the exception of students in the non-Orthodox dioceses of the empire. This course included study of the Russian Orthodox Holy Scriptures, the lives of saints, the catechism, and church singing.[12] In non-Orthodox dioceses, religious instruction in the faith that was predominant in the diocese was allowed for non-Orthodox living there, but was increasingly restricted by legislation in the last half of the century. Russian Orthodox believers living in a non-Orthodox diocese were not allowed to receive religious instruction or participate in any religious service other than Russian Orthodoxy. In the last half of the nineteenth century, the Orthodox Church began to construct imposing cathedrals in the most prominent parts of the capital cities of the western provinces, Poland, and Finland to provide services for Russian Orthodox believers and converts.

The state appropriated funds to support religious instruction in all religions within the empire. The Russian Orthodox Church received a disproportionately large sum, even considering that it had the largest number of members in the empire (some 70 percent of the total population by 1904, with approximately the same percentage of the population of the empire ethnically Great Russian, Ukrainian, and Belorussian). Despite significant increases in funding (it had increased to 53.9 million rubles in 1914), the total appropriation for the church never exceeded 2 percent of the total state budget for any year.[13]

State and police organs supported the Russian Orthodox Church in ways other than financial subsidies and protection of their monopoly on proselytizing. State and police were also obligated by law to prosecute all persons who attacked, or whom the police or clergy *suspected* of attacking, the Orthodox Church "by word or by deed." Of course, the church was also dependent on the secular power to prosecute church members who renounced the Orthodox Church to convert to another religion, or to join one of the sects created by former Russian Orthodox members.

The tsar and immediate heir to the throne, and their wives, were required by law to be members of the Orthodox Church. Protestants who married into the Romanov family were not required to convert to Orthodoxy, although many did. Only the wives of the emperor and immediate heir to the throne were forced to convert. Should they refuse, the male Romanovs would have been barred from succession to the throne. By law, the emperor was "the supreme defender and preserver of the dogmas of the ruling faith, and protector of the purity of belief and the decorum in the holy Church."[14]

In exchange for the state's role as defender and nurturer of the church's monopoly, the church aided the state by anointing the new monarch in Uspenskii Cathedral as "the Divinely anointed" ruler, preserving to the eve of the twentieth century, with Nicholas II's coronation in 1894, the ancient notion of the divine right of kings to rule over all the inhabitants of their kingdom. At the coronation, the church hierarchs also administered an oath to the entire Orthodox population that included the admonition that the population had an obligation to inform the authorities of anything that might be "of detriment, harm, or damage to the interests of His Imperial Majesty." Priests were to inform police of any dangers to autocracy that they might discover, even during confessional. And the churches were to serve as a communications network for the tsar and his government by proclaiming decrees and statutes during religious service.[15]

In 1800 the Russian Orthodox Church already had a set of educational institutions to train clergy. During the remainder of the century, the tsarist government created or maintained existing ecclesiastical institutions in annexed territories to train clergy for four additional groups of his subjects: Roman Catholic, Protestant (Evangelical Lutheran), Armenian, and Muslim. At the beginning of the nineteenth century, Russian Orthodox educational institutions were divided into four official types: (1) the ecclesiastical academies, which were "higher" educational institutions intended primarily to train the higher clergy and teachers for the Orthodox educational institutions; (2) seminaries, which were "middle" educational institutions intended primarily to train future priests and provide students for the ecclesiastical academies; (3) county (*uezd*) institutions, which were primarily to prepare people for family life; and (4) village schools, which were to teach practical lessons for life in the village. In practice, the "county" schools were merged with the village schools so that only three types functioned. Each of the ecclesiastical academies was in charge of one of the four spiritual-educational districts into which the empire was divided. Each ecclesiastical academy managed the seminaries; the seminary administration, in turn, managed the educational institutions in the educational-spiritual district. Each diocese could contain one seminary, up to ten county schools, and thirty village, or parish (*prikhodskie*), schools.[16]

In 1800 four Russian Orthodox academies existed in the Russian Empire, one each in St. Petersburg, Moscow, Kiev, and Kazan. The Kazan and St. Petersburg academies had been founded in the early eighteenth century; those at Moscow and Kiev originated still earlier, in the seventeenth century; and the one at Kiev, the oldest in the empire, had been established in 1615 and existed from 1631 to 1701 as Kievo-Mogilianskaia kollegiia (Kiev-Mogila College).[17] By 1890 the Russian Orthodox Church maintained the same four ecclesiastical academies, fifty-five seminaries, and 185 church schools.[18]

The educational institutions created for the non-Orthodox population began in a period of toleration under Alexander I, using native languages of the region to provide instruction in the region's dominant religion. But the Russian state and church soon began a coordinated effort to restrict teaching about religion in native languages and to expand Russian Orthodox Church institutions into these non-Russian areas. In the 1830s and 1840s, the state replaced local teachers with Russian teachers in higher educational institutions (closing them down temporarily, if necessary, while the change was being made). Simultaneously, the Russian Orthodox Church created a set of competing bishoprics and built cathedrals in the region to proselytize among the local religion. The final stage of this process came during intense Russification in the period from the 1880s to 1905, when all instruction in all schools and universities, except in Finland, was conducted in Russian. The only other exception was for children in the primary grades, who were allowed to receive religious instruction in their native language.

Educational institutions serving the tsar's Roman Catholic subjects reflect the fate of Roman Catholicism in Lithuania, Belorussia, and Poland. The institutions began in a period of toleration during the reign of Paul I and his son Alexander I, but suffered restrictions and repression after the Polish-Lithuanian insurrections of 1830 and 1863, and during Russification under Alexander III and Nicholas II. William James's essay in this volume presents a detailed analysis of the work of the Jesuits in creating schools among the Catholics in the territory of the former Grand Principality of Lithuania (now mostly in Belorussia) and of Paul I's support of that work. Where Paul's mother, Catherine II, had tried to restrict the Jesuits' activities to the Catholic population of Belorussia, Paul encouraged and aided them to open schools in St. Petersburg and other Russian cities. After Paul's death, Alexander I initially allowed the Jesuits to continue their work, but was not their advocate as Paul had been. Alexander I, despite his initial toleration of Jesuits and his promise in 1815 to respect Catholicism as the national religion of Poland, had come by 1820 to consider toleration of Roman Catholicism and Protestant pietism a means of opening Russia to an influx of politically liberal and revolutionary ideas from the West. In 1820, after several high aristocratic families had converted to Catholicism, he expelled the Jesuits from the Russian Empire in March, and in 1824 replaced Over-Procurator A. N. Golitsyn whose "new Christianity" had opened Russia's doors wide to the ideas of Protestant pietism.[19]

In 1803 Alexander created separate school systems and universities for Lithuanian Catholics and Polish Catholics. In doing so, he was continuing the policy initiated by his grandmother, Catherine II, of retaining Lithuania separate from Poland, with which it was united when the two passed into Russian hands during the partition of 1795. In Lithuania, Alexander transformed the Main School into Vilna University in 1803. Among its four divisions was the Faculty of Moral-Political Sciences, which was closely linked to the Main Vilna Seminary after the latter's founding in 1808. These two institutions served as centers for Catholic learning in Lithuania.

When Alexander granted Poland a constitution in 1815, he did not extend any of its privileges to Lithuania.

Students at Vilna University soon formed societies advocating reunification with Poland, and in 1830-31 supported the Polish insurrection against Russian rule. In response, the tsarist government closed Vilna University on May 1, 1832. The following year, the tsarist government combined the former Faculty of Moral-Political Sciences and the Main Vilna Seminary to create the Roman Catholic Ecclesiastical Academy in Vilna. In 1842, the tsar moved the academy to St. Petersburg, and from 1847 onward, after an agreement between Rome and the tsarist government, all Catholic seminaries in the Russian Empire were placed under the academy's control, the emperor provided it with an annual budget, and added the word "Imperial" to its title, to correspond to the title of Russian Orthodox academies. The Roman Catholic academy was under the jurisdiction of the metropolitan of Mogilev, who chose its rector from a list presented to him by the academy's administrative council.[20]

In Poland Alexander I founded a royal university in Warsaw, September 20, 1817, with instruction in Polish and with a department of theology to prepare clergy for his Roman Catholic subjects in the Kingdom of Poland. In 1830, the university council voted to change its name to Alexander University, but the insurrection later that year resulted in the university's closure. From 1830 to November 25, 1862, when the Warsaw Main School opened, Poland had no higher educational institution resembling a university. During this period, the Roman Catholic Academy in Warsaw served as the center of Catholic learning and the institution training clergy for the Catholic Church in Poland. In 1843 the tsarist government secularized the land belonging to the Catholic Church in Poland.[21] As reprisal for the Polish insurrection of 1863, the tsarist government closed the Roman Catholic Academy in 1867, and designated the St. Petersburg Roman Catholic Ecclesiastical Academy as the ecclesiastical academy to which all students graduating from seminaries in the Kingdom of Poland should apply for higher theological training. As a part of the agreement with Rome that established that arrangement, the academy's management passed exclusively into the hands of the metropolitan of Mogilev.[22] Because the Lithuanians supported the Polish insurrection again in 1863, Russian officials reorganized the school system to expunge all possible Polish and Roman Catholic influences, and applied other pressures for peasants to convert from Catholicism to Orthodoxy. Yet they did not totally remove Catholic influences from schools, in that the tsarist government allowed classes in religious instruction in primary schools to be taught in the local language, even as late as 1885 when it required that instruction in all other subjects be done only by Russian teachers using the Russian language.[23] From 1867 onward, any student applying to enter the Roman Catholic Ecclesiastical Academy in St. Petersburg had to obtain permission from the governor of the province in which the applicant resided.[24] When the Russian government reopened a university in Warsaw under the title Imperial Warsaw University on October 12, 1867, the university had no department of theology.[25]

In the period 1830-63, the lull between the two Polish-Lithuanian insurrections, Westerners and Slavophiles debated in Moscow and St. Petersburg the significance of Catholicism and Orthodoxy for Western and Russian cultures. The case that Petr Chaadaev made for the superiority of the Catholic culture of Western Europe over Russian culture is well celebrated in the literature on the period. Less well known, but contemporary with Chaadaev and sharing his admiration of Catholic culture, was Prince P. B. Kozlovskii, a Russian Catholic critic of Russian state and society. The essay by John McErlean in this volume is the first detailed study in English of the nature of Kozlovskii's dislikes of Russia and the similarity of his and Chaadaev's analyses of Catholic cultures. The similarity allows us to see that Chaadaev's was not a singular, lone Russian voice in the 1830s condemning Russian Orthodox culture and praising Western, Catholic culture. In that Kozlovskii was the person who informed the Marquis de Custine at length about the nature of Russian society, and the Marquis published his travel account (*Russia in 1839)*, upon returning to France, Kozlovskii indirectly contributed still another negative comparison of Orthodox Russia to the Catholic West during the Westernizer-Slavophile debate of the 1830s to 1840s.

It is against the background of two insurrections in Catholic Poland and Catholic Lithuania; the Westerner-Slavophile debates of the 1840s; and the negative comparisons by Chaadaev, Kozlovskii, and Custine that we should view the activities of those professors in the four Orthodox ecclesiastical academies who looked with relish at the rupture in the Roman Catholic Church and the emergence of the "Old Catholics." John Basil's essay in this volume probes their hopes that a segment of the Western Church might reunite with the Russian Orthodox Church, and traces the professors' pursuit of the Old Catholics at conferences in Holland and through other means during the 1870s. But, as Basil concluded, the Old Catholics' differences with the Orthodox proved as great as with their disputants in the Western Catholic Church, and the question of possible reunification of the churches remained open for later Russian scholars of religion, such as the distinguished Vladimir Soloviev, to contemplate two decades later.

Although Lutherans presented the Orthodox no challenge similar to that of the Roman Catholics, the tsarist government's policy toward them followed the same pattern. The government provided educational training for the Protestant clergy (limited to Evangelical Lutherans) in the schools of theology in Dorpat University (renamed Iur'ev University in December 1893) and Helsinki University, located in regions solidly Lutheran. Before 1893, instruction at Dorpat University was in German (as were church services in Latvia), while at Helsinki University the instruction was in Swedish and Finnish, and Finnish church services were in Swedish or Finnish.[26] Dorpat University, in existence since the seventeenth century, was made into an imperial Russian university in 1802 as a part of Alexander I's scheme for dividing Russia into six educational districts, each with its own university. Like Helsinki University (formerly the Abo Academy in Abo/Turku until it moved to Helsinki in 1827 and was renamed Imperial Alexander University), Dorpat University contained, among its four departments, a department of theology. Also like Vilna and Helsinki, instruction was initially in a non-Russian tongue. Consequently, Dorpat's student clientele were the residents of Latvia, Estonia, and the German colonies of southern Russia.

The Dorpat Department of Theology and the Lutheran church competed with the Orthodox bishopric created in Riga in 1836 that converted thousands of peasants to Russian Orthodoxy in the 1850s and 1860s. To aid the Orthodox in that contest, the tsarist government required in 1852 that the teacher of philosophy at Dorpat University be of Russian Orthodox faith.[27] When the peasants who converted to Orthodoxy during this contest attempted in the 1880s to reconvert to Lutheranism, the Russian government tried and convicted several of the Lutheran clergy for the "crime against Orthodoxy" of allowing these former Lutherans to partake of Communion.[28] The final intervention by the tsarist government in support of Orthodoxy was to close the university in 1893 and reopen it as Iur'ev University with a completely Russian-speaking faculty.[29]

The fourth religious group for which the tsarist government maintained educational institutions was the Armenian Church. An agreement of 1836 between the head (Catholicos) of the Armenian Church and the Russian emperor made the emperor president of the Holy Synod of Russian Armenia with the rights to choose the Catholicos from a list of names submitted to him by a church assembly, and to choose members of the Holy Synod and diocesan bishops from a list submitted to him by the Catholicos. Until 1874 the tsarist government trained teachers for the six Armenian seminaries, one in each of the six Armenian dioceses of Russian Armenia, in a special section in the Lazarevskii Institute of Oriental Languages in Moscow. In 1872, Catholicos George IV established minimum educational requirements for all persons entering the clergy. Two years later, he presided over opening ceremonies of the Armenian Ecclesiastical Academy that the tsarist government created and endowed with 335,000 rubles in the monastery village of Echmiadzin near Erevan.[30] Each seminary was administered by the diocesan administration, but the academy was under the jurisdiction of the Catholicos of Russian Armenia.[31]

The fifth religious group for which the tsars allowed training of religious servitors in the nineteenth century (although they gave this group virtually no financial support) was Muslims. As a means of integrating this religious minority into the Russian Empire with considerable religious autonomy, Catherine II had created in 1788 the Muslim Spiritual Administration, headed by a *mufti* with offices in Orenburg. In 1841, his seat was transferred to Ufa. This agency was responsible for administering a series of Muslim seminaries (*medresses*) and schools (*mektebs*) in which Muslim teachers taught by Koran and Muslim traditions. Thus an administrative-religious system already existed for the Muslims at the time the tsarist government added large numbers of Muslim believers to the empire during the conquest of Central Asia from approximately 1860 to 1880. When those new territories were integrated into the empire, the tsar prohibited the Russian Orthodox Church from proselytizing among the Muslims in those territories.[32]

The expansion into Central Asia and the Far East also added adherents to other faiths. Small in number and far from Great Russia, they were less a target for government repression. For instance, Buddhist Kalmyks received a charter in 1828 allowing religious autonomy. The government recognized an organization of lamas as head of the Buddhists' spiritual administration, and in 1841 vested authority in a senior lama as head of that group.[33]

Russia also acquired a sizable Jewish population at the same time it acquired Roman Catholics during the partitioning of Poland in 1795. By 1870, 93 percent of all Jews in the empire still lived in the original Pale of Settlement that Catherine II created for them in fifteen western and southwestern provinces. The Jews accounted for 11 percent of the population in the area of the Pale; outside it, they were only one-third of one percent of the population of the empire. Their area of settlement was in the educational districts of Vilna, Warsaw, Riga, Odessa, Kharkov, and Kiev. Cities such as Grodno, Kovno, Minsk, Vitebsk, and Vilna, each of which had a state gymnasium, acquired high concentrations of Jews.[34]

The competition from Roman Catholicism and other religions that precipitated Russification in the borderlands had its counterpart inside Great Russia in the secular challenge that developed in the educational institutions and among the educated public during the 1840s to 1880s. Within the universities and some secondary schools, the Russian Orthodox Church faced a challenge from secular and atheist views that flowed into Russia in the 1860s and 1870s. To remain strong enough to protect its recent territorial acquisitions and to compete with European nations in the arena of world imperialism, the Russian government came to realize after the Crimean War, and even more after the victories of the Russo-Turkish War faded into diplomatic defeat at the Congress of Berlin in 1878, that it must industrialize to increase military and economic strength. This desire to build modern industries forced the regime to undertake broad, though far from

universal, education to train specialists to perform the varied tasks required
in a technologically based society.

But life in a university city studying at a Russian university proved to be
a transforming experience for many youths from the provinces whose
previously unquestioned religious convictions and modes of thinking were
replaced by Western secular ideas. Dostoevsky created the character
Raskolnikov to illustrate this pattern of value displacement. Turgenev
illustrated the rapid change in values by positing a generational conflict
wherein sons rejected their fathers' values. Against the background of
significantly changed traditional categories, social status, and social groups
in Russian society, Alexander Herzen saw his own transformation in the
milieu of Moscow University. In his essay on the "native lineage" of
Herzen's thought, Alan Kimball explains how Herzen universalized his own
experiences to characterize everyone who had studied at Russian
universities in the 1850s and 1860s as creators, and members, of a new
social stratum of people alienated by their university experience from all the
traditional estates, classes, and other socio-legal groups spawned by the
Russian autocracy. Each year, a new class of students graduated, or left, the
universities to swell the ranks of this new group. Bound by the common
experience of alienation from society through education, this new group
(the *intelligentsiia*, a member of which he called an *intelligent*) formed a
brotherhood devoted to serving the people, the *narod*.

No longer did students seek university degrees primarily as a means of
obtaining a position in the tsarist civil service. The *intelligent* looked upon
an occupation not as a way of providing that particular service but as a
means of drawing closer to the *narod* to provide the ultimate service of
emancipating the *narod* from its miseries through social revolution.
Teaching in a zemstvo school was nearly ideal for an *intelligent*. He, or she
(women were allowed in Russian universities as auditors from 1863 to
1884, but not at all after 1884), could utilize his/her knowledge in the
village where an audience of young students waited. My essay, in this
volume, on the Rzhev Technical School is a case study of members of the
intelligentsia disseminating secular and revolutionary ideas they brought
from Moscow University to the classroom of a secondary school in a
county in Tver province in the 1870s. This case illustrates the paradox of

the tsarist government's need to construct a network of schools to develop a reservoir of citizens with technical skills, while radical students and teachers used that school to disseminate Darwinian and political ideas challenging the twin monopolies of autocracy and Orthodoxy.

This case also illustrates the vigilance the state exercised in its role as defender of the Orthodox Church's monopoly on interpretations of topics considered religious. True to its legal obligation to "defend Orthodoxy against word and deed" that might harm it, the provincial governor reported the "offenses against Orthodoxy" these *intelligenty* had committed, and the minister of education ordered the school closed. Despite its many ears in the countryside, the Ministry of Education could never ferret out all the *intelligenty*, such as teacher Mech and the radical students desecrating icons in their student apartments. As schools and students became more numerous in the 1870s and 1880s, tsarist officials could not completely stop the flow of secular and revolutionary ideas from the cities into the villages.

In the 1880s, Marxism entered the pool of ideas being disseminated inside educational institutions and among former students living in university towns. Disappointed that their assassination of Alexander II in 1881 failed to produce the changes they desired, many of the young *intelligenty* abandoned, or adapted, their populist notions to embrace Marxism. Alexander Ulianov, Lenin's elder brother, was executed during this period (1887) for plotting to assassinate Alexander III, and Lenin was expelled from Kazan University for discussing Marxist ideas. The essay, "Marxism and Aziatchina," abstracted for this volume by Gary Ulmen from the unpublished dissertation by our late friend and colleague Joseph Schiebel, is a careful analysis of the Russian Marxists' mental labors to reconcile Marx's interpretation of Russian state and society as Orientally despotic (i.e., not suited for a proletarian revolution) with Marx's certainty that the socialist revolution would occur first in Western Europe. Professor Schiebel argued that Lenin--by bending portions of Marxist thought to fit Russian conditions, and by minimizing Marx's warnings about the possibility of a restoration of Oriental despotism--established a concept of the revolution for Russia and built a Russian revolutionary party that precluded the emergence of a Marxist socialist state. The outcome, instead, was the creation of a bureaucratic state that, because it ostensibly rested on the immutable laws of scientific socialism, became a sacred object. The general principles of Marxism, mangled though they were, became the secular religion that legitimized the Soviet state.

The twin spiritual-political monopolies of autocracy and Orthodoxy had given way to a new set of twin monopolies: totalitarianism and bastardized Marxism, each supporting the other against outside challengers. As in the medieval inquisitions about which David Goldfrank wrote, criticism of the form of government became heresy, and the state, the new "secular arm," began to use the instruments at its disposal to defend the monopoly Marxist interpretation against competing interpretations. It is appropriate to observe here that under Soviet state tutelage the established religion of Marxism became as lethargic and superficial--as a body of thought for social analysis and action--as the established religion of Orthodoxy became under the tsarist government's tutelage. As caged exotic birds, both lost considerable ability to fly.

The popularity of Marxism, the emergence of social Darwinism, and the desecration of icons in Rzhev Technical School were but three signs of the "spiritual crisis" that existed in postreform Russia. Other signs were the appeal of sectarianism and Protestantism. The most celebrated sectarian was Leo Tolstoi, who renounced Orthodoxy and formed his own religious movement in the 1880s. Other sects came into existence, and the number of adherents increased in long-existing sects such as Old Believers and Molokans. With the rise of independent religious thinkers such as Tolstoi, the ecclesiastical academies lost their previously uncontested position as repositories for the nation's most capable religious thinkers.[35]

As was the case under Alexander I at the beginning of the nineteenth century, Protestantism began again to make inroads into the most respectable social circles in the major cities of Great Russia. This interest in foreign religions and sects, sometimes called the "spiritual revival" of the 1870s and 1880s,[36] was a response to "the spiritual crisis" that included Orthodoxy's loss of appeal to Russian intellectuals. The search for new values led Russian thinkers to sectarianism, Protestantism, still other religions, and to secularism. As Edmund Heier has written, Tolstoi's experience "epitomizes the struggle of Russian intellectuals" of the period,[37] but his formation of his own sect was hardly typical. Some

members of the aristocracy, close to the imperial family, embraced
Protestantism, illegal though it was to convert from Orthodoxy.

Protestantism spread among the St. Petersburg aristocracy as a result of
the effects of British evangelist Lord Radstock, who began evangelical
preaching in Russia in 1874. Among the upper aristocracy who became
evangelical Christians and joined his St. Petersburg group was Modest
Korf. By 1880, Radstock's Russian disciples were achieving success
proselytizing in the provinces.[38]

Confronted in the 1880s by religious and political opposition, including
assassination of Alexander II in 1881, the tsarist government and Russian
Orthodox Church began a coordinated campaign to combat the religious and
secular challenges to autocracy and Orthodoxy. In the borderlands, the
state's policy was cultural and political Russification, and the church's
policy was to increase the level of proselytizing. In Great Russia proper, the
state's policy was to revise the Great Reforms of the 1860s, and the
church's policy was to reinsert the church into the role of elementary
education to stop the spread of non-Orthodox religious influences
(Romanism, Protestantism, and sectarianism) and secular thought.

The essential tool of Russification in the borderlands was control of the
educational system. First, St. Petersburg removed the schools from local
control and placed them under direct control of tsarist ministries. Next, the
ministry replaced local teachers with Russians, or Russian-speaking
teachers, and required all instruction to be conducted in Russian. The only
exception was in the primary grades, where children were allowed to
receive religious instruction in the local language. But even they had to be
taught all other subjects in Russian. Simultaneously, the Russian Orthodox
Church began establishing bishoprics in these non-Russian areas and
building Russian Orthodox cathedrals in the most prominent spots of the
capital cities of these non-Russian areas.

In 1885-86 the tsarist government implemented this scheme in the Baltic
provinces. It transferred the Baltic school systems from local administrative
and local church control to the tsarist government and required all
instruction to be in Russian except for religious instruction in the primary
grades. In 1893, as noted earlier, the tsarist government closed Dorpat
University and then reopened it with the new name of Iur'ev University

with a Russian-trained professoriate. Because the statute of the new university admitted all students who had completed a course of study at any Russian Orthodox seminary, Russian students "came from every corner of Russia" to swell dramatically the number of Russian students among the student body.[39] In the same year, the Russian Orthodox Church erected an imposing cathedral in Reval and an Orthodox seminary in Pskov to train missionaries to work among the Baltic population.[40]

In Finland, the university and its school of theology remained intact. The main visible threat from the Russian Orthodox Church was the imposing Uspenskii Cathedral, completed in 1868 atop a hill in Helsinki just east of South Harbor, rivaling the Great (Nikolai) Cathedral,[41] the national symbol of the Finnish Lutheran Church, which had been erected nearly a century earlier atop a nearby hill overlooking the city's main square and South Harbor. These churches still face each other today from their respective promontories, symbolizing a relationship altered, but not totally expunged, by the events of 1917.

During this period of Russification and Orthodox assertiveness, the tsarist government also placed restrictions on Jewish attendance at secondary and higher schools. In July 1887 the central government (against the wishes of Minister of Education Delianov) published a circular announcing a quota on persons of Jewish origin in the gymnasiums and universities. The maximum number of Jews allowed was ten percent of the total number of students enrolled in gymnasiums and universities within the Pale of Settlement, five percent of the total student enrollment outside the Pale, and three percent for those within the cities of Moscow and St. Petersburg.[42]

In the Muslim areas, the Russian government was unable to expropriate the existing autonomous Muslim-financed network of schools, and in 1884 created a parallel educational system, called Russian-native schools, wherein native children were taught primary classes and received instruction in religion from Muslim teachers in their native languages and studied the Russian language. The tsarist government gave no financial support to the competing Muslim school system and confiscated an endowment which had previously helped fund the network of Muslim schools.[43]

In Russian Armenia the tsarist government closed the Armenian schools in 1897.[44] In 1903, it confiscated the endowment that helped support Armenian seminaries, alleging that the Armenian clergy was supporting revolutionaries. When Armenians protested and revolutionaries began assassinating tsarist officials, the tsarist government unleashed Tatars against Armenians in racial warfare that cost thousands of lives.[45] In 1894 the Russian Orthodox Church began erecting a large Orthodox cathedral on a prominent location in the central square in Warsaw.[46]

In Great Russia, the domestic equivalent of Russification in the borderlands was the government's counterreforms to alter the institutions created during the 1860s and 1870s. The church's policy, devised by K. P. Pobedonostsev as over-procurator of the Holy Synod, was to create a system of parish (*prikhodskie*) schools under church control, using local priests as teachers, and then have the government transfer control of existing village schools from the Ministry of Education to the Holy Synod. Fearful of the foreign ideas (Romanism, Protestantism, and secularism) that were sweeping into Russian villages, Pobedonostsev coupled an attack upon those ideas at their source with a program to strengthen the Orthodox fiber of the Russian village so that it would repel such influences in the future. The attack on the enemy at its source was not only the Russification in the borderlands and construction of Orthodox cathedrals opposite Catholic and Protestant churches discussed earlier, but also included expulsion of Lord Radstock and his disciple Colonel Pashkov from Russia in 1884.[47]

Strengthening the Orthodox fiber of the Russian village was the task of the system of parish schools. In his essay, "Pobedonostsev's Parish School: A Bastion Against Secularism," Thomas Sorenson carefully chronicles and documents the evolution of Pobedonostsev's plan, summarizing his argumentation that persuaded the government to increase funding from 55,000 rubles for 4,457 parish schools in June 1884 to 3,279,205 rubles in 1895, and 42,696 parish schools by 1905. This essay shows clearly that Pobedonostsev was a firm advocate of universal literacy, but wished to limit peasant reading materials to the Bible, prayer books, and the lives of saints--in short, the literature used in the required course *Zakon Bozhii.*

Although teaching in the parish schools was added work for local priests, they received no additional income. Pobedonostsev filled his annual reports with assertions that the priests loved their new responsibilities. Outside evidence casts doubt on such enthusiasm. Because the zemstvo schools were also required to teach *Zakon Bozhii* and were required to obtain the Holy Synod's approval of the teacher of the course, the zemstvos typically first approached the local priest, who was qualified automatically by virtue of his position, to teach the course. Thus, in zemstvo provinces where parish schools were founded the priests were in demand as teachers. Because the zemstvos paid the priests to teach the course, the church sometimes had more trouble finding priests who were willing to teach without pay in the parish schools than was suggested in Pobedonostsev's annual reports.[48]

The government tried in other ways as well to use religion as a glue to bind the pieces of a near-crumbling empire. Devout believers themselves, but also hoping to gain political benefit from revitalized Orthodox zeal, the imperial family acted upon counsel from political advisers to make greater use of Russian Orthodox symbols to rekindle religious fervor among the masses. From the end of the 1880s the imperial family had supported the Palestine Society's organization of pilgrimages from Russia to the Holy Land, its construction of spectacular churches at the scene of major Biblical events, and its construction of a separate world of lodging and events to prevent Russian pilgrims from chance encounters with Roman Catholics, Protestants, and other pilgrims visiting at the same time.[49]

A major event in the imperial family's efforts to revitalize religious fervor through increased use of ceremonies was the canonization of Serafim of Sarov. Robert L. Nichols's essay in this volume explains how the royal family worked with political advisers to weave from various political and religious threads a web of religious events aimed at promoting support for the autocracy. Impressed by gains some French politicians had acquired by manipulating the Catholic Church in France, the royal couple decided to impose its will, if necessary, upon the Holy Synod to create a series of religious ceremonies and rituals inside Russia. In this study of the canonization of Serafim of Sarov, Nichols lays bare the politics behind the event and shows that, while the autocracy might vigorously defend Orthodoxy from outside threats, it was not hesitant to appropriate the church's influence to advance the cause of autocracy.

No manipulation of symbols was adequate to save the autocracy from the buffeting it received in 1905. Among the many problems the autocracy addressed in attempting to preserve itself was the question of religious pluralism. On April 17, 1905, the Imperial Decree on Religious Tolerance promised that a person converting "from the Orthodox faith into another Christian confession or religious teaching shall not be subject to persecution"; thus persons registered as Orthodox, "but in reality practicing a non-Christian faith to which they themselves or their ancestors belonged before joining the Orthodox church," would be free to have their names removed from the Orthodox roll. In addition, Old Believers and sectarians would be allowed to "hold public religious services ... and perform religious ceremonies freely both in private houses and in houses of prayer, and in other necessary cases."[50]

The act merely "tolerated" other religious groups; it did not abolish the Orthodox Church's position as the established religion or remove the imperial family's obligation to protect it; the emperor and immediate heir to the throne and their wives remained obligated by law to be Orthodox. But, allowing the tsar's subjects to choose freely among Christian religions, or reconvert to a previous non-Christian religion, and allowing all the major religions and sects freedom to preach reduced the onus of the Orthodox Church's privileged, official position. Tsarist and Duma committees began work to determine precisely what rights the act would grant to other religions and to Old Believers, but liberals in the Duma could not agree with Prime Minister Stolypin's contention that the Duma's task was to "adapt Orthodoxy to the attractive theory of freedom of faith within the limits of our Russian Orthodox state," and Duma deputies could not agree among themselves that the Orthodox Church should be denied a privileged status in the new order. Such questions as freedom for atheists, or establishing equality between the Orthodox faith and religions of the *inorodtsy* (including Judaism, a measure Stolypin opposed), were not resolved before the end of autocracy. October 1917 established a new context for all questions related to religion in Russia.[51]

Nonetheless, from 1905 to 1917 the general principles stated in the act of religious toleration made spiritual life much simpler for the thousands who had converted, willfully or under duress, to Orthodoxy and wished to return to their original faith. Near Chelm, in Poland, where Uniats had been forced to convert to Orthodoxy in the 1870s and, as one Polish deputy in the Third Duma said, "the bloody nightmare of heavy memories" hung, some 200,000 overcame obstructions placed by local officials and reconverted to their original faith. Polish-language instruction also was allowed in state schools for teaching the Polish language and Catholic religion. In private schools, all instruction could be in Polish. In the Baltic provinces, local languages were permitted more freely; thousands of Lutherans reconverted from Orthodoxy, and Baltic German schools reopened.[52]

De-Russification and religious toleration in the borderlands after 1905 were limited. Full restoration of native languages in schools did not occur, and the government decided to retain Pobedonostsev's parish schools and the Russian-native schools that had been created in 1884. In the Third Duma, liberals and representatives of the national minorities favored transferring all elementary schools from control by the Holy Synod to control by the Ministry of Education. Kadet Party leader Paul Miliukov argued that religious schools wanted "to repress the personality" rather than free it as secular schools did. Spokesmen for Muslims, Poles, and Jews called the parish schools "a repressive instrument for the state." Muslim deputy Enikeev called the schools operating in the border areas "finished [as educational institutions]; they have been diverted into a missionary, political swarm."[53]

The essay in this volume by Edward Lazzerini examines in detail attitudes of Crimean Tatars in 1908 toward the Russian-native school (the Russian-Tatar school in this instance) on the Crimean Peninsula. At a conference, zemstvo deputies and several Tatars teaching in the Russian-Tatar school considered the broad question of the proper education for Muslims in the Russian Empire. Unable to agree on an answer to that question, the group was unwilling to blame the tsarist government alone for the deplorable condition of the schools (unanimously, they shared this assessment). Divided among themselves, fearing the emergence of radicalism, and seeing some advantage in their position in the empire, these members of this Tatar minority were still potential tsarist allies in the borderlands. But wise policies from St. Petersburg toward the borderlands were necessary to retain existing goodwill, and those were not plentiful after 1908. The year 1908 was the date that the fourth congress of Orthodox missionaries, the event with which we began this essay, decided that the major means for combatting socialism was to attack its premises through the curriculum of the educational institutions.

Professor Lazzerini's essay shows that socialism had its opponents among the Crimean Tatars. In Great Russia several members of the intelligentsia were also becoming disaffected with the materialism and secularism of Marxism. Significant numbers of the intelligentsia had evolved through stages from their initial rejection of the established Orthodox Church to a reassessment of its dogma. Some had found in Marxism a path back to religion. Having been weaned away from the established Russian Orthodox Church by revolutionary ideas, they applied their analytical training to philosophical questions that produced a more sophisticated comprehension of religion as more than the rituals of an established church. Further, religious toleration had removed some of the negative stigma that official status had given the Russian Orthodox Church.

Various scholars have noted religious characteristics in the thought and activities of the intelligentsia. They point to such things as the large number who were children of priests, their extolling the virtues of suffering and martyrdom, and the fact that one well-known radical proclamation was called the "catechism" of a revolutionary.[54] Well-known Marxists who returned to the Orthodox Church, but advocated religious and political reform, are Berdiaev, Bulgakov, and Struve. Still others on the fringe of the church engaged in philosophical-religious discussions at the turn of the century, seeking ways to revitalize the church so that it could make its "presence felt in our midst," as the Orthodox missionary whom we quoted at the beginning of this article said in 1908.[55]

In 1909 seven *intelligenty* who had abandoned Marxism published a critique of the revolutionary intelligentsia for its "fanatically upholding materialism and atheism." The "classical Russian intellectual," the authors chided, "is a militant monk of the nihilist religion of worldly well-being."[56] Convener of the symposium and editor of the collection of essays was Mikhail Gershenzon. In the essay "Mikhail Gershenzon's 'Secret Voice': The Making of a Cultural Nihilist," David Davies analyzes

Gershenzon's intellectual efforts to arrive at a new, nonmaterialist view of the world. Ethnically Jewish, Gershenzon did not follow his fellow former Marxists into the Russian Orthodox Church, but began searching for the "secret voice" that he considered the spiritual, religious presence in all humans. Unification of the external and internal "I" would create "wholeness," the characteristic he felt most lacking in the Russian revolutionary intelligentsia.

What moral values guided Russians through the period of social collapse between February and October 1917 when daily pressures of life made moral and survival questions quite real? Tsuyoshi Hasegawa has taken that question as his task in the essay on crime in Petrograd in 1917. Judging people's behavior and values by analyzing the types of crimes and the incidence of crime within the various categories, he shows how they came to police themselves through vigilantism.

The first thirteen essays in this volume were written by twelve scholars who received their Ph.D. degrees from the University of Washington. Donald Treadgold was dissertation director for eleven of those authors, and he was a member of the dissertation committee for the other. To round out this volume, which is dedicated to Don Treadgold, I asked two distinguished scholars, who are his peers among the generation that established the field of Russian and East European studies in the United States at the end of World War II, to write evaluations of Treadgold's contribution to that effort. The response is the last two essays in this volume. The essay by Nicholas Riasanovsky is an evaluation of his work as historian of secular and religious thought in Russian and Chinese history. The essay by Robert Byrnes tells of Treadgold's role as a promoter of Slavic and East European studies. In both of these roles, Don Treadgold's efforts to establish the field of Slavic studies in the United States have endowed us, the generation of his students, with rich human and material resources needed to continue the lines of inquiry into Russian secular and religious thought that he helped begin.

CHAPTER 2

THEOCRATIC IMPERATIVES,
THE TRANSCENDENT, THE WORLDLY,
AND POLITICAL JUSTICE IN RUSSIA'S EARLY INQUISITIONS

David M. Goldfrank

> So also the king of Moscouie seeing his people,who had receiued
> the rites and ceremonies of the Greekes, diuided into diuers sects
> and factions, by reason of the diuers preachings and disputations of
> the ministers: hee thereupon forbad them upon paine of death any
> more to preach or dispute of religion; and withall gaue a booke unto
> the bishop and parish priests, wherein was contained what he would
> haue euery man persuaded of, and to beleeue, concerning matters of
> faith and religion, which he commaunded them upon all festiual
> dayes to reade and publish unto the people: with a capital paine
> thereunto annexed, if by any mans exposition any thing were at all
> thereunto either added or diminished.
>
>   - Jean Bodin (1606 English edition)

An inquisition is quintessentially a secular organ of a monopoly church to deal with what it defines as heresy.[1] Requiring cooperation from the secular authorities and bolstered by pervasive superstition, inquisitions aim to defend the ecclesiastical organization and the doctrines that provide legitimacy for the clergy, and its property, power, and self-esteem.

 Justifications for inquisitions have varied. One type is purely practical: according to the relatively tolerant Erasmus, if a heretic incited public disorder, he was lawfully subject to punishment for his civil offense.[2] Another kind bridges the artificial barrier between the secular and otherworldly: the relapsed heretic, said Thomas Aquinas, was implicitly a danger to his own and others' salvation and must be executed.[3] The Old Testament enjoins all authorities to punish those guilty of offending God. Even the tolerant Bodin, who understood that trying to compel people to believe fosters atheism, sees the pragmatic logic of secular and clerical officials cooperating to prevent religious strife.[4]

30

Curiously, the pragmatic line of argumentation may call for limitations or even avoidance of repressive measures. Erasmus warned that persecuting Luther would serve only to support his movement. Even more curiously, the purely transcendent position allows for no inquisition at all. Let God, directly or via his prophets, punish those who offend Him.[5] The consummate inquisitor, on the other hand, must develop or follow a political doctrine. Within it, the "secular arm" represents simply a means by which the bearers of clerical routinized or institutionalized charisma avoid the physical sins associated with condemning heretics. In this respect, perhaps, pagan priests who killed with their own hands were more logically consistent concerning their sacramental pretensions.

This essay will show how Russian churchmen, with the participation and constraints of Ivan III, Vasilii III, and Ivan IV, developed a *sui generis* inquisition from about 1470 to 1570 to deal with a variety of intellectual and moral threats to their spiritual and societal authority. One can barely speak of a "secular arm" even for the formative period of this inquisition, when the Church had a great deal of autonomy. The Muscovite monarchy already had the power of supervising, if not managing, all elite purges. Since the state appointed the top churchmen, and the church needed state permission to initiate a heresy trial, such processes were thoroughly political, and differences between the purely transcendent and the worldly virtually disappeared.[6]

Byzantium supplied Russia with an inquisitorial model and skeletal apparatus. These came in the form of history and hagiography, canon law books, apologetic digests, catalogues of heretical movements and doctrines, and an ascending hierarchy of synods to supplement the bishops' administrative officials.[7] Contrary to established views, there is no evidence from the most reliable sources that the Russian Church had to deal with heresy prior to the late fourteenth century.[8] Does this mean that the early Russian Church was not about to shrink from employing the most brutal secular means to defend worldly or semiworldly interests? Not at all! The metropolitans before the Mongol conquest were ready to imprison or mutilate insubordinate bishops--one of whom was explicitly compared to an evil and unrepentant heretic who perishes in body and soul. A bishop might kill or maim his underling, while the authorities would burn shamans for their alleged sorcery.[9]

The Novgorod and Pskov *strigolniki* presented the Russian Church in the latter fourteenth century with its first heretical challenge: that an incipient sect might dispense with the sacraments. Abstractly, it appears, the *strigolniki* would have allowed for a lawful, nonsimoniacal officiating clergy, but objectively they were pushing for what Friedrich Engels called an "inexpensive church."[10] Whatever their views of the transcendent may have been, they were certainly attacking the existing Church's worldy interests. The initial response to them was twofold. On the one hand, Novgorod authorities killed three *strigolniki* in 1375--under whose initiative and with what normal or abnormal procedures is not known.[11] On the other hand, two outside prelates, Patriarch Neilos of Constantinople and the missionary bishop Stefan of Perm, composed special homilies, the latter calling for expulsion, the former empowering Bishop Dionisii of Suzdal to employ ecclesiastical measures against these errant "children."[12]

Since such moderate treatment failed to uproot at least the Pskov *strigolniki*, Metropolitan Fotii worked during 1416-27 directly with the local lay and ecclesiastical leaders to suppress the heretics. The metropolitan instructed them to investigate, excommunicate, confine, and physically punish short of killing--whatever would work to prevent the accused from "dying in their state of sin." His ultimate threat was to arrange for a special synod, which would formally condemn them if nothing else worked. Something evidently did, since the problem seems to have abated.[13]

The appearance in the 1470s and 1480s of the disparate and still rather mysterious late fifteenth-century group, lumped together by the Church under the name of "Novgorod Heretics," provoked a real inquisition. While the dissidents' actual beliefs may never be known, they clearly threatened the Church's worldly interests and authority in several ways. Occupying some key positions of functional authority, the archpriests, priests, and state secretaries (*diaki*), who constituted the heretical leadership, by their very existence and influence at court were dangerous. Conservative churchmen had to be concerned that their opponents had access to astronomical information at a time when a new calendar was needed and when Ivan III for raison d'état was casting hungry eyes on Church lands.[14] The

quasi-pansophism of Fedor Kuritsyn's *Laodiiskoe poslanie* and his brother's
secularizing canon law code that omitted the (Late Roman) Civil Law, and
thus protected heretics from a secular arm, epitomize the challenge of such
freethinking to the Church.[15]

Russia's first great inquisitor, the Moscow-installed Archbishop
Gennadii of Novgorod (1485-1503), claimed to have been bothered from
the moment of his "discovery" of these heretics by their combination of
dissimulating sectarianism, which rendered them impossible to discipline by
ecclesiastical measures, and their relatively broadly based learning, which
rendered him incapable of competing against their expertise with the meager
intellectual resources of the Russian Church.[16] Quite understandably, he
moved simultaneously to build the Church up and to cut the dissidents
down.

When Gennadii began his local investigation in 1487 with the
cooperation of the Moscow-appointed governors of Novgorod, the
Zakharin brothers, he found himself very much under the power of the
Grand Prince. It was Moscow, both sovereign and metropolitan, which in
1488 accepted the evidence against three of the four original suspects and
had them whipped, but rejected the fourth for lack of a second witness and
then directed Gennadii to continue the inquests in Novgorod. The
archbishop was free to hold a local synod, lay penances upon the penitant,
and turn the obdurate over to the Zakharins, who would then check the
evidence and administer physical punishment. At the same time, Gennadii
had to keep the Grand Prince informed. The latter, it turned out, lightened
the sentence of one alleged *strigolnik*-monk, who then fled to Moscow and
produced broadsheets against Gennadii. Others accused Gennadii of torture,
although he claimed only to have had a clerical official present at inquests
to prevent any bribery. Meanwhile, with or without aid from the
Dominican Veniamin, a member of the West's original inquisitorial order,
Gennadii developed his own bag of literary tricks, exaggerating and
dramatizing sacrilege and implicating all suspects in the actual offenses of
individuals.[17]

In a general *sobor* at the end of 1490, Moscow subjected some of the
accused to a trial with testimony from witnesses and live confrontations.
The defendants were charged separately with various doctrinal and physical

(iconoclastic) insults against Jesus, the Virgin, and other iconographic subjects and collectively of praising Jewish customs. They were thus made to appear guilty of blaspheming the positive transcendental and willfully adhering to the (Jewish, hence ipso facto) negative.[18]

The archbishop himself wished for the death penalty on two practical grounds: the heretics' independence, as evidenced by their dissimulation and willful relapsing after accepting a penance, and a fundamental (mixed transcendent and wordly) *raison du Gosudar'*--for the sake of his salvation and honor.[19] As an example of the latter, Gennadii presented a fanciful, Russianized version of the king's direction of the initial stages of the Spanish Inquisition. That action could have appeared to be a fiscally profitable model, since the property of 2,000 executed Jewish heretics had become available for the royal treasury.[20]

But late medieval Muscovy--lacking Aristotle, algebra, or the Talmud-- was not Spain. The Russian proceedings were limited to just one batch of dissidents, and their punishments were restricted to lashing and supervised confinement, with at least the theoretical possibility of the heretics' repentence and freedom.[21] On the other hand, the new metropolitan, Zosima, his suspected heterodoxy notwithstanding, did issue a circular instructing all the faithful to expose and shun any heretic, and threatened those who disobeyed his order or who protected heretics with ecclesiastical sanctions, including a synodal anathema.[22] Thus the Russian Orthodox Church had at least established the principle of a permanent inquisition of the faithful. Gennadii, for his part, was at liberty to arrange in Novgorod his famous *auto-da-fé*, which appears to have combined Eastern with Western elements and dramatized the culprits' countertranscendence.[23]

Ivan III's unwillingness immediately to sacrifice the remaining suspects led to a fourteen-year standoff, during which Hegumen (Abbot) Iosif Volotskii took over the leadership of the inquisitional faction. He added to the fight not only his outright mendacity (thus the "Judaizer" label in historiography) and the independent charismatic authority of the disciple-collecting elder (*starets*), but also the mentality of the coenobiarch, whose authoritarian social utopia (so long as it follows the "divine writings" and wards off satanic enticements) combines the best of both worlds: peace and prosperity here, salvation and honor afterward. On earth, where the physical is infused with both a divine presence and diabolic forces, the sovereign is just as duty-bound before God as is the abbot to "purify" his domain.[24]

In his campaign for repression, Iosif appears to have commenced with salvation-oriented arguments. He maintained that the (divinely established) laws commanded and the historical examples showed that Orthodox rulers executed the worst offenders, while clerics killed such people through the operation of the Holy Spirit. As the fight intensified and Iosif was able to take advantage of the turn-of-the-century succession crisis, he moved as well to the more practical argument that God punishes the whole land for the sovereign's sins. His procedural advice was simple: seize (and torture) two or three, and they will reveal everything.[25]

Iosif's political victory resulted in a new *sobor* in late 1504 under Ivan III. This *sobor*, of which we know very little, determined that some of the offenders would be burned, at least one with his tongue cut out first, and that others would be sentenced to corrective confinement. Of the eight known to have been executed, four were associated with the top leadership of the sect and had been important figures.[26]

The severity of the sentences of 1504 produced opposition from several quarters, including the leading *startsi* (elders) of the immensely rich Kirillov Monastery and the more consistent disciples of Muscovy's leading practising Hesychast, Nil Sorskii. As early as 1490 the purely transcendental argument that "it is a sin to condemn" had been circulating, and Iosif had responded with standard affirmations of ecclesiastical authority.[27] Now he added that historically holy men did "kill [heretics] by means of prayer."[28] This time, the opposition, led by Nil's chief politically minded disciple, Vassian Patrikeev, retorted with the sarcastic and practical suggestion that perfectly expressed the purely transcendent standpoint: Iosif should prove his correctness and sanctity by binding himself to Archimandrite Kassian while the latter is being immolated.[29] On the practical level, Iosif induced Metropolitan Simon (1495-1511) to issue a circular declaring that willful opposition by monks to a synodal decision would result in excommunication.[30] The opposition then moved to demand the release of the surviving, imprisoned (former?) heretics and claimed that the canons require the clergy to facilitate the heretics' repentence. In refusing to do so, they said, Iosif was guilty of the heresy of Novatianus.[31] Vassian also raised the classical practical argument that attracted his contemporary Erasmus: the fear that executing heretics would generate irrepressible civil strife.[32]

Iosif's final position, worked out in his "Extended" *Enlightener* and bolstered by his "Extended" (monastic) *Rule*, was to repeat his previous lies and arguments and to conjure up from his sources a staged treatment of heretics that stressed, primarily, their danger to society. He argued that the purely religious types, who "hold to some heresy" and repent of their own free will, could be handled by ecclesiastical discipline. But those who did not try to repent until they were indicted were worthy of punishment up to confinement, with communion withheld until they were on their deathbeds--a mixed civil and ecclesiastic sentence. Finally, worst of all were the dissimulating, falsely repenting, Judaizing "Novgorod Apostates," whose repentence could not be believed, who deserved the most brutal treatment, and who, if not executed, certainly should be kept in prison, lest the Orthodox realm perish as others have from heresy.[33] Against such diabolic foes, moreover, it is proper to employ "divinely wise cunning," the obverse of Satan's schemes.[34]

The struggle between Iosif and Vassian over the inquisition had a rather dirty side. Vassian revealed a willingness to use a "secular arm" against would-be inquisitors. Iosif, without calling Vassian's position heretical in doctrine, attributed its formulation to the "Novgorod Heretics."[35] Vassian, meanwhile, used his influence at court after 1508 to counter charges by two of Iosif's disciples that some of the northern "hermits" were in fact heretics. With license from Vasilii III, Vassian had the only other witness, a simple priest, tortured to death in an attempt to induce him to disclaim that he had seen a hermit throw a book into a burning stove to prevent it from being read. The Grand Prince then vented his wrath over this outcome by temporarily imprisoning Iosif's two men in Kirillov.[36] Iosif appears, however, to have secured their release and to have convinced Vasilii to continue to hold the surviving convicted heretics in prison. All the same, he did not receive his great wish to extend the inquisition to Vassian's faction.[37]

Iosif's successor as hegumen, Daniil, was more consistent than the master had been. When Ivan III sent the heretical merchant Semen Klenov to Iosif's cloister for imprisonment in 1504, Iosif raised the purist (transcendent) objection that the Grand Prince was saving society by "destroying" the monastery--as if to deny that its regular means of physical coercion and of insulating most of the brothers from one dissident were sufficient protection from one of Satan's adherents.[38] When he became metropolitan (1521-39), Daniil allowed Iosifov Monastery to be used as the prison for the most prestigious or dangerous of the "heretics." One leading family of Iosifov elders, the Lenkovs, actually specialized in handling convicted heretics deemed in need of personal supervision.[39]

Daniil devised a slightly more balanced version of Iosif's inquisitional theory. Paying greater attention to the clergy's otherworldly role in correcting heretics' errors, Daniil still affirmed the duty of the clergy to judge and condemn and the propriety of utilizing tricks and punishments of all kinds. He also insisted on the theocratic nature of any dealings with heretics: only the "divine writings" were to be used in debates. In a word, the monopoly church determines the procedures that may produce deadly secular consequences for the opponent.[40]

Daniil does not seem to have had the opportunity to apply these ideas to a genuinely heretical movement.[41] However, he did initiate inquisitional measures against rival Orthodox. His desire to take this action sprang from the presence of Maksim Grek, who was a *sui generis* visiting professor of theology in a country without a university, combined with Vassian's continued influence at court, where he lobbied for greater secularization (or rather desecularization of the Church). High politics also helped Daniil. Scattered opposition to some of Vasilii III's tyrannical policies; fears of Ottoman-inspired intrigues against this ruling descendant of the Byzantine Paleologues; anger engendered by the metropolitan's complicity in a matter involving Maksim's lay associates; and, perhaps, Vassian's opposition to Vasilii's uncanonical divorce and remarriage all combined to afford Daniil opportunities to act.[42]

Daniil's first inquisitorial move was his 1525 synodal trials of Maksim, his cell valet (*keleinik*) Afanasii, and another Greek, Archimandrite Savva of Moscow's Novospasskii Monastery. That the trials took place in the

Grand Prince's palace in Moscow attests to their political significance.[43]
Before the process, Maksim and Afanasii had already been interrogated
during the state-led inquest into the alleged seditions of the diplomat
Bersen-Beklemishev and the state secretary Fedor Zharennyi, the latter
recorded as having the audacity to charge the Grand Prince with seeking
false testimony against Maksim.[44] The "Brief Pafnutiev Chronicle," hardly
to be believed, but indicative of Iosifite propaganda, politicizes the issue in
a way that presaged the 1930s. Accordingly, the Grand Prince accused the
above five and a sixth of inviting the sultan to invade Russia. For this
Bersen lost his head, Zharennyi his tongue, and a third layman, Petr Mukha
Karpov, his freedom, while the Grand Prince was "merciful" and sent the
three clerics to a network of monasteries: Maksim to Iosifov, Savva to
Vozmitskii in Volokolamsk, and Afanasii to Pafnutiev, Iosif's original
cloister.[45]

Daniil's and Vasilii III's surviving instructions from 1525 to Maksim's
Iosifov jailers, on the other hand, reveal the operation of a real heresy trial,
in which the defendant was accused of at least two major offenses, one
purely doctrinal-transcendental, the other quite worldly. Accordingly,
Maksim held to a quasi-monophysitic interpretation of "Christ's
Enthronement on the Right Hand of God," and he also denied the
legitimacy of Muscovy's autocephaly. For these offenses he was
excommunicated, was to be held incommunicado under the supervision of a
confessor, and was allowed to read only works written by the church
fathers. Should Maksim give evidence of repenting, a new synod under the
metropolitan could review his case. Disregard for these instructions would
bring still "other spiritual swords" from the metropolitan and "disgrace"
(Vasilii's word) or "merciless punishment" (Daniil's term) from the Grand
Prince.[46]

When Ivan IV's birth in 1530 (from Vasilii's "uncanonical" marriage)
apparently compromised Vassian's position at court, Daniil was free to
move against the latter and his Russian colleagues.[47] In a rather
spectacular new show trial, staged against Maksim in the presence of the
Grand Prince, where some "heretics" were indeed set against each other,[48]
Daniil was able to secure the public testimony of a series of Maksim's
former co-workers as well as from others who knew him. The accusations

ranged from the countertranscendental to the purely secular, from normal insubordination to the ridiculous and more ridiculous. These included sorcery, doctrinal errors, mistakes in translations, blasphemy of Russian wonder-workers, disputing the validity of the Russian books and rituals, *lèse-majesté*, and treason. The most outlandish was the hearsay report by Mikhail Iurevich Zakharin (son of one of the governors who had helped Gennadii in Novgorod), that Maksim had earlier been one of over 200 disciples of a Judaizing philosopher in Italy, most of whom the reigning pope had burned at the stake.[49] Maksim denied almost everything, except his position concerning Russian autocephaly[50] and his questioning the sanctity of Russian monastic founders who had employed physical violence in their estate management. Concerning the latter issue, Daniil asserted that it was a proper means of instilling fear of the Lord and promoting salvation for Pafnutii of Borovsk to have chastized and imprisoned his peasants. Here the Orthodox Church was not about to cede an inch concerning the protection of its worldly interests.

Daniil had Vassian tried on charges of dogmatic and practical errors in front of a full ecclesiastical synod, attended by the same Mikhail Zakharin who testified against Maksim. The practical errors were related to Vassian's reform program: revising the Russian canon law books, including using (secular) classical thinkers in his argumentation (for partial secularization); disputing the validity of monastic villages and of the latest set of Russian wonder-working saints, and calling major sinners heretics and apostates with the implicit denial that their good (physical) works could save then. The dogmatic errors were that Christ was created of matter and that his incarnated body was incorruptible--that is, aphtharodocetism.[51] Vassian was also associated with Maksim's mistranslations and purported criticism of some minor liturgical practices. The most important issues for Daniil concerned canon law, monastic villages, and the aphtharodocetism, this last being a purely otherworldly issue that served as the metropolitan's doctrinal rope for hanging his great rival.[52] Vassian's canonical justification of an inquisition without the death penalty only in the case of obdurate heretics does not seem to have been an issue at this *sobor*, where such punishment was not inflicted.[53]

These trials resulted in at least five additional sentences of excommunication and exile. Vassian was sent to a supervised prison regime in Iosifov. Maksim was reassigned to a much more lenient confinement with the Bishop of Tver, but Savva Grek went back to Vozmitskii. Afanasii was sent to the metropolitan's palace, and two of the co-worker scribes who had testified were sent to the bishops of Riazan and Kolomna, while another went to Nilov Hermitage in Beloozero, and still another, Isaak Sobaka, went to Iur'ev Monastery in Novgorod.[54] Some of these places must have been locations of honorable exile, where the prisoners could put their talents to use. Sobaka, however, had not testified and proved to be recalcitrant. He was tried again and sent to a different cloister.[55] A murky case is that of the gifted Troitsa-Sergiev monk-copyist Selivan, who had begun to learn Greek before Maksim's arrival and by 1523-24 was making solo translations into Russian.[56] Rumors slightly later had him either killed by Daniil in his palace or imprisoned in Iosifov and suffocated by smoke, though an official source claims he died naturally.[57]

Sublime flights of monophysitic speculation are hardly likely to have had much to do with any of these sentences. It was rather that under Daniil conspicuous promotion of a (secularly) learned approach to theology or a dissenting concept of the church in the world could result in excommunication and a life sentence with only the theoretical possibility of parole for good behavior, especially if the Grand Prince's political sensitivities were also involved.

Two of the victims received pardons in the 1540s, but politics seems to have played as significant a role as sincere contrition. After Daniil's forced retirement in 1539, his replacement Ioasaf released Sobaka, ordained him a state secretary (*diak*) and priest, and may have tried to appoint him to the archimandricy of Simonov Monastery in Moscow.[58] Court politics soon forced Ioasaf to resign, but his successor, Makarii, generally a Iosifite supporter, continued reconciliation policies. Some time after the devastating Moscow fire of 1547, the learned, and rather open-minded, part-time hermit Artemii was residing at the Moscow Chudov Monastery, and Sobaka was soon appointed its archimandrite.[59] It was under these conditions that Maksim also had his excommunication lifted, though he was not permitted to return to Ottoman Greece.[60]

On the other hand, a genuine system of innerecclesiastical surveillance
and control came into place. Also after the 1547 Moscow fire, Makarii's
protegé, the talented master iconographer and priest Silvestr, became one of
the young Ivan IV's chief advisers and officiated as archpriest at
Blagoveshchenskii Sobor in the Kremlin.[61] By the early 1550s Silvestr
appears to have controlled many, if not all, of the major state and church
appointments.[62] For the latter, two stages of interviews might be held: one
by Silvestr and a second by a designated confessor, whose acquired
knowledge was not bound by any code of secrecy. To the contrary, if he
heard anything untoward, he was expected to inform. If he failed to do so,
he became a suspect. Failure to confess properly could also have pernicious
results. If a layman were involved in an investigation, he might be expected
to reveal what he had read and where he had obtained his books.[63] This was
a system made for abuses by the unscrupulous who could secure the support
of the chief authority for all matters--the tsar.

Four kinds of synodal trials were held during 1549-56, revealing the
different uses of what by now had developed into a distinct Muscovite
Inquisition. First came Sobaka, again a victim of ecclesiastical politics in
1548-49. For reasons that are not at all clear from the records, after Sobaka
was designated archimandrite of Chudov, Makarii, purportedly under the
direction of the seventeen-year-old tsar, started to research the history of
Sobaka's pardon. Finding a discrepancy between the words of Ioasaf and
Bishop Nifont Kormilitsyn (a former hegumen of Iosifov) concerning the
deceased Metropolitan Daniil's concurrence in Sobaka's rehabilitation,
Makarii held a full synod at his own palace. This was attended by bishops,
abbots, archpriests, and elders (*startsi*) from Troitsa-Sergiev, Kirillov, and
Iosifov, including Gerasim Lenkov.[64] Remaining proud and defiant
throughout, Sobaka was stripped of his priestly rank, but then sent off to
what appears to have been a relatively harmless exile at Nilov Hermitage
"for repentence"--a strictly ecclesiastical disciplinary measure. With church
reform in the air, the Iosifites and their allies apparently were not above
using mild inquisitorial means to purge the hierarchy of an obnoxious type.

The next to come to trial was the case of the state secretary for foreign
affairs (*posol'skii diak*), Ivan Mikhailovich Viskovatii, who, when the tsar
was deathly ill early in 1553, had supported the latter's request that his

infant son be recognized successor, while other advisers had leaned toward the tsar's adolescent first cousin Vladimir Andreevich of Staritsa.[65] At the same time, Viskovatii opposed as uncanonical and heretically Western some of the new icons that had been painted with Makarii's approval on the Novgorod and Pskov models for Blagoveshchenskii Sobor after the 1547 fire. When a regular synod met to finish work left over from the 1551 *Stoglav* Synod, specifically to deal with the problem of supervising iconographers, Viskovatii raised some objections. Makarii warned Viskovatii of the danger of falling into an iconoclastic heresy, and then the tsar allowed Makarii to recess the synod, so that Viskovatii could prepare a full position paper for examination.[66] The result was that in January the synod first subjected Viskovatii to a two-week excommunication and then, with the tsar attending, accepted the man's humble petition of repentance, answered his objections point by point, upbraided him for daring to speculate about theological matters, and laid a standard three-year staged and supervised excommunication-penance. The synod promised Viskovatii full rehabilitation if he cooperated, but warned him that if he continued to hold such ill-conceived opinions or disturbed others with them, he would be "terminally anathematized with the other heretics and apostates of the Orthodox Church."[67] On paper, Viskovatii's case was a lot like Sobaka's, in that fundamentally both revolved around the authority of the hierarchy: Sobaka's pride landed him in exile, while Viskovatii's humility gave him a way out and could serve as an object lesson to others. The fact that Viskovatii was basically correct about the icons hardly mattered.[68]

Even before the issue of the new icons came up for discussion, the case of the middle serviceman from Tver, Matvei Bashkin, surfaced. Since his confederates, the Borisov-Borozdin brothers, had been associated with Vladimir of Staritsa, the other candidate for succession during Ivan IV's illness, political rivalries may also have been involved.[69] During the tsar's illness, Bashkin had revealed to his confessor, Simeon (Silvestr's colleague at Blagoveshchenskii Sobor), a belief in the incompatibility of slavery with the New Testament and had given him a text with wax markings at certain passages. After Ivan's recovery, Simeon told Silvestr about this, and the latter informed the tsar and showed him the text. The tsar had Bashkin arrested and placed in a Kremlin palace cellar under the investigatory supervision of two Iosifov *startsi*. Bashkin's actual religious offense is not evident: was it interpreting the Bible on his own and thus intruding into the clergy's exclusive domain, or did he dare to propose social reform on the basis of a radical or chiliastic reading of Christianity?[70]

Viskovatii's testimony also implicated Artemii and the two priests Simeon and Silvestr who had investigated him two and a half years earlier, when he was appointed hegumen of Troitsa-Sergiev Monastery. The latter cleared themselves by pointing to their role in uncovering and reporting Bashkin and by implicating Artemii and his colleague Porfirii.[71] Artemii, for his part, had abandoned Troitsa-Sergiev without the tsar's permission after only six months. Summoned now to cooperate in the investigation of Bashkin, he refused and fled back to Porfirii's hermitage in Novoozero.

The inquisitorial authorities proceeded to lump Artemii and Bashkin together and try them and their friends as one clique, if not all at the same time.[72] Prodded, apparently, with generous doses of torture, as well as confrontations with live witnesses, Bashkin informed on and misrepresented both his comrades and Artemii's circle. In front of both the tsar and his younger brother and cousins, Bashkin confessed to a gamut of proto-Protestant, antisacramental, and iconoclastic beliefs (the old Novgorod Heresy, as described by Iosif, but minus the Judaizing, or, rather, Lutheranism without justification by faith), and the foreign origin of all of them. The evidence from Artemii's recorded opinions is that Bashkin's doctrinal deviation was much less, if any at all.[73] Nevertheless, he received the special sentence reserved for the "heresiarch" after the 1504-5 immolations: life imprisonment in Iosifov. One of the Borisovs was similarly sent off to Valaamo Monastery, but escaped to Lithuania.[74] Whatever the real crimes of the accused, the inquisitors wanted them convicted of direct attacks on both standard piety and the sacraments.

Artemii's trial was next. Along with Porfirii and "hermit" Savva Shakh, Artemii was charged with a variety of offenses, including iconoclasm, antisacramentalism, and dietary infractions.[75] The accusations receiving the most attention were connected with the old Nonpossessor issues: debunking the Russian wonder-workers and canon laws and, in the case of Artemii, failure to condemn Russia's heretics, and failure to believe that rituals can save major sinners. The surviving abstract of Artemii's trial shows a procedure similar to that employed against Maksim, with a host of witnesses that included Artemii's own cell valet (*keleinik*). Artemii denied most of the accusations and boldly pointed out that when he broke a fast he was the tsar's guest. Several witnesses also defended Artemii from certain accusations. Artemii actually debated with Makarii concerning the inquisition and claimed there were no real heretics, since no one was starting a public quarrel. Accordingly, Bashkin was guilty of no more than childish errors, at least in his theological thinking. Artemii's opinion concerning Bashkin's position on slavery does not seem to have been sought at the trial. At any rate Artemii would at least grant leeway for the private, otherworldly "heresies," which Volotskii had considered actionable by ecclesiastical discipline. Artemii, whose views seem to have approximated Erasmus's, certainly would not send someone to prison for life for having speculated.[76]

The tsar and the synod sentenced Savva and Artemii to the now normal, supervised life terms, the latter specifically for criticising Russian Orthodoxy, denigrating some rituals, and questioning the verdicts of previous heresy trials. Artemii, who was also stripped of his priesthood, absconded to Lithuania. The investigations also uncovered in the hermitages the ex-slave Feodosii Kosoi, who, along with two others, including (another or the same) Porfirii, underwent investigations in Moscow. They all likewise escaped to Lithuania, following which Feodosii was depicted as a genuine, socially radical sectarian, interested in realizing the kingdom of God on earth.[77] Meanwhile one pro-Artemii witness or his relative, a certain Ioasaf/Isaak Belobaev from Solovetskii Monastery, was tried for heresy in front of the tsar and metropolitan. Belobaev's disciple Kassian, who happened to be bishop of Riazan, attacked Iosif Volotskii's book when Tsar Ivan and Makarii tried to use it as an authority. Kassian is claimed immediately to have suffered a stroke, while the metropolitan proceeded to produce a witness to attest to another miracle by a Russian saint.[78] Once more the defense of the inquisition and promotion of new Russian saints went hand in hand.

Zealous inquisitors also locked up the very talented Hegumen Feodorit of Spaso-Evfimiev Monastery, who had earlier converted some Lapps and translated prayers into their language. Kurbskii and some other top officials were able to convince even Makarii to release this national resource, who was later sent on a delicate diplomatic mission to Constantinople on behalf of the Russian Church.[79] According to Kurbskii, the real instigators of this last purge of northern monasteries and hermitages were "cunning, property-loving monks." The secular interests of leading Russian ecclesiastics had become so pervasive that they apparently were losing the ability to understand what activated otherworldly energies. The steady growth of Russian Christianity outside the Church would tend to substantiate this thesis.

To recapitulate, after some interaction between local and central authorities in Russia's pre-unification experience in dealing with heretics, Russian inquisitional methods developed in part on the basis of Byzantine synodal practices and with scant regard for truth or legality. The targets were always explicitly depicted as threatening the church itself and its authority. The issues never focused simply on a set of beliefs concerning ethics and salvation. The metropolitan's *osviashchennyi sobor*, which was very much under the sovereign's control, functioned as a grand and petty jury and a panel of experts. In the first Moscow phase, Archbishop Gennadii of Novgorod, who was attracted to both Catholic concepts of the episcopacy and to what he knew of the Western inquisitions, was the moving spirit.

He was followed by the most genuinely fanatic and hence deadly of Moscow's inquisistors, the charismatic Iosif Volotskii, who came to grips with the reality of the autocracy and theoretically monasticised the secular arm, without retreating from the church's maximum demands for theocratic worldly authority and rich emoluments. His disciple Metropolitan Daniil then turned the inquisition against Russia's secularizing and more spiritually minded Orthodox reformers, who at one and the same time would have deprived the Church of some of its worldly riches but still enriched religious life with a few carefully chosen, nonthreatening fruits of worldly culture. Finally Iosifite monks and their allies, as authorized inquisitors under Metropolitan Makarii, brought the Muscovite inquisition to a climax, by blurring the distinction among Orthodox reformer, social dissident, and incipient sectarian, lumping them all together with other critics, and having scant regard for fact or religious impulse. The end result was that the

Church retained its property and authority, but continued to forfeit popular allegiances as popular heresy spread in the latter 1550s and 1560s.[80]

An interesting and hardly accidental thread throughout is the chronological coincidence of major trials and succession issues. The only attested direct linkage occurred in 1504, when the victory of the Iosifites followed the death of Elena of Moldavia and Vasilii's victory over his nephew Dmitrii. However, Vasilii III's treatment of his brothers and his remarriage were at least tangental to Maksim's and Vassian's travails and central to Daniil's success; and the crisis around Ivan IV's illness set the stage for intrigues, investigations, and trials, resulting in Silvestr's and Simeon's exoneration, Viskovatii's light penance, and the sentencing of Bashkin, Artemii, and others. The 1488-90 synods, of course, arose more from the problems accompanying Moscow's ecclesiastical conquest of Novgorod, but then the problem was not resolved until the succession crisis broke out. Succession questions at least intensified the stakes of high politics and gave inquisitors and informers a special opportunity to profit.

As a postscript, it is interesting to note which active intellectual and religious types escaped the clutches of the Russian inquisition. One group were immigrant Roman Catholic "experts" with immunity. Obviously the Orthodox Church was not about to turn against a Dominican who supplied a possible foundation for the Russian Church's worldly efforts, or against an astrologer-doctor, whose services were valued at court, though his doctrines might serve as the object of polemics. Better to attack an Artemii, even falsely, for approving the "Latins."[81]

A second type were relatively well-educated Orthodox, who delved into moderate social criticism, but served as commissioned writers for the Church and composed antiheretical tracts. It is significant, however, that even though they were useful as theologians, neither the moralist Zinovii Otenskii[82] nor the utopian Ermolai-Erazm[83] achieved a position of power. Also, Maksim Grek, his theoretical support of the inquisition notwithstanding, could not achieve his fondest wish: permission to leave.[84]

An intriguing problem is that two major secular critics who fell afoul of the state, lost their lands, and disappeared from the surviving sources are not known to have suffered ecclesiastical reprisals. This is hard to believe in the case of the Latin-reading Fedor Karpov, who had the nerve to use Aristotle to attack Metropolitan Daniil for placing the despotic political principle of endurance (*terpenie*) over justice (*pravda*).[85] Fedor thus came close to one of the issues that may have cost Bersen his head and another Karpov--Petr Mukha--his freedom: disgust with Vasilii III's system of rule. Attracted, as Fedor Kuritsyn had been, to natural science and astrology, and possessed of certain chiliastic hopes, Karpov was certainly a potential target for Daniil's inquisition as well as Vasilii III's security apparatus.[86]

Ivan Peresvetov's attacks on slavery, using a religious argument based on old Testament apocrypha, carried the danger of raising the same suspicions as had Bashkin.[87] On the other hand, Peresvetov was a crusading expansionist, who wanted to copy the Muslim Turks in order to facilitate Russia's conquering and converting the Kazan Muslims--a program supported by the worldly oriented Church. Like Silvestr, who freed his slaves for only the practical reason that they would thus be better workers, Peresvetov at least avoided Bashkin's fatal attempt to develop a secular social reform movement on the basis of trancendental principles.[88]

How Peresvetov expected to establish *pravda* via a doctrine of punishments more worthy of a Chinese legist than European Aristotelian eludes this writer, but his concept of "near paradise," a conquered and transformed Kazan, was down-to-earth and attractive to Russia's churchmen, who cashed in on the conquest just as the Spanish clergy did in Mexico and Peru.[89] Those reformers like Artemii, however, who believed not only that the tsar should rule with *pravda* and *krotost'*, but also that "peace, justice and joy in the Holy Spirit constituted the Kingdom of God," could not avoid crossing the dangerous and thin sixteenth-century line between tolerated reformer-critic and actionable heretic.[90]

CHAPTER 3

THE JESUITS' ROLE IN
FOUNDING SCHOOLS IN LATE TSARIST RUSSIA

William A. James

Once the Jesuits were assured of Catherine II's protection in the early
1700s and satisfied with the legality of their existence as a religious order in
the Russian Empire, they knew they were in a unique position. In an
Orthodox country that was far behind Western Europe in cultural and
intellectual achievements, the Society of Jesus was the only organization in
the empire with the talent and facilities to offer the Russian nobles the type
of sophistication they desired. Through the attraction that their scientific
and artistic achievements exerted on the nobility, the Jesuits hoped not only
to improve the cultural level of the empire but to alter its creed as well. In
this attitude, they were faithful to the spirit of their founder, Saint Ignatius
of Loyola, as commemorated in the liturgy celebrating his feast day: "I
have come to bring fire to the earth. How I wish it were already blazing!"[1]

The apostolic thrust of Ignatius's spirituality was that a good Christian
should be interested not only in his own eternal salvation but in that of his
fellow man. The application of this principle to Jesuit education is easily
discerned. For the Society of Jesus, education is not an end in itself but a
means of helping the Jesuits and those they teach to achieve their ultimate
goal as creatures of God.[2] The Jesuit teacher is expected to be a
distinguished academician who encourages the intellectual growth of his
students so that they might pursue successful careers in secular society, and
he is also expected by his personal example to lead his pupils to a
knowledge and love of God.[3] Therefore, a Jesuit teacher believes that his
work in the classroom, though it may be immediately concerned with
physics or Latin, has a spiritual function. He is helping his students gain
eternal salvation.

Several conditions served as opportunities for the Jesuits to expand
their activities inside the Russian Empire. Because the tsarist government's
finances were encumbered in other areas and the nobility did not support

government-sponsored education, Russia had an acute shortage of educators and educational facilities.[4] The foreign policy of Catherine II's predecessors, as well as her own military expenditures, had deprived education of its share of the budget. Although her government attempted educational reform and innovation, these efforts were too few and their effects too restricted. The standards of the existing institutions of higher education were quite poor, and the empire had no organized system of education that reached into the villages. Thus the nobility were not interested in the educational enterprises of the government. If they sought an education at all, they generally went abroad, hired a tutor, or enrolled in a private school.

In short, the empire had no institutions that could provide the competence and services of the Jesuit schools. The University of Moscow was the sole institution in Russia that approximated a Western university, but having been founded only in 1755, its standards were still quite low.[5] Although the academies of Kiev and Moscow were influential, they were primarily concerned with theological studies. Finally, while Catherine aspired to create a native enlightenment and sponsored various educational projects, the "Semiramis of the North" did not establish any new university.

The schools supported by the Russian Orthodox Church were also relatively poor. Consequently, Russian Orthodoxy was quite vulnerable to a concerted Jesuit campaign. Although the theological schools established by Peter the Great had improved the intellectual level of the Russian clergy, the Jesuits were far more learned and articulate than the Orthodox priests.[6] Furthermore, the Russian Orthodox Church had been steadily losing its own vigor because of government controls and the influence of Protestant theology and spirituality.

Since the Jesuits were dependent on the autocrat's favor for their existence in Russia, they could only subtly suggest their interest in changing conditions in her empire. These Jesuit overtures took place during visits by the empress or other important personages to Jesuit schools. In addition to solemnly receiving the visiting dignitaries, the Jesuits took the opportunity to show them the scientific inventions of the faculty and the academic achievements of their students. In an age fascinated with the physical sciences and in a society anxious to imitate the culture of Western

Europe, these visits were tantalizing spectacles for a Russian autocrat. They were demonstrations of what could be achieved throughout the empire if the Jesuits were allowed to expand their facilities and influence beyond Belorussia.

A typical example of the Jesuits' tactics is the reception given to the future tsar Paul I when he visited Polotsk in 1781. The following is an eyewitness account of this event:

> The 9th Inst the Grand Duke and Duchess arrived here in the Great Square where our Church is very conspicuous. All our Fathers, with our Pensioners & Scholars were drawn up in a long line, & when they made a low reverence to the Princes, they rose up in their Carriage & returned the Salute: immediately, the whole Square was illuminated, but the front of our Church made the finest appearance; an ingenious & simple piece of Machinery, invented by Father Hieukeuri had the appearance of a splendid Throne, erected amidst lucid columns, from which hung a transparent representation of the Royal Couple: the Porch, & Steps of the Church were surrounded with a blaze of Tapers, with Pyramids rising at equal distances in the intervals; & transparent Images with Epigrams on the Bases. The Prince seem'd delighted with the sight, & said, that these were indeed marks of sincere love & esteem. The following day, after having receiv'd the respects of a few of the Nobility, they came on their own accord to our Church, where speaking to us with great affability, they examined every thing with great attention, & after Vespers, they wou'd see & examine the Vestments, & other Furniture, & desired to be taught the different rites & uses of them. The Grand Duke said, that he was highly satisfied & approved of every thing; & that it was the first time he had ever seen a Catholick Church, & Catholick rites & service.[7]

Catherine II had also visited Polotsk and had been afforded a similar treatment, but mother and son had strikingly different responses. Unlike his mother, Paul showed a deep respect for the liturgy during the service that was offered for him and even participated in the ceremonies.[8] This significant gesture demonstrated an aspect of Paul's character that would later make him a sympathetic supporter of the Jesuits' plans for Russia.

For the present, however, the Jesuits had to limit their activities to Belorussia. Catherine was content to retain them for the stabilizing influence they provided in the area. Through the ukase of December 14, 1772, the Russian empress had already placed definite restrictions on their proselytizing,[9] and relations with the Vatican during her reign were adequate testimony of her opposition to the spread of Catholicism in the Russian Empire. Although the Jesuits were fine educators, they were also excellent missionaries. Catherine wanted to restrict their teaching to the predominantly Catholic population of Belorussia.[10]

Until the end of Paul I's reign in 1801, approximately two hundred Jesuits lived and worked in Belorussia. They concentrated their efforts on two tasks: parish work and education. About a dozen Jesuits were involved in staffing parishes or missions scattered throughout the rural sections of the province. These men performed liturgical and sacramental functions and taught the illiterate to read and write. By teaching these basic skills the Jesuits hoped to solidify the beliefs of the faithful and bring the unbaptized into the Catholic Church. Usually, one or two Jesuits would be sent to a location for this purpose. Although conditions were rather primitive, the rigors of the mission were offset by the zeal of the Jesuits for this type of work.[11]

The vast majority of the order were employed in the Jesuit schools at Polotsk, Vitebsk, Dunaburg, Orsha, Mstislavl, and Mogilev.[12] These schools were the basic type of educational establishment that the Jesuits had maintained throughout the world previous to the suppression of their order in 1773. Sometimes referred to as colleges, from the Latin *collegium* or the French *collège*, these schools might be better described in English as Latin grammar schools or middle schools.[13] The contemporary American educational system has no counterpart to these schools: in a Jesuit school a student was taught the subjects that fall between the rudimentary skills learned in an elementary school and the knowledge gained in a modern junior college. Consequently the ages of the pupils could range from seven years to the early twenties.[14]

The Jesuit schools in Belorussia followed the format described in the *Ratio Studiorum* (Plan of Studies) of the Society of Jesus published in 1599.[15] While this document was the culmination of much experimentation and superseded earlier versions of the *Ratio*, the Jesuits in Belorussia were utilizing it two hundred years after its promulgation. Critics might argue, as they did at the time, that the Jesuits were following an outdated educational formula.[16] Yet it is only fair to note that the *Ratio* was a model allowing for adaptation. The curriculum at Polotsk and the other Jesuit schools in Belorussia reveals alterations in the courses outlined in the *Ratio* that can be attributed to the scientific achievements and the growing popularity of modern languages during the intervening two centuries.[17] Moreover, it was only in the mid-nineteenth century that a definite change took place in the overall academic aims of the best academic institutions in Europe. Until that time, the mark of an educated man was eloquence.[18] Through its broad humanistic curriculum, the *Ratio* handsomely achieved this goal.

Furthermore, the Jesuit schools in Belorussia were very popular. Since the area was predominantly Catholic, the Society of Jesus competed for students with the other religious orders engaged in teaching: Dominicans, Piarists, Franciscans, and others.[19] Yet in 1801 the Jesuits taught 865 students, approximately three-quarters of all males enrolled in the Archdiocese of Mogilev.[20] Logically, a parent wishing a progressive education for a son would have chosen a Piarist school using the methods developed by Stanislaus Konarski or a Dominican school maintaining the standards of the *Komisja Edukacji Narodowej*.[21]

With the exception of Polotsk, the Jesuits had only a Faculty of Letters in their schools. This faculty was divided into five sections, or grades: lower grammar (*infima*), grammar, syntax, poetry, and rhetoric.[22] Advancement through this system was determined not by the calendar but by mastery of the subject matter in a particular section. Conceivably, a student could spend a year in a grammar class, but two years in rhetoric.[23] Examinations were held a few times each year in the presence of the school's rector, the prefect of studies, and various teachers.[24] Also, public examinations were conducted at the end of the year. At Polotsk, and probably at the other Jesuit schools, a Jesuit seminarian, known as a scholastic, traditionally began teaching a class in the lower grammar section and remained with that class through syntax.[25] This practice might indicate the existence of a promotion system in which an entire class advanced through the lower grades in the Jesuit schools in the empire.

Polotsk had the only complete educational structure as outlined in the *Ratio*.[26] In addition to a Faculty of Letters, it had a Faculty of Liberal Arts and a Faculty of Theology. After completing the five sections (through rhetoric) of the Faculty of Letters, a student could take logic and physics in the Faculty of Liberal Arts. The last section (theology) usually attracted only seminarians. Finally, on the other end of the scale, Polotsk had a section called *fara* in which students learned to read and write "as well as the beginnings of grammar and Christian studies." All students in this section had housing in town, paid no tuition, and once per day received "bread and food at the gate of the Jesuit College."[27] The *Ratio* does not mention this grade in its program, and it apparently was not a feature of the other Jesuit schools in the empire.[28]

Most of the details available about daily classroom organization concern the school at Polotsk. There, the school day began at 7:45 with morning prayers in the college chapel. Classes began at 8:00 and continued until 11:30. The midday recess lasted until 1:00, when classes resumed for an afternoon session about the same length as the morning one. Classes were taught in Polish, Russian, or Latin and usually lasted thirty or forty-five minutes. In the lower grades, classes were occasionally very short, usually catechesis, lasting only fifteen minutes. Ordinarily no classes met on Tuesday or Thursday. The students had three vacations: one during summer and a two-week vacation at Christmas and at Easter.[29]

The Jesuits in Russia employed the basic Jesuit teaching method called the prelection. In this method, a teacher of Latin, for example, would read aloud a text as a means of preparing the class for the next day's assignment. The process served a number of functions. The students learned the correct pronunciation and rhythm of the piece. The teacher also involved the class by asking various students a range of questions concerning the grammar and possible nuances of meaning of the words in a passage. This exercise promoted not merely memorization of a subject but an involvement with and eventually a mastery of the material presented.[30]

In order to achieve their academic goals, the Jesuits had developed a number of skills and incentives for their students. For example, a Latin class would be divided into various sections named after some of Julius Caesar's legions. These divisions would compete with each other for the top honors of the class. Public disputations were also conducted, pitting one class against another, and prizes were awarded according to the ability of the contestants. Finally, in order to promote a more thorough knowledge and appreciation, they formed "academies" devoted to languages, the arts, and other fields.[31]

Dormitory life at Polotsk was closely circumscribed. At the beginning of the year an inventory of a student's possessions was made in duplicate. The owner retained one copy and the other was kept by the custodian. Residents were not allowed to have money of their own, but could deposit it with the treasurer. Permission was required to write letters and to take a long walk. Even short walks with servants required a prefect's permission. Reading material was censored, and obedience to the regulations of the dormitory was strictly enforced. Although the students enjoyed a four-course dinner and a three-course supper, they read during the meals.[32] In short, student life at Polotsk resembled the routine of a seminary.

The Jesuit colleges at Polotsk and Dunaburg, in addition to classroom buildings, library, and dormitory, had a pharmacy and a resident doctor.[33] To help support itself, the school at Polotsk had a printing press,[34] a linen factory, and considerable timber holdings. Dunaburg had a cloth factory and a well-stocked lake for fishing. The revenue from these projects was substantially increased by Catherine II's exempting the Jesuits from a land tax.[35]

The Jesuits apparently provided a pleasant study environment for their students. A Russian school inspector visiting Polotsk in 1803 described the classrooms as light, large, clean, and in order. The library was described as enormous and furnished with cabinets and a large variety of study aids.[36]

Virtually all the students who attended the Jesuit schools in Belorussia were from upper-class Roman Catholic families. For example, approximately half of the students at the Jesuit school in Vitebsk in 1801 were sons of noblemen.[37] In addition to "noblemen" the categories used to designate the social background of the students' families were "merchants," "petty bourgeoisie" (*meshchane*), "clergy," "residents of Vitebsk," "the mayor of the City of Vitebsk," and "a doctor." Of the sixty-four students enrolled, fifty-six were identified as Roman Catholic, five as Uniat Catholics, and three as Russian Orthodox. Since the Jesuits charged no tuition for these schools, we can conclude that this sociological and religious profile indicates the sort of people who were interested in Jesuit education, rather than those who could afford it. The only charge in the Jesuit schools was for living in the dormitory, and a number of alternatives were open to students who could not afford to pay this fee. They could receive a grant from the school, do odd jobs on the campus, or find a private benefactor.[38] Thus the only criteria for admittance to a Jesuit school were sufficient aptitude and good character.

The establishment of a novitiate in 1779 had encouraged a number of ex-Jesuits from Western Europe to join their colleagues in Russia.[39] Moreover, after the election of a vicar-general, Stanislaus Czerniewicz, in 1782 and the establishment of a tertianship (the final stage in a Jesuit priest's formation) in 1783, the organization of the order in Russia was complete. As a result, the number of ex-Jesuits who made the journey to Belorussia increased. Although several locally prominent Jesuit educators lived in Belorussia, this influx of new men improved the stature of the Jesuit schools.[40] Furthermore, the addition of French, German, Austrian, and Italian Jesuits added a cosmopolitan atmosphere to the schools that composed what was once derisively referred to as "the tail of a Polish province."[41]

Among the ex-Jesuits who arrived in Russia during this period was Gabriel Gruber, who more than any other Jesuit was responsible for the successes the Society was to achieve in the empire.[42] Soon after his arrival at Polotsk in 1784, he began to make a strong impression on his co-workers. Some of those works were recorded by one of his contemporaries as follows:

The City of Polosko, has never yet had a well, this Father is now employed in digging one for the College, & the Building over it is to be adorned, by his desire, with the Emblems of the Sacred Hearts of Jesus & Mary. He now hopes, to exchange the mission of China for which he was destined, for that of Siberia. He quickly accommodated himself to the manners, Language, & regular observance of our Fathers; we think, in this one Father alone, we possess the value of many.[43]

The writer's assessment was to prove quite accurate, for in addition to the practical talents that Gruber displayed, he possessed a vision of what the Jesuits could accomplish in Russia, and he was a perceptive diplomat.

Shortly after Gruber's arrival, Catherine II asked the Jesuits to send a delegation to St. Petersburg to acquaint themselves with a new plan for schools that she hoped they would adopt. During a recent visit to Russia, Joseph II had informed the empress of the new educational methodology that he had implemented in the Austrian Empire. In July 1784, Fathers Kareu, Gieryk, and Rzewuski went to St. Petersburg to inspect a model school and to hold discussions with the appropriate authorities. They returned to Polotsk in August, but evidently made no changes in the curriculum or method used in the Jesuit schools.[44]

Further discussions about educational innovation were held at the general congregation convened on September 20, 1785. The death of Vicar-General Czerniewicz on July 7, 1785, necessitated convoking a general congregation to elect a new superior.[45] Shortly after writing to Potemkin, Gruber was informed that imperial permission had been granted for the assembly. The congregation not only elected Gabriel Lenkiewicz as vicar-general but also directed its attention to educational reform. While the meetings were in session, a letter arrived from the empress expressing her wish that the Jesuits implement "the form of teaching in use in the schools in St. Petersburg."[46] The congregation established a committee composed of Gruber and Fathers Kareu and Borowski. However, there is no evidence that the Jesuits ever seriously responded to the imperial request. The only apparent concession they made was to establish a polytechnical institute at Polotsk to train science teachers.[47]

Despite the traditional approach to education, the Jesuit colleges underwent several changes in atmosphere and appearance. Having been elected an assistant to the vicar-general at the general congregation, Gruber directed his attention to establishing Polotsk as the preeminent center of the small cluster of Jesuit schools in Belorussia. He had the college theater refurbished and a series of dramas presented for the school community and visitors. He enlarged and improved the school library, and personally contributed an original painting of Saint Ignatius for the vestibule. A new two-story building soon housed a museum, laboratories for chemistry and physics, and rooms where students studied mechanics, hydrostatics, geodesy, optics, astronomy, and civil and military architecture. It was also during this period that a linen factory and a printing press were established at the college. In addition to providing leadership, Gruber also formed a team of competent artists and technicians to continue the progress that had begun. As a result of these achievements, Russian officials who visited the grounds of the Jesuit college soon came to consider Polotsk an oasis in the desert.[48] Encouraged by the activities at Polotsk, the Jesuits at the other schools in Belorussia increased their efforts so that a restricted Jesuit renaissance developed under Gruber's inspiration during Catherine's reign.[49]

A twofold effect resulted from Gruber's efforts. The Jesuits gained the respect of the Russian nobility, and the nobles had greater access to the most recent scientific and artistic achievements. Once again, as in Europe over a century earlier, it became fashionable for nobles to correspond with Jesuit scholars. This increased popularity gained some public support for the expansion of the Jesuits' educational institutions. Moreover, by attracting the nobility to learning, the Jesuits helped raise the cultural level of Russian society. Russians no longer had to travel to Western Europe to see exciting scientific discoveries, for significant intellectual work was being done in their own country.

For the moment, the Jesuits had to be content with their impressive but limited successes under Catherine II. Their experiences during her reign had taught them a valuable lesson. Autocracy had preserved them, but it had also restricted them. If their sovereign shared their sentiments, the Jesuits could realize their objectives more fully throughout the empire.

Obviously, when Catherine died November 6, 1796, the Jesuits were quite anxious to learn her son's attitude toward them.

The Jesuits' first opportunity to meet their new sovereign, Paul I, occurred on May 7, 1797, when the emperor visited their college at Orsha. Their concern about making a favorable impression is shown by the fact that Gruber had already sent a letter and gifts to Paul I and Maria Fedorovna.[50] The emperor's gift was a specially designed clock; the tsarina's, a miniature icon of the Madonna. Moreover, on the day of the tsar's visit Gruber traveled with Father Lenkiewicz, the vicar-general, to Orsha to renew his past acquaintance with Paul. Certainly Gruber's status as a scientist and a man of learning was adequate reason for his presence, but on that day his concerns were diplomatic rather than academic.

The Jesuits' fears were groundless. After meeting the assembled superiors and men of the Society of Jesus, Paul assured them that he had no intention of emulating Joseph II's harsh treatment of religious orders. Turning toward Gruber, the tsar said, "You have many enemies." Gruber observed that the Jesuits' enemies were also enemies of God and kings. The priest concluded his remarks by expressing his gratitude for the safe and favorable refuge he found in Russia.[51]

Obviously, Gruber already knew the new tsar's deepest concerns, and used them to the Jesuits' advantage. Although the Society of Jesus did have its enemies, Paul, a devoted autocrat and defender of Christianity, was threatened by the same enemies. Gruber attempted to show the emperor that the Jesuits cherished values similar to his. Impressed by Gruber's words, Paul said while leaving, "I want all of you to be preserved in my realm as you have been until now. I deeply respect your order."[52] Instead of the eccentric martinet who often entered into well-intentioned but poorly planned projects with an impatient exactitude that made his subordinates tremble with anxiety, Paul at Orsha appeared to be a thoughtful and compassionate ruler. Reflecting on this meeting with the tsar, the Jesuits must have hoped that they finally had a sovereign who would allow them to pursue their objectives in the empire.

The Jesuits' best opportunity to expand their influence through educational institutions came on August 22, 1800, when Paul I ordered Gruber to Lithuania, Volynia, and Podolia to conduct a survey of existing

educational institutions in that area. The Jesuit returned to the emperor's
estate at Gatchina on October 10 of that year for further discussions. The
results of Gruber's survey and his conversations with Paul were soon
apparent. Several schools and tracts of land that the Jesuits had once owned
in Lithuania, Podolia, and Volynia had been confiscated by the Polish
government after suppression of the order. This property remained in
private or government hands after annexation to the Russian Empire during
the second and third partitions. On October 12, 1800, two days after
Gruber's arrival at Gatchina, Paul I issued an ukase returning these former
possessions to the order and placing the schools under the order's direction.
The same decree augmented their training facilities by allowing the Jesuits
to enlarge the novitiate at Polotsk, a testimony to the anticipated growth of
the order in the empire. Furthermore, the Jesuits were also to take control
of the University of Vilna, except for its medical faculty, by May 1801.[53]
Six days later an ukase of October 18 gave the Jesuits the church and
property of Saint Catherine's parish in St. Petersburg, where the Jesuits
were to perform pastoral works and establish a school.

    Despite opposition to his new decrees, Paul I firmly supported the
Jesuits. Having occupied former Jesuit lands, local nobles strongly
protested the ukase of October 12, which forced them to give up this
property.[54] Furthermore, the faculty of the University of Vilna were not
happily resigned to their fate. Indeed, it seemed that Gruber's discussions
with Paul had caused more trouble than they increased stability.
Nonetheless, Paul would not change his policies, and his critics were either
imprisoned or exiled.

    The tsar's attitude can be explained by reading some of the sentiments
he expressed to Gruber:

I see no other way to arrest the flood of impiety, illuminism, and of
Jacobinism in my Empire than to entrust the education of the young
to the Jesuits; it is in childhood that one must begin; one must repair
the edifice at its foundation, if not everything will collapse, and
there will not remain either religion or government.[55]

Encouraged by Gruber, Paul had obviously become convinced that in order to eradicate the dangers he feared and build the type of society he desired, the Jesuits had to have a greater influence in the education of his subjects.

A natural consequence of Gruber's achievements was the disgrace of Archbishop Stanislaus of Siestrzencewicz-Bohusz, the head of the Catholic Church in Russia. By the ukase of October 18, Paul had in effect evicted the archbishop from his residence in the capital, for Siestrzencewicz lived in one of the buildings attached to Saint Catherine's on Nevskii Prospekt. A few days after being informed of the new decree, he was notified that he must move from his apartments so that the Jesuits could occupy the church property. The actual decision to dismiss Siestrzencewicz had been made by November 11, and the archbishop was given the opportunity to resign before he received the final order to leave the capital on November 14. Although the prelate stated that he was in poor health, his gesture was an obvious excuse to save face. He was exiled to his estate near Mogilev under police supervision and remained there for the rest of Paul's reign.[56]

Meanwhile, the Jesuits had responded to Paul's request to operate Saint Catherine's church in the capital. Four Jesuits left Polotsk for St. Petersburg on November 10 and arrived there November 20.[57] The number and nationalities of the priests conformed to the provisions of a law of 1769 that sought to provide clergy for the major Catholic nationalities in the capital. Thus the four Jesuits were Gaetano Angiolini, an Italian; Joseph Kamielski, a Pole; Desiré Richardot, a Frenchman; and George Rottensteiner, a German.[58] Gruber had personally selected these talented men because of their homiletic abilities. In addition, the Jesuits renewed the liturgical life of the parish by employing all the richness of the Latin ritual and by selecting the most appropriate sacred music for the occasion. Whether the celebration was solemn or festive, the Jesuits provided the appropriate religious atmosphere to appeal to both the mind and the spirit. They also had the good sense to install stoves to allow services year-round.[59]

Obviously, the Jesuits directed their attention beyond the concerns of the Catholic community in the capital. Their new parish provided them with an unprecedented opportunity for increasing their influence and spreading their faith among the nobility in St. Petersburg. Consequently, they established a pharmacy on the church grounds and set up a permanent display of Jesuit inventions and manufactured goods in one of the church halls.[60] However impressive these attractions might have been, the Jesuits used them only as a means to interest the citizenry in the liturgies offered in the Jesuits' church. An interested worshipper could witness a service conducted by well-educated men who could express their religious beliefs articulately and competently. Thus, unlike the Orthodox Church, which never confronted the prevailing challenges to organized religion, the Jesuits offered the thinking Russian nobleman the possibility of reconciling his intellectual and spiritual concerns within the structure of a traditional church. As a result of their activities in the parish, the Jesuits managed to convert a number of nobles from the ranks of prominent Russian families.[61]

In addition to establishing the Jesuits in his capital, Paul encouraged them to expand their activities into other parts of the empire, and even into foreign countries. Jesuit missions were contemplated in the Caucasus, Saratov, Astrakhan, and New Russia, and a college was planned for Odessa.[62] During a visit by King Gustavus Adolphus IV of Sweden to Russia in December 1800, Paul asked the king to allow the Jesuits to return to their former parish in Stockholm.[63] Finally, on December 8, 1800, Paul instructed his ambassador in Constantinople to request that the Ottoman Porte return former Jesuit properties located in the Ottoman Empire.[64]

As in Paul's previous acts favorable to the Jesuits, Gruber played a significant role in these plans to expand Jesuit activities. When the king of Sweden visited St. Petersburg, Gruber met with him on at least one occasion.[65] Paul's letter to his ambassador in Constantinople was the result of a memorandum Gruber wrote for the tsar on Jesuit missions in the East.[66] Furthermore, he was frequently seen in the presence of the tsar and important members of St. Petersburg society. It seemed that Gruber could be found wherever there was a person or a group that could promote the interests of the Jesuits.

Although at one time Gruber said he would be much happier having the lowest position in the most obscure Jesuit college than living in St. Petersburg among immoral people who were antireligious and despised the

Jesuits,[67] he was eager for the Jesuit college in Saint Catherine's parish to begin its classes, and spent time developing a curriculum and assembling a faculty. Teachers of the Russian language were especially needed. The health of his men worried him, for they not only worked in the parish but spent time helping the sick and burying the dead. Debts for the parish and the new school had to be paid. He often had to quiet his vicar-general's anxieties about opening the University of Vilna and assure him that all would go smoothly.[68] His whole life in the capital seemed involved with the success of the Jesuits. Gruber's place of residence might have changed, but his concerns had not.

During the early months of 1801, news began to reach St. Petersburg concerning the restoration of the Society of Jesus. Pius VII personally supported an official confirmation of the Jesuits, but wanted to accomplish the task in a way that would be least offensive to the order's opponents. Thus he selected four cardinals, known to be hostile to the Jesuits, to form a commission to examine the case.[69] However, even their antagonism toward the proposal must have been diminished by the fact that it was Paul I who had suggested the project. His support had enabled the cardinals to convene for the recent papal election, and the church needed his continued favor. A denial of his request might jeopardize the planned nunciature in St. Petersburg, as well as the welfare of the Catholics in Russia. Thus, despite the inevitable opposition of Spain and other hostile parties, Paul's support of the Jesuits carried enormous weight and probably was the decisive factor in overcoming the scruples of the cardinals.

On February 23, 1801, Pius VII signed the papal brief, *Catholicae Fidei*, restoring the Society of Jesus. While this event granted Gruber and his companions virtually all their desires, the document's diplomatic phrasing and stipulations accomplished this task in a way that was sensitive to the objections of the opposition. The brief contained no praise of the Jesuits; it restored the Society of Jesus in the Russian Empire only, but did not endorse or sanction the Jesuits' continued existence in Russia prior to this restoration. Furthermore, only the privileges granted the order by Pope Paul III, the pontiff who originally approved the Society, but none of the subsequent favors of his successors, were extended to the Jesuits.[70] Thus the Jesuits and their friends had finally accomplished their long-sought goal.

In receiving papal approbation, as in other aspects of the Jesuits' progress, Paul I's support was essential. Their expansion and achievements had been built on Gruber's close relationship with the tsar, and their future growth depended on the tsar's continued benevolence toward them.[71]

The two prerequisites for a major Jesuit impact on Russian culture were imperial support and time. During the latter part of Paul's reign, the Jesuits had the type of support necessary to foster their growth. The need for such support in an autocratic system is obvious. Unfortunately for the Society, time was against them. The question of time refers to the nature of the Jesuits' program and the circumstances in the empire. Because they were essentially elitists, the Jesuits concentrated on attracting the nobility. They believed that if the upper classes of Russian society were converted, the rest would follow. Moreover, the Jesuits used their technical and artistic skills only as a means of converting their admirers to Catholicism. Proselytizing requires patience and conducive conditions. Unlike Freemasonry, which had adherents among the Russian nobility, the Jesuits had very little indigenous support among the nobility when they appeared in the empire. Most of their support they cultivated themselves. Later in Paul's reign they were aided by a considerable number of French émigrés and Poles. However, their growing acceptance and support was cut short by the tsar's assassination. Thus the Jesuits never had, for a sufficient length of time, the kind of favorable climate they needed to make a lasting impression on Russian culture.

In previous periods of Russian history, Jesuit education had some influence on the curriculum in Russian theological academies. However, in the eighteenth century, newer, European models were being introduced and the Jesuits' methods never played a significant role in this field. In fact, rather than serving as the source of inspiration in education, the Jesuits were conservatives who refused to adopt the government's plan for schools in the empire. Thus, in a certain sense, the influence of the Jesuits even in this traditional area of their activity was qualified.

While they might not have been innovators, the Jesuits were still highly competent educators who shared their scientific and artistic skills with their students and any visitors who became interested in their work. But because their audience was not sizable and was dispersed over a wide area of the empire, the Jesuits' influence was rather limited. Within the areas where they were active, they were another source of West European culture to their guests and patrons. Because they were the only Roman Catholic organization to attain the high level of prominence they achieved in the Russian Empire, their activities helped to make Paul's reign the most favorable period that the Church of Rome experienced in the empire for centuries. For their role as disseminators of Western culture and champions of a Roman Catholic orientation, the Jesuits are entitled to a special place in Russian history.

CHAPTER 4

CATHOLIC, LIBERAL, EUROPEAN:
A CRITIC OF ORTHODOX RUSSIA, THE
DIPLOMAT PRINCE P. B. KOZLOVSKII (1783-1840)*

John M. McErlean

To posterity, defined here as readers of the Marquis de Custine's *Russia in 1839*, Kozlovskii may be known as Prince K**: elderly, an unwieldy body propped on crutches, his head disconcertingly reminiscent of that of the late decollated Bourbon monarch, his manner that of an amateur cicerone on a Russian Baltic cruise, by turns hesitant and voluble, confiding iconoclastic and penetrating insights on Nicolaevan Russia and its origins-- "and beyond this, nothing." For friends and acquaintances, Petr Borisovich Kozlovskii was a legend in his own time. Some thought of him primarily as a brilliant conversationalist, a tremendously gifted, witty, and learned man of letters, master of many languages and literatures, remarkable for his knowledge of mathematics and physics. Like a meteor, to borrow the description by N. I. Turgenev, he flamed across the heavens, but once lost from sight left nothing by which the world at large could remember him.

Kozlovskii's diplomatic career was short, because his liberal views on such questions as the advantages of constitutions became incompatible with his official role as representative of the Russian autocracy. In one respect Kozlovskii resembled such contemporary Russian diplomats as Prince A. K. Razumovskii in Vienna or Count S. R. Vorontsov in London who retired in the countries to whose courts they had been accredited, married into local families or let their children do so, and did not return to Russia. He too

* I wish to acknowledge the support extended to me by the Faculty of Arts, York University, and the Social Sciences and Humanities Research Council of Canada. At the Archives Nationales in Paris, I was assisted in consulting the original Napoleonic index to the police files. At the Quai d'Orsay, Mme Bompart saved me much time. I was able to consult many of the published Russian materials at the University of Illinois Summer Research Laboratory, and rare items in Helsinki University Library.

was conspicuously more at ease in Western Europe than in his native Russia where his visits between 1803 and 1840 added up to perhaps five years. Major elements of Kozlovskii's analysis of Russia were propagated by the Marquis de Custine in *La Russie en 1839*, a book widely published and in many translations in its own time and since. The continued popularity of Custine's book has contributed to a growing interest in Kozlovskii, mirrored in numerous recent studies, while other aspects of his career and activities have also attracted attention in widely scattered publications.[1] Since the book on Custine by former U.S. Ambassador to the Soviet Union George Kennan helped rekindle interest in Kozlovskii, and since few of the other recent studies have appeared in English, it seems timely to look again at his career and opinions.

Kozlovskii was a part of the early nineteenth-century phenomenon of Russian nobles who were born into the Russian Orthodox Church but fascinated by Roman Catholicism. By the 1830s, many such Russians had converted to Roman Catholicism, while others, most notably P. Ia. Chaadaev, were very interested but stopped short of conversion.[2] The best known and most influential Russian convert was Sofia Soimonova, more usually known as Madame Swetchine. Among her contemporaries were three major thinkers who shared her convictions: M. S. Lunin, Kozlovskii, and Chaadaev. All of them were formally converted except Chaadaev.[3] Among converts living abroad were princes Kozlovskii and Razumovskii. Unlike Razumovskii, who converted very late in life, Kozlovskii's religious views came to color his perceptions of Russia.

In many respects, Kozlovskii's perceptions were similar to those of his much better known contemporary, Chaadaev. By birth and education Kozlovskii was certainly well qualified to become a member of an European cosmopolitan elite. His family, although nearing impoverishment by the time of his birth in December 1783 (by official order, one of his father's estates was sold to pay debts),[4] traced their origins from Rurik, the legendary founder of the Russian state. Since Gallomania then raged in Moscow, where he was educated, it was not surprising that Kozlovskii learned French and German before Russian, or that he met some significant French émigrés in his father's Petersburg house. Varnhagen von Ense later referred to his speaking brilliantly in French, English, and Italian, and fluently in German. Later, Kozlovskii considered that he had been ill-educated and forced to remedy the deficiencies by himself. His complaint is similar to one made by Lunin.[5] By 1800, at age sixteen, Kozlovskii was a published poet in Russian, but his translations of Goethe's *Werther* and Gray's "Elegy" remained unpublished. In January 1801 he was appointed to the civil service and had already started work in the archives of the chancery of the College (Ministry) of Foreign Affairs, then presided over by a relative, Prince A. B. Kurakin. It is at this period in Moscow that his friendship began with the four brothers Turgenev and two brothers Bulgakov and by extension their friends--a "band of brothers"[6] indeed![7]

In April 1803[8] he was sent as legation secretary to serve under I. E. Lizakevich, Russian minister at the court of the king of Sardinia. Victor Emmanuel I, whose predecessor had lost Savoy and Piedmont in the French revolutionary wars, was living in exile in Rome. Thus the young diplomat's duties were light if any. He profited from this leisure by taking lessons in Latin, history, and mathematics from a Jesuit, Father Lamy. While the date of Kozlovskii's formal conversion is a matter of some controversy, it seems reasonable that his comparison of the Russian Orthodox Church with the Church of Rome occurred at least as early as this time. It seems probable also that he was swayed by Chateaubriand, who in 1805 was appointed to a diplomatic post in Rome, and who had published in 1803 his influential *Génie du Christianisme* (*The Spirit of Christianity*), to which Kozlovskii referred in 1810 in his letter to Chateaubriand. He showed Chateaubriand around Rome and the two made a trip together to Naples.[9] In Rome he also met Madame de Staël, on whom he lavished much attention.[10] He became a lifelong friend of both of these great French writers. But this enriching cultural dolce vita came to an end when, with the resumption of European war, Napoleon found the presence of a Sardinian king and Russian diplomats in Rome inconvenient. Consequently, the king moved to Cagliari, the capital of Sardinia, and Lizakevich and Kozlovskii accompanied him, in February 1806.

Compared with Rome, Cagliari could be considered a "hardship" posting, since it was a town with no redeeming features on an island little more than a mountainous desert. It made Kozlovskii homesick for Russia.[11] After the treaty of Tilsit in 1807 between France and Russia,

Lizakevich abandoned his post on November 5, leaving Kozlovskii as chargé d'affaires. A bon vivant, and visceral opponent of the French Revolution, Lizakevich pleaded illness. Boredom, lack of pay, or personal inability to implement the new policy of friendship toward France may be better explanations for his withdrawal.[12] Only twenty-five years old, with no instructions and only fitful communication with Russia, Kozlovskii did his best to follow what he assumed to be the line of Franco-Russian cooperation established by the treaty of Tilsit. Consequently, he ransomed French soldiers captured in Spain and held in Minorca, and helped them to regain French territory in Corsica.[13] Also he acted as intermediary between Sardinia and France (who had no diplomatic relations) in settling disputes over fishing rights.[14] He was in contact with General Morand, the governor of Corsica, to whom he entrusted at least a part of his correspondence, since Sardinia was isolated from the rest of Europe by the British navy and corsairs. Much of his correspondence was read by the French police and other ministries. Some was forwarded after copying. This was difficult for dispatches in Russian, as there was a shortage of translators.[15]

Among letters intercepted and retained by the French in 1810 were two addressed to Chateaubriand and Madame de Staël, who were both in disgrace and regarded as enemies by Napoleon.[16] Kozlovskii's correspondence was conveyed to and from Corsica by Sardinian and Corsican fishermen and smugglers, who formed part of the intelligence network run by Sardinian and British officials. These officials were very suspicious of Kozlovskii, and kept him under surveillance. British Minister Hill referred to him as a "Jacobin."[17] Though in later years, at Turin, Hill came to modify his views on Kozlovskii, the Sardinian king and his circle continued to regard him as a revolutionary at heart, and this judgment explains in part their requests for his replacement before 1818. In fact Kozlovskii considered Napoleon "the destroyer of the Universe" and had privately expressed hopes for French defeat in the campaigns that preceded Tilsit. But this privately held view did not become known to his contemporaries.[18]

Kozlovskii certainly found his situation in Cagliari uncomfortable. Britain and Russia were technically at war, and no contact seemed possible between their representatives. Relations between Russia and France were becoming more strained. He rarely heard from his government, and in reply to requests for advice he heard not from Count N. P. Rumiantsev, then in charge of foreign affairs, but from Joseph de Maistre, the Sardinian minister at Petersburg.[19]

He wrote to his successor in September 1811 that in more than a year he had received "neither salary nor letters."[20] The Russian government named Count G. D. Mocenigo as minister replacing Lizakevich in 1810, but he reached only Vienna, and never arrived in Sardinia. Mocenigo received the instructions from Emperor Alexander I for which Kozlovskii had asked. They were more flexible than the line to which Kozlovskii hewed.[21]

In 1809 Kozlovskii's father died and he wished to return to Russia to help his family settle the estate. His mother died in December 1811, when he was on his way home. On the eve of his departure, Kozlovskii communicated with Hill, indicating his true feelings about the Napoleonic regime, but the British minister remained suspicious.[22] Arriving in Naples in November 1811, Kozlovskii went to Rome, where he stayed with Mme de Staël's banker, Prince Torlonia, and then to Genoa, where he was awarded the Gold Eagle of the Legion of Honor for his services to France.[23] Accompanied by N. I. Turgenev (a future Decembrist), whom he had just met in Rome,[24] he returned to Russia, where he was appointed to a position under the direct orders of Rumiantsev, in April 1812.[25]

Kozlovskii's stay in Russia was short. Perhaps the story that he gleefully told against himself was true, and he indeed did spill ink over the fresh white breeches of Chancellor Rumiantsev.[26] Whatever the cause, he was appointed minister to the Sardinian court, rather to general surprise and to the dismay of the king in Cagliari. Since Kozlovskii had reported from Sardinia on the Peninsular War, he might have hoped for a Spanish posting, but, to his disappointment, he lacked the required military experience.[27] However, while in Russia he had for a while cultivated Alexander I, who appreciated many of his qualities,[28] and he had become better known to Joseph de Maistre,[29] with whom he would continue to correspond, and who was at the height of his influence in Russia, both in government circles and with putative and actual converts to Catholicism.

Leaving Petersburg in November 1812, Kozlovskii arrived in London in December or early January, after a memorably rough sea voyage from which he had some respite in Sweden.[30] After Cagliari, England came as a delightful and formative experience. The caricaturists immortalized his rotundity, he met Byron, became a popular celebrity and the incarnation of Russian resistance to Napoleon, and received the first honorary doctorate conferred at Oxford on a Russian in the nineteenth century.[31] Hill's suspicions seem to have been dismissed. Hardly had Kozlovskii landed than he fell "desperately in love" but in vain, just as Count A. A. Balmain, attached to the Russian Embassy, had done the month before.[32]

For Kozlovskii, arrival in England was the most decisive stage on a political road to Damascus. He became an instant Anglomaniac, as many Russians of his generation did.[33] Ever after England was his touchstone for a whole range of things, especially political, but even food (he liked the great dinners of the aristocracy).[34] Of all the people he met he was most impressed by the statesman George Canning, about whom he often spoke and wrote in later years. Indeed it was to Canning that his final letter from England was addressed, when he finally tore himself away in early August to regain his post.[35] Shortly after the overthrow of Napoleon, he accompanied Emperor Alexander I to London.[36] Some writers have claimed that Kozlovskii became a friend of the prince regent. However there are no traces of him in the Royal Archives,[37] and at Vienna he referred slightingly to the regent in terms much like those of Beau Brummel.[38] From London he returned to Turin[39] and then attended the Congress of Vienna, where if he made no great diplomatic impression, he established a European reputation as a conversationalist and wit.[40]

One of the major questions discussed at the congress was the future of Poland. Alexander I wished to set up a Kingdom of Poland, presided over by himself as a constitutional monarch. Surviving evidence strongly indicates that of all Alexander's ministers and advisers, only Prince Adam Czartoryski was in favor of these plans. Gleb Struve has argued that Kozlovskii also supported the emperor, and has directed attention to an anecdote recounted by Kozlovskii to Pushkin.[41] According to this, at Vienna Alexander I charged Kozlovskii to declare orally to Count C. A. Pozzo di Borgo, the Russian minister in Paris, that the emperor rejected the arguments Pozzo had advanced in a memorandum against the emperor's Polish policies. The incident in itself is inconclusive as to Kozlovskii's own views. However, in August 1814 he had written to Pozzo di Borgo, whom he had almost certainly met in January 1813 in London, and given his views on Poland. He prefaced them with the remark, "I have never been afraid to say what I think to men whom I respect and admire." He continued:

> Russia acted unjustly in 1772, but she wiped out this wrong by the immense service of 1814 in liberating Europe.... After all, it is no wiser once more to discuss this acquisition than to examine the positive and negative aspects of the English conquest of Ireland under Henry II or whether France ... should or should not have acquired Alsace at the Treaty of Westphalia.... The Archbishop of Malines said to someone: The partition of Poland is a good thing, because it has condemned the Poles to a state of peace and quiet, and freed Europe from the trouble of having continuously to restore it.[42]

These remarks, in a private letter to one of the leaders of the opposition to an independent and constitutional Poland, do not suggest that Kozlovskii had arrived in 1814 at the views on Poland that he was to express in the 1830s.

At the end of the congress, he returned to Turin, where he was an effective participant in multilateral talks to settle frontier problems involving Sardinia-Piedmont, France, Switzerland, and Austria.[43] Less satisfactory, from the Sardinian point of view, was the solution of rivalry over the disputed territory of Lucedio. Maistre would have preferred a more effective Russian representative, such as Pozzo di Borgo, "who exercises a good deal of influence," whereas Kozlovskii "always allows himself to be led by others, as if he had no head on his shoulders."[44] However, it seems that Kozlovskii in fact closely followed orders from St. Petersburg.[45] The only other major concern to occupy Kozlovskii's official time was the withdrawal of Maistre from Petersburg, which he tried to prevent.[46]

There was little to do at the excruciatingly dull Turin court.[47] In March 1817 he filled four pages of a letter to his colleague in Paris, Pozzo di Borgo, with witticisms on the dullness of court life at Turin, and in 1818 he again referred to the "monotony of a monastic existence."[48] By way of diversion he turned to his studies, much as he had done at Rome. In July 1816 he wrote to Pozzo di Borgo that he was studying speculative mathematics with a Mr. Plana, professor of astronomy at Turin: "You may expect to receive from me a well argued report on the time-honored revolutions of the moon. Of these only is it proper to speak." The previous October, J. de Maistre had given him advice on studying jurisprudence in Turin.[49] The Austrian ambassador claimed that Kozlovskii's speech was now sprinkled with legal maxims, most of which he got wrong. He also noted that the Russian minister had a taste for low company.[50]

We may suppose that it was the combination of boredom and low company which prompted Kozlovskii's morganatic marriage, sometime in this period, to an Italian, a servant in a Milanese inn. As she was a Catholic, the marriage was not legal in Russia and hence kept sub rosa.[51]

Very important for Kozlovskii was a trip to Paris in 1816-17 to visit Mme de Staël.[52] It was in the course of their discussions about the French Revolution, while she was preparing her *Considérations sur la Révolution Française*, that she said to him, "You are not a Russian, dear Prince, you are a European." In two long letters to Secretary of State Capodistrias he reported on his discussions with Mme de Staël, and after her death gave his views.[53] Some writers have commented on his courage in discussing with Capodistrias her *Considérations sur la Révolution Française*, which was banned in Russia. It may be worth noting that Kozlovskii had permission to make the trip to Paris.[54] Since it was an exceedingly rare privilege for a Russian diplomat to receive permission to absent himself from his post, this trip is a strong indication that Kozlovskii was held in high regard in St. Petersburg.[55] In return, he may have wished to demonstrate to his superior that he had benefited from his leave.

In July 1816 Kozlovskii showed the French chargé d'affaires Gabriac a dispatch that he had just written. Because George Canning had recently been in the news, the prince wrote about Canning, demonstrating how much

he knew about him and English political life, and discussing the
implications of Canning's possible ministerial career. This dispatch,
claimed Gabriac, was a bid to earn a posting in London for which
Kozlovskii was very ambitious.[56] If indeed Kozlovskii had hopes for a
better diplomatic posting, the announcement of his transfer to the dual
position of Russian minister to Baden and Württemberg, alternating
between Karlsruhe and Stuttgart, must have come as a very painful surprise
when it was made at the Congress of Aix-la-Chapelle in the fall of 1818.
Kozlovskii's attendance there was apparently pro forma. In fact,
Kozlovskii left Turin in July 1819 after a delay caused in part at least by a
severe illness.[57]

There can be no doubt that Kozlovskii himself considered his new
posting an inferior one, and that he resented the choice of Count Mocenigo
as his successor and the way the announcement of his successor was
made.[58] Most commentators then and since have considered his change of
posting a disgrace provoked by his behavior and views. An attractive but
probably ill-founded theory is that Metternich was responsible.[59] Certainly
Metternich did not care for him either as a person or as a liberal,[60] but no
document has yet been cited to show that Metternich attempted to dislodge
him from his post, as he certainly attempted to do to other Russian
diplomats.[61] Moreover, he made favorable comments on Kozlovskii in a
letter to the Austrian minister in Turin on hearing of the Russian prince's
new posting.[62]

Kozlovskii's departure was doubtless welcomed by the Turin court.
The Sardinian Minister, Count Vallaise, with whom Kozlovskii was "on
bad terms personally,"[63] twice asked the Russian court for his recall, but
received an answer calculated permanently to discourage him.[64]
Mocenigo, though in contrast to Kozlovskii a colorless functionary, shared
his liberal views about Italy,[65] which may be a further reason to suppose
the rotation of Russian diplomats at Turin was not a response to Sardinian
displeasure. Kozlovskii's views irritated the court at Turin, and perhaps the
Russian emperor as well. In reporting to London Kozlovskii's new posting,
the British minister in Turin referred to the Turin "Court to which he has
long given great offence by his extremely liberal opinions . . . his
attachment to England and its institutions."[66] Kozlovskii, he wrote, had

been overwhelmed by enthusiasm at the inauguration of a constitution in the
Congress Kingdom of Poland in 1818 and hoped this example would be
widely copied, and eagerly pushed these views to the Sardinian
government. His suggestions were badly received. He was warned by both
Capodistrias and Nesselrode to be more circumspect, and some talked of his
being sent to the United States.[67]

Evidence abounds that Kozlovskii was sympathetic to the movement for
national unity in Italy and understood feelings provoked by the absolutist
regimes of the Italian states and the Austrian administration in Lombardy-
Venetia.[68] At the same time, he took a keen interest in Spanish affairs,
prompted perhaps additionally by his intimate friendship with Eusebio
Bardaxi y Azara, the Spanish minister in Turin, and with Prospero Balbo,
the former Sardinian envoy in Madrid.[69] He had written to Alexander I in
1815 that to abolish institutions on the grounds that they had not previously
existed, as was done in Spain, was to strangle the interests of the people.[70]
A criticism of Ferdinand VII, not made to Alexander I, was that through
favoritism he had given office to the wrong people.[71]

A particular reason for Kozlovskii's departure from Turin, it has been
suggested, was his meetings with the Prince de Carignan, the eventual heir
to the throne (ruling as Carlo Alberto), whose progressive views were
regarded as subversive in court circles, perhaps with reason. Kozlovskii's
reports on these meetings in May 1818 may have contributed to the decision
to transfer him.[72] Yet other reasons advanced include his allegedly
excessively close relations with the French minister, the Duc Dalberg, a
"loud" liberal, denounced by Capodistrias in a meeting with Kozlovskii in
1819.[73] Kozlovskii's lack of discretion was well known. Starhemberg
noted to Metternich, "This good prince really does not know how to keep
any secrets."[74]

In 1819 the British and French representatives were surprised to be
shown an official Russian circular which revealed continuing Austrian
hostility to France despite the congress in 1818. The French government
reviewed its policies in consequence.[75] In April 1816 Nesselrode had
written to Kozlovskii warning him not to enter into discussions with Joseph
de Maistre, on the latter's return to Turin, on how to improve the situation
in Russia. "Conversations," or "superficial remarks--born of a transient

intuition," he warned, could not remedy matters but could embarrass the Russian government.[76] Compelling reasons for transferring Kozlovskii, it is apparent, were not lacking. Nevertheless, the official explanation-- transfers of other Russian diplomats, all senior to Kozlovskii (from Madrid to Vienna, from Vienna to Naples, from Naples to Turin), that resulted in his own--may be the plain and unexciting truth.

In his new station in Germany, Kozlovskii enjoyed a great deal of social success. There were already colonies of Russians in German spas, much as later depicted by the novelist I. S. Turgenev. He made a very strong and lasting first impression on Varnhagen von Ense, then the Prussian representative at the Baden court,[77] as evidenced by Varnhagen's memory of him long after his Russian friend's death.[78] Varnhagen's famous wife, Rahel, also recorded her favorable impressions of the bulky prince after his visit to her Berlin salon in 1824.[79] Varnhagen and Kozlovskii shared similar political views and literary tastes, but Varnhagen published enormously in comparison. Varnhagen, a vociferous supporter of the Baden constitution, left Baden not long after Kozlovskii's arrival. He had been recalled by the Prussian government at the instigation of the duke of Baden, and Metternich saw to it that he had no further diplomatic career. There was some question of his representing his court in the United States, just as there had been with Kozlovskii. In the late 1830s he took up Russian literature and became an authority,[80] and as a friend of Custine's was one of the human resources exploited for *Russia in 1839*. This scholarly interest seems not to have been a product of his meeting with Kozlovskii nor of his service with the Cossacks against Napoleon.

A success in some quarters, Kozlovskii followed Varnhagen in relinquishing his diplomatic position. His departure was noted in December 1820 by the British minister at Stuttgart:

The Prince has been recalled in consequence of his indiscreet manner of expressing his opinions upon political subjects and even of the measures of his own Court. He is of a most amiable disposition, with a highly cultivated mind, but professes Principles, which in the present day are called Constitutional, but which I fear

tend much to convert the blessings of Constitutional Liberty into the
horrors of Revolutionary Licence.

It appears from the same letter that the king of Württemberg asked Emperor
Alexander to allow Kozlovskii to stay.[81] This account shows that
Kozlovskii was the victim of his reputation, deserved or not. The British
diplomat was not alone in reacting to the public indications of Kozlovskii's
departure, while in ignorance of the unpublicized facts.[82] The judgment of
Nikolai Pahlen, who shared many of Kozlovskii's political views, is very
revealing. To a friend he wrote that Kozlovskii had been recalled from
Stuttgart--"I do not know why; apparently he must have talked too frankly.
When one has the misfortune to be in the service, one should respect its
conventions."[83]

On March 28, 1820, Kozlovskii wrote privately to Pozzo di Borgo to
tell him that he had resigned, and asked him not to mention the news to
anyone and to burn the letter, "for I fear archives." He was careful not to
give the grounds for his decision in the letter, though they might be made
known to Pozzo later.[84] He claims that he would not have been so bored
and depressed in Stuttgart if he had left Turin in other circumstances. There
was still a possibility that he might be sent elsewhere: "It seems I am too
much liked here to remain here."

Much of his letter is concerned with the revolution that had broken out
in Spain in January. Kozlovskii seemed to think that the developments
there might have turned out very differently had he been the Russian
representative in Madrid.[85] Certainly he would have been more
experienced and knowledgeable than the young chargé d'affaires, Count N.
M. Bulgary, and more alive to popular grievances than the latter's
predecessor, the reactionary D. P. Tatishchev. So the disregard of his
dispatches on Spain may be part of the explanation for his resignation. He
considered that his representations were not taken sufficiently seriously:

Had my opinions, that for reasons I do not know have been accused
of liberalism, whereas this charge is absolutely false, been better
known and better judged, it would have been known that no one is
a greater monarchist than I, and that I often quarreled with Dalberg

trying to prove to him that the King of Sardinia should not try to repair what is not broken. Finally, I believe I am a reasonable man. Others perhaps do not believe this; they are wrong.[86]

Some support to these claims may be found in a letter dated January 5, and consequently before he heard of the events in Spain. In this he assured Pozzo di Borgo, "This is not the curse of the constitution which has withstood the test of that fanaticism that corrupts even the purest things."[87] Kozlovskii seems to have shown Varnhagen some of his dispatches and perhaps his letter of resignation. He told Varnhagen that the institution of a parliamentary regime in Russia would be the start of a new epoch in the history of the world.[88] It is certainly clear why Varnhagen's account is favorable to him. Kozlovskii in his letters to Pozzo and dispatch to Nesselrode[89] was a strong supporter of the Final Act of Vienna of May 15, 1820 (Wiener Schlussacte) with respect to the German states.[90] This position may not have been appreciated in Petersburg. Kozlovskii was, however, a proponent of the (very limited) parliamentary institutions that still functioned in southern Germany. It appears from the dispatches of the well-informed French diplomat, Vicomte de Ségur, that Kozlovskii and the king of Württemberg saw the events in Spain in exactly the same way, and that the king was a strong liberal whose maintenance of a representative legislature was not appreciated in Vienna and Berlin.

Kozlovskii complained that the favor the King showed him was a disservice, and that Emperor Alexander disliked William I, his brother-in-law. Kozlovskii had been reprimanded by Capodistrias for expressing opinions on German affairs not identical with those of his government.[91] Shortly after the assassination of a member of the French royal family, the duc de Berry, Kozlovskii confided in Ségur: "I have little hope that the Emperor might agree with my personal opinion. His Majesty's character has entirely changed as well as his views on France; those liberals that he liked so much four years ago, today he detests."[92]

It seems likely that some earlier writers assumed that because Kozlovskii's recall from Stuttgart was announced after the Italian uprisings, which began in July, there was a link between his move and these events. According to one French diplomat, Kozlovskii wrote to the emperor opposing any offensive enterprise against Naples.[93] However, the Italian disturbances may have influenced Alexander I in his decision not to give Kozlovskii another post, and Kozlovskii's stand on principle may be an echo of the differences that came to separate the two Russian secretaries of state for foreign affairs, Counts Capodistrias and Nesselrode, at this period.[94] What seems clear in this episode is that Kozlovskii remained the enthusiastic partisan of the constitutional policies he had thought Alexander championed. Now that the emperor took the opposite view, Kozlovskii resigned.

General K. Benkendorf replaced him in December 1820. The prince remained on the active list of Russian diplomats, on reduced salary,[95] waiting for an assignment. Some indication of his interests while he waited can be found in his collection of newspaper clippings about political disturbances or trials of alleged revolutionaries in France.[96] After the uprising in Piedmont, one of its leaders, the Marquis St. Marsan, sent Kozlovskii leaflets in the hope that the prince might be able to get them reproduced in the European press.[97] In the years from 1821 to 1834, Kozlovskii's most visible activity was travel, incessant not to say febrile. He spent much time in England, Germany, and France. He had a wide and eclectic circle of friends and acquaintances, ranging from various English poets and Heine, not forgetting Varnhagen, to members of the itinerant Russian nobility and intelligentsia.

It is not surprising that Heine should have written of himself and Kozlovskii after their meeting in 1826 that they were "inseparable."[98] Heine was an Anglophile, an admirer of Canning, influenced by Byron, a supporter of Catholic Emancipation, recommended England and America to his Jewish friends who sought toleration, and earlier had said of himself, "though I am a radical in England and a *carbonaro* in Italy, I do not belong to the demagogues in Germany."[99]

In December 1826, Kozlovskii fell victim to a restructuring (*perestroika*)--a staff and pay reduction that new emperor Nicholas I implemented in the foreign service. Kozlovskii was transferred to the retired list. Nicholas's decision was probably prompted by rational and economic considerations rather than dislike of Kozlovskii's political views. The new emperor and the prince had met in Germany the previous year, but it is not clear how well Nicholas knew Kozlovskii's views. More significant was the fact that, unlike others affected by the restructuring, Kozlovskii had no patron to intercede for him with the emperor.[100]

At about this time he became very close to the Decembrist Nikolai Turgenev, and probably spent more time with him than with any other Russian in Western Europe (much of it in Cheltenham). He also knew Nicholas's brother Alexander, with whom he had begun working in 1800, and who also began in 1827 to spent long periods in the West.[101] Alexander shared many of his brother's ideals. Kozlovskii had probably kept up to date with developments in Russia through his old friend Alexander, and may have read, for example, early hand-copied versions of Chaadaev's "Philosophical Letters" that circulated in Paris.

A frequently asked question is: what were Kozlovskii's relations with the Decembrists?[102] He was not a conspirator or a member of any of their organizations, since he lived outside Russia, but he certainly agreed with some of their ideas. His main interests lay in the area of constitutional reform, decrease of bureaucracy, and abolition of serfdom. He was not a republican nor a revolutionist. These are some of the conclusions of a recent study, based on manuscripts in Soviet archives, that investigated Kozlovskii's views and links with the Decembrists.[103] This subject is too large to be given any further treatment here, especially since some elements are discussed below in a different context. Allegedly, Heine reported to Varnhagen that in 1826 Kozlovskii was apprehensive about returning to Russia.[104] He probably felt close to the Decembrists who were still undergoing interrogation.

In the late 1820s, the American writer James Fenimore Cooper was in Paris, where he recorded a memorable encounter, probably made in 1827:

I have made the acquaintance of a Russian of very illustrious family, and he has always been loud and constant in his elogiums of America and her liberty. Alluding to the subject the other day he amused me by *naively* observing, "Ah, you are a happy people - you are *free* - and so are the *English*. Now, in Russia, all rank depends on the commission one bears in the army, or on the will of the Emperor. I am a Prince; my father was a Prince; my

grandfather, too; but it is of no avail. I get no privileges by my
birth; whereas, in England, where I have been, it is so different -
and I dare say it is different in America, too?" I told him it was,
indeed, "very different in America." He sighed and seemed to envy
me.[105]

It is tempting indeed to conclude that this anonymous Russian prince
was Kozlovskii. There is no proof, but the sentiments expressed were
certainly his. Kozlovskii was an Anglomaniac, and interested also in the
United States. In a letter to Pozzo di Borgo he expressed his admiration of
Henry Clay's oratory. Rosalie Rzewuska once asked him, "Of what use is
an illustrious birth when you despise the nobility?"[106] Later, in 1839, he
also discussed with Custine the nature of nobility in England. In his
unpublished "Essai sur l'histoire de la Russie," he denounced Russian
officialdom, which was the prop of despotism, and Peter the Great's Table
of Ranks that facilitated the elevation of officials into the nobility.[107] In
1816 he had told the Swiss diplomat, Pictet de Rochemont, that he regretted
not having been born in Geneva and asked if it were possible for him to
become an honorary citizen.[108] These are suggestive arguments for an
identification. Beyond these, one could add that Cooper when in Paris was
often in the company of Princess Praskovia Golitsyna, and that one of
Kozlovskii's aunts was a Golitsyna.[109] Cooper was beginning to become
very well known and appreciated in Russia in the late 1820s[110] (even the
saintly Mme Swetchine was an enthusiastic reader), and Kozlovskii, a
personal acquaintance of many English writers, would surely have been
glad to meet a famous American author.[111]

In 1834 Kozlovskii set out for Russia. With the loss of his salary at the
end of 1826 he clearly found it harder to make ends meet. His wife and
children, who were living in Versailles, required support.[112] He turned to
Mme Swetchine, a close family friend of the Nesselrodes, to intercede for
his return to government service, claiming that it had been Metternich's
influence that had denied him a posting. He wrote to many of his
friends.[113] Konstantin Bulgakov described him as "eternally without a
kopeck, sick and in a grievous situation, having three children."[114]
During the revolution of 1830 in Belgium, Kozlovskii had acted on behalf

of the prince of Orange in some abortive negotiations with the insurgents, in what seems to have been a desperate attempt to improve his income.[115]

Emperor Nicholas took the view that the proper place for Russians was in Russia and the worst place was in the Paris of the July Revolution. Accordingly, he put extreme pressure on obdurate expatriates to return. The most stubborn in staying in Paris, Princess Bagration, lost her Russian estates in consequence.[116] Fear of a similar outcome, or just his poverty, may explain Kozlovskii's sale of his part of the Smolensk estate to his sister Daria.[117] Both Ambassador in Paris Pozzo di Borgo and Foreign Minister Nesselrode interceded for him, apparently to good effect, since the prince wrote to thank Pozzo after hearing that his cause was making progress.[118] He also wrote to the emperor himself.[119] In the end, however, the only hope of persuading the emperor to help him was to return to Russia and plead his cause in person. Kozlovskii's return to Russia is quite similar to Mme Swetchine's temporary return to Petersburg. Her Catholic salon in Paris was well known, and it probably was not a coincidence that she and Kozlovskii left Paris for Russia the same year.[120]

In Warsaw Kozlovskii broke a leg in a horrific traffic accident and thereafter permanently retained a crutch. As a consequence of his protracted recovery, he did not reach St. Petersburg until late in 1835.[121] This unexpected year in Warsaw provided him with the opportunity to become better acquainted with Polish society and to become an intimate of Field Marshal Paskevich, who had been appointed viceroy of Poland after the failed Revolution of 1830. He had met Paskevich in Italy in 1818.[122] During this year, Kozlovskii was able to exercise some influence in favor of the Poles. He would later be rewarded for his efforts.

Having reached the Russian capital, he had the great social success of becoming a friend and collaborator of Pushkin's.[123] His relations with Pushkin and the articles he published in Pushkin's periodical, *Sovremennik* (*The Contemporary*), have been extensively studied, and additional materials on relations with Pushkin have been found in Soviet archives.[124] He had some literary success and befriended Prince Petr A. Viazemskii, whom he had met in Germany in 1834.[125] It was at this time that the manuscript of Chaadaev's "First Philosophical Letter" was somehow passed by the censor and published in the *Teleskop*.

This publication provoked a great scandal. Readers construed the argument that Russia differed from the West because Russia lacked the influence of Roman Catholicism as an attack on Russia.[126] The tsarist government suppressed the *Teleskop*, declared Chaadaev officially insane and confined to house arrest, and disciplined the censor who approved the publication. It is impossible that Kozlovskii did not at this time read much of Chaadaev's writings, if he had not already. Furthermore, many of his friends were also close friends of Chaadaev, such as Alexander Turgenev, Pushkin, A. Ia. Bulgakov, and others.[127] There is a certain congruity between the ideas of Chaadaev and those of Kozlovskii about the significance of the absence of Catholicism in Russia. Chaadaev wrote some of these ideas in the late 1820s; Kozlovskii had expressed them in 1816.[128] Perhaps by 1836 these views had become commonplace within their circle of mutual friends.

If Kozlovskii had any public association with Chaadaev's ideas, his fortunes in St. Petersburg did not suffer from it. Taken under the support of Grand Duke Michael[129] and his wife, the Grand Duchess Helen,[130] daughter of Prince Paul of Württemberg, Kozlovskii moved in the highest circles. Eventually even Emperor Nicholas succumbed for a while to the charm of the conversation of this prince he had first met in Germany in 1824.[131] On one occasion their conversation was something of a confrontation.[132]

Kozlovskii regained his former place in the Russian foreign service, and at the very end of 1836 was sent to Warsaw as an aide to Paskevich.[133] This new appointment he owned, to a considerable extent, to British Ambassador Lord Durham, who urged it because he knew Kozlovskii to be a friend to the Poles.[134] Soon afterward Metternich learned of Kozlovskii's intention to mitigate Paskevich's attitude toward Polish Catholics and that Kozlovskii's religious ideas were similar to Chaadaev's.[135] In Warsaw he met Countess Rosalie Rzewuska, who noted: "The goodness of Prince Kozlovskii was unlimited, and his touching solicitude for the unhappy beyond praise." Her account suggests he remained in Warsaw until his final illness. Kozlovskii became the director of the department of church affairs and additionally was charged with school reform. His friend, Prince Paskevich, with whom he lodged,

deplored in February 1838 his lax attitude to the hostile Polish clergy. In
March 1837, Paskevich had assured Nicholas I that since Kozlovskii was
under surveillance, the field marshal knew Kozlovskii had not written an
ironical article as the emperor supposed.[136] He seems not to have left
the Russian Empire except for trips to spas, in vain attempts to restore his
failing health. It was on one of these journeys that he met the Marquis de
Custine, and on the next that on October 26, 1840, he died in
Baden-Baden.

* * * *

Having set out for Russia in 1839,[137] the Marquis de Custine met
Kozlovskii in Germany.[138] Both were friends of Varnhagen. The two
traveled together from Travemünde to St. Petersburg on the ship *Nicholas
I.* According to Custine's account, Kozlovskii (Prince K**) gave him his
views on Russia aboard ship. While Custine claimed that he reproduced
Kozlovskii's view in his Letter V. Prima facie, it seems unlikely that
Kozlovskii would have spoken so openly on board ship, especially when a
fellow passenger was the notorious Nikolai I. Grech, referred to by the
Polish community in Paris as the Russian emperor's "Grand Spy."[139]
Thus it seems likely that if these were indeed Kozlovskii's views, he had
given them to Custine in Germany before their departure by ship.

It is also possible that they met again in Russia.[140] On the other hand,
in reworking his book for the final draft, Custine was extremely careful to
conceal the real sources for his account, and may have put words into
Kozlovskii's mouth, confident that he could do him no disservice since the
prince was safely dead when the book was published in 1843.[141] One of
the best authorities, nevertheless, considers that Custine's account of
Kozlovskii's views is for the most part genuine.[142] Custine's own starting
point in considering Russia was his own Catholicism. Meeting a Russian
Catholic, whose expressed conclusions coincided so closely with his own,
must have been a godsend.[143]

Probably unknown to Custine, Kozlovskii had been looking for someone
who could explain Russia to Europeans. He had encouraged Mme de Staël
to go to Russia in 1810. It is likely that he gave her the benefit of his

views on Russia in conversations in Petersburg and Stockholm in 1812, in
England in 1813 and during her visit to Turin, as well as in their
discussions in Paris from October 1816 to February 1817. Can one trace
his influence in her posthumous account of her visit to Russia, published in
Dix années d'exil? Kozlovskii may well have contributed some Russian
folklore elements to Byron's poems "Lara" and "Manfred," and his own
name appears in "Don Juan."[144] Byron was critical of Russia and
favorable to Poland in poems that were eagerly read in Russia.[145] Can one
trace Kozlovskii's influence in them? He may have met and influenced
Balzac (who later wrote about Russia) when visiting his family in
Versailles, where Balzac then lived. He had hoped that Joseph de Maistre
would give an account of Russia, but in vain.[146] But we may suppose
that Kozlovskii was the source for Maistre's accounts of the Table of Ranks
and of respect for rank (*chinopochitanie*) in general that filled out his
dispatches in 1812.

   Maistre's criticisms of the Orthodox clergy and other Russian subjects
in his letters to Kozlovskii in Turin indicated his agreement with points
made to him by Kozlovskii. Kozlovskii himself claimed to be incapable of
a sustained long account,[147] and after the treatment accorded Chaadaev
would not have attempted such a task. He had, however, written in the
1820s at least one chapter of "Essai sur l'histoire de la Russie," which
survives in a Soviet archive.[148] Furthermore, as happily suggested by M.
Cadot, it seems likely that several liberal Russians, including Kozlovskii's
own friend A. I. Turgenev as well as Chaadaev, were happy to assist
Custine in giving to Europe the true account of Russia that they dared not
publish themselves, because of the failed Decembrist uprising of 1825 with
which they had sympathized.[149] So to each for his own reasons,
collaboration between Custine and Kozlovskii seemed mutually
advantageous. There can be little doubt that Custine did indeed meet
Kozlovskii. The physical description of the aging prince[150] and the
biographical data[151] given by Custine are accurate. The comments
allegedly made by Prince K** on the ship reproduce comments Kozlovskii
made years earlier. Gabriac in 1816 reported:

An ardent supporter of representative government, he laments
Russian serfdom, and would like to establish the basis of general
civilization and political liberty in his country by the abolition of
slavery and by replacing the Greek religion and the ignorance of the
popes by the Catholic religion and an enlightened clergy, and by
repressing from today onward the unlimited despotism of the
sovereign by bringing in organic law.[152]

Prince K** discusses the genius of Canning's political speech. To
Pozzo di Borgo, years before, Kozlovskii had compared French oratory
unfavorably with Canning's on India and with Mr. Clay's against General
Jackson.[153] On the ship, Prince K** discussed Byron and Scott. In fact,
Kozlovskii was a personal acquaintance of Byron's and perhaps something
of a publicist for his writings.[154] In Russia, because of despotism, Prince
K** claimed aboard ship, "evidence has no more voice than justice." To
Pozzo, Kozlovskii had written that the young Grand Duke Nicholas, then
touring England, should not go from factory to factory, but rather to the
assizes: "It is there that a Prince can learn what advantages should be
accorded to a defendant, and what feelings of justice good laws must have
inspired in a country where false witness is almost never seen."[155] The
ship-bound prince was generally critical of Peter I; and Kozlovskii had
written to Pozzo in 1820: "Peter the Great said to Russia: Internally you
will have no liberty, this is true, but externally you will have much glory;
and there she is, as he created her."[156]

In his memoirs (1825), Kozlovskii refers to Peter's cruelty.[157] To
Custine, Prince K** declared himself an opponent of serfdom, as
Kozlovskii had to Gabriac and one of the Turgenevs, and presented that
point of view in his famous oral novel.[158] In practice he seems to have
reduced the quit-rent (*obrok*) of some of his own serfs,[159] while others
purchased their freedom.[160] Prince K** stated that in comparison to the
West, and Poland in particular, Russia suffered from not having
experienced chivalry; to Pozzo, Kozlovskii wrote in 1815, quoting Burke:
"The time of Chivalry is gone."[161] In claiming in his memoirs in 1825
that Princess de Solms had shown political insight by enumerating several
of Kozlovskii's negative characterizations of Russians, Kozlovskii was

laying the groundwork for the more elaborate criticisms that he would supply to Custine.[162] These details suggest that Kozlovskii reiterated to Custine remarks he had often rehearsed to more familiar collocutors.

Among the more significant assertions made by Kozlovskii to Custine as Prince K** were the following: "Russia, to-day, is scarcely four hundred years removed from the invasion of the barbarians, whereas the West was subjected to the same crisis fourteen centuries ago";[163] "The influence of chivalry and Catholicism has been missed by the Russians; not only have they not received it, they have reacted against it with animosity";[164] "The Poles find themselves today vis-à-vis the Russians in exactly the same position the Russians were in, vis-à-vis the Mongolians, under the successors of Batu."[165] These remarks evidence a similarity between the views of Kozlovskii and Chaadaev.

Recently M. Cadot has drawn attention to remarks the Austrian ambassador in Petersburg made in 1836 when Chaadaev's views were published, about the similarity of his religious principles to Kozlovskii's, and the ambassador's observation that Kozlovskii would be dangerous in Warsaw.[166] M. Cadot noted that many of Kozlovskii's remarks to Custine were far from exclusive to Kozlovskii. But the suggestion that Poland might serve as a shield for Europe against Russia was original, and fits well with Kozlovskii's reputation as a Polonophile. Kozlovskii repeatedly stated that Russian civilization lagged behind Western Europe. In 1810 he made the point to Mme de Staël[167] by the humorous reference to himself as a Scythian. In Rome, in 1811, he surprised Nikolai Turgenev by asserting that the Russian people lacked character.[168] In 1818, writing to Mikhail Vorontsov, he used the protracted arrival of Karamzin's *History* as occasion to reflect negatively on the Russian past.[169] In his memoirs of 1825, he wrote further critical remarks.

Kozlovskii was also a convinced disciple of Adam Smith and eager to convince others that the state should not interfere in the workings of the market. His analysis of the food shortages in Piedmont in 1816 might have been written in Chicago in the 1980s. In contrast to some of his contemporaries, he did not see people's cries of protest as signs of revolt, but rather the need for greater education.[170]

The centrality of Catholicism to Kozlovskii's assessment is obvious to the reader of Custine's pages. Kozlovskii discussed not only Nicholas I's religious persecution of Poland; he seems to base his interpretation of the differences between Russia and Poland on a Catholic point of view. The question has been asked: Was Kozlovskii, like Chaadaev, impressed by Catholicism without being a formal adherent of that church? Kozlovskii was not a bigoted church hen (*punaise de sacristie*) and may have been a Don Juan.[171] Rosalie Rzewuska and Mme Swetchine, judging his behavior, wondered about his religious beliefs. Father Gagarin, however, affirmed from personal knowledge the sincerity of Kozlovskii's personal conviction.[172] Dependent on a salary from the tsarist government, Kozlovskii may have found it politic, as a servant of two successive Russian emperors hostile to Catholicism, to make no public demonstration of his Catholicism nor to mention his marriage to an Italian Catholic.

But he defended Catholic interests in his dispatches and the pope's interests in letters and discussions with the Dukes Dalberg and Richelieu, and Count Pozzo di Borgo.[173] He wrote a pseudonymous defense of Catholic Emancipation in Britain.[174] Clearly Kozlovskii's enthusiasm overcame his reticence, or the Austrian ambassador in Petersburg would not have been impressed with his Catholic views. It is worth noting that Kozlovskii's finances were exiguous, as Custine notes, because Kozlovskii was generous (or improvident). As a boy he had given away all his money to the poor; in Sardinia he spent all he had on French prisoners of war; when his father died he allowed his sisters to have the larger part of the inheritance despite his legal rights to most of it.[175] With his friends he had no reason for caution, and quite plainly told Nikolai Turgenev that he had become a Catholic.[176]

In his letter to Pozzo di Borgo in 1820 announcing his resignation, Kozlovskii objected to his views being labeled "liberal."[177] No doubt he disliked the blanket application of a stereotype. Yet in a letter to the Marquis Cavour in 1818, he gave a scathing denunciation of accepted morality and hypocrisy in political life.[178] To Mary Berry in 1819 he had written:

I am ready to obey my sovereign blindly in everything respecting
the interests of his State relative to those of other states, but as for
the activities of individuals, I believe that above all one should obey
God. I despise with all the strength of my soul the baseness with
which Governments make war on the opinions of a poor, unarmed
individual, who has the misfortune not to think as their courtiers,
who receive so many pence a day to praise them.[179]

This affirmation is perhaps the best explanation of Kozlovskii's failure
as a functionary (*chinovnik*). However loyal to the tsar he was as an
official, when he was off duty, *glasnost'*, or candor, "would keep breaking
in." Indeed, where might one find a better description of *glasnost'* than in
Countess Rzewuska's account of how his lack of control led him "to parade
opinions displeasing to the government, to expose abuses that he would
have done better to hush up, to extol institutions quite the opposite of those
of his own country."[180] Kozlovskii was judged on widely publicized salon
monologues such as those the countess evoked, rather than on his formal
dispatches. A number of his friends had difficulty reconciling his great
gifts and intelligence with his occasionally baffling behavior.[181] As he
himself wrote: "I can claim always to argue well and always to act badly,
at least so far as my own interests are concerned."[182] This conclusion is
echoed by Rosalie Rzewuska's. It was his destiny, she wrote, to harm no
one but himself.[183]

* * * *

Many interpretations that Prince K** expounded to Custine have
become the staples of contemporary historiography.[184] For these insights
and as a personality representative of his own times, Kozlovskii deserves
greater recognition. The recently uncovered materials merit further
research. Should the text of his "Essai sur l'histoire de la Russie" ever be
published, dare one suppose it might come to be seen as an equivalent to
Chaadaev's "First Philosophical Letter"? In 1853, Varnhagen visited
Baden-Baden after an absence of many years, and noted, "Kosloffski is
supposed to be buried here. I found no monument to him."[185] But

Prince Viazemskii composed a fitting epitaph in his necrology of 1840:
"Kozlovskii did not live in vain,"[186] a formula lapidary enough to deserve
an engraver. Though neither of Kozlovskii's friends could have foreseen it,
Kozlovskii's permanent memorial may be his contribution to, and
appearance as Custine's Nestor in, *Russia in 1839*, a book which has
apparently become a perdurable classic, better known to us as *Journey for
Our Time*.

CHAPTER 5

THE RUSSIAN THEOLOGICAL
ACADEMIES AND THE OLD CATHOLICS, 1870-1905

John Basil

When the Vatican Council promulgated the dogma of papal infallibility
in 1870, an articulate body of dissenting opinion began to grow within the
Catholic Church. Its first appearance came in the form of small, scattered
groups of educated Germans in Munich and the Rhine area. They called
themselves Old Catholics, a name deliberately selected to embarrass Pope
Pius IX, who was now supposed to represent "new catholicism."

Similar dissenting groups soon appeared in Switzerland, where they
became known as Christo-Catholics, and in Italy, where they were known
by the title of their short-lived journal, *Emancipatore Cattòlico*. Several
years later, the opinions associated with Old Catholicism were used in
Poland by the Mariavitian sect. In most parts of Europe, however, such
groups identified themselves as Old Catholics and founded small religious
societies or joined the Dutch Little Catholic Church, a congregation of the
former archdiocese of Utrecht that had been in schism from Rome since the
eighteenth century. The chief intellectual figure in the movement was the
aging Ignaz Döllinger, a professor of ecclesiastical history at the University
of Munich. His writings were heavily influenced by Romanticism and
expressed little sympathy for the papal-centered Catholicism of his day;
other names associated with the early activity of the Old Catholics include
Joseph Langen, Johannes Friedrich, the French priest Eugène Michaud, and
Joseph Reinkens, who was elected by the Old Catholics in Germany to
serve as their first bishop.

In the early 1870s some Vatican officials feared that Old Catholicism
could become destructive, particularly because many European bishops had
reservations about the definition of papal infallibility and were slow to
announce this new dogma in their dioceses. They were especially
concerned about Joseph Strossmayer, the bishop of Zagreb, who, they
thought, held strong sympathies toward the Old Catholics. As an outspoken
critic of papal infallibility, his defection from the Roman hierarchy would

have dealt the Ultramontanes a devastating blow. As it turned out, however, Pius IX and his defenders had little to fear. The bishops remained faithful, and infallibility was readily accepted by most European Catholics. The appeal of Döllinger and his associates was taken seriously by only a small number among the faithful, and many of them, like the Munich professor himself, were intellectuals who harbored long-standing grudges against Roman authority.

Today, it is not generally known that many Russian clergymen and laymen took a keen interest in the Old Catholic movement as it developed in late nineteenth-century Germany. The ultimate failure of Old Catholicism was so complete that few people recall the name "Old Catholic," and still fewer realize that some Russians saw the movement either as a sign of moral regeneration in the West or as an opportunity to weaken Roman influence among Slavic peoples. The reaction when the doctrine of papal infallibility was promulgated is still remembered, but the relations between the small group of West European Catholics who gained notoriety by rejecting the dogma and the Russians who encouraged this resistance have been forgotten. This is regrettable because a study of the Russian response to the Old Catholic movement can reveal much about the intellectual life of the Russian Orthodox Church in the last decades before the revolution.

An active Russian interest in the Old Catholics came about in 1871, soon after Döllinger began to criticize his bishop for publishing and circulating the decrees of the Vatican Council. The learned Catholic historian and his outspoken followers attracted the attention of Orthodox theologians by their defiance of Pope Pius IX, and also by their own well-publicized conviction that Orthodoxy still professed the true dogma taught by the ancient Christian church. In fact, the central themes of the Old Catholic religious argument seemed like an Orthodox apologetic. They were antipapal; they called for grounding all Christian dogma in the ecumenical councils of the ancient undivided Christian church; they emphasized the importance of the writings of the Eastern fathers, and they absolutely rejected the major theological points identified with the Protestant Reformation. Moreover, many Russians were curious about the ultimate goal of the Old Catholic leaders, which was to reunify all Christian churches into one communal body. When the dissenters held their first important meeting at Munich in September 1871, both the Russians and Greeks who attended were eager to become acquainted with Döllinger and to reach a better understanding of his plans.[1]

By the middle of the 1870s contacts between the Old Catholics and the Russians had become so extensive that close relations between the two, or even intercommunion, appeared to be within the realm of possibility. For the purpose of opening a semiofficial channel of communication with the Old Catholics, the Russian Orthodox Church founded a branch of the Friends of Spiritual Enlightenment in St. Petersburg.[2] Its office was to publish and disseminate in Russia a Russian translation of all the basic documents and correspondence related to the new movement, and to publish in German many texts that the Russians considered essential for an understanding of the Orthodox Church. The society was placed under the directorship of its secretary, General Aleksandr Kireev, aide-de-camp to the Grand Duke Constantine, and an enthusiastic promoter of the Old Catholic cause in Russia. In 1872 in Cologne, and again in 1874 in Bonn, contingents of Russians as well as groups of clergy from Greece, Romania, and Serbia attended the Old Catholic congresses. In 1875 the Russians played an important part in the so-called Unification Congress held in Bonn among Anglican, Old Catholic, and Orthodox theologians.[3]

All this action came to nothing. By 1876 hopes for union or even continued interest on the part of the Russians were quickly fading. The political weakness of Old Catholicism was probably the principal reason. It simply made no sense to waste energy on a small group of religious activists that was not likely to grow beyond the stage of an unpopular sect. Despite the efforts of Chancellor Bismarck to bolster the Old Catholics with state aid, the dissenters attracted only scattered groups of laymen, a handful of priests, and no bishops from the Roman fold.[4] The weakness of the Old Catholics may have caused the Russian imperial government to make no effort on their behalf. In 1872, when asked by the German ambassador if he would support the Kulturkampf against the Roman Church and thus lend moral support to Old Catholicism, Alexander II gave an uncharacteristic reply: "We are at this moment not at all unhappy with the pope."[5] Since the Russian Orthodox Church yielded to its government in all political matters, clergy support for the anti-infallibility dissenters in Germany was not likely to grow to proportions that would be unfriendly to the emperor. By the end of 1876 the Old Catholic episode appeared to have run its course in Russia. No explanation was given as to why Russians lost interest. The name "Old Catholic" simply disappeared from the pages of the Russian ecclesiastical press.[6]

Ten years later, in 1889, the Old Catholics made an unsuccessful effort to revive their dying movement. Troubled by the shrinking number of priests serving in the Dutch Little Catholic diocese of Utrecht, Bishop Johannes Heykamp invited the Old Catholic leaders Hubert Reinkens of Germany and Eduard Herzog of Switzerland to visit Utrecht to discuss the possibility of sharing resources among the dioceses. He also invited the Dutch Little Catholic hierarchy to participate. At the meeting, the small assembly affirmed some common beliefs that it presented in a document that became known as the Declaration of Utrecht. While this assembly did not solve the practical problems facing the movement, it agreed to hold an Old Catholic international congress in Cologne in 1890 and another one in Lucerne in 1892. Subsequent congresses were held in Rotterdam in 1894, Vienna in 1897, and the Hague in 1907; the last important gathering of Old Catholics, the Eighth International Congress, was held in Vienna in 1909.[7]

The Russians quickly took an interest in the efforts to revive the Old Catholic movement. Scholars and clergy who had been sympathetic to the Old Catholics in the 1870s attended the international congresses in the 1890s and were joined by a new group of colleagues who encouraged close relations or even union with Orthodoxy. A great deal was written on the topic, which now spread beyond the pages of the ecclesiastical press, and much of it was devoted to polemics among Russians and Greeks about how Old Catholicism should be received in the East. The reason for polemics was the growing strength of a body of opinion that rejected Old Catholicism and advised the Orthodox Church against taking an interest in the sect beyond an indifferent curiosity. As Georges Florovsky observed in his brief discussion of the topic: "A vigorous controversy ensued."[8]

One Russian scholar who took a sympathetic interest in the Old Catholic cause was Vladimir Kerenskii, a professor of Western church history at the Kazan Theological Academy. In his many works, Kerenskii

identified the Old Catholics as representatives of an antipapal phenomenon
that had been reappearing in European history since its early medieval
period. The Old Catholics were a symbol of a very long struggle carried on
against the illegal action perpetrated by the bishop of Rome. If immediate
political or social motives contributed to the force of the movement,
Kerenskii rejected their influence. In a long explanation of the rise of the
sect, he criticized Popes Innocent III (1198-1216) and Boniface VIII (1294-
1303), and presented a various collection of papal enemies such as Arnold
of Brescia (d. 1155), Marsiglio of Padua (d. 1342), and Franz Baader (d.
1841) as earlier Old Catholic-like figures. The chief manifestation of these
Western troubles had been, of course, the Protestant Reformation.
Kerenskii was indeed well aware of the people who protested against the
direction taken by the Vatican in 1870, although the evidence he consulted
about the Council was naively drawn only from Old Catholic accounts. But
he was primarily interested in using them as historical types, as conscious-
stricken sufferers trying once again to restore the West to its original
purity.[9]

Kerenskii's work is important because it was typical of the explanations
of Old Catholicism found among its Russian supporters. N. Ia. Beliaev,
who preceded Kerensky as professor of Western church history at Kazan,
for example, used the same pattern. According to Beliaev, the rejection by
the Old Catholics of the papal decrees of 1870, as well as their thirst for the
regeneration of ecumenical Christianity, was best understood by reviewing
Western medieval and modern history. He skillfully used the antipapal
polemics of Döllinger himself to present his views. His history criticized
the Spanish Dominican, Torquemada (d. 1468), the papal positions taken up
at the Councils of Lyon (1245 and 1274), Florence (1438), and Constance
(1414-18), the Roman political claims supposedly based on the Donation of
Constantine, and the legal scholarship defending the papal courts in the
works of Ivo of Chartres (d. 1115) and Gratian (early twelfth century). The
Old Catholics were arranged to fit into this big Manichean picture.[10]

What was said of Kerenskii and Beliaev can also be said of others.
Ionnes Leontovich Ianyshev, for example, wrote less history than the
professors at Kazan, but this rector of the St. Petersburg Theological

Academy may have been the most influential Russian supporter of the Old Catholic cause. Ianyshev began his most profound discussion of the Old Catholic movement and the Vatican Council of 1870 with the following significant statement: "One of the prime causes of Church division in the 11th century rested on the ever increasing aggression of the Roman bishop not only over the West but over the whole Christian Church. . . ."[11] It was a nineteenth-century phenomenon, in Ianyshev's opinion, but its explanation was to be found in the Middle Ages. The same conclusions were reached by V. V. Bolotov, A. Katanskii, I. T. Osinin, and many authors who wrote articles in *Tserkovnyi vestnik* indicating that the Old Catholic supporters in the East saw in this sect of anti-infallibility Catholics an interpretation of Western history that placed blame for all the woes in Europe at the feet of the Roman pope.

General Kireev, the secretary for the St. Petersburg branch of the Friends of Spiritual Enlightenment and an aggressive Panslav, followed the same order, but he should be separated from the others because a strong political motive was obvious in both his history writing and his criticism of Russian foreign policy. In a long series of articles and letters written in response to his critics in Russia and abroad, Kireev explained that the evil deeds of Rome rested at the base of Western history and the Old Catholic movement. To illustrate his point, he used incidents of popes embarrassing government authorities. Gregory VII had been wrong to force Henry IV into a humiliating position at Canossa in 1076 and John XXII had been wrong to excommunicate Louis IV of Bavaria in 1324.[12] The Society of Jesus was significant in Western history only for its political defense of the papacy, and it was Kireev who expressed most clearly the sentiment that the 1870 decree of papal infallibility was essentially a political act aimed at strengthening Pius IX against the authority of Bismarck in Germany and the Italian liberals in Rome. The Catholic Church was essentially a political system, and the Old Catholics had resisted this tyranny as had so many figures in past Western history.[13]

Among the Russians favoring close relations between the Old Catholics and the Orthodox Church, it was General Kireev who found what may be called practical reasons to forge a strong bond. Old Catholicism, according to General Kireev, should be supported by the Russian imperial

government, because it would be useful as a weapon to weaken the force of
the Roman Catholic Church in Poland, the Western Ukraine, and
Bohemia.[14] Inhabitants of these areas were Slavs, the general pointed out,
who had been forced or tricked into facing toward the West but who were
naturally drawn toward Orthodoxy, a religion that understood the proper
relationship between the church and the state. Old Catholicism could serve
as a stepping stone or a halfway point for Catholic Slavs on their way to
Orthodoxy. It was General Kireev who presented the befuddled
Mariavitians to the Old Catholic congress in Vienna in 1909 with the aim of
strengthening antipapal Catholicism in Poland.[15] So ambitious was
Kireev's plan that he encouraged the imperial government to support the
Old Catholics in the Balkans, where the Roman Catholic Church during the
pontificate of Leo XIII was undertaking a propaganda offensive among the
local inhabitants.[16]

The other Russian champions of Old Catholicism were not as obvious
as Kireev in revealing their political motives, if they had any political
motives to reveal. Katanskii did once make reference to "our Slavic
brothers" and Kerenskii showed a considerable interest in the development
of the Old Catholic movement among the Czechs.[17] Moreover, since
these men knew Kireev quite well, it may be argued that their failure to
renounce his plans constituted collusion of some sort. This evidence all
seems somewhat flimsy, however, and does not prove that Panslavism
enjoyed a strong base of support in the imperial theological academies.[18]

It can be concluded, however, that the Russian sympathizers of the Old
Catholic movement depended heavily on a one-sided view of Western
history that probably had its origins in the thought of the Slavophiles. They
pursued a romantic vision that saw Old Catholicism returning Western
Europe to a period of history that had passed away at least a thousand years
earlier. They took seriously the Old Catholic claim that life without the
pope would bring about harmony, a religious revival, and a religious
reunion based on a general commitment to the dogma taught by the
ecumenical councils.[19] It is unlikely that such a dream could have
remained in focus without the continued belief in the reign of a satanic-like
figure who had disturbed European life.[20]

The positive approach toward Old Catholicism encouraged by Ianyshev, Kireev, and Kerenskii did not reflect all Orthodox opinion. A strong and determined group of Russians and some Greeks were hostile to Old Catholicism and warned against taking steps that would tie the Eastern churches to this Western sect. Criticism had been present since 1872, but its voice grew particularly strong in the period between 1896 and 1905.[21] Reservations first began to focus on dogmatic problems, then doubt expanded to include the validity of Old Catholic priestly orders, questions of Church discipline, and ultimately the strength of the Old Catholic commitment to Christian belief.[22] A great deal of hostile reaction was evident in the debate on the *filioque.*

Filioque is the Latin word that the Roman Catholic Church added to the most important of Christian creeds to help describe the nature of God in the Trinity. It simply means "and from the Son," but its presence changed considerably the Trinitarian formula derived at the ecumenical council of Constantinople in 381. By supplementing the initial wording, Rome made the Son of God an equal participant with God the Father as the origin of the Holy Spirit. The Holy Spirit, the so-called third Person of the Trinity, now had two sources, not just one. The majority of the faithful in the Eastern churches opposed both this change and what was later to become known as the *filioque* theology. They insisted that both scripture and church tradition revealed the Father to be the sole origin of the Holy Spirit. Rome protested against the way in which this criticism was made, and refused to delete the *filioque* clause. It came into traditional usage in the Western Christian Church.[23] As a countermeasure, some Eastern churches introduced into the creed a word μόνον, "only," following the word "Father," to emphasize their rejection of the *filioque.*[24]

Because the Old Catholics wished to enter into a union with the Eastern church, they soon realized that they were expected to reject formally the *filioque* theology as a condition for close relations. After all, if Döllinger and his colleagues based their faith on the teachings of the undivided church of the early centuries, as they said, why object to discarding what was clearly a corruption introduced by Western medieval churchmen and held steadfastly by the Roman See? The seriousness of the issue was obvious. The two Old Catholic congresses held in Bonn in 1874 and 1875 devoted a

great deal of time to a discussion of the *filioque* and many well-known
European theologians addressed this question, either at the congresses or by
writing learned analyses that were published in the late 1870s. When the
so-called Unification Congress ended in Bonn in 1875, the Old Catholic
leadership seemed prepared to drop the questionable clause from the creed.
But the question was not yet settled.[25]

Some Russians remained suspicious. Even in 1875, after the Old
Catholic leaders had agreed to delete the *filioque*, there was reason to
believe that the official Old Catholic position was not being accepted by all
the groups that made up the sect. Moreover, it was suspected in some
quarters that the Old Catholic leadership had agreed to delete the clause in
its official statements only to attract support from the East. It was a sop
given away by men who did not take the dogma seriously and were
indifferent to its place in or out of the creed.[26] In 1896 when the subject
was again raised, newly formed committees of both the Russian Orthodox
Church and the Old Catholic international congress were expected to
resolve the issue. Instead, their efforts opened a controversy, proving that
earlier skirmishes had more than simply semantic significance.[27]

Aleksandr Gusev, professor of philosophy at the Kazan Theological
Academy and president of the Russian Friends of Leibniz Society, was an
important figure in this controversy. In a series of rather hyperbolic
arguments, he prodded the Old Catholics into taking a stand that made
agreement on the *filioque* issue unlikely. Gusev pursued the Old Catholics
and their Russian sympathizers from 1896 until his death in 1904; at one
point two Jesuits entered the debate, forcing Gusev to fight on two
fronts.[28]

His approach to the problem was based on historical and philosophical
evidence, but in some important respects his goals were political. As the
argument unfolded, everybody agreed with Gusev that the Eastern Church
fathers would have rejected the *filioque*, had it been presented to them.
But, the Old Catholics argued well that the Western Church fathers,
particularly Augustine, would have supported the *filioque*. The debate
seemed evenly balanced, but problems were arising because many Eastern
Christians were unwilling to accept the *filioque* under any circumstances
and because the discussion was drifting into much more dangerous areas.

Gusev must have realized what was occurring and saw that troubles lay ahead for his adversaries. When efforts were made to reconstruct the steps taken at Constantinople in 381 (the place and time of the creed's acceptance), the obstacles became formidable for the friends of union.

At this point the Old Catholics took a position that was difficult to defend. They held that the authors of the creed stated and indeed fully intended to conclude that the Holy Spirit proceeded from the Father, but, they added, this statement did not say or mean that the Holy Spirit proceeded μόνον "only" from the Father. In 381, according to the Old Catholics, the door was left open for those who might later wish to believe that procession came from both the Father and the Son. In other words, the creed did not contain the *filioque*, but its authors did not expressly forbid its later addition. Gusev was quick to point out that the Old Catholic argument was stretched thin at this point, but he scored an even greater victory. The Old Catholics had now done violence to the version of the creed used throughout most of the Christian East, and also had made themselves look like theological speculators.[29]

V. V. Bolotov made a vain effort to avoid the negative consequences of the *filioque* debate. Bolotov was a learned scholar and a devout Orthodox Christian who taught ancient church history at the St. Petersburg Theological Academy. He was a good historian and in sympathy with those who wished to establish close relations between Old Catholicism and the Orthodox world. In his thesis on the *filioque*, which was written in German and first published in the Old Catholic journal *Revue Internationale de Théologie*, Bolotov introduced a strategy that may have overcome the obstacles confronting the contestants. He advised the use of three categories in which to place all church teaching: dogma, theologumen, and theological opinion. He then recommended reducing the differences in the *filioque* controversy from the category of dogma, where it demanded a strong commitment of faith from Christians, to the less imposing category of theologumen. In this category, each side of the argument could marshal whatever evidence it wished, but neither could force the other to accept all its conclusions.[30]

Bolotov's thesis did not resolve the controversy. The Russian and Greek enemies of Old Catholicism rejected it, and even as recently as 1948, an Orthodox theologian reviewing the issue commented that Bolotov lacked a dogmatic sense.[31] Nor did the thesis make a strong impression on the Holy Synod's committee on Old Catholic relations, even though Bolotov himself was one of its advisers. Nor was the *filioque* controversy the only obstacle confronting the Old Catholic allies in Russia.

The question of qualifications for church membership also arose to confound the friends of an Old Catholic-Orthodox union. It seemed to be a harmless matter, but soon became the focus of a serious argument. In 1892 at Lucerne, the delegates to the Second International Congress of Old Catholics defined the church as a body of believers who accepted the dogma of the seven ancient councils, considered themselves to be followers of Christ, and lived a good life. Like so many stands that had already been taken by the Old Catholics, this position was inspired by an animosity toward the papacy (now in the pontificate of Leo XIII), and by a desire to root all dogmatic teaching in the period prior to the eighth century. Characteristically, the Old Catholics were looking for religious revitalization in the distant Christian past, and by doing so took a long step toward freeing believers from obedience to ecclesiastical regulations presently in force. To emphasize this stand, they were fond of citing the canon of the fifth-century saint, Vincent of Lerins, who described the faith as being "what has been believed everywhere, always and by all." Inside these vague limits, one enjoyed church membership and freedom.

In 1895, the argument came under attack from some Greek and Russian theologians, but at the same time it was defended by other Greeks and Russians. In 1896, the Greek theologian Zikos Rossis took the Old Catholics to task in an article that described the formulas derived at Lucerne as being too vague for Orthodox approval. He worried that the Old Catholics had come to view most Eastern Christian teaching formulated since the eighth century as pious opinion that need not be accepted as dogma. Where there was no common acceptance of dogma among Catholics, Protestants, and Orthodox, according to Rossis, the Old Catholics felt free to reject ecclesiastical authority and even appeared to regard the present institutional church in an advisory or Protestant perspective. As a corrective measure, the Athenian theologian wanted union only after the Old Catholics agreed to accept the 1672 Synod of

Jerusalem as binding on all Christians.[32] Since the Synod was devoted to a rejection of Calvinism, its acceptance would accomplish two purposes.[33] It would help to commit the Old Catholics to an ecclesiology that recognized the authority of the Orthodox churches into the modern period, and it would place Protestantism out of their reach.

This argument was quickly carried into Russia,[34] and in 1898 it was forcefully used by A. Mal'tsev, the Russian chaplain at the Berlin embassy. He declared that union was impossible if the Old Catholics wished to remain free of the teachings and canonical regulations that now bound all Eastern Christians. The Old Catholic thirst for freedom made it appear as if Orthodox teaching defined since the eighth century did not rest in divine sources. If they wished to join with Orthodoxy, according to Mal'tsev, they must accept all that was now taught in the East or join the imaginary ideal (Protestant) church that seemed to appeal to their aesthetic taste.[35] As in the case of Rossis, this reaction was inspired by a fear that Protestant skepticism toward the institutional (visible) church would enter Orthodoxy by way of union with the Old Catholics. It was a defense of the Eastern tradition with its hierarchy and regulations, and it enjoyed the approval of K. P. Pobedonostsev, the government-appointed over-procurator of the Holy Synod.

In 1902, this argument against the Old Catholics was expanded by Bishop Sergii (Stragorodskii), at that time rector of the St. Petersburg Theological Academy and later the bishop of Iamburg. He saw in the Old Catholic desire for theological freedom an extreme danger. He first denied the Old Catholic assertion that no one Christian church enjoyed full ecumenical authority. Church unity had not been split asunder in the eleventh century, he declared. The Orthodox Church itself represented and had always represented the one true church. It was conscious of its divinely inspired authority, and the so-called split of A.D. 1054 was nothing more than heretical groups falling away from the true Christian body. In the opinion of Sergii, this falling away placed Rome, the Nestorians, the Protestants, and the Old Catholics outside the realm of grace. Thus neither union nor salvation could be achieved unless the Old Catholics were first "reconciled" with Christian tradition by agreeing to submit to all the discipline and canons of the Orthodox Church. Following this act of submission, the Orthodox Church would then follow its well-known path of toleration and allow Old Catholics the right to use liturgical and canonical regulations that conformed to Western rather than Eastern culture.[36]

Sergii used the formula often attributed to Cyprian, the third-century bishop of Carthage, *Extra ecclesiam nulla salus* (Outside the church there is no salvation). To Sergii, being "outside the church" meant outside the institutional Orthodox church. This position was later adopted by Antony Khrapovitskii during his efforts to establish an anti-Soviet Russian Orthodox church. It reflected an extremely conservative ecclesiology that aimed at protecting the Russian Orthodox Church against all outside influences. It went far beyond Rossis's demand that Old Catholics must agree to accept only some Orthodox teachings that had been defined after the eighth century.[37]

The defense of the Old Catholics on this issue was inspired by a desire to salvage union of some sort and also to criticize the ecclesiology of Rossis and of Sergii. Of course, the Old Catholics themselves rejected the conclusion that their love of freedom carried with it either a Protestant interpretation of church authority or a denial of the Orthodox tradition that had developed since the eleventh century.[38] In addition, they were not prepared to accept submission to Orthodoxy as a qualification for membership in the Christian church. They were supported in 1896 by the Greek church historian D. Kyriakos, who argued that as long as the Old Catholics accepted the dogma of the seven ancient councils, their idea of the church as a single authority with visible and invisible qualities remained sound.[39] There was no need for submission to Orthodox authority as defined by Sergii. This defense from the East was reinforced in the contemporary work of the Greek historian H. S. Alivisatos, who rejected Rossis as naive and pedantic. Both Kyriakos and his colleague J. E. Mesoloras were moved by a genuine desire to reject Sergii's and Mal'tsev's standards for church membership, but they were also interested in reaching another goal, one that was typically found among Old Catholic supporters in the East. They wanted to cultivate an antipapal force in Western

Europe, and giving support to the Old Catholic cause seemed to be a good way to achieve this objective.

In 1904, P. Ia. Svetlov, professor of theological science at the Kiev Theological Academy, wrote a series of polemics against Sergii and Vladimir Kerenskii, the former supporter of the Old Catholic cause in Russia who switched sides in 1902 when he thought that the Old Catholics were drifting into Protestantism. Svetlov rejected Sergii's conclusion that the Western church fell away from the Christian body in 1054. He denied that such an argument could be defended by evidence found in the writings of such notable Russian theologians as Makarii or Filaret, or by the liturgical prayers recited in the Orthodox liturgy. The division of the Christian church into many separate components was indeed a serious shortcoming, but unity would not be achieved by submission to Orthodoxy, in its institutional form, nor could disunity among Christians be properly understood by viewing Orthodoxy as the only true Church. Svetlov praised the efforts of Vladimir Soloviev, the Russian intellectual then writing on the question of church unity, and even discussed the possibility of a final union with Rome.[40] His arguments were clearly efforts to reduce the importance of the institutional and cultural lines that divided Christians and to reduce the importance of modern tradition in determining who qualified for church membership. His actions drew the charge of Protestantism from his detractors.

The debate that took place in Russia over the question of union with the Old Catholics continued until 1914 and came eventually to include discussion about the validity of Old Catholic orders, transubstantiation, the veneration of icons and relics, and other subjects, but by 1905 the cause of union was lost. Those Russians and Greeks who promoted union, intercommunion, or close relations with the Old Catholics could not overcome the Orthodox opposition that depended on dogma as it had been written at the ancient ecumenical councils and as it was being interpreted in the nineteenth and early twentieth centuries. The friends of union had been attracted to Old Catholicism by their animosity toward the papacy and by a vision of a renewed Christianity based on circumstances long since passed into history. These motives were not strong enough throughout the Christian East to overcome its long-standing fear of heresy. If the Old Catholics had converted to Orthodoxy, compromise may have been reached in the East and union may have been achieved, but the Old Catholics had no intention of carrying out what they saw as an act of submission.

CHAPTER 6

ALEXANDER HERZEN
AND THE NATIVE LINEAGE
OF THE RUSSIAN REVOLUTION*

Alan Kimball

In the past few years Soviet scholars have shown a fresh interest in the native lines of historical descent in their revolutionary tradition. Historians with a nativist inclination have never been content with the thought that the revolution in Russia could be explained solely by reference to vast, international historical trends. Heavy concentration on the ideology of the German-born scholar and socialist theorist Karl Marx, and commitment to the single party of the émigré theorist and then national leader Vladimir Lenin, have sometimes slanted the historical imagination toward relatively artificial images of what was at work down in the *Unterbau* of Russian political history.[1] Of the two main lines into the Finland Station--one from Western Europe into Russia and the other from the heart of Russia itself--the international route has been most exhaustively studied.[2]

In mild reaction, Grigorii Vodolazov has used the expression *skvoznaia liniia* to describe his approach.[3] The unusual phrase translates literally as "through line," and the meaning is as unsure in Russian as in the clumsy English translation. It could be that the phrase comes from the traditions of the theater, from K. S. Stanislavskii, who speaks of *nepreryvnaia liniia*, *sploshnaia liniia*, and *skvoznoe deistvie* or *liniia skvoznogo deistviia*. These phrases describe the consistency of theatrical motivation by which coherence is imposed on fragments or details, from act to act, through the whole production:

---

* In November 1982 I presented the first outline of the central ideas of this essay in an address to a meeting of the Central States Slavic Conference in Lawrence, Kansas, dedicated to the retirement of Professor Heinrich Stammler, Professor of Russian Literature at the University of Kansas. In November 1986 I discussed the social content of Herzen's *Byloe i dumy* with the *Beseda* seminar at Hokkaido University in Sapporo, Japan. This essay owes much to participants in these two sessions.

If there be no *skvoznoe deistvie*, all the flavor and problematics of
the play, all suggestions of circumstance, all communion, all
agreement, all instances of truth and faith, everything would be just
as scattered seeds, without any hope of resurrection. But the *liniia
skvoznogo deistviia* unites everything into a whole, and like a thread
which draws together various beads, it pierces through all elements
and links them with the general, central theme [*k obshchei
sverkhzadache*].[4]

The phrase *skvoznaia liniia* (plural *skvoznye linii*) is perhaps as useful in
historical scholarship as in the theater. The historian, particularly the
national historian, seeks to draw together the various beads of the past and
link them through a general, central theme. The phrase in this application
might be translated as "straight lines [of descent]" or "interior courses" or
"indigenous traditions." I will translate the phrase as "native lineage."
When Vodolazov urges the search for *skvoznye linii*, he is urging the search
for native lineage of the Leninist ideology, the main lines through Russian
history, as distinct from global history, to the present. He suggests that
there is an interior route to the Finland Station, and he identifies N. G.
Chernyshevskii in the 1860s as the station of initial departure, thus
reinforcing a now standard Soviet exaltation of the radical journalist.

Vodolazov is, of course, not alone in this search; he is just a touch more
explicit about it than most. M. V. Nechkina's monumental
accomplishments as historian of the Decembrist movement and of the "first
revolutionary situation" in Russia (1859-62) have as their subtext to reach
back a generation or so before the 1860s to confirm the Soviet historical
claim to the traditions of K. F. Ryleev and Alexander Herzen, as well as
Chernyshevskii. The histories of more recent epochs reflect some of the
same search. I. I. Mints's monumental history of the Bolshevik Revolution
makes a great deal more sense when its mind-blunting length and detail are
seen as "various beads of the past" drawn skillfully onto the string of
Russian/Soviet history.[5]

But there has been a disproportionate emphasis on surface, textual,
intellectual traditions. Fundamentally, that is all that Vodolazov was
saying. Historians have so far failed to incorporate one of the wisdoms of

the theater, namely that the components and overarching themes cannot be lodged singly in the script, but must be expressed in the whole production-- the staging, costumes, and lighting. They must be intrinsic to the action itself. The historian may seek to ensure "communion," "agreement," "truth and faith"--a sort of "resurrection" in the current generation of the spirit of the forefathers. But this must be done by working with all the materials of historical experience. All historical actors, but particularly those who are most eloquent and engaged, reflect and contribute to the native lineage, not only allies and "good guys" but antagonists as well, even rogues and villains. The central theme should resonate in the being of every creature shaped by history.

No figure in the long and rich Russian tradition of political opposition was more eloquent or engaged than the radical émigré pundit Alexander Herzen. And few present such a wonderful challenge to historical understanding.[6] At the same time, few have left such an endearing record of self-examination. No one expressed better than Herzen his own generous and theatrical vision of the native lineage, and few have done as well as he in defining his historical relationship to it.

Herzen's memoirs would ensure his place in the history of Russian literature and culture even if the revolutionary movement were but an insignificant moment. The creative power of his words is considerable. He was a master of the memoir genre. In this genre life must be like a story. Life becomes more than reportage; it combines the qualities of both literary--or dramatic--and historical truth.

His words continued to inspire readers even when, almost simultaneously with publication of the memoirs in book form in 1861, Herzen's personal influence began its final heartbreaking decline during the last nine years of his life. Thus his words spoke even to the "sickly representatives" of the new generation, as he called Dobroliubov, Chernyshevskii and other leading radicals of the reform epoch. He had himself prefigured their cavalier rejection of him in his own rejection of Polevoi a quarter-century earlier. Tension, conflict, crisis, and resolution were all part of the drama. When historians seek instances of division, or split (*razmezhevanie*), in the ranks of political activists, they might well remember that all parties add their bit to the larger, native lineage.[7]

Herzen's brilliant muckraking was closely read even by the minions of tsarist authority.[8] His influence on them, all but neglected as historians search for the *skvoznaia liniia*, may well have been as great as his influence on the political opposition. The words of Herzen were greater than the man. But that is so because his life and thought reflected and gave some shape to the *skvoznaia liniia*.

Most pointedly, his words describe the position, within Russian circumstances, of that sector of the population that in the 1860s received its indelible name, "intelligentsia." The word has a recognizable Latin root, and it came to Russia probably from Germany. Since then it has been assimilated into nearly all the world's languages.[9] Efforts to erase it have failed.[10]

Herzen's words express with powerful clarity the interior routes of Russian political history, the native lineage. Herzen has been much admired for writing both philosophically and poetically; the bulk of the literature devoted to him, and to the intelligentsia, has concentrated on these intellectual and aesthetic dimensions.[11] But Herzen's words rebound off the hard surface of social reality. His life was one of painful uprootedness and profound alienation, but neither he nor most of those whom he continued for decades to inspire can best be described as "socially unattached." It has been too often forgotten, or almost explicitly denied, that intellectuals, especially aristocratic and wealthy intellectuals, have faced hard social realities. Our scholarship prefers to deal with working people as if only they reflected larger social realities. It prefers to deal with intellectuals as if they dined on precisely cooked ideas, or were possessed by saintly, demonic, or psychopathic powers. Thus our scholarship suffers two shortages: the history of popular mentalities--on religion, for example--and the daily realities of the intelligentsia.

Herzen must bear a large measure of the blame for the airy treatment the intelligentsia has received. He was touchy about his own comfortable financial situation and its social foundations. He easily shifted toward purely moral and intellectual grounds as he thought about why men revolt. But he was also among the first to give extended personal testimony to what was then already a recognizable pattern of the Russian historical process: the alienation of those who were educated and talented from the official, statist Russia above them socially and from the great primitive agricultural population, bound in servitude, below. [12] Alienation is neither the same thing as "detachment" nor merely an intellectual or spiritual experience. It is rooted in everyday realities and it grips the whole person, not just the writing pen. Representatives of this social stratum were forced to make a hard choice: to surrender to the state or join their destiny with that of the people. [13] The third option, or so it seemed, was resignation to a life of dismal compromise. Herzen's memoirs, almost casually and metaphorically, defined for the first time this central *skvoznaia liniia* or *sverkhzadacha* of modern Russian revolutionary history.

His memoirs appeared abroad in fragments over several years, mainly after 1855, on the pages of the very popular almanac *Poliarnaia zvezda* (*Polar Star*). From London in 1861 under the title *Past and Thoughts* (*Byloe i dumy*) they appeared in book form when Herzen's influence was beginning to wane. Half the book is devoted to the oppositional movement of his youth, thirty years earlier, in 1831-32. Two remarkable passages pierce to the heart of the matter, the first in a chapter on student life at Moscow University and the second in a chapter on his return to legal life after his first exile in the 1840s. Quite unconsciously he sketched the main features of the other route to the Finland Station, the native lineage of the Russian Revolution.

A small and privileged student body was admitted to higher education in Herzen's time. Moscow University boiled them down, he said, to a common, "democratic" humanity. It stripped them of their homebred identity, transforming and reforging them. The university in a sense severed them from their natural families and shaped them into a new one. The university graduated a new "brotherhood," but gave them back to a world that had no place for brotherhoods that were mind-forged--"conceived out of wedlock," so to speak.

What sort of family did the university create? As Herzen's narrative unfolds, the reader sees clearly that the university had made them something altogether unprecedented and unknown to the domestic, or inherited, environment. Alien and hostile to established ways and structures, these students were by no means unnatural or superfluous to them. The university helped make them a brotherhood defined by mind, by intelligence. Herzen did not use the word *intelligentsiia*; the term came into usage only in the months after publication of his memoirs, in part under their influence.[14] But he meant something very much like what the word later came to mean--a social formation much more permanent and thoroughgoing than what we mean when we use the English word "intellectuals." The term he used was *uchenyi*, a direct translation of *savant,* from the Saint-Simonian tradition that his generation, his brotherhood, first inherited. Here he announced the meager beginnings of political opposition in young Russian savants, the intelligentsia in embryo:

> . . . the youthful strength of Russia streamed to it [Moscow University] from all sides, from all strata [*sloev*] of society, as into a common reservoir, in its halls they were purified from the prejudices they had picked up at the domestic hearth, reached a common level, became like brothers and dispersed again to all parts of Russia and among all strata [*sloi*] of its people.[15]

The word *sloi* appears twice in Herzen's explanation of the university's impact on him and his generation. He said students came from all "strata" and were sent back into all "strata" of the world. The word is most often translated as "class." The formal imperial Russian word used to describe divisions within Russian society is not *klass* or *sloi,* but *soslovie,* which is best translated as a social estate with specific legal privileges and duties. Herzen used *sloi* and studiously avoided the words *soslovie* and *klass.* The native term *soslovie* had become meaningless, and "class" (as a Russian word or a concept) had not yet--perhaps never would--become appropriate. Thus the question of social attachment of intelligentsia in Russia must be raised in the context of a peculiarly "unattached" social structure in general.

Russian law formally defined five estates (*sosloviia*) in two large divisions: taxed and not taxed. The nontaxed *sosloviia,* "privileged classes," were *dvorianstvo* (nobility, or aristocracy), *dukhovenstvo* (clergy), and *kupechestvo* (merchants who nonetheless had to pay a guild fee). The taxed *sosloviia* were *meshchane* (a "middling" group with assets below the minimum for joining a merchant guild), and *krest'ianstvo* (peasantry). After 1722, in the reign of Peter the Great, the "ranks" (*chiny*) of state

service and the whole system of state service (*chinovnichestvo*) seriously
compromised the integrity of the legal *soslovie* distinctions.[16] The estate
(*soslovie*) system was overlaid with degrees and categories of state service.
Just as the *chin* (rank) system seriously undercut the coherence of the
sosloviia (estate) system, so also *soslovie*, especially the privileged
sosloviia, attenuated the system of *chin*. Service rank and social status were
so seriously diced, sliced, and blended by the early nineteenth century in
Russia that it is virtually impossible to separate them.

   One of the few things that can be said with certainty is that the Russian
bureaucratic stratum, or "class" (*sloi*), grew to such monstrous proportions,
and its power and influence expanded to such unprecedented dimensions,
that even the fondest defenders of the state became alarmed. The number of
bureaucrats continued to grow rapidly in the years that Herzen's memoirs
were published, as shown in the table below.

Year	State Servants
1856	82.3 thousand
1874	98.8 "
1902	161.0 "

Year	Third Class	Fourth Class
1860	200	805
1870	343	1,210
1880	540	2,040

[Source: Shepelev, *Otmenennye*, 77, 78, 95]

Little was done about the *chin* system in the time of Alexander II, except
that he responded favorably to recommendations that wages should be
raised. As a significant index of the end of "aristocratic rule" in Russia,
Alexander took measures to ensure that those who had no other source of
income could make a living in the bureaucracy. By 1880, wages had
increased 1.5 to 2 times.[17]

   Herzen was born into the nobility *soslovie*, the *dvorianstvo*. As a
soslovie the aristocracy had ceased to be a significant political force

independent of the state and state service system. Noble status carried real force only in connection with state rank. This is not to say that individual nobles ceased to be significant political activists or that their privileges were insignificant in the daily struggle for existence. But as an estate, they never recovered from the centuries of dependent state service. As "noblemen," or aristocrats (i.e., nobles with their roots in the local agrarian economy, based on servile labor and feudal dues), they had all but ceased to exist as a coherent social force even before Emancipation.

As an estate, the nobility were approaching complete bankruptcy by midcentury. They were forced in great numbers to mortgage serfs as well as land. In 1859, 75 percent of the serfs owned by gentry were mortgaged. In Kazan province, 84 percent of all the landed estates and the peasants attached to them were mortgaged. As of January 1859, 44,166 of the 111,693 noble estates were mortgaged to various banks, with a total indebtedness of 425,503,061 rubles. The 1858 census register showed that nearly half the gentry possessed no more than twenty serfs each, and were therefore disenfranchised even from noble committees.[18]

Even before 1861 the *dvorianstvo* were clearly a "dying class," supported selectively out of the autocrat's purse. In 1861 they were fatally damaged by the autocrat's emancipation of the serfs. The rapid decline of the *dvorianstvo*, the estate that many inexplicably still call the "ruling class" of imperial Russia, was the starting point of political opposition in the nation. That phenomenon was the basis for much that was later apparently motivated simply by ideas, ideals, personality, or happenstance. We are not yet talking about philosophy or ideology, Slavophilism or Westernism; nor are we talking about self-abnegation, duty, sacrifice, charity, or altruism; nor, furthermore, are we talking about oedipal inclination or any other psychosis. We are talking about the very tangible social origins of Russian political opposition, the native lineage, the other route to the Finland Station. We here view the large, glacial social and economic circumstance that gives rise to and dominates the first Russian revolutionary epoch. Old ways were collapsing, and new ways had to be found. Choices had to be made.

The autocracy itself perceived the problem and understood that it could never allow its heritable nobility to be destroyed altogether. That would have simultaneously neutralized the most persuasive social justification of the autocracy itself. However far the Russian imperial state went toward a systematic social "meritocracy," toward the thoroughgoing implementation of the Petrine Table of Ranks, toward the replacement of estate (*soslovie*) with rank (*chin*), it could never let service replace birth altogether as the ostensible or official basis of highest prestige. The tsar did not earn his title by working his way up the ranks; he was born to that highest position. However far the state went toward the actual evisceration of the aristocracy as a class of noble landowners, it did not allow the outer surface to be scarred too deeply. The state itself tried simultaneously to modernize and bolster traditions of social privilege that had at best no functional relation to modernization at all.[19]

But even here it is important to remember that privilege is not the same thing as rights. Similarly, comfort is not the same as power. The emperor favored the aristocracy with a deference that was insufficient to give them, as a corporate whole, as an estate, any real political position or independent power. Autocratic deference was insufficient to the corporate needs of the aristocracy, but was sufficient to rankle the sensibilities of the ignoble and capable, those from other estates (*sosloviia*) who advanced up the ranks (*chiny*), and whose efforts were the real motive force of the Russian Empire as it entered the specialized era of modern technical development. The autocracy thus immobilized the nobility in its relationship to state power and public leadership. The nobility's servile position also rankled a proudly aristocratic democrat like Herzen.

While preserving the nobles' *soslovie*, largely as a reward for state service, the state struggled to maintain a similar political control over the formation of all other *sosloviia* and social categories. The Russian middle class was minuscule and, like the nobility, much under the debilitating tutelage of the centralized state. The merchants (*kupechestvo*) suffered as a group from a chronic instability and progressive enfeeblement. The state rushed in and began defining its fledgling "bourgeoisie." A law in 1800 tried to bring into the system of *chin* a whole category of persons in manufacturing (*manufaktur-sovetnik*) and trade (*kommertsii sovetnik*). In 1824 the right to this rank was given to all merchants (*kuptsy*) after twelve years in the first guild. By midcentury, 258 persons had been thus designated. Additionally, in 1832 the state created the title "honored citizen" (*pochetnyi grazhdanin*), as a personal and heritable status primarily, but not exclusively, for merchants. It freed them from army recruitment, personal taxation, and corporal punishment. Thus, in pre-Emancipation Russia, the social category that was becoming the center of gravity of a vast historical transformation in Western Europe was a category of civil servants.[20] It is nearly impossible to say for certain whether the critical social category that defined their status was estate (*soslovie*) or rank (*chin*). The two systems had become inseparable in the case of late-blooming social formations. Here more clearly than at most levels of the social structure one sees the justification of the old formula: the state grew stronger than society, and thus society was always the creature of the state.

The merchantry was a "weak and amorphous social group" to the end of tsarist Russia.[21] State interference contributed to the instability of the class. In mid-nineteenth century, some of the major investors were those who directly benefited from the state-controlled franchise (*otkupka*) system and other corrupt and dependent forms of access to the state treasury.[22]

Some of the instability in the corporate body of the merchantry is suggested by the astonishing fact that in 1873 only 108 of 623 merchants who had achieved the rank of first guild in Moscow could trace their ancestry back two or three generations to eighteenth-century merchant families. More than half of the members of guilds in the early years of Alexander II's reign (1855-81) were new to that status.[23]

The clergy (*dukhovenstvo*) were a pitiable class, though still larger than the middle class in the 1860s. Since the reign of Peter the Great, the clergy had been members of the civil service under the directorship not of a patriarch but of a layman in the Holy Synod. The 1860s witnessed the first significant modern "grass-roots" movement against state dominance. Father Flerov attacked the harmful effects of the Petrine reforms of the church, deploring the church's dependence on state servitors who ultimately justified themselves by the old law that "might makes right." Flerov presented a moving description of clerical poverty and misery.[24] Clerical reformers during the time of Herzen's memoirs concluded that the primary task "was to transform the traditional service estate into a more professional class of servitors, armed with the requisite education, status, and zeal to carry the church's mission to society."[25]

For a brief while in the 1860s and, in a more sustained fashion in the early twentieth century, a part of the clergy restlessly stirred under state incubus. But it still would not be possible to argue that the clergy, as an estate, or their church, as an institution, played an independent role in the political life of the empire. At least since Peter, a "two-swords controversy" was as unimaginable in Russia as regional patrimonial independence of the aristocracy.[26]

This slow, grinding disintegration of the estate system was the background for Herzen's words about the effect of the university on its students. While still enjoying many of the juridical privileges of their estate, the nobility as a whole progressively lost control of the source of their economic power--the land--and the revenues from that land. At the same time, a general moral crisis, related to the impropriety of their privileges, ate away at easy, heritable self-esteem. Wealth and position based on servile peasant labor came to seem repugnant to a growing number of the very class whose customary existence depended on it. The solution of that problem--emancipation--not only financially wrecked them but demonstrated that they no longer performed a genuine role in the empire. Beggared landowners, sensitive about superannuated privileges, became a standard target of scorn or nostalgic pity. As a consequence, many sought a new self-justification through world views foreign to traditions, and a more reliable livelihood through commercial investment and careers no less foreign than their new outlooks.

Some could and did find ways to adjust themselves to the rapid changes that came upon Russia at midcentury. Without derogating themselves, some accepted new conditions and made a good life as gentlemen farmers.[27] These few survived the last decades of the old regime without breaking the traditions of their *soslovie*. The politics of this group consisted typically of retreat to the protective wing of the autocratic state. Although it seems ironic, the representatives of this group who played a political role did not represent the traditional interests of their *soslovie*. They were what we usually call "liberals." They opposed the autocracy, understandably, because it was their primary enemy as they sought to assert themselves as an independent social and political force outside the confines of the state-created *soslovie* system.[28]

A much larger number of nobles did not break with the traditions of their *soslovie* but quietly faded from the scene. The last decades of the old regime were a time of economic and political marginality for them, even though the zemstvo institutions offered some economic relief and political outlet. Many found state service a necessity. These latter, we might say, deserted *soslovie* and surrendered to *chin*.[29]

Finally, a small but significant number found neither *chin* nor *soslovie* adequate to their sense of self and their instincts about the future. These were the nobles who joined the *raznochintsy*, an amalgam of social elements spun off from the clergy, merchant, and agrarian groups as they experienced dislocations equal to those experienced by the aristocracy.[30] Their new, positive self-image was best reflected in the term "intelligentsia." At first they typically angled toward professional careers in fields such as journalism, the arts, law, and medicine, where training and personal achievement, rather than inheritance, were the keys to success.[31] Many concluded that the autocratic state was as antiquated and objectionable as aristocratic serf-owning; certainly many found the state to be a significant obstacle to the realization of the sort of world where their new identities would best prosper. These turned eventually, and sometimes immediately, to political forms of self-definition.

For aristocrats, the urge to free themselves from dysfunctional *soslovie* traditions, to dissociate themselves from the fate of a "dying class," was the impetus for their early leadership within the Russian political opposition. Furthermore, the impulse to escape the fate of their social estate and redefine themselves, rebaptize themselves in mind-forged brotherhoods, was directly related to the perfectly natural impulse, having inherited a past without a future, to seek an apparently functional future, to associate themselves democratically with the whole nation, particularly with the fate of an apparently ascendant class: the working people, the *narod*.

The word *narod* is critical to the mentalities of nineteenth-century Russia. It was a vital component of both conservative nationalism and revolutionary populism. Count Uvarov's triune formula ("Orthodoxy, Autocracy, and *narodnost'"*) and the theories of the radical "populists"

(*narodniki*) share the same inspiration: to escape the dilemmas of Russian
social history. Herzen himself is most widely known for having supposedly
popularized a radically romantic vision of the *narod*.

The word *narod* is no more precise than the phrase "the people." In
various settings and mutations it implies most narrowly "peasants,"
somewhat more broadly "the folk," even more broadly "the working
people," and most broadly "the nation." We can now see something of
how the word and concept served as a renegade social category. Is the
narod a *sloi*? That may be unclear, but it cannot be called a *soslovie*, nor a
class. Even in its narrowest use, it is not precisely a synonym for
krest'ianstvo, a term that encompassed only the peasantry. It is almost
always an abstraction implying a "native" congregation to which a very
large and diverse group of people may belong.

Whether used by Nicholas I as a statist formula or by Mikhail Bakunin
as a revolutionary slogan, the concept of *narod* (the people) represented an
escape from the concatenation of *chin* and *soslovie*, really an unstable
solution of the dysfunctional legal definitions of social estate and rank.
With their idea of *narod*, both the emperor and the anarchist vaulted shakily
over the tangled confusions of the actual Russian social/service structure.
For refractory aristocrats and others from various ranks and classes
sloughed off by the tsarist system, association with the *narod* could appear
to promise a transcendent future of progress and justice. The concept of the
narod smelted down the junky confusion of *chin* and *soslovie*.

Herzen launched a discussion of *narod* in the course of his essay on
Petr Chaadaev.[32] He called the *narod* his "faith." Chaadaev, he said, did
not believe in a special path for Russia. He believed in a salvation of
individuals, but not of a whole *narod*. The Slavophiles (*Slaviane*) thought
otherwise. They believed in a quite glorified potential of Russian popular
traditions.

"But history won't let us go back," said Herzen in his memoirs.
"Political life in pre-Petrine Russia was freakish, impoverished,
primitive--and it was just to this that the Slavophiles sought to return. . . ."
Chaadaev joked about the effort to return to the people, to "go to the
people" in this way. He told of a Slavophile intellectual dressed in a
murmolka (ancient fur hat) whom the peasants mistook for a Persian when

they met him on the street. The Slavophiles think the people are ready for
them, Chaadaev scoffed. In this "they show themselves naive like certain
Western democrats [*zapadnykh dimokratov*]. They don't appreciate the real
condition of the folk." Neither the "Byzantine church" nor "the Granite
Palace" (i.e., the chief spiritual and secular institutions of Russia) has
anything more to offer the folk.

Herzen argued that the *narod*--not "peasants" or "serfs" as such, but that
rescuing abstraction "the people"--still must be the choice for Russia's
future:

But it is quite another matter to return to the village, to the
workers' artels, to the village assembly, to the Cossacks. But do
not return in order to bind them in a stagnant Asiatic crystallization,
but in order to develop the foundations on which they grow, free
them from everything artificial and false, from the scars they have
suffered--that is our natural calling.

In this case, the word "our" stands for what would soon be called the
intelligentsia. Clarifying this point, Herzen continued by emphasizing how
some new force, independent of state power, must turn to the *narod*, the
nation. Neither the old-fashioned Muscovite state nor the modern Petrine
state was capable of the task. Herzen also deflated the hopes of those who
had grasped at the Novgorod *veche* (town meeting) bell as a symbol of a
third political option suggested by Russian history: that bell had long ago
been melted down to forge a cannon in the arsenal of the Muscovite state.

The Russian state adulterated our inheritance, our homebred ways, said
Herzen; it compromised our *soslovie* origins and corrupted our *chin* future.
But the Petrine reforms had pointed the way toward enlightenment and
modernization. The university was as much a consequence of Peter I as was
the awful emasculation of Russian society. The university "mercifully
stripped all this from our backs." It melted us all down "as into a common
reservoir," then recast us in a better shape, he said. The *veche* bell had
been reforged as a canon, but the youthful strength of Russia was cast into
something very fine. The university had endowed them with a new identity
which precisely foreshadowed a better future for all Russia. But at the end,

the university sent them back into a world where the old *soslovie* and *chin*,
however logically contradictory, however morally outrageous, still reigned.
Herzen blamed Nicholas I: "Until 1848 the organization of our
universities was purely democratic. Their doors were open to everyone
who could pass the examination, who was neither a serf, a peasant, nor a
man excluded from his commune. Nicholas spoilt all this. . . ."
He spoiled the university when he placed restrictions on student
intellectual and organizational life that choked the life of this young stratum
(*sloi*) as it first stretched and felt its new strength. Herzen and his confreres
resisted Nicholas, in actions that were motivated by nothing more
complicated than self-organization and self-defense, and they suffered.[33]
As they made the first efforts in the direction of organizational substitutes
for the broken sodalities of *soslovie* and *chin*, the state intervened in the
classic pattern to smash them.[34]

It was natural for these energetic youths, whose tendency toward active
organization was blocked by the state, to channel their energies into
thought. N. A. Polevoi introduced Saint-Simon's ideas to the circle of
which Herzen was a member. Polevoi was an influential progressive
journalist, historian, and critic, initially something of an intellectual guide
for Herzen and his brotherhood. A son of a provincial merchant, he was
self-taught and generally what one would call a "self-made man." These
passages, which Herzen wrote originally in 1856, tell us something of
Polevoi's position, and oddly prophesy Herzen's troubled relationship with
the younger forces in his own time:

> The new world was pushing at the door, and our hearts and souls
> opened wide to meet it. Saint-Simonism lay at the foundation of our
> convictions and remained so in its essentials unalterably. . . .
>
> For us Saint-Simonism was a revelation; for him [Polevoi] it was
> insanity, a vain Utopia, hindering social development. . . .
>
> [Polevoi warned:] "The time will come when you will be
> rewarded for a whole life-time of toil and effort by some young man
> saying with a smile, 'Be off, you are behind the times.'"[35]

In what way did Saint-Simon recommend himself to Herzen and his brotherhood as they sought to solve real-life problems of their social existence? We must disencumber ourselves of many of the specifics of Saint-Simon's life and teachings, stand back a step or two, and observe his happy larger fit with the problems of the Russian state service system and social structure; we must see how he and his ideas appeared to offer solutions to problems of *soslovie* and *chin*.

First, Saint-Simon was an aristocrat who derogated himself in order to greet and embrace the future during one of its most dramatic appearances, the French Revolution. Second, he waltzed crazily through the bloody wreckage of that revolution and emerged whole and undaunted with a healthy appetite and fabulous recipe for industrial, technical, and scientific progress. Finally, he predicted that in the future savants would rule: *uchenye*, or *intelligenty*, would be the first estate of the new order.[36] Saint-Simon thus represented to Herzen's generation a precise, comprehensive, and beautiful subversion of the Russian social and service system.

With this in mind, we can make greater sense of one puzzling passage in Herzen's memoirs. Attempting to explain what value the efforts of young savants could possibly have, and specifically the good that comes of their seemingly idle deliberations and scheming, Herzen contrasted their efforts with those of other Russian groups:

> Work, "business!" Officials [*chinovniki*] recognize as such only
> civil and criminal affairs; the merchant [*kupets*] regards as work
> nothing but commerce; military men call it their work to strut about
> like cranes and to be armed from head to foot in time of peace.[37]

Herzen highlighted three leading career possibilities that presented themselves to his generation: service in the bureaucracy (*chinovnichestvo*), commercial enterprise (*kupechestvo*), or service in the military. In his memoirs he did not bother to deliberate on the "work" of the landowner, nor of the peasant or industrial laborer. He did not wish to say that these do not "work," but that no young *intelligent*, in his view, could possibly consider these options. He rejected them all--civil and military service, business, commercial farming, and rural or factory labor--in order to affirm the value of another sort of useful work particularly appropriate to the Russian scene:

> To my thinking, to serve as the link, as the center of a whole circle of people, is a very great work, especially in a society both disunited and fettered [*razobshchennom i skovannom*]. [N. V. Stankevich] drew a large circle of friends into his favorite pursuit [philosophy]. This circle was extremely remarkable: from it came a regular legion of savants [*uchenykh*], writers and professors, among whom were [V. G.] Belinskii, [M. A.] Bakunin and [T. N.] Granovskii.[38]

Herzen, of course, came from that group himself.

In Herzen's view of Russian society, the bureaucrat (*chinovnik*) ran others' lives, the merchant (*kupets*) bought and sold to his own advantage, the military officer strutted and prepared to make war. The nobleman (*dvorianin* or *pomeshchik*) lived off the labor of peasants. These less than savory activities represented the work of a "disunited and fettered" Russian society. This surprising and agreeable phrase describes how, strangely both bound and disunited, Russian society suffered from the extreme opposites of two virtues: community and freedom. Was it idle then to become an *intelligent* (an *uchenyi*)? On the contrary, it was of the highest practical importance to build cadres for the future when these skewed virtues would be restored. Stankevich created "a regular legion of savants," said Herzen, pridefully exaggerating the size of his brotherhood if not the size of their task. The work of the savant, in contrast to the fettered and disunited work of other strata (*sloi*), amounted to a grand, nation-building task, purging the people of *soslovie* and *chin*. The university (modern scholarship and thought) formed savants from the shambles of this decrepit system, shaping them into a social force able to defeat *soslovie* and *chin*.

Herzen's savants were inspired more directly by Saint-Simon than were subsequent generations of *intelligenty*. But the Saint-Simonian spirit pierced through factions and decades, from the earliest beginnings up to Herzen's day. The Saint-Simonian spirit inspired wholesome welcome of the modern world, the next stage of human maturity, up from aristocratism and militarism to egalitarian humanitarianism and peaceful productivity. It promised leadership for savants. Savants were different from old-fashioned leaders--the men on horseback or in bishop's miter--because their position resulted from what they did, not from birth or privilege, not from *soslovie* or *chin*. The Saint-Simonian spirit thus promised the triumph of savants over aristocrats, bureaucrats, and clergy. It promised also the triumph of reason and science--collectively the main instrument of the savant--over ceremonial mumbo-jumbo. It promised the triumph of the future over the moribund past. Most thrilling, it promised the triumph of creativity and quality over militarism and dull middle-class or bureaucratic routine. It promised the triumph of humane cooperation over inhumane exploitation. It did not address the problem of the urban or rural laborer, but the Saint-Simonian spirit happened to fit very nicely with the predicament that Herzen's small and talented brotherhood faced in the very real bog of their social, economic, and political relations.

From the perspective of the late twentieth century, enthusiasm for Saint-Simon seems rapturous and naive until we look at the organic roots in daily life from which that enthusiasm grew. Herzen's generation, and subsequent generations, embraced the essential elements of Saint-Simonism even when they did not bother too much with the actual texts, the precise ideas.[39] They did this because Saint-Simon so perfectly solved the riddle of their social existence. He taught them who they were--savants (*uchenye*)--and promised that it was they who had the future stored within them.

In those instances and eras when Saint-Simon ceased to have a dominant influence, when other figures like Fourier or Guizot or Proudhon or Mazzini or Ledru-Rollin or Lassalle or Marx came to have influence, their influence stemmed from this same source. To have influence in Russia, these thinkers had to solve the questions of identity and mission for Russian *intelligenty*, whatever else they did, or their influence remained pinched and partial.

When Herzen appealed to the students of the new universities of Russia, in the aftermath of their expulsion and the closing of the halls of learning in 1862, to go into the countryside, to the people, to where the action was, he was not just expressing a wildly democratic hope for the vitality of the peasant masses, but was without a second thought asserting that these fledgling *uchenye* were essential to the unfolding of events in the countryside. One should never forget that Herzen's call to go to the people was voiced in tandem with an equally relevant appeal to them to establish printing presses. Both appeals were made at the same time that his close associate, Nikolai Ogarev, was penning model plans for nationwide political organizations, in harmony with the direction of events in Russia itself.

When Herzen composed the first chapters of his memoirs in the 1850s, the heavy hand of Nicholas I still lay upon Russian universities. By the time he published them in book form, the situation had notably changed. Restrictions had been removed, admissions were open again, even more widely than in Herzen's day, and student activism had taken on such scope and intensity as Herzen and his brotherhood could never have anticipated.

Herzen was slow to absorb the implications of the growth of the state bureaucracy and the expansion of the student body at the universities. Nor could he perceive the close connection between them. University enrollments grew as higher education increasingly came to be a requirement for a service career and as the need for trained administrators expanded so broadly. Life in St. Petersburg and Moscow--to some degree in the other provincial administrative, university, and market towns--changed along with social and institutional changes. Society had changed as much as the cities in which society centered itself, as much as the universities with which society was every day more closely associated, as much as the ubiquitous administration where society worked.

Society at midcentury bore some family resemblance to society in the 1830s, Herzen's youth. But it had reached a stage that--if we follow Herzen's imagery--might be called adolescence. In that stage of life, society was not the same being Herzen had known earlier. He greeted it tentatively, as an uncertain parent. And he held it at arm's length in some disparagement for its gangly unrecognizability. His hesitancy with respect to the new Russian society is analogous to his hesitancy with respect to West European bourgeois culture. He anticipated both, needed both, but on direct confrontation, found neither quite palatable. For its own part, society in that adolescent stage was hardly more secure in its sense of identity or its relationship to its "parents."

For all these changes, in one important respect society in 1861 was not so different from society in Herzen's university days. The student rebellion of 1861-62 was like that of Herzen's day in that it was motivated by the same uncomplicated and directly perceived self-interest. But, in the later rebellion, many hundreds of people became involved, not all of them students.[40] That is why 1861, rather than 1831, more nearly represents the beginning of those oppositional movements that were to have a relatively unbroken history into the twentieth century, that were to add their weight to the collapse of the Russian Empire in 1917, and that would oversee the construction of the Soviet system. Herzen understood much, but after more than a decade in exile, he had lost touch with the pulse of political life--the native lineage of revolution--in his homeland.

Herzen inserted the following words into the book edition of his memoirs, as he witnessed with sorrow these first awkward steps of the "new men," the "new people." Listen to his distress, his startling ungenerosity. As a representative of the founding generation, he, metaphorically speaking, greeted brash teenagers, sired by his own brotherhood, in these words:

> After our affair . . . , fifteen years passed in tranquillity before the Petrashevsky affair [1849], and it was those fifteen years from which Russia is [in 1861] only just beginning to recover, and by which two generations were broken, the elder smothered in violence, and the younger poisoned from childhood, whose sickly [kvelykh] representatives we are seeing to-day.[41]

Directly after this bilious insertion, the original narrative picked up again with what now seemed an almost apologetic recollection of how his brotherhood in its own time offended its elders. Herzen's clash with Polevoi in the 1840s--especially the latter's warning that Herzen would someday be greeted: "Be off, you are behind the times"--acquires a special poignancy, introduced by the reference to "poisoned" and "sickly" representatives of the current "smothered" generation, by which Herzen meant Chernyshevskii and others with whom he had most recently been feuding.

Their plebeian origins and manners were as offensive to Herzen as were those of the European bourgeois revolutionists of 1848 who had so badly failed his *raffiné* expectations. The generation of Chernyshevskii and Serno-Solovevich defined the role of the savant even more precisely, and they gave themselves a lasting name, "intelligentsia." But all the elements were present, in embryo, in Herzen's memoirs.

Herzen wrote these final passages after the first rancorous dealings with the "men of the Sixties." He summed up the reign of Tsar Nicholas I in the following manner:

The pestilential streak, running from 1825 to 1855, will soon be completely cordoned off. . . . Thirty years ago the Russia of the future existed exclusively among a few boys [*mal'chikami*], hardly more than children, so insignificant and unnoticed that there was room for them between the soles of the great boots of the autocracy and the ground--and in them was the heritage of the 14th of December. . . . [Here he refers to the dramatic but limited and ineffectual Decembrist uprising in 1825, at the outset of Nicholas's reign.]

In the very jaw of the monster these children stand out unlike other children. . . . They are the rudimentary germs [*iaicheiki*], the embryos [*zarodyshchi*] of history, barely perceptible, barely existing, like all embryos in general. . . . The objection that these circles, unnoticed both from above and from below, form an exceptional, and extraneous, an unconnected phenomenon . . . seems to us quite groundless.[42]

These boys were few in number and short of tooth, but were not at all superfluous or foreign to the world that produced them: they and only they represented the natural and native living force of the Russian future. They were alienated and hostile, but that's different. Their alienation and their hostility had a natural and central place in the vast scheme of things. Notice Herzen's instinctive use of genetic metaphor: embryo and germ.

This helps us make better sense of the father/child and other generational imagery, so central to his message. The intelligentsia were native to the Russian historical process, and from them would be generated the Russian future:

> The very appearance of the circles of which I am speaking was a natural response to a profound, inward need in the Russian life of that time.
>
> Below this great social sphere [of privilege], the great world of the people maintained an indifferent silence; nothing was changed for them: their plight was bad, but no worse than before, the new blows fell not on their bruised backs. Their time had not yet come. Between this roof and this foundation the first to raise their heads were children [*deti*]. . . .
>
> The number of educated people among us has always been extremely small; but those who were educated have always received an education, not perhaps very comprehensive, but fairly general and humane: it made men of all with whom it succeeded.

Herzen's definition of education and its effect is vital. Education made his circle into persons who simply could not allow themselves to become officials, landlords, or generals; certainly it was out of the question to become a peasant or worker, at least so far as Herzen was concerned. Education came to the rescue, providing a future when all other avenues provided by history were blocked or thoroughly repugnant. Dan Brower has shown that education continued to have just that effect through the 1860s and into the years of Lenin's schooling.[43]

Very clearly we are in need of a significant adjustment in one of our standard clichés about Russian history. Herzen, and most of those who followed him, were less inclined to idealize the *narod* than they were to idealize themselves. Education, their *alma mater*, nurtured them toward a portentous adulthood. But Russia, in the meantime, had no place for them:

> But a man was just what was not wanted either for the hierarchical pyramid or for the successful maintenance of the landowning

regime. The young man had either to dehumanize himself again--and the greater number did so--or to stop short and ask himself: "But is it absolutely essential to go into [state] service? Is it really a good thing to be a landowner?" After that there followed for some, the weaker and more impatient, the idle existence of a cornet on the retired list, the sloth of the country, the dressing-gown, eccentricities, cards, wine; for others a time of ordeal and inner travail. They could not live in complete moral disharmony, nor could they be satisfied with a negative attitude of withdrawal; the stimulated mind required an outlet. The various solutions of these questions, all equally harassing for the younger generation, determined their distribution into various circles.

In these passages Herzen traced the native birth of the Russian oppositional intelligentsia and described, even if only in embryonic form, the larger features of the social and political organism that cradled them in their infancy, that threatened them with suffocation, that tilted them toward opposition. The conception was far from immaculate and the birth was labored in the extreme. He may have grasped only partially the actual process then altering beyond recognition the Russia he had fled over a decade earlier. But he managed to captivate and speak to its spirit. The "sickly youths" who crowded into the universities read his memoirs and found guidance in them.[44] That is so because they instinctively recognized the *skvoznaia liniia* that ran from Herzen's time, through their own, into the twentieth century.[45] Squeezed between state and nation, the intelligentsia had only one meaningful choice: alliance with popular freedom and national progress, against the imperial state.

CHAPTER 7

TVER ZEMSTVO'S TECHNICAL SCHOOL
IN RZHEV: A CASE STUDY IN THE DISSEMINATION
OF REVOLUTIONARY AND SECULAR IDEAS[*]

Charles E. Timberlake

Technical schools were virtually nonexistent in Russia in 1866, the year
that zemstvo institutions were introduced into Tver province. Four special
institutes classified as "higher" educational institutions existed in the
empire,[1] and the statute of November 18, 1864, on *real* gymnasiums and
progymnasiums established schools at the "middle" level to prepare students
for entrance into these higher special institutes. But not enough *real*
gymnasiums had been created by 1866 to form an integrated system. By
1870 only nine gymnasiums were included on a list of educational institutions supported by the tsarist government.[2]

In addition to the *realschulen*, three technical schools were founded at
the "middle" level by private patrons from 1865 to 1869, among them the
Aleksandrov Technical School founded by the Miliutin brothers in
Cherpovets.[3] Technical schools at the "middle" and "lower" levels
appeared in Russia in more significant, although still small, numbers only
in the 1870s after the government promulgated the law of August 27, 1869.
In response to urging from persons inside and outside government service
that the government encourage "professional education" in Russia, the
government established, through this statute, procedures by which private
persons or groups could found and maintain technical schools. From 1865
onward, the zemstvo institutions ("private" bodies in government parlance)
that were being created in thirty-five provinces of European Russia became
collectively a major advocate for elementary and secondary education and a
major force in founding all types of schools at the middle and, especially,
elementary levels. Among these were a few technical schools.

* I am grateful to the International Research and Exchanges Board
(IREX) and the University of Missouri Research Council for support of the
research in the Soviet Union on which this chapter is based.

128

Another voice urging the government to aid the dissemination of useful technical knowledge was the Russian Technical Society, founded in 1866. It later founded and supported a series of its own technical schools under the jurisdiction of the Ministry of Education.[4]

In response to such requests, the tsarist government promulgated the statute of August 27, 1869, stating that the government would approve technical schools proposed and financed by city or social estate (*soslovie*) groups and by private persons. When the level of the curriculum in a proposed technical school qualified it for status at the "middle" or "higher" level, the government ministry within whose jurisdiction the school would exist would decide whether to issue permission for founding the school. Anyone wishing permission to open a school whose curriculum would be at the "lower" or "county" level was required to obtain the joint permission of the superintendent of the educational district and the governor of the province in which the school would be located. At all levels, the tsarist officials making the decision required people proposing a school to submit a special charter explaining the administrative structure of the school, the school's curriculum, the number of teachers to be hired, fees to be charged, and other such pertinent details.[5]

When the government conducted a census in 1872 of all educational institutions in the Russian Empire, except for Finland, three years after promulgation of the statute of August 27, 1869, the census revealed that only 36 technical schools of all types--from "higher" through "lower"--existed in the empire. Of these, 18 were located in provincial capitals, 14 in other provincial cities, and 4 in cities that were county seats. Collectively, these schools had 5,094 students. Among these schools was the "middle" technical school that the Tver provincial zemstvo founded in Rzhev, the county seat of Rzhev county, in 1871. According to the census, the school had 141 students in the 1872-73 academic year.[6] But, by academic year 1873-74, it had been closed by the tsarist bureaucracy for disseminating revolutionary and secular ideas.

An analysis of the short history of the Tver zemstvo's technical school in Rzhev illustrates clearly that the tsarist government wished to protect the values of the official church--the Russian Orthodox Church--against secular incursions. In the end, the government was willing to sacrifice 141 much-needed technicians and a training center for many others in order to preserve those values. The decision to take the action was exclusively the affair of the state, with no participation from the church hierarchy.

* * * *

The Tver provincial zemstvo assembly decided within a month after promulgation of the 1869 statute on technical schools to found the Rzhev Technical School. At the assembly's fourth regular session, in December 1869, the deputies voted, upon hearing the provincial zemstvo board's report on the status of education in the province, to found two schools as a step in developing a general plan to promote education in the province: a teachers' seminary in Torzhok, the county seat of Novotorzhok county, to train teachers for the web of elementary schools the zemstvo was developing; and a technical school in Rzhev to prepare students for further study at higher technical institutes or for work in state or private industrial enterprises.

During debate on the zemstvo board's proposal to found a technical school, A. A. Bakunin of Novotorzhok county strongly supported opening the school as a necessary step in the industrialization of Russia. Besides Russia's need for more factories and industrial enterprises, he said, the country must also "open up the intellectual and material riches that are now in a primitive condition. We have, of course, good bakers, saddle-makers, cabinet-makers, and other artisans, but they all live within a routine. Their mental capabilities are not developed, and they must, therefore, be led out of such a situation." Supporting his assertion with a case study from Novotorzhok county, he noted that "a semi-literate German technician" had recently built there a small mill that utilized "all the latest methods provided by science; everyone fell in love with it, and has said good-bye to the coarse flour ground by the old methods." In a technical school, he felt, Russian students would learn

in practice the data worked out by science, the strict, scientific step-by-step preparation necessary for higher education. The study of physics and other subjects that occurs in courses of a technical school can be done by methods used in the schools of France, England, America, and Belgium where the barely literate can studyscience with textbooks that are completely understandable, so that they complete their training and leave as people of genius. Thus, one educated geologist discovers in a baker a brother in science, but [one] much superior to him in degree of practical knowledge."[7]

At the conclusion of the debate, the zemstvo assembly passed the resolution by a plurality of one vote. While the specific reasons for locating the school in Rzhev were not discussed in the debate on the proposal, one might reasonably assume that the characteristics of the city made it a logical setting for a technical school. Located on the Volga River, Rzhev was the second largest trading center in Tver province, second only to Tver, the provincial capital. In the 1870s Rzhev had a population of more than 3,000 residents, but its importance later waned relative to other cities after railroad transportation provided competition with river transport in the province.[8]

After accepting the commission's proposal for a technical school and appropriating funds for it, the zemstvo assembly and board began immediately to take necessary measures to open the school by autumn 1870 for academic year 1870-71. The assembly chose a three-person committee of A. N. Tolstoi, A. A. Grubnikov, and S. D. Kvashnin-Samarin to draft a program for the school, and elected (as required by statute) three persons from the zemstvo to be members of the councils of the two schools: V. N. Lind from the zemstvo board; Prince B. V. Meshcherskii, from the county school council where he was the zemstvo's elected representative; and to the council of the technical school from the provincial zemstvo assembly, A. N. Tolstoi.[9] Unknown to the zemstvo board, the governor wrote a letter to the minister of the interior approximately two months later, on February 1, 1870, complaining that as a member of the provincial zemstvo board Lind had "repeatedly attracted attention to himself by his lack of success in choosing [suitable] teachers" to be hired for zemstvo schools in Tver province.[10]

Early in 1870, the provincial zemstvo board hired Professor D. I. Mendeleev and E. A. Evnevich, director of the Moscow Technical School, and other teachers and scientists to help draft the charters and determine the curriculums of the technical school and the teachers' seminary.[11] The plan for the technical school projected opening a four-year school in 1870 with a commitment of 12,300 rubles from the zemstvo assembly for its support. The last two years of the curriculum would be divided into two specializations: mechanical and chemical. In hours free from class work, all students who wished could study one of two crafts: woodworking or metalworking.[12]

The provincial zemstvo board contacted the superintendent of the Moscow educational district, in which Tver province was located, and various officials in the Ministry of Education in St. Petersburg, to file necessary petitions and documents for opening the two schools. But at the time of the regular session of the zemstvo assembly in December 1870, the board had not yet received a response to its petitions to found the two schools. The zemstvo assembly merely approved the board's report and asked it to continue its efforts to complete the necessary steps for founding the schools.[13]

Although the zemstvo board was not aware of the governor's reasons for hesitation in approving the charters of the new schools, archival data show that he was displeased with the zemstvo's choice of personnel for its boards, school councils, and teaching staff. On March 13, 1871, some three months after the zemstvo ended its regular session of 1870, the governor wrote the minister of the interior a letter that the former marked "secret," reminding the minister of the warning about Lind in the letter of February 1 of the previous year. The governor recalled that he had objected to Lind's having been chosen as one of the teachers in the zemstvo's Maksimovich school for girls. He had written, he said, that he preferred that Lind be replaced by a teacher "more suitable in his teaching abilities, [and with more] seriousness toward the obligations he has taken upon himself." But, the governor had since talked with Prince Meshcherskii and zemstvo deputy P. P. Maksimovich (who had contributed the funds to found the school that bore his name), who told him that Lind intended to retire soon from his activities related to schools. Therefore, the governor had decided "not to intervene officially in this particular instance" and not to delay approval of the Maksimovich school for girls. But, he promised, if he should see anything worthy of note in Lind's future actions, he would immediately inform the minister.[14] On the first page of the governor's letter, someone in the Ministry of the Interior wrote in the margin: "It seems that we had something about Lind." Below that was another person's comment: "On Lind, see the file on Nechaev."

Perhaps because of the governor's many warnings about Lind, the minister of education said that all teachers at the Novotorzhok Teachers' Seminary and the Rzhev Technical School would have to be approved by the director of educational institutions for Tver province. Thus the board sent the names of the two potential directors it had provisionally hired: N. P. Val'berg, who held the title Technologist of the First Order from St. Petersburg Polytechnic Institute and who would teach chemistry and be head of the Rzhev Technical School, and N. S. Lvov, a landowner from Chernigov province and holder of the Candidate (*kandidat*) degree from St. Petersburg University, who would be head of the Novotorzhok Teachers' Seminary. On August 20 the district superintendent informed the zemstvo board that he would allow Val'berg to serve as acting head of the technical school prior to his confirmation as permanent head, and that shortly the exact information that he had requested about Val'berg would arrive and the final decision could be made. He approved appointment of Lvov as head of the teachers' seminary.[15]

The request for further information came from the governor of Tver province. Although he had met in his office with Val'berg, the governor was hesitant to reach a decision approving him and the other two teachers the zemstvo proposed to hire for the technical school. "As far as I knew," he wrote later to the minister of the interior, their "degree of desirability and moral quality was not fully suitable to the government's demands for people working closely with the young generation." When the superintendent gave the teachers a positive rating, the governor called Val'berg to his office a second time and told him "to follow strictly the course of the teaching in the school, and once again pointed out to him the circumstances which served as the basis for such demands from me."[16]

On November 13, the governor wrote to the minister of the interior saying that he had been informed by the "main head" of the Third Department of the chancellery, General-Adjutant Count Levashev, that several of the teachers being named to the technical school, the teachers' seminary, and the Maksimovich school for girls were "undesirable people." The governor tried to assure the minister that "needed measures were taken to prevent evil consequences from these institutions." In the margin beside this phrase, someone in the ministry added the note: "Request the detailed information." In compliance with the warning from Count Levashev, the governor "considered it necessary to place the Tver zemstvo's schools under the closest surveillance of the local school official," and asked the minister if he would try to find a way to have the Tver zemstvo "move both of these schools to the city of Tver where the necessary oversight of them by the responsible officials would be more convenient and practicable."[17]

Despite the governor's foreboding, he informed the minister of the interior on November 26, after recounting his many steps to prevent all possible foreseeable problems, that he and the superintendent had permitted the technical school and the Novotorzhok Teachers' Seminary to open. He sent the minister copies of the charters on which they would operate, and listed the names of the teachers with the courses they would teach. Thus far, he reported, teaching in the schools was going properly.

Nonetheless, in view of the fact that these schools, in particular the Novotorzhok school, are under surveillance and extremely undesirable because Mr. [P. A.] Bakunin was chosen a member of the Novotorzhok county school council, and chairman of the Novotorzhok zemstvo board Mr. Lind, whose reputation is known to Your Excellency, . . . [They] must be denied the possibility to deviate from the program and charters of the schools. I would propose it necessary as much as possible for the ministry of education to strengthen the surveillance of these schools.[18]

When the technical school opened for academic year 1871-72, it had four teachers plus the priest A. Popov, who taught the required course on religion (*Zakon Bozhii*) and a supplementary course on Russian language on an overflow basis. The four subject teachers were: N. P. Val'berg, who served as head of the school and taught chemistry, mathematics, and natural history; A. N. Diakov, holder of the Candidate degree from Moscow

University, who taught zoology, Russian, and German. A. I. Knipper, holder of the Candidate degree from St. Petersburg University, who taught physics, algebra, geometry, and geography; and V. M. Chausov, who taught handwriting, drawing, and drafting. Because of the uncertainties regarding opening date, the zemstvo was unable to find a teacher for courses on Russian history and geography. This position would be filled for academic year 1872-73.[19]

At its regular session for 1871, in December, the Tver zemstvo assembly heard a report from its board on the status of the technical school. A. N. Tolstoi, member of the technical school's council, reported that he had visited the school and found the teaching and overall operation "completely in keeping with the purposes for which the school was founded." The peasant boys he knew who were students there had been quite unprepared academically, but were proving to be successful in mathematics and other subjects. In response to his proposal that the zemstvo find a better building for the school, the assembly voted to buy a building in Rzhev for the technical school and one in Torzhok for the teachers' seminary. The assembly instructed the board to present a plan for both at the 1872 session. The assembly again reelected Lind a member of the provincial zemstvo board; Prince Meshcherskii and Bakunin members of the provincial school council, and to the council of the technical school: Tolstoi, Meshcherskii, and Kvashnin-Samarin.[20]

On April 8, 1872, during the first academic year, the minister of education approved the two schools in the two cities where they were located. He said he would inform the superintendent of the Moscow educational district to have the inspector of public schools of Tver province, along with the director of schools, send somebody out once a month to check the schools and make a report, and at the end of each year to file a detailed annual report. Further, the superintendent should name specific officials from the educational district to be present at the final examinations in these two schools.[21]

Although the technical school seemed far more pain than joy to the bureaucracy, the Free Economic Society, charged with the enormous task of disseminating knowledge about agriculture and technology in a virtually illiterate society, noted with delight at the beginning of 1872 in its publication, *Trudy*, that the school had been opened, summarized its curriculum and extracurricular activities for students, and reported that those students who finished were eligible to enter three special institutes--technological, transportation, and agricultural--or they could take positions in factories and industries. Attendance was free for residents of Tver province.[22]

Entering academic year 1872-83, the technical school retained its staff from the previous year. But, early in the school year, Diakov, who was now teaching physics and natural history, became ill and had to resign his position. For approximately the two months from November 1872 to February 1873, when a replacement was found for Diakov, Val'berg and Knipper divided his courses between them and taught them in addition to their own courses. In February, S. N. Mech, who had the Candidate degree from Moscow University, joined the staff to teach physics and natural history. At the same time, the school hired a fifth teacher.[23]

During academic year 1872-83, the Tver provincial zemstvo assembly, at its regular session for 1872, in December, again took up the question of finding a permanent home for the technical school. After discussing a report by the zemstvo board on this topic, the assembly created a six-person special commission to locate two suitable buildings--one in Rzhev for the technical school, and one in Torzhok for the teachers' seminary--and authorized the board to spend up to 35,000 rubles to buy any two buildings that the special commission might find and determine satisfactory for the purposes intended. Tolstoi, because he was moving to Nizhnii Novgorod, resigned his position as member of the technical school's council, and the assembly elected T. N. Pavalo-Shveikovskii to replace him.[24] The special commission placed advertisements in local newspapers, and soon located a suitable building for 15,000 rubles, and used 500 rubles to convert it for school purposes for academic year 1873-74.[25]

But the technical school began to have domestic problems soon after teacher Mech arrived in February 1873. Director of the school Val'berg came to Tver on April 11 to report that a lot of "nasty rumors" were circulating in Rzhev about poor conduct of students in the school. The technical school council investigated conditions and found four students living in one large room guilty of "poor conduct," without specifying the students' specific acts. Zemstvo deputy N. A. Chaplin visited the school and found "certain omissions" and noted that students were "insufficiently punctual" in attending classes. The zemstvo board informed the governor of these details.[26]

In April, at the zemstvo's request, Val'berg resigned as director and teacher at the school. The courses he was currently teaching were dropped or given to other teachers. Chemistry and world history were temporarily suspended; Russian language and geography were taken over by two other teachers. Kvashnin-Samarin, a member of the provincial zemstvo board, replaced him as acting director.[27]

On May 1 the technical school council met to resolve the problem of the "poor conduct" of the four students. In no official zemstvo report, during or after this case, were the students' misdeeds identified. It is clear that the zemstvo sought to minimize the negative publicity by using the vague term "poor conduct" to describe the problem. Only in the governor's report to the minister of the interior (in which the governor cited the report of the Rzhev county administrator [*ispravnik*]) can one learn of the specific acts that constituted poor conduct. In the governor's words, four students-- Upervshchkii, Kolmovskii, Lukin, and Sergeev--who lived together in a rented apartment in town, had "allowed themselves the worst kind of disgraceful acts with holy icons; they glued pieces of paper to them; mortgaged the metallic edge [*riza*] of the sacred image for smoking tobacco, etc."[28] Because none of the four would plead guilty to these acts during the school council's inquest, the council members decided to expel all four students, and resolved to increase its oversight role at the school.[29]

On May 4, the governor informed the minister of the interior by letter of the events of April and May. He reported that he had recently been hearing rumors that the students in the technical school were extremely "undisciplined," that they had "absolutely no supervision outside class," and that they had "total freedom about attending classes and about doing their homework assignments." He reported that he had ordered the new Rzhev county administrator, whom he had just hired, to pay particular attention to the students' life and attitudes, to find out personally whether the rumors had any substance, and to report to him on this subject. Within a few days, the *ispravnik* reported that the rumors were based on fact, that many of the students did anything they wished, without supervision. The situation there was one of extreme lack of discipline; students had no homework assignments and were often seen, even during class hours, walking around the city with nothing to do. The school administrators did not ask why they missed classes and did not consider it necessary to determine whether students had valid reasons for missing classes.[30]

Having received such a report from the *ispravnik*, the governor asked the inspector of public schools, who had immediate jurisdiction over the technical school, to verify the accuracy of the *ispravnik*'s description of conditions. The inspector not only agreed with the description but reported that he had already told school director Val'berg of "the abnormality of such a situation and of the harm that could come from it for students at the school."[31]

After hearing the same negative report by two appointed officials, the governor called the members of the Tver provincial zemstvo board to his office on May 7 where he pointed out to them the "disorders" in the school for which they had the main administrative responsibility, and demanded that they "immediately adopt measures to rectify the situation, specifically the irrevocable firing of director Val'berg for his inability to perform the duties assigned to him, naming someone else in his place, and then screening all students at the school and immediately expelling those who have no right or reason to be in school." Zemstvo board members told him at that meeting that they had already asked Val'berg to submit his resignation and that he had already resigned both as director and as a teacher. In his letter to the minister of the interior later that day, the governor claimed that the board had named Kvashnin-Samarin director "for the purpose of implementing my remaining demands."[32]

The governor's next step was to ask the superintendent of the Moscow educational district to strengthen surveillance of the technical school. The Ministry of Education's two responsible officials--the director of schools and the inspector of public schools of Tver province--were unable to provide adequate oversight, he said, because the ministry had already freed the director from that task; and although the inspector was visiting the school monthly, the governor felt that level of surveillance insufficient. Not only did the continued "disorders" in the school attest to that fact, but the inspector had warned him independently that in cases like this, "measures limited to official warnings to the director of a school could not quickly restore order."[33]

During this first week of May, the governor reminded one Tver zemstvo deputy that the charter for the technical school had still not been approved in its final, detailed form and that events at the school "could give occasion for various interpretations and omissions from the demands of the charter and curriculum. . . ." He also told Kvashnin-Samarin that by confirming him as acting director, he "was not naming him permanently to that position."[34]

On May 7, the governor, having received further information from the *ispravnik* and names of five "student radicals" from the inspector of schools for Tver province, summoned the provincial zemstvo board to a private meeting in his office, and gave them the names of the five students whom the inspector of schools and he demanded be expelled from the technical school. The zemstvo board reminded him at this meeting that the council had already expelled four students, but the students' names on the new list were not the same as those of the four who had just been expelled. The zemstvo board promised to look into the records of these five students. Shortly after the zemstvo board members left his office, the governor wrote to the minister of the interior informing him of all these events and described the specific acts of the four students the technical school council had expelled. He reported that the *ispravnik* would continue to investigate matters at the technical school, and promised to transmit any further information that might come from that investigation.[35]

On May 25, the superintendent of the Moscow educational district sent the Tver provincial zemstvo board the same list of five students that the governor had presented, repeating the request that they be expelled from the technical school. On June 14, the chairman of the zemstvo board Prince Meshcherskii responded to the superintendent's letter saying that the board was unable to determine why the inspector (who had given the superintendent the list) wanted these students expelled. Of the persons he mentioned, no Reinval'd had ever been a student in the school; Obrazuov had withdrawn from school himself; Vydenskii was not a regular student, but an auditor; and Kuznetsov and Rumiantsev were students on stipend from the zemstvo. "All four of these persons are characterized by completely good conduct and diligence [in their studies]." Rumiantsev, he said, was particularly gifted.[36]

In a letter of July 9 to the superintendent of Moscow educational district, Inspector of Public Schools in Tver Province A. Druzhinin presented his side of the story to his superior. He reported that he had told Meshcherskii and Kvashnin-Samarin--in the presence of the Tver governor--all the reasons Rumiantsev and Kuznetsov should be expelled, and the governor had agreed. About Kuznetsov, he reported that before entering the technical school, he was known in Rzhev as "a drunken nihilist, not hiding his inclination. Many have told me," the inspector said, "that he was persuaded to leave service, where he received 300 rubles a year, and to enter school to raise the school's morale [dukh], and for that he was given a zemstvo stipend!" Former school director Val'berg had told the inspector that Kuznetsov "does not look at things right" and that he had great influence on the students. The inspector said that the Rzhev ispravnik and Tver gendarme lieutenant "see in Kuznetsov a harmful person."

Rumiantsev he called "a friend and follower of Kuznetsov." He called the Tver board "mistaken about their quality as students," asserting that Kuznetsov and Rumiantsev had not even shown up for several of the final examinations held at the school in June. Vydenskii was over 22 years old, and Obrotsuov over 23. Both were earlier expelled from Tver seminary. "I consider it harmful," the inspector wrote, "to allow such grown-ups into the second class, where people 13-14 years old are students." As concerns Reinval'd, even though the board maintained that he had never been in school, the official letter of July 4 from the Rzhev ispravnik stated that Reinval'd attended school from February to June of that year. The inspector allowed that perhaps the school had not considered him its student because "the school did not have any kind of list of students until the end-of-the-year exams so that neither the school nor anyone else could tell who was and was not a student." Reinval'd had been a junker in the Narva regiment, quartered in Tver, until forced to leave service for insubordination. The inspector had heard from "a reliable source" that Reinval'd wanted to enter Rzhev school and that he considered himself a student in the technical school at the time of the inspector's letter.[37]

On July 23 Inspector Druzhinin supplied further evidence that the entire technical school at Rzhev was saturated with revolutionary and secular ideas. Writing to his superior, the superintendent of the Moscow educational district, he was transmitting information that he had, in turn, received from the vice-governor, who was acting in the governor's place during the latter's absence. The vice-governor had learned "through private, but trusted sources," that the situation at Rzhev Technical School had not improved with the firing of Val'berg, and it "will not improve because Val'berg did not give it direction, but other people, mainly the teacher Mech." The vice-governor had accumulated a good deal of information about Mech. Added to existing knowledge, these facts proved fatal to the technical school. First, in his classes at the technical school Mech "discussed the morals and life of bees, comparing the structure of a bee colony with the structure of our society." Mech said that the Russian "aristocrats correspond to the worker bees; peasants and workers correspond to the drones; and the tsar to the queen bee."

Second among Mech's faults was a secular act that would cause him trouble in some classrooms of the world even today, on the eve of the twenty-first century: He "explained to the students the origins of man according to the theory of Darwin." Further, "when a student interrupted him with the question: 'How is it that the priest says otherwise?' Mech answered: 'I am not a priest and do not recite fables, but speak about scientific facts; if you want to hear fables, go to the priest.'" The vice-governor volunteered that although he had no facts about the situation in the Novotorzhok teachers' seminary, he was confident that "student fulfillment of their religious duties . . . and student thoughts and convictions" were "the same as in the Rzhev school."[38]

In addition to the information about teacher Mech, the inspector also supplied two personal observations of student life that he felt were illuminating about the morality of the students in the technical school. One incident that he considered worthy of narration occurred June 13 while he observed the final examinations in the Rzhev school. Awaiting the beginning of the examination, he was in the director's office with acting director Kvashnin-Samarin and the religion teacher, priest Popov, when

Into the room came a student, about 14 years old, bowing to no
one, turned sharply to Samarin with the question, "Why did you
call me?" Samarin answered, "You petitioned me to leave school,
but your father was just in my office and asked you to remain
one more year." The student answered "and what's it any of his
business what I do?" Samarin repeated, "Your father asks to keep
you another year," and the student said again, "and what is it any
of his business what I do?" and turned and was gone from the
room.[39]

The inspector offered this anecdote without comment, apparently certain
that its content was adequate condemnation of the technical school at Rzhev.

The second anecdote he reported falls into the same category as the
first: lack of respect for elders. Two days after leaving the examinations in
Rzhev, the inspector reported, he was on a steamboat on the Volga River
traveling from Rzhev to Tver. On the boat there were also about a dozen
students on zemstvo stipends for study in Rzhev Technical School. During
the evening, while the passengers waited for a mechanic to repair one of
the boat's paddle wheels, he heard one of the students say to his
compatriots: "'You know, brothers, why the wheel broke? It was from
caused by disrespect for our parents.' And all the students laughed loudly at
this."[40]

Not only did the Rzhev students lack respect of their parents, they also
did not respect priest Popov, the religion teacher at the technical school,
Inspector Druzhinin wrote, as the final item in his long list of ills. But
Popov not only enjoyed "absolutely no respect" among the students, he
lacked respect "generally among the residents of Rzhev." Druzhinin
delivered a scathing characterization of Popov as a teacher:

[He pays no] attention to the students' success, or to their
morality, allows the students to skip his classes and to take various
school absences on their own. They have told me how he,
narrating to the students about the discussion of Jesus Christ with
the Good Samaritan, was asked by one student: "and what do you

think, little father? Was this Samaritan good?" To this he merely smiled.[41]

The minister of the interior was so impressed by the information in the report that on August 19 he verified that N. P. Val'berg was Nikolai Pavlovich Val'berg, who was then studying technology in Austria, found the place and date his passport was issued for the trip to Austria to be certain of his identity, and then put his name on a list of teachers "never to be given a position in educational service" in Russia. Two days later, the minister of education sent a letter to Acting Minister of the Interior Demianov repeating all the information, which the acting minister had already seen, that the minister of education had just received from the superintendent of the Moscow educational district. Citing those reasons, he asked the acting minister to take measures to close the technical school completely.[42] On September 18 the acting minister of the interior instructed the governor of Tver province to close the school. On September 20, the governor informed the Tver school board informally of St. Petersburg's decision. The reasons he gave the board for closing the school were the students' "lack of moral discipline and their frivolous attitude toward religion." While he appreciated the recent efforts made by the school council, "matters had not improved significantly."[43]

On October 3 the zemstvo board received the governor's official letter ordering the school closed. The zemstvo board demanded the "true" reasons for closing the school. They requested the evidence that served as the basis for the decision to close the school. They had, of course, seen none of the governor's letters, the *ispravnik*'s reports, nor the inspector's reports. The governor pleaded with the minister of the interior to be allowed to come to St. Petersburg to present his reasons in a personal report, and to explain why he did not feel at liberty to reveal to the zemstvo board information that had been gleaned by various people during the course of the investigation.[44]

Tver zemstvo board members never obtained the detailed information they sought. Even in 1914 when B. B. Veselovskii wrote of this incident in his history of the Tver zemstvo, he could merely repeat some of the bureaucracy's phrases to explain that the closing "was motivated by 'student mischief' and 'the inability of the teachers to guide the school along the desired path.'" Rather than seeing their adversaries in local officials, zemstvos blamed the central bureaucrats in St. Petersburg. Such vagueness, Veselovskii said, made a "heavy impression" among zemstvo activists in Tver and elsewhere and caused them to see in this act "the appearance of a new course taken by Minister of Education D. A. Tolstoi in relation to the zemstvo."[45]

Whether the governor was granted his junket to St. Petersburg is not clear. The technical school, nonetheless, remained closed, and the zemstvo expenditure of some 41,000 rubles had come to naught. The secular power had intervened, without even a request for assistance from the monopoly church, to destroy a source of secular and revolutionary ideas. Educational institutions, and the zemstvos as their promoters, could train specialists necessary for industrialization, but they could serve simultaneously as disseminators of unacceptable values. How to make the changes industrialization demanded, but leave traditional values of Orthodoxy and autocracy unchallenged, became an increasingly acute problem as the country began intense industrialization in the mid-1880s. The story of the Rzhev Technical School shows that reconciling those two objectives was probably impossible.

CHAPTER 8

MARXISM AND *AZIATCHINA*: SECULAR
RELIGION, THE NATURE OF RUSSIAN SOCIETY,
AND THE ORGANIZATION OF THE BOLSHEVIK PARTY[*]

Joseph Schiebel

Marxism is often called the "science of society," even the "science of
revolution." But when Marxism moved east it took on a religious character.
If the doctrine had its basis in Marx's analysis of Western "bourgeois"
society, the gospel spread by the Bolshevik Party was peculiarly Russian.
In being Russian, its character was more Asiatic than Western. Just as the
character of the Russian Orthodox Church was shaped by the despotic
nature of the post-Mongol Russian state and society, so also was the
character of Russia's secular religion. It is the contention of this essay that
these factors also shaped the organization of the Bolshevik Party.

The Asiatic character of the Russian state and society not only became
an integral part of Russian Marxist doctrine in the decades before the
Russian October Revolution of 1917; it profoundly determined the
theoretical concepts and practical actions of Plekhanov and Lenin. To a

---

[*] *Editor's Note*: Joseph Schiebel died from a heart attack on October 9,
1976, while attending the convention of the American Association for the
Advancement of Slavic Studies in St. Louis. This essay is an abstract from
"Aziatchina: The Controversy Concerning the Nature Of Russian Society
and the Organization of the Bolshevik Party," the dissertation Schiebel
wrote under the supervision of Professor Donald W. Treadgold in 1972 to
complete the requirements for the Ph.D. degree in Russian history at the
University of Washington in Seattle. I have focused on his central
argument as developed from Marx and Engels to Plekhanov and Lenin, but
Professor Schiebel's research is, of course, much richer in the history of
Marxism and the Russian revolutionary movement. Reasons of space have
also made it necessary to avoid any mention of Professor Schiebel's critique
of the relevant Western historiography concerning the focus of his
argument. Only the absolutely essential references are given here to
support the thesis. For full documentation, the reader is referred to
Professor Schiebel's dissertation on file with University Microfilms in Ann
Arbor, Michigan, order number 72-28662. -G. L. Ulmen

somewhat lesser degree, this was also true for other members of the Russian revolutionary movement. In Marx's terms, as well as in those of the classical and Western Marxist precursors of the Russian revolutionaries, this meant that they believed Russia's old order was characterized by a despotic state which, supported by a bureaucratic ruling class and a dependent service nobility, dominated a society unable to resist state power--what Miliukov called a "state stronger than society."[1] During Russia's post-1861 transformation, this old order was unable to generate the political and economic energies necessary for a thoroughgoing "Westernization."

The Asiatic character of Russian state and society presented Russian Marxists with a particular and fundamental problem because they also believed that the Paris Commune was the prototype of the Russian revolution. Even though this prototype did not fit Russian conditions, the myth of this "Western" example lived on. The conflict between Western and Asiatic Marxist perceptions before the October Revolution led to internal debates within Russian Marxism. The most important were between Plekhanov and Lenin, whose doctrinal positions and disputes reveal not only the Marxist heritage of their understanding of the problem and prospect of Asiatic Russia but the ultimate shape of Soviet state and society. They reveal the intimate relation between the secular religion and political reality of Russian Marxism.

At the end of his life Lenin saw the emerging danger of an "Asiatic restoration": a resurrection of the institutions of tsarist despotism, in the structure of the party and the state he had created. But the religious dimension of Russian Marxism and revolution was already tied to that structure, whereby the "total power" of "Oriental despotism" would become "totalitarian" in a new type of society which Karl A. Wittfogel calls a "total managerial order."[2] The struggle between Western and Asiatic elements in Russia ended with the total eradication of those very Western influences that had brought about the revolution. When Marxism moved east, it had necessarily to falsify Marx and Engels's analysis of "Asiatic society" and "semi-Asiatic" Russia; it had to obscure the doctrinal positions and disputes of Plekhanov, whom Lenin called the "father of Russian

Marxism," and of Lenin himself. It had also to destroy the concept of what both Plekhanov and Lenin called Russia's *Aziatchina*.

The founders of Marxism characterized Russia's peculiar institutional system as "Asiatic," an "Oriental despotism." With respect to the prospect of revolution and the appropriate revolutionary methods for Asiatic Russia, Marx and Engels left a legacy in the form of an institutional analysis and a practical guide to action. Several attempts have been made to attribute their adoption in 1853 of an Asiatic interpretation of Russia to their anger at Russia's behavior in the aftermath of the revolution of 1848--to their hatred of Russia as a bastion of European reaction and their fear of Russian aggressiveness.[3] There is no doubt that Russia's participation in crushing the Hungarian revolution of 1849 came as a shock to Europe's Social Democrats and other socialists, and that Marx and Engels shared this feeling when they condemned Russian participation in the oppression of the Poles. But Russia's political behavior in Eastern Europe had nothing to do with Marx and Engels's sociohistorical analysis of Russia. The Marxist view of an "Asiatic" Russia did not emerge until after they had lost their faith in the reemergence of revolution in Europe.

Taking his cue from Engels, Marx first publicly introduced his concept of Oriental despotism in an article published in the *New York Daily Tribune* in July 25, 1853:

There have been in Asia, generally from immemorial times, but three departments of government: that of Finance, or the plunder of the interior; that of War, or the plunder of the exterior; and, finally, the department of Public Works. Climate and territorial conditions, especially the vast tracts of deserts, extending from the Sahara, through Arabia, Persia, India and Tatary, to the most elevated Asiatic highlands, constituted artificial irrigation by canals and waterworks the basis of Oriental agriculture. . . . This prime necessity of an economical and common use of water, which in the Occident, drove private enterprise to voluntary association, as in Flanders and Italy, necessitated, in the Orient where civilization was too low and the territorial extent too vast to call into life voluntary association, the interference of the centralizing power of

Government. Hence an economical function devolved upon all Asiatic governments the function of public works.[4]

Marx clearly distinguished "Asiatic despotism" from any European form of state and society. "Two circumstances" had produced among "all Oriental peoples" a "social system of particular features--the so-called *village system*": a central management of waterworks and the dispersed nature of agricultural and commercial pursuits for which those public works were a primary condition.[5] It was precisely this system of self-contained, dispersed village communities that "had always been the solid foundation of Oriental despotism."[6] Despite civil wars, invasions, revolutions, conquests and famines, the "internal economy" (i.e., the "social condition") had remained unaltered from the earliest times. Although Marx later noted the disappearance of the village commune in China, he and Engels continued to consider that country, together with India and Persia, as characterized by Asiatic despotism.[7] Similarly, when Marx characterized Russia as "semi-Asiatic," because it lacked one of the "two circumstances" (public works for water control), he nevertheless considered Russia to be a full Oriental despotism.[8] Marx and Engels might have made their analysis more sophisticated had they noted the considerable presence of public works other than those for irrigation in the pre- and post-Petrine periods, particularly those concerned with defense and transport. But the fathers of Marxism were mainly interested in the sociohistorical typology and political system of Russia.

Marx did not understand the origin of Russia's Oriental despotism from the nature of its geographical requirements of water control, as in China, but from the events of Russian history, most importantly the Mongol invasions. In his *Secret Diplomatic History of the Eighteenth Century* (1856), he asserted: "The bloody mire of Mongolian slavery, not the rude glory of the Norman epoch, forms the cradle of Muscovy, and modern Russia is but a metamorphosis of Muscovy," and "the Muscovite Czars [had been] obliged to *tartarise* Muscovy, [while] Peter the Great . . . was obliged to *civilize* Russia." As Marx saw it, Peter the Great had "coupled the political craft of the Mongol slave with the proud aspiration of the Mongol master," producing a foreign policy that blended "the encroaching method of the Mongol slave with the world-conquering tendencies of the Mongol master." Peter the Great had "adapted" the Russians "to the technical appliance of the Western peoples, without imbuing them with their ideas": he had "metamorphosed Muscovy into modern Russia by the generalization of its system."[9] Marx and Engels were well aware of the Westernizing elements in Russian society since Peter the Great. But they saw these as supporting rather than challenging the power of the despotic state. They continued to equate Russia institutionally with India. Unlike India, Russia had not been directly occupied and colonized, but had suffered great military defeats that had shattered its sociopolitical structure. Russia's proximity to the West had also accelerated and intensified the development of those internal forces pushing for an antiautocratic (anti-"Asiatic") bourgeois revolution.

Beginning in 1875, Marx and Engels considered it increasingly likely that the Russian antidespotic revolution would precede the socialist revolution in the West. In that event, the Russian revolution would trigger the socialist revolution in the West. To the extent that the ameliorative potential of capitalism was being realized, it would be essential for the Western revolution. It was not essential for the Russian revolution. But if the Russian revolutionaries wished to preserve the village commune in their advance toward a social revolution, they would need a socialist revolution in Europe to show them "how it's done" (*wie mans macht*).

Marx and Engels's agreement with the idea of building Russian socialism on the remnants of the village commune was both conditional and limited. Not only did it require the watchful sponsorship of a socialist Europe; it could only be used to accelerate, but not to bypass, a period of capitalist development in Russia. Since they did not consider the preservation of communal institutions desirable elsewhere, it seems clear that these limited theoretical concessions were intended to mute a considerable difference of opinion between Marx and Engels and their Russian friends (whom they did not wish to antagonize). They left it to the Russian Marxists to work out their own problems. But they insisted that the Russian Marxists could do so only if they realized that their sociohistorical development was different from the West's, that they would have to effect a special type of an anti-Asiatic bourgeois revolution.[10]

George Plekhanov (1856-1918) adopted many of the classical elements in Marx and Engels's thought. Owing to the immediate relevance to the revolutionary situation in Russia, he was particularly interested in their classification of Russian state and society as "Oriental" or "Asiatic"--a classification Plekhanov appropriated, elaborated upon, and from which he drew specific conclusions about the practical tasks of the Russian revolutionary movement. He communicated this Asiatic interpretation of Russian history and institutions to that sizable portion of the Russian revolutionary movement that came to rely on his judgment. It was through Plekhanov that Marx's Asiatic understanding of Russia became one of the fundamental assumptions of revolutionary Russian socialists in the period prior to the October Revolution.

Plekhanov probably startled many of his Western socialist listeners in his speech in Bern, Switzerland, in 1884, when he said that the primary task of the Russian socialists was not to fight capitalism but rather absolutism, that combating capitalism under Russian conditions would lead "to the strengthening of *Eastern despotism.*" As Plekhanov saw it, "capitalism is bad . . . [but] despotism is even worse. Capitalism develops the beast in man, despotism turns him into a trained animal; capitalism lays its filthy hands on literature and science, despotism kills literature and science."[11] It was acceptable for the Russian socialists to struggle for political freedoms and to organize a revolutionary proletariat. But, Plekhanov cautioned, Russian absolutism could not be combated and conquered in association with the commune, only in association with the capitalists.

Plekhanov's so-called conversion to Marxism was more a clarification and formalization of Marxist ideas already held. These ideas centered on a rejection of the notion that the village commune could serve as the basis of a socialist order-- the notion that a stage of capitalist development could be skipped. His rejection was rooted in two fundamental considerations. First, he believed that the commune was the foundation of Russia's despotic order and that its preservation would only serve to perpetuate that order. He described the commune as the "most basic element of barbarian society," the "centuries-old foundation of national life," the basis of "the Muscovite despotism." Second, he was convinced that, regardless of what uses might be made of the commune, it was rapidly and inexorably breaking apart. He was careful to point out that Marx and Engels had limited the possibilities of integrating the commune into an emerging socialist order by the condition that it be attempted only when a socialist state in Western Europe guaranteed its success. Even so, not having Marx's problem of soothing the feelings of Russian socialists, Plekhanov asserted that even this condition would not justify the attempt. He preferred the inevitability of a socialist revolution after all the "objective conditions" had been met, rather than to explore possibilities for developmental and revolutionary shortcuts.[12]

Plekhanov showed himself fully aware of Marx's notion of the self-perpetuating village commune as the "secret of the unchangeable character of Asiatic society." But he made no attempt to explore its meaning for Russia. Concurrent and inconsistent with his understanding of the Asiatic character of Russian state and society, he considered the appearance of industrial capitalism irresistible and universal--neither the feudal institutions of Europe nor the communal system of Russia and other Eastern countries could withstand it. His commitment to the idea that the development of a money economy and commodity production for the market necessarily portended the destruction of the economy of communal agriculture and the appearance of capitalist institutions was later, in 1898, to characterize Lenin's attempt to describe and document the development of capitalism in Russia. Plekhanov even went so far as to suggest that capitalism might develop in Russia more quickly than in the West, where it prevailed only after overcoming the tenacious resistance of feudal institutions, precisely because of Russia's "centuries-old stagnation." The decisive fact for him was that the Russian bourgeoisie had advanced to the point where it had become the enemy of Russian absolutism.

Had Plekhanov believed that Russia had ceased being an Asiatic despotism after the emancipation of the serfs, that it had become fully Westernized, his historical and institutional conception of Russia would not have provided the focal point for his debates with Lenin. He did assume that Russia's Westernization had advanced considerably after 1861 and that it had become an irreversible process. But he never described the Russian state as exclusively or predominantly bourgeois-democratic (i.e., as the tool of the capitalists), and he never referred to it as "feudal." On the contrary, he variously characterized Russian absolutism as "despotic," "Asiatic," "Eastern," or "bureaucratic."[13] As a Marxist, Plekhanov believed a decisive change in the political "superstructure" of a society occurs only after a prolonged period of transformation in the socioeconomic "foundation." Thus he distinguished between Russian *society*, which was transformed (Westernized) by bourgeois capitalist elements, and the Russian *state*, which retained the centralized-bureaucratic structure of the old Asiatic-despotic order. Once begun, the evolutionary process had to await its ratification by a revolutionary transfer of power in a general antiautocratic, anti-Asiatic revolution. The end result would be a "socialist" order, regardless of whether the development of capitalism led to a bourgeois regime or merely served to undermine the existing political order by the establishment of new forces and classes. There is thus no ambiguity in Plekhanov's characterization of Russian state and society. He realistically stressed both their European and Asiatic features and attempted to distinguish their respective natures and rules.[14]

While Plekhanov saw Russia's bourgeoisification as imminent, he did not foresee a socialist seizure of power in the near future. More specifically, he was less interested in the seizure of state power than in a full-fledged socialist revolution. In a truly remarkable insight, which occurred neither to Marx nor Engels, he discovered a retrogressive possibility and a restorationist potential in the socialist revolution. Warning against a premature seizure of power, which would put authority in the hands of a revolutionary committee lacking popular support and control, he insisted on the necessity of such support and control, which could be counted on only "in the event that the people are sufficiently alienated from the autocratic tsar." Plekhanov warned: "If at the time of the outbreak of the revolution the said alienation is not sufficiently great, there can be no popular government, and the revolution which has been carried out can lead to a political deformity like the ancient Chinese or Peruvian empires, i.e., a restoration of tsarist despotism on a communist foundation."[15]

From the 1880s Plekhanov was primarily interested in social and institutional history as a guide to action. Thus his analysis fell short of providing an adequate account of the nature and origin of Russia's Asiatic despotism. Perhaps for this reason, he made no effort to evaluate Marx's writings on India, which describe the nature of Asiatic society and particularly the role of the village commune; nor did he refer to Marx's historical survey of Russia's Asiatic despotism in the *Secret Diplomatic History*. Until 1890, when direct confrontations with the tsarist state began to stimulate their interest, other Russian Marxists appear not to have been influenced enough by Plekhanov's analysis to elaborate their own ideas about the nature of Russian society and institutions. But then, together with the increasing interest of European socialists in Russia's peculiar conditions, many Russian Marxists began to follow Plekhanov's lead.

In the new literary and political review, *Sotsial-Demokrat*, V. N. Alekseev wrote an editorial stating: "The foremost of all contemporary Russian social questions is the question of the struggle against our Asiatic despotism, which not only crushes all life inside the country but also menaces the cause of progress in all of Europe." Writing in the most prestigious theoretical journal of the strongest Marxist party in Europe, *Die Neue Zeit*, Paul Axelrod described the revolutionary Russian intelligentsia as "a kind of European oasis in the immeasurable desert of the Russian *Aziatchina*," a desert "which becomes smaller every day with the expansion of the popular masses in the grip of Europeanization."[16] Like Marx and Plekhanov, he saw the basis for the Russian revolution in the emerging tensions between an Oriental state and a Westernizing society. He was the first (to my knowledge) to coin the term *Aziatchina*. But his understanding of the Russian revolution was shared by broad circles. Vera Zasulich was one who took up the theme when she decried the small size of the Westernized intelligentsia opposed to the Russian state--those "colonies of intellectual aliens, deserted in Asiatic tsarism."[17]

If the views of these and others, like Petr Lavrov, had come to resemble several of the major conclusions Plekhanov had reached by the early 1890s, there was still the question of whether the commune should be retained and capitalism could be avoided. On this, there was considerable disagreement. But Plekhanov continued to maintain that Russia was "an altogether 'original' country, a kind of China in Europe," and that the main support of Russia's Asiatic despotism had been and still was the commune system. He saw the breakdown of the Asiatic state resulting from the loosening and decline of the commune, which in turn was presumably causing the development of new economic conditions in the cities, giving rise to capitalism. Specifically, he argued that the "transfer of West-European political institutions" could be accomplished only after the Russian intelligentsia abandoned such "Asiatic ideas" as the maintenance of the commune: "The Russian intelligentsia wanted to establish a new political edifice on the old economic foundations--to maintain the peculiar economic quality of Russia and at the same time to be forever rid of Tsarism, i.e., the peculiar quality of Russia, . . . to achieve an Asiatic Europe. But that is nonsense, an impossibility."[18] It is clear that Plekhanov did not at this time anticipate a thoroughgoing bourgeois revolution for Russia, which could only be achieved by a radicalized peasantry led by a Marxist intelligentsia: "If this intelligentsia were finally to become imbued with the idea of scientific socialism, . . . it would understand that there is now internal work going on among the people . . . which will transform it from a loyal subject '*muzhik*' altogether similar to that of all Asiatic countries into a *class-conscious toiler* related by his spirit and in his demands to the revolutionary proletariat of the West."[19]

    The evolution of the Russian Marxist outlook on Russian state, society, and revolution in the period from 1890 to 1895 can be characterized by two important traits--the intensification and spread of the recognition of Russia's peculiar Asiatic features, and an increasing optimism regarding the rate and efficacy of the growth of capitalism in Russia. If it can be said to have originated in Alekseev's call for the Russian socialist movement to take up the issue of Russia's *Aziatchina*, it culminated in Plekhanov's integration of the concept of the Asiatic type of society into both his and the movement's understanding of the historical process. If the continued evolution of Plekhanov's thought was in large part the consequence of his own interest in elaborating a comprehensive theory of social and historical development in general and of Russia's transformation in particular, the concrete explanation for the growing acceptance of the Asiatic interpretation of Russian institutions and the belief in the imminence of capitalism in Russia must be sought in Plekhanov's prevailing intellectual influence among the Russian Marxists. But there is no doubt that Engels's renewed interest in

the Russian situation, the famine of 1891-92, and the reforms that Sergei
Witte initiated in 1892 also provided impetus.

Engels's continued interest in the Russian situation was kept alive in the
early 1890s by his concern for the role of Russian foreign policy in
European diplomatic and political issues, and by his close contact with
Plekhanov and other émigré Russian socialists. He learned much from
Plekhanov and generally identified with his work. But Engels also sought
to contribute directly to the direction and content of Russian socialist
thought by attempting to influence Plekhanov. Most important, he made
Plekhanov aware that he wanted him to be the one to "work seriously on
agrarian problems in Russia." He expected from Plekhanov no less than a
systematic analysis of Russia's agrarian, industrial, and social development,
which would integrate the best insights of Marxism with the real conditions
of Russia and thus serve as the ideological basis for the Russian-Marxist
movement to advance toward a socialist revolution.[20] That is precisely
what Plekhanov accomplished in *The Development of the Monist View of
History*, begun late in 1894 and published in 1895, which in the next
decade was the outstanding statement of the fundamental beliefs of the
Russian-Marxist movement. It not only profoundly influenced those who
were to make up the core of that part of organized Russian social
democracy which became politically predominant, and of that faction which
eventually prevailed in the revolution, but it also influenced those who
otherwise retained serious reservations and disagreements with Marxist
theoretical formulations and the organizational course of the party.

As it turned out, the Russian Marxists drew entirely correct conclusions
about the meaning of the famine. Not only did it remind them that Russia
was still a very backward country, particularly with respect to the state
apparatus and the agrarian order, but they saw the weakness of the
government in its inability to deal with the crisis. They also saw the
urgency for the government to proceed with its modernization--its capitalist
economic development. Their revolutionary hopes thus strengthened, the
course of events seemed to bear out what Plekhanov had been saying for
some time. Moreover, the course adopted by the government served to
confirm the Marxist-Plekhanovite analysis.

When he was appointed finance minister in August 1882 and put in charge of dealing with Russia's poverty, Witte had already come to the same conclusion as the Marxists: that rapid industrialization via capitalist development was Russia's only hope. He differed from them in that he was primarily determined to eliminate hunger rather than to manipulate it for political ends, and he saw capitalist development as deterring rather than fostering a social revolution. However, this mattered little to the Russian Marxists, who were only too ready to see in the actions of the authorities a confirmation of their theories.

Plekhanov had stimulated the intensive study of Russia's real social, political, economic, and institutional conditions as essential to the determination of revolutionary ideology, organization, and tactics. If for now the contemporary growth of a capitalist economy loomed larger for the Russian Marxists than the state economy of the old Asiatic order, they would be persuaded in a few years that neither that old order nor Marx's concept of the Asiatic mode of production could be so easily overcome.

When Lenin appeared on Russia's political and revolutionary scene, a dramatically accelerated pace of Westernization in the sense of industrialization made it practical to approach the issues of revolution and socialism from a more sophisticated doctrinal, organizational, and tactical perspective than the one that had characterized the earlier anarchic phase. His "conversion" to Marxism has engendered much controversy; like that of Plekhanov and other Russian revolutionary leaders, it is best understood as a shift from one understanding of socialism to another. Since Marx and Engels were almost everyone's source when it came to understanding the meaning of socialism, whatever a particular Russian adherent's original commitment may have been, it might well be appropriate to speak of "conversions" from one kind of Marxism to another.

The development of Lenin's ideas on state, society, and revolution in Russia until 1906, both on its own terms and in relation to that of the revolutionary socialist movement, can be divided into four distinct periods or stages. From 1888 to 1894, he studied and mastered Marxism and applied it to Russian conditions. From 1895 to 1897, he followed other members of the movement in becoming increasingly optimistic about the extent of capitalist development in Russia and the prospects for revolution.

Like his comrades, he believed the revolution awaited only the formation of a social-democratic party, which would imbue the proletariat and its revolutionary allies with the understanding that Russia's prebourgeois government, fortified by surviving "Asiatic" political features, would first have to be destroyed before a socialist revolution could be attempted. From 1898 to 1901, he took a keener interest in the Asiatically despotic features of the state and the economy, owing to the failure of the antiautocratic revolution to unify the movement. From 1902 to 1906, he promulgated new concepts of organization and tactics designed to deal more effectively with Russia's old order. Combined with the experiences and observations of the 1905 revolution, these concepts led in 1906 to Lenin's formulation of the model for revolution that the Bolsheviks would adhere to in their struggle for power.

In the first period, 1888-94, Lenin generally viewed Russia and its social revolution in strictly European terms. However, there are indications that he was already becoming aware of what Plekhanov and others had concluded about the peculiar nature of Russian state and society. On several occasions he observed that Russian absolutism was more rigid than that of the West, was based on a much more powerful and pervasive bureaucracy and police system, and that Russian institutions were "semifeudal." At one point he directly approached his later position when he wrote with respect to the "small rural world exploiters" who were controlling the emerging markets for the growing surplus produced by capitalist agriculture: "In view of the barbarism of the countryside, caused by the low productivity characteristic of the system, . . . and *by the absence of communications*, [their exploitation] constitutes not only robbery of labor but also the *Asiatic abuse* of human dignity that is constantly encountered in the countryside."[21]

In the second period of Lenin's theoretical development, 1895-97, he identified the tsarist bureaucracy as the main instrument of absolute rule, as "omnipotent, irresponsible, corrupt, savage, ignorant and parasitic." For Lenin, bureaucracy represented "a special category of persons specializing in the work of administration and occupying a privileged position as compared with the people." In this connection, he offered a comparative example: "We see this institution everywhere, from autocratic and semi-

Asiatic Russia to cultured, free and civilized England, as an essential organ of bourgeois society. The *complete* lack of rights of the people in relation to government officials and *complete* absence of control over the privileged bureaucracy correspond to the backwardness of Russia and to its absolutism, [whereas in England] powerful popular control is exercised over the administration, [and even this] *is far from being complete.*"[22]

The line was clearly drawn. The duty of the Russian workers was to organize a revolutionary party and to prepare themselves for a political struggle against semi-Asiatic Russia and its pervasive, uncontrolled bureaucracy, to carry out a social revolution against the exploiting bourgeoisie. In the political struggle, the proletariat was to find allies among all classes opposed to the state and interested in developing a capitalist mode of production. In the social revolution, the proletariat and its social-democratic vanguard was to stand alone. But most significant in this context, Lenin both implicitly and explicitly rejected the idea that the Russian Social-Democrats should adopt what took place in the West "as an unfailing model."[23]

The third period, 1898-1901, signaled a significant transition in Lenin's perception of Russia's social and political conditions and the ensuing tactical and organizational consequences. His book, *The Development of Capitalism in Russia*, written between 1896 and 1899, represents the high point of his optimism regarding the widespread growth of capitalist relations in Russia and their effect on the political and social transformation of the country. But almost immediately after the book was published, Lenin began to depart from the position stated therein for reasons having to do both with his increased understanding of the nature of the Russian state and society and his perception of what was happening.

In "The Heritage We Renounce," written toward the end of 1897, Lenin restated his awareness of Russia's "stagnation and backwardness" and reaffirmed his belief that, although the development of capitalism in Russia was following a general and universal pattern, tsarist political institutions both supported and sabotaged this development. Progressive as these changes were, they involved the conversion of "Asiatic forms of labor, with their infinitely developed bondage and diverse expressions of personal dependence, into European forms of labor."[24] In *The Development of*

Capitalism in Russia, Lenin indicated the kind of precapitalist, economic
system that had prevailed in Russia before the coming of capitalism: *"a
network of small local markets which linked up tiny groups of small
producers, severed from each other by their separate farms, by the
innumerable medieval barriers between them, and by the remains of
medieval dependence."*[25]

Lenin particularly emphasized the "Asiatic" remnants in Russia's
agricultural institutions and the new form of rural capitalism which served
to perpetuate them. In early 1900 he defended his book against certain
criticisms, arguing that capitalist development in the countryside would
have been much more rapid had there been a greater distribution of land
among the peasants, that the problem lay in the fact that "poverty of land
and the burden of taxation have led to the development over a very
considerable area of Russia of the labor-service system of private farming,
i.e., a direct survival of serfdom and not at all to the development of
capitalism."[26] Here, as in many other places, Lenin emphasized that "the
Asiatic government" was seeking support from "large Asiatic landowners"
of its own creation.

Already at the end of 1899 Lenin had stressed the need to base the
revolutionary program of Russian social democracy on "the *specific features*
of Russia" in general, and the *"peasant"* question in particular.[27] In
February 1900 he concluded that the specific features of Russia's rural
economic conditions gave an "Asiatic" quality to the whole country's social
system and that the struggle against the state was dependent on the peasant
revolution. In practical terms, this meant that "the peasantry as a class"
would serve as "fighters against the autocracy and the survivals of
feudalism." Lenin assured his followers that the peasantry would not
become "the *vehicle* of the revolutionary movement," that "the
revolutionary mood of the peasantry" would not "*condition* the
revolutionary character of [the] movement."[28] Nevertheless, Lenin's view
was clearly that the Russian socialist revolution had become dependent on
the correct analysis of Russia as an "Asiatic" despotism.

The increasing shift to the theory of a peasant-based anti autocratic
revolution did not signal any change in Lenin's concept of the two
revolutions: "The Russian proletariat will throw off the yoke of autocracy

in order to continue the struggle against capital and the bourgeoisie for the complete victory of socialism." Because conditions in Russia were "quite different from those of Western Europe," the political revolution had to precede the economic and social revolution.[29] In late 1899 Lenin described Russia as "an absolute and unlimited monarchy" in which "the tsar alone promulgates laws, appoints officials and controls them"; he likened the Russian system to that of Turkey, and held it to be different from those of "Germany and all other European countries" principally with respect to political representation.[30]

The following spring he utilized the characterization Marx and Plekhanov had applied to Asiatic despotism--"political slavery"--to describe all those "oppressed by the present political system of Russia"; and in December 1900, he specifically linked Russia with China: "The Chinese people suffer from the same evils as those from which the Russian people suffer--from an Asiatic government which squeezes taxes from the starving peasantry and suppresses by military force every aspiration to liberty."[31] In January 1901, he stressed "the Asiatic nature even of those of our institutions which most resemble European institutions";[32] in February, he spoke of the "imprint of Asiatic backwardness on the entire social system of our country";[33] and in July he even berated the editors of the journal, *Novoe vremia*, for struggling against the non-Russian factory owners instead of the "Asiatic government."[34] By the end of 1901 Lenin had concluded that it was necessary to work out a practical plan for a successful revolution against that "Asiatic" government.

The fourth period of Lenin's development, 1902-5, begins with his famous pamphlet written between the autumn of 1901 and February 1902, *What Is To Be Done?*, wherein he sketched a theory of organization of a political revolution against an absolutism of the "Asiatic" type. This organization of a socially heterogenous popular movement represented by a proletarian mass movement was to be led by a professional Marxist elite. Lenin did not propose to establish a small, professional revolutionary organization to take the place of a broad-based proletarian socialist party; he insisted on the need for two organizations, with his Marxist elite forming a core within the mass party. The organization of the Social Democratic Party had to be approached from the premise that it would be the function

of that party to "bring about the political revolution," which specifically
required an "organization of a *kind different* from the organization of the
workers designed for this struggle." The first was to be an organization "of
revolutionaries"; the second, a "trade union organization."[35]

Such a centralized organization of professional revolutionaries to lead
the Social Democratic Party was necessary because of the dual aspect of the
struggle and because of the impossibility of politicizing economic
agitation--of turning economic agitation into a political challenge to the
system. There were also other reasons, but the most important was the
necessity to effectively lead the proletarian and nonproletarian opposition in
a struggle against an Asiatic despotism:

> The Russian proletariat will have to fight a monster beside
> which an anti-socialist law in a constitutional country [i.e.,
> Germany] is but a dwarf. History has now confronted us with an
> immediate task which is the *most revolutionary* of all the
> *immediate* tasks confronting the proletariat of any country. The
> fulfillment of this task, the destruction of the most powerful
> bulwark of not only European but (it may now be said) Asiatic
> reaction, would make the Russian proletariat the vanguard of the
> international proletariat.[36]

The purpose of Lenin's organization was thus to lead a successful political
revolution against all manifestations of the Asiatic despotism of tsarist
Russia.

Until the middle of 1903, Lenin elaborated on his insights into the
peasant base of the Russian revolution, stressing the Asiatic character of
both the social and political institutions of Russia which blocked
fundamental change. But from June 1903 to December 1905 he attempted
to get his analysis of the Russian social situation and his organizational
program for revolution accepted by the movement and the party. In June
1905, he was still of two minds on the issue of whether a bourgeois
revolution could overcome Russia's Asiatic social and political structure.
But he had no doubt that the success of such a revolution would "for the

first time really clear the ground for a wide and rapid, European not Asiatic, development of capitalism."[37]

Given both Lenin's and Plekhanov's understanding of the Asiatic character of Russian state, society, and revolution, the Fourth ("Unification") Congress of the All-Russian Social Democratic Labor Party held in Stockholm from April 23 to May 8, 1906, gains a more historical perspective and sheds new light not only on the organization of the Bolshevik Party but on the essential nature of the Russian Revolution and its aftermath. Even as Plekhanov and Lenin were agreed on the Asiatic question, they disagreed about what was to be done. Plekhanov stressed the ultimate social and historical consequences of not appreciating the *specific kind* of revolution required to completely destroy the old order. But only Lenin understood the *organizational necessity* for the seizure of power in an Asiatic society. Such a seizure of power in Asiatic Russia was probably only possible for a party organized along Leninist lines. But a party so organized was incapable of destroying the socioeconomic foundation of the old order precisely because its organizational structure was not only kin to that order but contained within it the seeds of its restoration. In a sense, Plekhanov was a prisoner of his revolutionary theory, and Lenin was a prisoner of his revolutionary practice. Ultimately, Russia became a prisoner of both.

By 1906 it was apparent to both Plekhanov and Lenin, as it was to most of the Mensheviks and Bolsheviks, that the 1905 revolution had failed. Plekhanov and the Mensheviks attributed this failure to the fact that the majority of the troops and the masses had remained loyal to the autocracy; Lenin and the Bolsheviks attributed it to a lack of organization. Plekhanov had welcomed his country's defeat in the Russo-Japanese War of 1904-5 because it shook the foundations of the Russian autocracy. He was preoccupied with relations between the proletariat and the bourgeoisie during the 1905 revolution because he considered it a "bourgeois" revolution. He presumed that the proletariat, aligned with the bourgeoisie, would strike the final blow against the autocracy. But now his conception of revolution in Russia caught up with his understanding of the peculiar Asiatic character of his country. Like Lenin, he discovered the revolutionary potential of the peasantry; like Lenin, he came to understand the predominantly agrarian nature of the Russian revolution. But he understood it differently.

Concerning the agrarian situation in Russia, Plekhanov said: "If we must choose between nationalization and division, then we must choose division."[38] The overriding advantage of nationalization would in practice amount to an attempt to restore the old order. The overriding advantage of division was that "it would strike a definitive blow to our old order, under which both land and the tiller are the property of the state, and which represents nothing other than a Muscovite version of the economic order which lies at the base of all great Oriental despotisms."[39] More specifically:

> The question arises as to *exactly why* the revolutionaries *were able* to influence the peasants in a given instance. . . . I replied: the psychology of the peasants, which historically was formed on the basis of the *"nationalization"* of land which I have described. But this psychology existed long before the peasantry began to fall under revolutionary influence. It was created not by the revolutionaries but by the "history of the Russian state."[40]

He left no doubt as to his meaning: "We have no need of a Chinese system. Therefore, we support the peasant movement *only* to the extent that it destroys the old order and not to the extent that it seeks to reestablish something in comparison with which this old order would appear as a new and progressive phenomenon."[41]

On his part, Lenin, early in 1905, emphasized Russia's "virginal" Asiatic despotism, and at the end of that year still found capitalist conditions "covered by the contradiction between 'culture' and the *Aziatchina*, between Europeanism and the *Tatarshchina*, between capitalism and bondage."[42] Shortly before the Stockholm Congress he saw the autocracy "completely restored."[43] Nevertheless, at the Congress Lenin argued against Plekhanov and for nationalization. It is true that he viewed nationalization, as he viewed the alignment of the proletariat with the peasantry, as a temporary necessity. According to him, it was based on

definite political circumstances. But Plekhanov's objection to
nationalization was based on the "objective conditions" of the old order.
To make his point, Lenin specifically criticized Plekhanov's linking
Russia with the "Chinese system." Plekhanov responded:

> The agrarian history of Russia has greater resemblance to the history
> of India, Egypt, China and other Oriental despotisms than to the
> history of Western Europe. There is nothing surprising in this,
> because the economic development of every people is carried out in
> its own particular setting. With us the development was such that
> land, together with the tiller, was enserfed by the state, and, on the
> basis of this enserfment, despotism grew. Therefore, I am against
> nationalization now. . . .[44]

Plekhanov demanded a guarantee against a "restoration" of the old
order. In Lenin's concluding statement on the agrarian question at the
Stockholm Congress he not only questioned Plekhanov's demand, he
emphasized the crucial significance of a socialist revolution in the West to
the success of the Russian revolution:

> Comrade Plekhanov asks: Where is there a guarantee against
> restoration? I do not think that posing this question is closely and
> indissolubly connected with the program we are examining. But
> since this question has been asked, it must be answered very
> precisely and with no ambiguity. If one is to speak of a real and
> actual economic guarantee against restoration--a guarantee that
> would create the economic conditions which would exclude
> restoration--then it must be said that the sole guarantee against
> restoration is a socialist revolution in the West; there can be no
> other possible guarantee in the real and full meaning of the
> word. . . . Without this condition, restoration is inevitable even
> with municipalization [Plekhanov's plan], even with nationalization,
> even with division, since the petty proprietor under all forms of
> possession and property will be the bulwark of a restoration. . . .

Our democratic republic has no kind of reserve other than the
socialist proletariat in the West.[45]

Lenin was begging the question. But Plekhanov had the last word. In
his concluding statement at the Stockholm Congress he answered not only
Lenin's arguments but those of the others as well. He indicated that his
differences with Lenin were serious and that he was not interested in unity
at any price. The party's decision concerning these differences would
decide the fate not only of the party but of the country. For Plekhanov, the
issue was "Blanquism" or "Marxism," since "*Lenin himself has
acknowledged that his agrarian scheme is closely linked with his idea of the
seizure of power.*"[46]

Given their previous predisposition, Lenin and the Bolsheviks quite
naturally viewed their defeat at the Stockholm Congress as a temporary
setback. Lenin's formulation of "democratic centralism" had in fact little
or no practical meaning for the wider social democratic party and the
central committee elected at the congress. The latter, which was dominated
by the Mensheviks, came out strongly against "the existence within the
party . . . of efforts to create some special, centralized organization
designed to prepare and lead an armed uprising."[47] But a secret Bolshevik
"Center" was in fact set up during the Stockholm Congress and was to
provide the model of the revolutionary party that Lenin would lead to
victory in 1917.

Late in 1907 Lenin wrote that it was "absolutely necessary" to revise the
agrarian program of the Russian Social Democratic Party along the lines he
had suggested at the Stockholm Congress. He admitted that the Stolypin
reforms were progressive from an economic standpoint, but said they
should not be supported because that would be tantamount to aiding the
bourgeoisie in its struggle against the old order. He castigated Plekhanov
and the Mensheviks for doing so, characterizing their position as "vulgar
Marxism." But most striking in this case was Lenin's deliberate attempt to
obscure the Asiatic character of Russian conditions by introducing the terms
"feudal" and "feudalism" into his discussion, even using them
interchangeably. Another tactic Lenin employed was to polarize the
alternatives in his own favor: "The choice is between the Stolypin agrarian

reform and the peasant revolutionary nationalization."[48] By so doing, he attempted to make it look as though his plan for nationalization was the real bulwark against the bondage conditions of Russian agriculture and that Plekhanov's plan (municipalization) would lead to their preservation.

Having turned the tables on Plekhanov by obscuring the central issues of the agrarian revolution, Lenin was ready to tackle the problem of a "guarantee against restoration." "What is restoration?" he asked: "It is the reversion of state power to the political representatives of the old order. Can there be any guarantee against such a restoration? No. . . ."[49] He pushed his argument to its limits:

Since we have no guarantees against restoration, to raise that question in connection with the agrarian program means *diverting* the attention of the audience, *clogging* their minds, and introducing confusion into the discussion. We are not in a position to call forth at our own will the social revolution in the West, which is the only absolute guarantee against restoration in Russia. But a relative and conditional "guarantee," i.e., one that would raise the greatest possible *obstacles* to restoration, lies in carrying out the revolution in Russia in the most far-reaching, consistent, and determined manner possible. The more far-reaching the revolution, the more difficult it will be to restore the old order and the more gains will remain even if restoration does take place.[50]

Then, having stolen Plekhanov's fire by presenting his own plan against a restoration, Lenin proceeded to put down the whole idea: "If there had been any real grounds for Plekhanov's fears of a return to Asiatic despotism, the system of landownership among the state peasants (up to the '80s) and among the former state peasants after the '80s should have turned out to be the purest type of 'state feudalism.' Actually, it proved to be freer than the landlord system because feudal [*sic*] exploitation had already become impossible in the latter half of the nineteenth century." Thus, said Lenin, it was "high time to put away forever the vague fear of 'Asiatic' restoration raised by the peasant movement." He even went so far as to claim that the "bogey of restoration" was a "political weapon of the bourgeoisie against the proletariat."[51]

In concluding his analysis of the agrarian program of social democracy, Lenin revealed all the inner contradictions of his position. He spoke at one and the same time of the Russian autocracy as being "permeated with the Asiatic interference of a hide-bound bureaucracy" and of the "economic necessity" of transferring all lands to the state.[52]   In criticizing Plekhanov, he stressed that Marx and Engels's theory was not a dogma but a *guide to action.*[53]   But in forging the party as he did, he made it organizationally possible for Marxism to become the secular religion of the Soviet state and the Communist revolution. Centralization had become for Lenin the key not only to the organization of his revolutionary party but to the success of the agrarian revolution. Nevertheless, said Lenin, "the peasantry cannot carry out an agrarian revolution without abolishing the old regime, the standing army and the bureaucracy."[54] He would later consider the last two conditions as "relative" guarantees against an "Asiatic restoration."[55]

Lenin's organizational dictum and tactics were certainly schooled by Plekhanov's "objective conditions." But in order to defend his conception of revolution he had to attack both Plekhanov's and his own understanding of the "Asiatic" character of Russia. The result was both revolution and restoration. The new *Aziatchina* was soon to become both quantitatively and qualitatively more total and despotic than the old order. Even as it defied Marx and Lenin and made Marxism the religion of the revolution and the Soviet state, it destroyed Marx's concept of the Asiatic mode of production and Plekhanov's and Lenin's concept of an "Asiatic restoration" in Russia.

CHAPTER 9

MIKHAIL GERSHENZON'S "SECRET VOICE":
THE MAKING OF A CULTURAL NIHILIST

David Davies

> For what is at stake is nothing other than the
> celebrated "reunion of intellect and soul"!
> -- Thomas Mann, 1920

Few educated Russians at the time of the revolutions of 1917 questioned
so fundamentally the idea of civilization in both its religious and secular-
humanist manifestations as did Mikhail Osipovich Gershenzon in his
fascinating "correspondence" with the symbolist poet Viacheslav Ivanov.
Yet Gershenzon himself had been a prominent exponent of Russian
civilization throughout the early years of the twentieth century, during
which Russian high culture flourished so notably. The nihilist views he
expressed in 1919 seem to contrast strikingly with his previous persona as a
learned and cultivated man committed to cultural heritage and civilized
values in Russia--producing, if not a paradox, at least an irony worthy of
investigation. This essay will explore what might be called the underside of
Gershenzon's mentality --revealed in letters he wrote early in his
career--which gave him a sharp awareness of a wider and wilder reality,
denied, or at least obscured, by his more civilized consciousness.

By no stretch of the imagination can Gershenzon be regarded as a major
historical figure of the late tsarist and early Soviet periods in which he
lived. But he was well known to educated Russians of his time and has
continued to be familiar to students of Russian culture outside the Soviet
Union since his death in 1926. Among his contemporaries Gershenzon's
reputation rested primarily on his scholarly work as a literary critic and
historian of previously neglected cultural topics from the era of Nicholas I,
a time when many of the enduring features of independent Russian social
thought appeared. Gershenzon chronicled not only the emergence of new
ideas, but even more so new values, concerns, and personalities, which he
presented in a series of finely etched biographies. His technique made use

of extensive primary sources--especially letters--many of which he himself had discovered. To these he applied a lively imagination and a knack for discerning what Renato Poggioli has termed the "originality of soul" in each of his subjects.[1]

Today he is better known for his polemical commentary on the salient cultural traits of Russian educated society in his own lifetime, a period which coincided with the fall of the tsarist regime and the October Revolution. His views were expressed most memorably during participation in two noteworthy debates which took place a decade apart, in 1909 and 1919, each of which became a classic in its own right. The first was the well-known *Vekhi* dispute, a volume of essays that critically reappraised the heritage of the Russian intelligentsia and challenged its prevailing social and political concerns. Gershenzon was the organizer and editor of this project and contributed one of its more controversial essays.[2] The second was the "correspondence" he carried on with Viacheslav Ivanov during the Russian Civil War, when both men were recovering from illnesses and occupied beds in opposite corners of the same room. This famous "corner-to-corner correspondence," as it came to be known, consisted of twelve letters in which Gershenzon debated one of the most learned persons of his generation.[3]

If the *Vekhi* exchange was about cultural values, the exchange with Ivanov dealt with something even more fundamental: the value of the whole heritage of Western civilization Russia had been painstakingly acquiring over the centuries and which was most conspicuously embodied in cultivated individuals such as Ivanov and Gershenzon. In their discussion, Ivanov ably defended the achievements of this heritage both in its religious aspects (Christianity) and its secular features (Classicism and the humanist tradition stemming from the Renaissance). In doing so, he was fully consistent with his own past, in which these values figured prominently. Gershenzon, on the other hand, chose to attack much of the world he had inhabited as well as the civilized values that had guided his life. In his final statement in this exchange, he fully acknowledged the dichotomy of his position and offered a glimpse of its source. His revelation is worth quoting in full:

I lead a strangely double life. From childhood accustomed to
European culture, I deeply absorbed its spirit and not only am I
completely familiar with it, but I also sincerely love much of it. I
love its cleanliness and comfort; I love science, art, poetry,
Pushkin. I mingle easily in the cultural family, converse in an
animated way with friends and acquaintances on cultural themes.
And I am genuinely interested in these themes and in the methods
of developing them. In all this I am with you. We share a common
cult of spiritual service to cultural achievement, common habits and
a common language. Such is my daytime life. But in the depths of
consciousness I live otherwise. For many years, insistently and
inexorably, a secret voice has been saying to me: "This is not it,
this is not it!" Some kind of another will in me with yearning turns
away from culture, from everything that is being done and being
said around me. . . .[4]

* * * *

Gershenzon's assertion in 1919 that for many years he had been hearing
a "secret voice" in the depths of his consciousness is confirmed by a series
of remarkable letters he wrote to his brother from Dresden eighteen years
earlier at the age of thirty-one. These letters convey a sense of urgency
and intensity that remind one of the memorable reunion of Ivan and
Alyosha in Dostoevsky's *Brothers Karamazov*.[5] In them he described in
some detail the extraordinary experience that first led him to take seriously
this inner voice and to clarify--at least to his own satisfaction--what it
meant. He confessed to his brother in the first letter that he had always felt
a restless anxiety in his life, that he was "internally not tranquil, just as a
telegraph apparatus unceasingly taps out an unhurried piece of news.
Confusion and disturbance in the soul and something not captured. That's
the main thing: Something not captured for fullness, but what--you do not
know"(p.88).

He began the second letter with the statement that he continually heard
inside himself "a voice, which determinedly and insistently repeated over
and over again to me 'this is not it!'" Gershenzon said that he had always

previously ignored this voice, regarding its prompting as "unsubstantiated," and as simply a sign of "bilious irritability": "If someone had said to me then that this sad voice, always negative, and . . . scraps of thoughts concerning the aim of life . . . which often passed through my mind but without any results--were one and the same, this would have seemed to me to be fantastic. I had, as did others, such a relation to these questions that they did not belong to the category of reality"(p.90).

Gershenzon also recalled a visit to the country during which his host's sister startled him by mentioning that she had overheard him groaning while asleep. It occurred to him then that these mournful sounds had come from another part of him--a realm that could not find expression during his waking hours--and that this "he" was profoundly unhappy and suffering. But, Gershenzon wrote, these fleeting thoughts soon passed and he forgot about them (p.87).

In Dresden an incident occurred--outwardly prosaic but inwardly pro-found--that dramatically altered his view on this matter. He had given up smoking two months earlier, apparently with considerable withdrawal pangs. After dinner on his first evening in the city, he left his hotel for a stroll and was overcome by a particularly strong desire to smoke. He entered a nearby cafe and occupied a table in the corner where he ordered coffee and "a couple of Russian cigarettes." What happened next was a psychological experience the account of which is worth quoting in full (pp. 86-87):

From the first inhalation such a powerful wave of feelings gushed into me that it is impossible to communicate them. There was bliss without bounds and the conviction that now I will begin a new, another life; but most of all, with terrifying force, I was enveloped with an immeasurable sorrow about that which I am and all the years that have flowed by. Lord, how this burned and seized my soul. How these marvelous, blue, comfortable rings of smoke before me so wrapped everything within me. And here, amidst the inhalations surrounding me, suddenly a certain thought was presented to me with full clarity. And when drinking coffee and smoking the second cigarette I rose in order to leave--I felt myself reborn.

The "thought" to which Gershenzon referred was a kind of self-discovery, a belief that another dimension of his being--hitherto repressed--had found expression and that he was now in touch with his own "true essence," with what he called "elemental cosmic feeling" (*stikhiinoe kosmicheskoe chuvstvo*, p. 94). He says that as a result of the transformation experienced in the Dresden café, he began to hear inside himself "an amazing and irresistible song." And euphorically he concluded: "Now finally it has broken through that my whole life was suppressed and obstructed, and I heard clearly the voice of my true self" (*istinnoe "ia"*).[6]

He regarded this as a voice of the elemental and spontaneous side of his nature as opposed to the externally acquired side that had previously filled his consciousness. It seemed to him that his own personal crisis was symptomatic of a malady afflicting educated Russians in general, that civilized habits of mind tended to produce a split "between our external 'I' and our true essence, *he* in imprisonment." And Gershenzon lamented the prevailing recent heritage of Russian intellectual life in which "people were occupied with externals--the life of nature and society--forgetting about their own personality" (p. 88). These statements foreshadowed the main argument he would advance in the *Vekhi* debate eight years later.

Gershenzon's Dresden letters also argue that the kind of rational consciousness acquired in civilization not only is often divorced from one's more personal, spontaneous self, but that such consciousness has a diminished awareness of the wilder elemental dimensions of reality outside the self. In providing a zone of comfort, rationality, and security, civilization offers a haven for human existence, but at the expense of a more impoverished sense of what actually constitutes the wider world (pp. 94-95):

Just as a person who, wishing to preserve warmth, tightly seals the doors and windows of his dwelling and putties all the chinks, so we hermetically are locked on earth. This seems at first unusually comfortable. Not disturbed by boundlessness and the terrible mystery of life, a person quickly and skillfully adapts his dwelling to his needs. But oxygen becomes less and less [available] and as a result everything falls from his hands, he is heavy, he is suffocating. Look at the lives of the people in our circle. They don't even have to putty the chinks [since] this was all accomplished by grandfathers and fathers through institutions, customs and mockery. Just as indecently speaking aloud about the bodily functions of a person [is unacceptable] so it is laughable to speak about the cosmic mystery. The first is resolved only by doctors; the second, only by poets [based] on the rules of arbitrary convention. And even more than that: defending oneself logically from in front and aesthetically from behind, we try in every possible way to paint over these two transparent walls, so that eternity would cease to be seen through them.

Gershenzon suggested that the only way to avoid suffocation is to culti-vate the idea of "boundlessness," and to allow the sense of mystery in the universe (*mirovaia taina*) "to circulate in our consciousness, like fresh air in our lungs." He wrote of the need to "open to God my feelings . . . to open to Him my consciousness," and he implored his contemporaries "to dream, to think and to speak about eternity, about the unfathomable in yourself and outside yourself. . . ." He sensed that there is no firm basis for human values and spiritual life within the framework of positivistic science and felt the need to break out of its confines. "To us there is only one way--into infinity. I am an undivided atom of a single unfathomable psycho-physical world substance; I should live in clear consciousness of my universal elementalness (*stikhiinost'*), like a drop in the ocean" (p. 95).

In these letters, especially toward the end, religious themes begin to emerge more and more. Gershenzon not only made reference to God and eternity, but said that religion provides the kind of "uninterrupted per-ception or consciousness of the universe" that he sought.[7] Clearly he was much more sympathetic to the religious dimensions of civilization than he was to modern secular trends. In his view, each founder of a religion "opened up to people a new, more vivid and more forceful perception of infinity than they had known previously." And for the masses of ordinary followers, every religious ritual offered a doorway into infinity; each religious sacrament, a presentiment of the eternal mystery. Those who sincerely carried out the rituals of any religion, therefore, lived more naturally than persons who deliberately locked their consciousness inside the four walls of the earth (p. 96).

It should be emphasized, however, that neither Gershenzon's sympathetic view of religion nor his use of the word "reborn" to describe his experience of self-discovery should be regarded in fundamentalist Christian terms. Ethnically Jewish, he distanced himself from all creedal religions and regarded religious doctrines, as he did all doctrines, as ultimately limiting. At the conclusion of his Dresden letters, he asserted that he did not wish "to surround myself with the fence of some kind of dogma. I want to be freely conscious of the unfathomable (of that which is beyond human understanding); I want to contemplate it with a clear gaze in the light of day, and not blindly grope in the morning twilight of symbols and sacraments or to guess in arbitrary hypotheses about the significance of life" (p. 96). Gershenzon apparently regarded any definite answer to the riddle of life as suspect, and perhaps even undesirable, since a clear answer, expressible in words, consciously grasped, already would lack some of the attributes of "mystery" and "unfathomableness" that he wished to preserve at the center of his view of reality.

Nevertheless, Gershenzon's Dresden experience can be viewed in spiritual terms no less than in psychological ones. The repressed side of him that surfaced dramatically in 1901 had not been able to find a place within the intellectual and secular culture that made up his "daytime life" in Russia. He regretted very much that in his previous life there had been "no piety at all, not at all--I mean that instinctive piety toward things which imparts authority to everything momentary and elevates life. Everything was prosaic, humdrum" (p. 89). That the Dresden letters document the formative experience of Gershenzon's adult life is clearly indicated by the fact that virtually all the major ideas and themes found in his later writings were first elaborated here in embryo form. Given his later emphasis that one's beliefs should be governed not by thoughts acquired purely intellectually but by personal experiences in which feelings coexist with an intellectual effort to understand them, it is wholly appropriate that his own views were ultimately rooted in (and derived from) a personal experience of his own. This experience centered on an extended idea of reality, which civilized consciousness--based on positivistic science, rational habits of mind, and religious doctrines--could not grasp.

* * * *

Prior to this time, Gershenzon does not seem to have possessed a strong sense of personal identity. A bachelor when he went to Dresden, he had been living a somewhat uprooted existence without connections to a definite career or to a settled family life.[8] He was constantly nagged by a feeling of regret about his past and uncertainty--even terror--about the future. In his letters, he wrote about the aimlessness of his earlier existence and of the fact that it did not seem "real." Several years later he argued that the "rootless flexibility" of modern life weakened personality development because it included constant change in "habits, tastes, needs, ideas; few of us even remain living in the place where we spent childhood and almost no one [remains] in that social circle to which his parents belonged."[9] Yet, he regarded too strong an identification with one's roots or heritage as a negative influence as well, since the "tyranny of tradition"--no less than acceptance of currently fashionable ideas--represented an externally acquired sense of self. Both types of self-definition derived from sources other than contact with the deeper spontaneous core of an individual. In terms of the categories used by sociologist David Riesman in the 1950s, Gershenzon seems to reject both "inner-directedness" (identity stemming from family tradition) and "other-directedness" (identity stemming from fashions among one's peers) in favor of an identity rooted in the elemental self.

One may legitimately question whether attaining identity in this way is indeed possible. Many of Gershenzon's assertions about finding one's true self sound curiously similar to the pop-psychology ideas on self-realization prevalent in North America in the early 1970s. Some of his utterances display the same kind of narcissistic excess as the more extreme claims of the human potential movement. Nevertheless, what has been called the "problem of the self" has long been and still is a genuine issue hardly confined to recent America. It was evident in eighteenth-century Europe (for example, in Rousseau's *Confessions* and Goethe's *Sorrows of the Young Werther*) and became acute after the turmoil of the French

Revolution and the Napoleonic Wars, during which status and identity seemed less tied to class and to ascribed roles; it became even more widespread as the Romantic idea of one's "self" being distinct from one's "role" gained currency.[10]

Gershenzon's initial biographical studies were in fact focused on this period of Russian history precisely because he discerned in the "idealists of the 1830s" a generation faced with having "to work out for themselves a personal conscious world view, to decide . . . the question of how to live personally and socially."[11] His biographies in *The History of Young Russia* were intended primarily as psychological investigations in which he chronicled these voyages of self-discovery. Notable Russians from this generation were contrasted with Russians from the previous generation who, Gershenzon believed, had inherited their values and ideas about life ready-made.[12]

Because of his sympathetic biographical sketches of Ivan and Petr Kireevskii as well as Iurii Samarin, Gershenzon has sometimes been labeled a Slavophile (or "neo-Slavophile").[13] But this designation seems ultimately misleading since he did not share the ideas about Russian national identity and Orthodoxy common to Slavophile thinking. He did, however, share some of the original Slavophiles' sympathy for European Romanticism, especially a fascination with the more distant reaches of the mind and a predisposition to the idea of the unconscious. His interest in the Slavophiles was limited almost entirely to their ideas about the self and their concept of wholeness (*tsel'nost'*), which, in psychological terms, denoted an integration of feeling and intellect. For him this "teaching about the soul" was the "essential kernel" of Slavophilism, and he regarded the other dimensions of Slavophile thought as almost accidental accretions.[14] Gershenzon saw Russian Slavophilism as part of European Romanticism, portraying, for example, the Zhukovskii circle's influence on the Kireevskii family in the following terms:

In closely tied communion, in tender letters, in full everlasting sincerity [*zadushevnost'*] they, without affectation, obeying spontaneous inclinations, wholeheartedly cultivated sensitive feelings *(chuvstvitel'nost')*. . . . In this circle . . . was accumulated

enormous experience of feeling and of internal listening by means of which were caught the most subtle and most complex experiences of one's soul.[15]

It is clear that Gershenzon looked with longing and nostalgia to this period of Russian history. If he exaggerated and misread some of its features, it was no doubt because his own inclinations corresponded closely with earlier Romantic ideas about the "subtle and most complex experiences of one's soul," and about important realities just beyond the outer edge of human consciousness.

The distinctive elements of Gershenzon's thought suggest a close affinity with Romantic presuppositions.[16] Among them perhaps the most prominent is the idea that reality is much more multifarious and complicated than it seems. Beneath the visible surface of a person, or the clearly articulated workings of the mind, are additional unseen dimensions of psychological activity; and beyond, or behind, immediately sensible phenomena are "overtones" and potentials which can be glimpsed in rare moments of intuition, or communicated by a poet of genius. Gershenzon shared with the Romantics a strong belief in this extended notion of reality, as well as a sense of longing (*toska*, in Russian; *Sehnsucht*, in German) which reached out towards these regions of the indefinable and the incomprehensible (*nepostizhimost'*). He also shared the notion that each individual is unique and that even perception itself involves subjectivity leading to a specifically personal way of viewing the world.[17] In particular, Gershenzon was predisposed to draw on one of the most important legacies of nineteenth-century Romanticism to twentieth-century thought: the idea of the unconscious.

Gershenzon's understanding of the unconscious was not always clearly developed or internally consistent. Since he was not a professional psychologist, it is hardly surprising that his terminology lacked precision or that many of his more extreme claims were unwarranted empirically. His assertions--often the product of introspection and intuitive leaps--were nevertheless not without some basis. He had, after all, his own noteworthy psychological experience to draw on, and he certainly made a concerted effort to clarify it. Moreover, he was quite well informed about contemporary psychological research into unconscious realms of the mind.

Sigmund Freud is often popularly credited with the "discovery" of the unconscious, at least in the sense of a systematic elaboration of this concept (as opposed to impressionistic treatments in imaginative literature). While it is true that Freud's work in this area was deservedly "historic," this truth has masked the considerable contributions made by his contemporaries, as well as those of nineteenth-century predecessors in establishing the unconscious as a serious category of study. In his monumental book on the history of this idea, Henri F. Ellenberger assigns to the "speculations and findings of German romantic philosophy" a crucial formative role, culminating in Eduard von Hartmann's famous *Philosophy of the Unconscious* (1869). It was in this book that the term "will," as used by Schelling and Schopenhauer, "finally took the more appropriate name of unconscious."[18]

In 1882 the Society for Psychical Research was founded in Britain by Frederic Myers, and at the end of the century Pierre Janet's Institut Psychologique International was established in Paris. These institutions had considerable interaction. Within them--and at an increasing number of world congresses--psychologists such as Janet, Myers, and William James were able to discuss findings on various unconscious and partially conscious states.[19] They also exchanged observation on such related phenomena as dual (and multiple) personalities, hypnosis, and hysteria.

These points are worth making because, while Gershenzon does not appear to have been familiar with Freud, he was fairly well acquainted with the ideas about the unconscious that were emerging from these other centers. Moreover, these ideas are of more than mere historical interest since non-Freudian approaches to unconscious states, particularly those of Janet, have regained considerable stature in recent years within the discipline of psychology itself.[20]

This is not to say that Gershenzon's use of this work was always as judicious, balanced, and careful as it might have been. He believed that he had found in this contemporary research scientific confirmation of his own views on the Dresden experience. That he seemed to find the ideas of Myers particularly congenial is not surprising, since Myers had contributed some important interpretations on dual personalities, arguing that the second or hidden personality might be superior to the main one. According to Ellenberger, "Myers was . . . one of the great systemizers of the notion of the unconscious mind," whose view was that the "subliminal self" (the term is Myers's) "could be understood as the 'subliminal uprush' of rich storehouses of information, sentiment and reflections that lie beneath the consciousness of the creative thinker."[21]

Gershenzon favorably reviewed Myers's work in *Vestnik Evropy* and often cited him in support of his own arguments, as, for example, in the following passage:

> Beyond the . . . region of consciousness [Myers] considers the scientifically proven existence of another self, subconscious or subliminal. Each of us, he says, possesses a psychological life more stable and more vast than he guesses, a personality which the organism can never reveal in full. Thus customary consciousness comprises only part of our personality; all of our roots lie in a subconscious sphere; the activity of the latter usually remains hidden, but sometimes, under certain conditions, it is revealed spontaneously and the character of these revelations leads to the thought that part of our essence lies beyond the conscious self.[22]

In his work on the Slavophiles, Gershenzon referred positively to the writings of both Myers and William James. He also gave expression to his own view, which echoes quite vividly his previous personal experience:

> Inside of every person is his underlying self (*podlinnoe* "*ia*") which has been buried as if in a landslide and become muffled, for the most part unknown to him. It happens that a particular action or some kind of staggering unhappiness suddenly shatters the scab and the underlying personality suddenly is freed and the person knows what he really wants.[23]

A central argument in this book is that a person can achieve wholeness "only in the identification of his feeling with his consciousness."

Intellectual effort should be directed toward the more elemental self in order "to be conscious of it as the . . . fully authoritative organ of one's personality . . . to organize your 'I,' to convert the chaos of your feeling into a constructed unity."[24]

Gershenzon's contribution in the *Vekhi* collection is an essay in social psychology. In it he contends that most educated Russians in his time were not characterized by "wholeness"; on the contrary, they were split personalities: "Our consciousness, like a locomotive that has broken away from its train, has purposelessly sped far away, leaving our sensual-volitional life far behind."[25] As a result, "we all became cripples, with a deep schism between our real selves and our consciousness."[26] Such "disembodied thinking," Gershenzon wrote, was the product of ideas that had been acquired impersonally and externally, the result of the positivist values that had reigned in Russian intellectual life. A healthy spiritual life demanded that a person "assimilate a set of convictions . . . because of their precise, instinctively necessary correspondence to the innate features of his will." Such ideas, acquired "in this deeply individual process of selection" would not be a "sterile twinge" within the consciousness but an "inner motive force"; rather than "purely speculative and lifeless ideas," they could be called "idea-feelings or idea-passions."[27]

* * * *

In all of Gershenzon's later writings, he drew contrasts between ordinary consciousness--contained within the logical structures of civilized thinking--and an "elemental" reality not reducible to rational categories. "Life" continually confounded human attempts to capture it in formulas, abstractions, and doctrines.[28] If he had earlier portrayed the Russian intelligentsia--and all Russian educated society--as too removed from direct, unmediated experience with life, he now extended this criticism to so-called practical men of affairs: those who governed Russia. His characterization of Nicholas I is perhaps an extreme example, but one that he believed applied to other officials within the regime as well:

A doctrinaire by nature, he directly pressed life into his formulas. . . . He . . . wanted to know all and to manage all . . . to contain the unbounded and to bring life into symmetrical order.

The many-sidedness and chaotic nature of life . . . brought him to despair. All his strength was directed to find the means by . . . which it would be possible to bridle this turbulent disobedience of things and people for the sake of the full triumph of principles.[29]

Poggioli suggests convincingly that Goethe's dictum, "the tree of knowledge is gray; and the tree of life is green," nicely encapsulates Gershenzon's view.[30] This idea was extended to question not only "knowledge" but the very ability of words to convey full meaning:

Logical consciousness, translating deed into word, life into formula, does not fully capture the subject. . . . To draw a plan [does] not at all mean to build a house; therefore when it comes to real building, it is difficult for us to find a stone instead of a pencil. This, by the way, clarifies the well known fact that everyone experiences whereby a thought can often move us deeply until it is put into words. Then our attention on the living subject is transferred to its representation and it suddenly ceases to act on us, like a drawn flower that doesn't grow or smell.[31]

On closer inspection, however, Gershenzon's suspicion of words seemed to be mainly directed against the clichés, stereotypes, and congealed formulations of ordinary consciousness. In his debate with Ivanov, he argued against "well-worn paths of consciousness . . . routines of thought and . . . perception . . . [that] lie in wait for budding spiritual intuition, immediately enveloping them as if in a loving embrace, and luring them along the beaten paths."[32] In contrast, he admired how the fresh use of language--as in a particularly arresting line of poetry--"cuts through the gloom like lightning," thereby enhancing consciousness.[33] In particular, Gershenzon admired the great writers and poets of modern Russian literature precisely because it seemed to him that their works powerfully conveyed a contingent universe--a wilder, more problematic reality--beyond the tidier, antiseptic world constructed by civilized consciousness. In *Vekhi* he laments that the Russian intelligentsia did not take more seriously the added dimensions suggested by Dostoevsky's "underground," Tiutchev's "primordial chaos," and Fet's "eternity."[34] And in later works he attempted to elucidate the "dreams and thought" of Turgenev and the "wisdom" of Pushkin. Gershenzon argued, for example, that Turgenev had an acute sense of the "elemental" nature of reality, but that critics and teachers--with their clear, well-ordered interpretations--often failed to communicate this dimension of Turgenev's work. It was as if a disturbing, "wild territory, where nothing will . . . soothe you," had been remade into an English garden "with clear, straight walk-ways . . . an even lawn among shady trees, wonderful flower beds and gazebos."[35]

Among the writers of his own time, he was especially close to Andrei Bely, to the point where each considerably influenced the other.[36] Curiously, however, he had little connection with Russia's foremost poet of the "elemental," Alexander Blok, even though their views coincided quite remarkably. As this paper has argued, a central image in Gershenzon's thought was that of civilization as an enclosed capsule, within which human existence could proceed in logical, ordered, and comfortable ways--but at great spiritual expense. Cut off from the wilder dimensions of reality outside the capsule and from the untamed depths of the self, secular civilized consciousness represented a diminution of life. Commenting in 1908 on a story by Andreev in which city lights and signs flashing "chocolate" and "cocoa" obscure vision of stars in the night sky, Gershenzon said that the souls of urban dwellers are crippled by the city. It is as if they are saying: "I don't want eternity and mystery. I want chocolate and cocoa. I want something to be written in the sky that I can understand, that is sweet and doesn't frighten me."[37]

The city, in contrast to the ocean and forest, is a shelter from the elements; but for that very reason it represents a confinement, a prison. Blok's images of the elemental--as expressed in his poetry and also forcefully in his prose essays, such as "The Decline of Humanism" (1919)--are much better known. This attitude is perhaps expressed most succinctly in Blok's diary entry for April 5, 1912: "Unspeakably overjoyed yesterday by the destruction of the *Titanic* (there is still an ocean)."[38] For Blok, the untamed elements mocked civilization's presumption of an "unsinkable" ship, and his sense of the "elemental" offers dramatic contrast to the predictable world implied by the work of his father-in-law, the famous chemist Dmitrii Mendeleev, in which the elements are neatly contained within the well-ordered rows and columns of the Periodic Table. In one of his last works, Gershenzon also referred to the *Titanic* as an appropriate symbol of civilization set within a wider elemental universe:

> The inflexible method of science is good and stupendous, rendering to man some power over a limited sphere surrounded by darkness "wherein God is." Modern man, intoxicated by science, forgets this darkness, and that the unknown may at every moment dispose otherwise than he proposes; his self-complacency is so thick that he does not see the signs . . . he reckons, measures, lays one brick on another, works even without rest. Then suddenly a thunderbolt falls, or the power slumbering in objects awakens, according to some secret order. Lisbon is destroyed by an earthquake; the magnificent and ingeniously built *Titanic* sinks to the bottom of the ocean, a war breaks out and specialists in demolition destroy what art has built with eager zeal; or sometimes in a man a strange passion will surge, so that he will in a frenzy leap into the flaming pile. . . . There are some forces which are inaccessible to reason forever.[39]

Both Gershenzon and Blok were nihilists not only in their preoccupation with destruction but in the way they questioned, fundamentally, some of the legacies and tendencies of humanistic civilization. Interestingly, at the same time that Gershenzon was challenging Ivanov's views on the value of culture, expressing a desire to shed the whole heritage of Western civilization--along with his clothes--and plunge naked into the waters of Lethe, Blok was having similar conversations with Maxim Gorky.[40]

* * * *

Born into a "generation of materialism," when positivistic values were dominant in Russian educated society, Gershenzon's life nonetheless unfolded in an era when the seemingly rational and ordered surface of life gave way to a more dimensioned and disturbing kind of world. The year of his birth, 1869, also marked a more widespread acceptance of the idea of unconscious mental life as worthy of serious study in psychology. A year later, Nietzsche's *Birth of Tragedy* began a revaluation of ancient Greece away from an emphasis on rationality, and "sweetness and light" toward a consideration of the irrational and Dionysian elements in Greek culture. At the end of the century, when Gershenzon was just beginning his career, Joseph Conrad's *Heart of Darkness* appeared. These events in the literary life of Europe document a growing awareness of a wilder reality just beyond the threshold of consciousness and civilization.

Turgenev, too, had experienced such a feeling while viewing classical Greek sculpture from the excavations in Pergamos in 1880. "These high-reliefs," he wrote, "represent the battle between the gods and the titans. . . . The victory is without doubt won by the gods, who represent light, beauty and reason; but the dark, savage forces of the earth are still offering resistance--and the battle is not over."[41] By 1919, after five years of war and revolution, the "elemental" was perhaps all too palpable throughout the whole civilized world.

Gershenzon's disposition to see in these forces signs of spiritual renewal--as well as his expectation that the narrowness of civilization would give way to a more open-ended existence--showed little awareness of how Bolshevik "consciousness" would seek to contain the Revolution and direct its energies along a far more restricted path.[42] He had made his earlier reputation by portraying voyages of self-discovery taken by figures from the past. His biographies often focused on individuals who, while not the movers and shakers of history, nonetheless expressed in their personalities some of the strongest urges and features of their times. Gershenzon's own attempts to understand himself and his society are no less worthy of study. His inner life provides the historian with an intriguing vantage point from which to view the crucial era through which he lived. The questions he raised about the relationships between civilized consciousness and elemental reality--between intellect and soul--endure.

CHAPTER 10

POBEDONOSTSEV'S PARISH
SCHOOLS: A BASTION AGAINST SECULARISM

Thomas C. Sorenson

Throughout his life, Konstantin P. Pobedonostsev believed that popular education in Russia must be based on religion and that it was especially important for the clergy to be directly involved in providing elementary education to the *narod*. One of his clearest and strongest statements of this point was expressed as early as 1864, in the book that he and I. Babst published that year:

No matter how many systems of popular education we organize, none of them will be completely popular and practical if it does not depend on the activity of the village clergy. If willing teachers of the *narod* cannot be found among this group, it can hardly be expected that any other group will be in a position to provide dependable teachers who would enjoy the same degree of confidence with both the government and the *narod*.[1]

Working throughout his tenure as over-procurator of the Holy Synod to implement this idea, Pobedonostsev achieved remarkable success.

Popular elementary schools run by the clergy had existed in one form or another for decades before Pobedonostsev became over-procurator in 1880. The Spiritual Regulation of 1721, which created the Holy Synod and the office of over-procurator, directed the bishops to create schools. By 1727 they had created forty-six "diocesan schools" with 3,056 pupils in eighteen dioceses. In 1740, Empress Anna Ivanovna directed the Holy Synod to create more of these schools.

Despite these favorable beginnings, schools run exclusively by the clergy had not become a major part of Russia's educational system by the end of the eighteenth century. In the educational reform of 1802, including the creation of the Ministry of Education, the basic school was called a "parish school" (*uchilishche prikhodskoe*), but it was not managed by the clergy. It was, rather, the first school in a ladder system leading to the university, and only the course on religion was taught by a priest. In fact, this layer of schools remained a plan, and very few, if any, came into existence.

By the 1830s, a true parish school operated by the clergy had developed. In 1836 the Holy Synod issued rules "on elementary education of village children," and by 1839 some 2,000 parish schools (*tserkovno-prikhodskaia shkola*; the same term was later applied to Pobedonostsev's parish schools) functioned with 19,000 pupils. According to official statistics, these schools grew at a rapid pace. In 1851, for example, there were 4,713 schools with 93,350 pupils. It appears, however, that many of these schools also existed only on paper or that instruction in them took place only when the local priest could spare time from his other duties. The numbers are nonetheless significant if we compare them with the figures for the schools of the Ministry of Education. In 1855, for example, that ministry maintained only 439 district schools (*uezdnoe uchilishche*), and a total of only 1,641 elementary schools.[2] It seems that the parish school had become a vital part of Russia's educational system.

The parish schools sank to a low level of significance during the era of the Great Reforms of the 1860s and 1870s. An imperial order of January 18, 1862, assigned primary responsibility for public elementary education to the Ministry of Education. After 1864, the zemstvo institutions also became active in elementary education. Conflicts developed between the secular zemstvo and ministry schools and Russian Orthodox parochial schools. Government statistics for 1865 listed 21,420 parish schools,[3] but these figures are probably inflated, and hard times lay ahead for the parish schools.

The years between 1866 and 1880, when Dmitrii Tolstoi served simultaneously as over-procurator of the Holy Synod and minister of education, were a period of sharp decline for the parish schools. When Tolstoi became minister of education in 1866, the clergy had twenty times as many schools in the thirty-three provinces of European Russia as the ministry. In his study of Tolstoi's educational policies, Allen Sinel claims that Tolstoi began with great hopes for the clergy as elementary school teachers because the priests already had extensive experience in primary education, they required only meager salaries, and their close proximity to the village population gave them an understanding of its needs. Moreover, the Orthodox seminaries were capable institutions for training teachers. Tolstoi's high hopes were soon dashed by the hard facts of life in the countryside. Qualified seminary graduates frequently rejected teaching as a profession. Many of the schools the Holy Synod claimed existed did not, and those that functioned did not appeal to anyone. As Sinel concludes, "It was unrealistic for Tolstoi to expect the relatively untrained parish priest to conduct school in addition to his other obligations." Consequently, the minister/over-procurator decided to work toward a totally secular school system.[4]

Tolstoi's plans for elementary education were embodied in the statute of February 14, 1874. The principal thrust of this legislation was to give the Ministry of Education greater control over elementary education. During discussion of this legislation in the state council, Tolstoi was, in Sinel's words, "chided . . . for neglecting the clergy's vital role in education." The State Council changed Tolstoi's proposals by declaring that moral and religious education in all schools was the special concern of the bishops and the parish priests. It also warned that primary education could not succeed without the clergy's cooperation. Sinel concludes that "Tolstoi thus received a sharp reminder that the government was not ready for the completely secular school system he envisioned."[5]

Toward the end of Tolstoi's tenure in his "dual ministry," people who favored reviving the parish schools became more influential. This group was led by head of the Third Section of the Chancellery (i.e., the secret police) A. R. Drentel'n and Minister of Finance S. A. Greig. In 1879, the Committee of Ministers, in Sinel's words, approved "the principle of clergy predominance in primary education." Sinel editorializes, "In the next decade K. P. Pobedonostsev would transform this retrogressive principle into an unhappy reality."[6] Despite the existence of such pressures working against Tolstoi's plans, only 4,440 parish schools remained in 1881.[7]

Thus when Pobedonostsev became over-procurator in 1880, he faced a trend toward secularization of elementary education that he wanted to reverse. Although his position was strengthened by the Committee of

Ministers' decision of 1879, among other factors, the number of parish schools had declined precipitously during the previous fourteen years, and much work would be required to open new ones and improve the quality of those already in existence. At first, Pobedonostsev saw the key to solving this problem in funds the Holy Synod would provide for these schools. He included the proposal in his first official report on the condition of the Russian Orthodox Church in 1880. The parish schools, he wrote,

> established by the priests and [other] members of the clergy with
> their own meager funds, with funds of church trustees and of private
> philanthropists, or maintained in monasteries at the monasteries'
> expense, satisfy the needs of the population, especially in localities
> far removed from large, established schools. The *narod* in general
> trusts and is attracted to these frequently wretched schools, which
> are managed exclusively by the clergy, and schools of this type
> would without doubt develop significantly for the spiritual well-
> being of the population if the Church administration had its own
> funds for their support and for the remuneration and encouragement
> of persons who devote their efforts to them.[8]

Including a request for state support for priests operating parish schools shows that Pobedonostsev had such funding as a primary objective from the beginning of his tenure as over-procurator.

Pobedonostsev quickly achieved some success in increasing the number of parish schools. From 4,400 in 1881 their number rose to 4,500 in 1882.[9] Additionally, in 1882 some schools began receiving approximately one hundred rubles each directly from the government. It is significant that a disproportionate number of the parish schools (2,401, or more than half) were located in the non-Russian western border regions of the empire in 1882. These numbers indicate a close connection between the spread of parish schools and nationality issues in the empire, and show that such schools were not aimed primarily at the Russian *narod*.

Pobedonostsev's plans for reforming and reviving the parish schools gathered momentum in 1883. The lengthy discussion of parish schools in his official report for that year merits a detailed examination. Not

surprisingly, Pobedonostsev began with a history of the clergy's role in
elementary education in Russia. His romanticized account is full of
inaccuracies. He asserted that teaching children had been the clergy's task
since "from the very beginning of the enlightenment of the Russian *narod*
by Christianity." In addition to Christian priests' duty to "lead people to
baptism," they were obligated "to make children literate." Since the time of
Saints Vladimir and Iaroslav, "throughout the entire expanse of the vast
Russian land, the first and almost the only teachers and educators of the
narod in the course of many centuries have been its spiritual pastors. Their
educational activity corresponded to the spiritual needs of the *narod*."[10]

The parish schools, he wrote, had been highly successful. The *narod*
"related to these schools with trust; parishioners gladly sent their children
to them, fathers and mothers rejoiced that their children were being taught
to read church books and to sing in the [church] choir." By the middle of
the 1860s, according to Pobedonostsev's figures, 18,000 such schools
offered instruction to 100,000 pupils. (Pobedonostsev's figure is less than
the government statistic of 21,420 schools in 1865 cited above.)

Pobedonostsev blamed educational reforms of the 1860s and 1870s for
the "deterioration" of the parish schools. Elementary education was
removed from the Orthodox Church's responsibilities and reorganized on
foreign models using foreign pedagogical methods. The reforms transferred
the former parish schools to control by secular school authorities. The sad
result, in Pobedonostsev's estimation, was that the clergy lost its influence
on education to secular officials "who did not always have behind them the
authority of experience and moral strength." The *narod*, he said, although
it funded education of its children as much as possible,

    was not satisfied with what the children found in the schools and
    brought home from the schools. Given its profound devotion to the
    Church, the *narod* desires that the schools have a close tie with the
    church, so that literacy may open to them the published treasures of
    religious edification and comfort, that their children may participate
    in reading and singing the church service and may read at home to
    their illiterate parents the holy books and other books for the
    salvation of [their] souls.

Having sketched this self-serving history of the parish schools that the peasantry allegedly desired, Pobedonostsev built a case for reviving them. He praised actions by the Committee of Ministers as an example for further government policies. He referred to their resolution of 1879, which said that "the spiritual and moral development of the *narod*, which constitutes the cornerstone of the entire state order, cannot be attained without assigning the clergy the predominant role in managing schools for the *narod*." Later, in an address to the Committee of Ministers, he again cited the resolution of 1879 and requested the committee take another step in the direction of that resolution by creating a special commission to conduct a thorough reexamination of the clergy's role in elementary education. Apparently the committee acted on his request, for on January 22, 1882, it directed Pobedonostsev, in conjunction with other concerned agencies, to develop "the present matter." This vaguely worded directive was used by Pobedonostsev as a mandate to revive and expand the parish schools.

New measures soon followed. In agreement with the ministers of education and finance, Pobedonostsev proposed that 55,000 rubles be transferred from other agencies to the Holy Synod to support the parish schools. In response, the committee drafted a law to this effect, and it was signed November 2, 1882. At the same time, Pobedonostsev proposed that the Holy Synod create a special commission of experts on popular education. The commission, to be chaired by one of the synodal bishops and to include a representative of the Ministry of Education, was to find ways to increase the clergy's role in education and to finance the parish schools. The synod agreed to this proposal in September 1882, named Archbishop Leontii of Kholm-Warsaw as chairman, and authorized Pobedonostsev to appoint the other members of the commission.

On April 29, 1883, the commission presented the synod a draft statute on the parish schools and proposals for increasing the clergy's influence in the secular schools as well. Pobedonostsev claimed that these efforts enjoyed the full sympathy of Minister of Education I. D. Delianov and the enthusiastic support of the clergy themselves. The stage was thus set for issuing the new statute, formulated according to Pobedonostsev's ideas and under his close supervision, on the parish schools. Alexander III signed the statute on June 13, 1884.

In his official report for 1884 Pobedonostsev discussed the new statute in detail. He began by listing three principal reasons for linking popular elementary education to the Russian Orthodox Church and clergy. First, he argued, the popular school "should have a historical basis." Second, it "should be based on the firm principles of the Orthodox faith, whose guardian and interpreter can be only the Orthodox clergy." Third, the school "should correspond to the religious feeling and desires of the *narod* itself." The statute of June 13, 1884, he claimed, met all these requirements.[11]

In support of the first point, Pobedonostsev presented a brief history of Russian education that paraphrased the sketch history in his report for 1883. He added a quotation of Minister of Education Delianov to the effect that until the 1860s virtually alone the clergy had taught the *narod* in parish schools that they had maintained at their own expense.

The new parish schools met the second requirement, Pobedonostsev explained, through the curriculum. By teaching religion (*Zakon Bozhii*, literally "God's law")--consisting of church singing and reading the Bible and hymnals--supplemented by lessons on the Russian language and rudimentary arithmetic, the parish schools provided peasant youths the practical knowledge they needed for their daily lives.

Pobedonostsev considered the third point (that elementary education must correspond to the religious needs of the *narod*) the most important of the three. Thus he discussed it in more detail than other points in the report of 1884. Experience shows, he argued, that the masses would attend and support only the type of school that provided the education they felt useful, both practically and spiritually. Only to such a school would the *narod* "attach itself, consider it its own property and not consider it an institutional burden prescribed from without." In Russia, he asserted unequivocally, "any such school had to be tied inseparably to the [Russian Orthodox] Church and to the teaching of faith." Pobedonostsev claimed that when children brought secular knowledge home from school, their parents rejected the school. But when the children came home reading religious books, and when the parents heard their children reading and singing in church, they realized the tremendous value of the school (pp. 105-7).

The three points that Pobedonostsev made in his discussion derived from his populist conservative ideology. His statement that the schools must rest on a historical basis is a clear example of the historicism that was a key element of his ideology. Pobedonostsev sought to arm the schools with the sanction of prescription that he knew any institution requires for legitimacy. His second and third points, that education must be based on Orthodoxy and must correspond to the religious sensitivities of the *narod*, reflect the prejudice that was the other central component of his ideology. Thus, meeting Russia's needs for elementary education was relatively simple if one accepted all of Pobedonostsev's premises. First, the educational system must be based on the *narod*'s desires. Second, the *narod*'s most profound attachment was to the Russian Orthodox Church. Third, the parish schools Pobedonostsev had designed corresponded to the peasants' desires as he understood them. Thus the parish schools were the most complete expression of Pobedonostsev's ideology in action.

It is clear that Pobedonostsev saw the parish school movement as a logical complement to the other counterreforms that the government of Alexander III enacted between 1884 and 1890. The consciously reactionary nature of the statute on the parish school is clearly illustrated by the following statement that Pobedonostsev inserted into his report for 1884 immediately after his discussion of the three main points we have just considered. He asserted that the "ideal of elementary education," shared by the peasantry and the Russian Orthodox Church, had, "unfortunately, been distorted during the last twenty-five years by a false and unrealistic conception of the popular school as a means for spreading practical knowledge among the *narod* through artificial institutional methods borrowed from the practice of other countries" (p. 108). He was asserting, in short, that the era of the Great Reforms had been a disaster for Russian elementary education, and he was calling for a conscious return to conditions that, he claimed, existed before the fateful reforms. His denunciation of the educational policy pursued by Alexander II as based on foreign models was fully characteristic of Pobedonostsev's approach to reform, and recalls the statements he made in the 1860s about the judicial reform of 1864.

One disingenuous statement in the official report for 1884 reveals the means Pobedonostsev thought might win Minister of Interior Tolstoi's support for the parish schools. Citing a directive Tolstoi had written as minister of education in 1879, Pobedonostsev tried to show that Tolstoi supported the principles embodied in the new legislation on the parish schools. Pobedonostsev totally ignored the fact that in 1879 the Committee of Ministers had rebuked Tolstoi for the excessively secular nature of his educational policies. In fact, most of Pobedonostsev's activities as over-procurator were attempts to reverse Tolstoi's policies in fields ranging from education to parish administrative structure. By 1884, of course, Tolstoi had become a symbol, ranking second only to Pobedonostsev himself, of Alexander III's reactionary policies. Pobedonostsev could hardly afford to antagonize Tolstoi, and the government needed to present a unified front to public opinion if its policies were to succeed. These factors no doubt explain Pobedonostsev's attempt to minimize the differences between himself and his immediate predecessor as over- procurator. The fact remains, however, that Pobedonostsev's policies were a reaction not only against the liberal measures adopted under Alexander II but also against the earlier policies of Tolstoi. The difference in approach between these two great statesmen of counterreform is nowhere seen more clearly than in their attitudes toward parish schools (p. 110).

Pobedonostsev explained in some detail, in his report for 1884, the structure and administration of the three types of parish schools created by the statute of June 13, 1884. Two types were related. The basic school was a two-year school consisting of only one class, or grade. For parishes that could afford the additional cost, a second, related type of parish school was approved. It added a second class and two years to the basic one-class, two-year parish school to create a two-class, four-year school. The third type of school was not a parish school but a "peasant home-school of literacy," the so-called literacy schools. Very primitive schools, maintained by literate peasants in their own homes, had long existed in Russia, but they were not regulated and had no officially recognized structure. The statute of 1884 brought these schools under the control of the clergy. Such schools were intended for localities too remote and too poor to support even the basic one-class parish school (p. 111).

To administer the schools the synod established the Council on the Affairs of the Parish Schools, chaired by one of the synodal bishops. The over-procurator had authority to name an assistant chairman, who would preside in the absence of the chairman, and to appoint the four other members "from persons closely acquainted with the condition of popular education" (pp. 25-27). This council was clearly Pobedonostsev's tool for controlling the schools. Given the generally passive nature of the synodal bishops and the frequent turnover among them, the bishop chairman was probably only of symbolic significance.

In the dioceses themselves, the bishop was designated as the official responsible for the schools. Each diocese was to create a diocesan committee on parish schools, which included among its members the Ministry of Education's local official, the director of elementary schools. The bishop was to choose a "priest-supervisor" to serve as inspector of the schools. The schools themselves were to be managed by the parish priest, who was also the instructor of religion in the schools. The school's teachers, selected by the priest, were given the same rights as teachers in the schools of the Ministry of Education. The inspectors, members of the diocesan committee, and the priests in their capacity as teachers of religion, were all to serve without pay. Interested laymen wishing to assist the work of the schools were authorized to serve on the diocesan committee or make financial contributions directly to the schools. This is the structure that Pobedonostsev considered the best possible to administer the basic unit in Russia's educational system (pp. 112-14).

Pobedonostsev naturally distrusted legislative solutions to problems. Arguing that people were "far more important than laws," he complained that the liberals of Alexander II's reign had believed they could solve any problem simply by passing a new law. Nonetheless, he had great faith that his new law, the statute of June 13, 1884, on the parish schools, would produce major improvements. Aware that his enthusiasm was in conflict with the long-held views he had stated so often publicly, Pobedonostsev discussed this problem in a letter to N. I. Il'minskii on the day the statute was ratified. "Regulations are necessary," he said, "and every institution needs a plan. It may be more or less formal or true. And when it is possible to prevent falseness and indicate the truth, that is a good cause and worth an effort of will."[12] If Alexander II's liberal minister P. A. Valuev or N. Miliutin had made the same statement, as well they could have, Pobedonostsev would have objected mightily. But tsarist policy-making affected him quite differently after he had become a tsarist bureaucrat.

Pobedonostsev stated his objectives for the 1884 statute more simply in his letter to Il'minskii than he did through the vague terms and generalities he used in his official reports. He told him that the purpose of the new statute was "to disentangle the knot that ties these schools to the [Ministry of Education's] school councils and to subject them to the exclusive management of the church."[13] Indeed, the only formal link the new statute retained between the parish schools and the Ministry of Education was the presence of the local director of public schools on the diocesan committee on parish schools. For all practical purposes, Pobedonostsev had created, via the statute of 1884, a school system totally independent of the Ministry of Education. Henceforth, Russia had two elementary school systems--one parochial and one secular. Competition between them remained a basic fact of Russian education until the Bolshevik seizure of government in 1917.

According to Pobedonostsev, the church began to implement the statute immediately after its enactment. In June 1884, according to his statistics, Russia had 4,457 parish schools with 105,150 pupils. After the bishops had "soon created diocesan committees everywhere," the committees took inventory of the existing schools and searched for means to increase their support and to open new schools. Always with an eye toward next year's budget, Pobedonostsev noted in the report that available means in 1884 were "meager and should be supplemented from state funds." Despite this hardship, the church had, between October 1, 1884, and January 1, 1885, created 1,167 new parish schools serving 33,771 new pupils. In addition, it opened 840 new literacy schools with 15,074 pupils. The synod provided 55,500 rubles and 101,485 free books to schools in the poorest dioceses.[14]

For the remaining twenty-one years of his tenure as over-procurator, Pobedonostsev's major project was to build the most extensive system of parish schools possible on the basis of the statute of 1884. While he had not written the statute himself, his ideas guided the hands that wrote it, and it embodied his ideas, plans, and dreams. The number of parish schools began to increase significantly after 1884. In 1885, 2,447 new schools (including all three types) were opened with a total of 84,668 pupils, both boys and girls. By January 1, 1886, the total number of all types of parish and literacy schools was 9,001 with 238,663 pupils. Of these schools, 5,570 were one-class parish schools, 100 were two-class parish schools, and 3,331 were literacy schools.[15] Compared with 18,000 parish schools that Pobedonostsev said existed in the mid-1860s, these figures show that the Russian Orthodox Church had not regained its previous role, and that the parish schools were serving only a very small segment of the potential pupils. But their number continued to increase for the next twenty years.

In 1885, the synodal council called for in the 1884 statute came into being under the altered name of the School Council of the Holy Synod. The chairman was a synodal bishop, but as assistant chairman Pobedonostsev appointed V. K. Sabler, then director of the synodal chancellery. Later, Sabler would become Pobedonostsev's trusted deputy over-procurator and still later his immediate successor as over-procurator. In appointing Sabler assistant chairman of the council (the person who actually directed its work), Pobedonostsev demonstrated that he valued the council's work and wanted to eliminate any doubt that he, personally, had final authority over its decisions.

Having achieved the statute of 1884, Pobedonostsev began in earnest the campaign, of which he hinted in the report of 1884, to increase the amount of money the imperial government allocated to the synod for the parish schools. His ultimate objective was funding equal to the tsarist government's allocation to the Ministry of Education for its schools. He noted that despite the increased number of schools, the Holy Synod had at the end of 1885 only 55,000 rubles for their support, the same sum as in 1884. The total amount spent--from all sources--on parish schools in 1885 was 528,067 rubles. Thus the synod, which had assumed responsibility for the parish schools and was working hard to create new ones, had control of only slightly more than a tenth of their total income. The remaining 90 percent came from local sources. Pobedonostsev compared these figures to those for schools administered by the Ministry of Education. To illustrate the incongruity he chose the provinces of Arkhangelsk, Astrakhan, and Orenburg, in which 1,801 of the ministry's schools had a total budget of 968,546 rubles and 65 kopeks, of which the ministry supplied 339,266 rubles, or six times more than the synod's total for the whole empire. Citing similar figures for other regions of the empire, Pobedonostsev argued that the parish schools should have equal funding with the ministry's schools. Without equal funding, he warned, the Holy Synod could not possibly "organize and strengthen the condition of the parish schools to the extent that they would satisfy the legitimate desires of the *narod* and serve it as a moral bulwark against all sorts of spiritual and material calamities" (p. 180).

It was, of course, clear that state support for the parish schools could not be increased so dramatically at once. Aware of the imperial government's chronic shortage of revenue, Pobedonostsev first submitted proposals that were modest. In November 1885, he proposed to the State Council that current annual funds of 55,000 rubles be increased to 120,000 rubles. To support his position he reminded the council of the government's commitment in 1879 to increase the clergy's role in elementary education. Calling once again upon the name of Dmitrii Tolstoi, he noted that as minister of education in 1879, Tolstoi had proposed government support for parish schools of 119,000 rubles annually. However, the state treasury had refused for lack of funds. In 1881, Minister of Education A. A. Saburov had reintroduced this proposal, but, Pobedonostsev lamented, it again produced no financial support for the schools.

Pobedonostsev next invoked in his behalf a comment Alexander III had written on his personal copy of the statute of 1884: "I hope that the parish clergy will prove worthy of its high calling in this important matter." Pobedonostsev claimed that the clergy had been greatly impressed by this statement and had worked zealously without pay. The number of schools had more than doubled since 1882, and requests for more schools were being received from all over the country. These requests were, alas, usually coupled with pleas for money from the government because local resources were insufficient. He concluded by pointing out that the minister of finance had agreed to his proposed increase. This time, Pobedonostsev's plea was successful. This argument, among other factors, won Pobedonostsev 112,000 rubles for the following fiscal year of 1886-87.[16]

In 1886, Pobedonostsev reached another significant milestone. That year, the synod created and adopted a mandatory program of study for all the parish schools. Pobedonostsev explained the principal aim of this program as "training the pupils in the spirit of the Orthodox Church." With obvious pride, he described the nature of the program in some detail:

> Religion is the main subject: sacred history of the Old and New
> Testaments, the catechism, and explanation of the service. All other
> subjects, except arithmetic, are a kind of supplement to and
> development of the main subject. The readings in [Old Church]
> Slavonic strengthen in the memory of the pupils the events of sacred
> history studied in religion class; church singing promotes the
> learning of church songs and the order of the service; the books for
> reading the Russian language contain articles predominantly of
> spiritually edifying and historical content. The mechanical study of
> numbers, which has previously predominated in the *narod*'s village
> schools, is excluded from the teaching of arithmetic and is replaced
> by the study of functions and by solving problems immediately
> related to the peasants' way of life.

Pobedonostsev was so excited by this new course of study that he let his imagination get the better of him when he exclaimed that even some district zemstvo assemblies were deciding to adopt it in their schools. He fantasized that, beyond doubt, his program would "be introduced into all popular elementary schools, with primary responsibility for its application assigned to the Orthodox clergy."[17] He had apparently temporarily forgotten that significant opposition to all his plans for Russian elementary education still existed in zemstvo circles and elsewhere in society. Nonetheless, this statement reveals that Pobedonostsev's ambitious plans were to use the parish schools to influence all of Russian education.

Five years after the introduction of the statute of 1884, the numbers of parish and literacy schools had risen to 19,135 with 530,480 pupils,[18] an increase of 400 percent in the number of schools during the nine years

Pobedonostsev had served as over-procurator. In his official report for 1888-89, Pobedonostsev gave a detailed evaluation of the schools' first five years under the new statute. Apart from the very gratifying increase in their number, Pobedonostsev believed that the schools had become a positive moral force in Russian life. He contended that the schools had not only

> succeeded in exercising a beneficial influence on the pupils, but on the local population, that everywhere is demonstrating, by its material offerings, its sympathy for the children's inclination toward the church that they acquire in these schools. The parish schools have exercised no less significant influence on schools administered by other institutions. [These institutions] have recognized the necessity of strengthening in their schools the study of religion, the Church Slavonic language, and church singing.[19]

Pobedonostsev cited some significant statistics to demonstrate the parish schools' impact on Orthodox children. For every 1,000 Orthodox residents in the Russian Empire, seven were pupils in the parish schools. Ironically, but not by coincidence, Pobedonostsev's statistics were most impressive for the non-Russian borderlands. Attendance was greatest in the Ukrainian dioceses. In Kiev, there were 22.5 pupils per thousand residents, in Mogilev 21.2, and in Podolsk 19.7. The figures were considerably less impressive in the central Russian regions of the empire. The relevant statistics for the diocese of Moscow showed only 6.3 pupils per thousand Orthodox residents, in Tambov 6.2, and in Novgorod 4.6. The situation was worst of all, in Pobedonostsev's opinion, in Siberia, where the diocese of Kamchatka reported only 2.0 pupils per thousand residents, and Iakutsk lowest of all with 0.6. The schools had also failed to take root in Poland, with only 0.8 pupils per thousand Orthodox residents.

Pobedonostsev analyzed the attendance figures for the diocese of Tambov in central Russia to demonstrate the unfinished task facing the parish schools. According to his statistics, 340,000 Orthodox children of school age lived in Tambov diocese. Of 1,057 elementary schools, half (525) were parish schools. Only 54,000 pupils, or less than one school-aged child in six, attended any type of elementary school. Of these pupils, 16,000 attended parish schools. Thus only 4.33 percent of all children of school age, and only 27 percent of all pupils, attended parish schools. Pobedonostsev also noted that of all 54,000 pupils, only 6,000 were girls. He deplored that this condition of the Orthodox population was found to some degree in all dioceses: "millions of children grow up in the darkness of ignorance. The light of the Orthodox doctrine of faith in Christ does not touch them." The problem lay not so much in an insufficient number of schools, he said, as in an insufficient number of pupils--an average of only 35 per school (pp. 345-49).

Still pursuing his ultimate goal of equal funding for the parish schools, Pobedonostsev laid out a detailed assessment of their material conditions. Their total budget during the 1888-89 school year was 1,948,000 rubles, of which only 175,000 rubles came from the synod. The government contributed another 162,000 rubles to schools in provinces that had no zemstvo institutions. Other sources of income included the zemstvos (140,000 rubles), philanthropic organizations and private contributions (180,000 rubles), fees paid by pupils' parents (83,000 rubles for the 39 diocese for which Pobedonostsev had figures), and, most important, parish welfare societies (460,000 rubles).

Pobedonostsev listed three major reasons why local resources for the schools were not more plentiful. First, in some areas people considered the parish schools solely the clergy's responsibility, with no outside help needed. Second, the peasants were frequently reluctant to make voluntary contributions because they already made obligatory payments to the secular volost and zemstvo schools. Third, many zemstvo workers and other local lay officials were not sympathetic toward the parish schools, considering them an infringement on their prerogatives. Cooperation between secular and church schools had not, Pobedonostsev said, developed as it should. Some important consequences of the low level of financial support for the schools were poorly trained teachers, a high turnover among them, and very poor facilities. The parish schools were frequently housed in peasant huts with dirt floors and no heat.

At the end of their first five years, the parish schools presented a mixed picture. While the number of schools and pupils had increased significantly, millions of children remained without any school system, and existing parish schools suffered from a serious shortage of funds. Having laid this statistical base for his argument, Pobedonostsev made an eloquent plea for greater funding for elementary education and, specifically of course, for the parish schools. "The time has come," he wrote at the end of his report (pp. 382-83),

> to take effective measures to create the possibility that, if not all, then at least the majority of Orthodox children can receive an education in the church schools. During the past thirty years tens of thousands of schools have been opened and hundreds of thousands of pupils have been added, but those same millions of children of school age remain without instruction in literacy because each year the population of Russia increases by more than one and a half million . . . , and each year up to 200,000 children reach school age. It is necessary to prepare many schools for them, since fewer children leave school than reach school age. If popular education continues to go at the same pace as it has gone and now goes, Orthodox Russia will not attain universal literacy for a long time and will grow in ignorance. Now more than ever before, given the development of a network of railroads in Russia and of steam power in agricultural and industrial production, literacy and school training in general are extremely necessary for the growing Orthodox population of both sexes, from whom must come loyal citizens for the state, Orthodox sons of the Church of Christ, and conscientious and more capable workers in all types of activity. At the same time, the number of law-breakers and prisoners must be reduced, the habit of alcoholism must be weakened, and the well-being of the *narod* must be increased. It is essential to seek measures for the education of the *narod* and to implement them. Social institutions and private persons, having felt the guiding direction of the state and the church in the development of popular education, will meet

the Orthodox children's obvious needs for learning with great zeal, thereby simplifying their [the state's and the Church's] task by half.

This appeal is one of the clearest pieces of evidence that Pobedonostsev was an advocate of universal literacy in Russia. He believed ignorance to be the *narod*'s greatest danger, and literacy was a prerequisite for abolishing ignorance. But his concept of the ideal curriculum and his efforts to spread literacy have been, and still are, frequently dismissed or badly distorted. In 1901 N. I. Lagovskii attempted to assassinate Pobedonostsev because, he said, the parish schools spread ignorance and superstition. More recently, a Soviet writer branded Pobedonostsev as the architect of a policy not of public enlightenment, but of "public endarkenment." Such was clearly not his intention. His populist conservative ideology and his own religious convictions led him to believe that education should be primarily religious education. Since neither political conservatism nor religious education has been in vogue in the Soviet Union or the West in recent decades, his work has been overlooked or attacked by liberal and radical politicians and scholars. He had, however, identified one of Russia's major social problems, and he attempted to formulate a realistic solution that the country's meager economic resources could support. The effort should not be dismissed so lightly.

In 1895, Pobedonostsev achieved another major victory in obtaining increased state financial support for parish schools. As we have seen, support rose from the tiny sum of 55,000 rubles in 1884 to a mere 175,000 rubles in 1889. In 1895, Pobedonostsev requested an allotment of 3,279,205 rubles from the State Council. In defense of such a large increase, he lauded the record of the parish schools in the decade since 1884, and attacked the Ministry of Education's efforts to provide elementary education. He claimed that between the years 1864 and 1884, while under the exclusive control of the ministry, popular elementary education had spread very slowly. Citing figures for 1880, Pobedonostsev alleged that European Russia and Poland had only 22,770 elementary village schools of all types with a total of only 1,140,915 pupils, less than 10 percent of the children of school age. This meant "an illiterate *narod.*"

The parish schools, although they received only 700,000 rubles from the state treasury in 1895, had begun to change that situation. Pobedonostsev claimed that the activity of the clergy had produced "such significant results that it fully deserves encouragement and support in the form of a permanent monetary grant from the treasury." He drew a contrast between the cost of funding schools maintained by the Ministry of Education and the parish schools. While in the 1892-93 school year the Holy Synod and the Ministry of Education each maintained about 30,000 schools, the ministry's budget for elementary schools had long ago passed six million rubles. The ministry's inspectors alone cost the state 650,000 rubles annually, and its teacher seminaries cost one million rubles. The church's inspectors worked without pay, and parish school teachers came from the ecclesiastical seminaries and diocesan girls' schools, both of which were supported by the church. Pobedonostsev stressed that the parish schools were well worth the government's investment, providing at a very small cost a service that the ministry had failed to provide at great expense.

Pobedonostsev attempted to strengthen his argument by invoking the narod's love of the church, the priests' traditional loyalty to the state, and the alleged fact that secular education in the West was leading to the spread of atheism, socialism, and anarchism. Moreover, the high educational level of Russia's Lutheran, Catholic, Jewish, and Muslim populations was a result, Pobedonostsev said, of the work of their respective churches. If the Orthodox Church was to provide the same service to the Russians, it needed more money from the state. He admitted that the requested sum was an enormous increase, but it was justified by the reality that only the parish schools could spread literacy and Orthodoxy among the masses.[20] Having won Finance Minister S. Witte's support,[21] his request was approved. With the imperial government's assumption of the major responsibility for supporting the parish schools, Pobedonostsev's ten-year battle had been won.

With greater funding, the parish schools grew rapidly in the following years. In 1899, 41,402 parish schools taught 1,554,229, the first year in which the number of pupils exceeded one million.[22] By the end of Pobedonostsev's tenure as over-procurator in 1905, the number of pupils approached two million.[23]

Pobedonostsev's final evaluation of his own work on behalf of the parish schools is perhaps best seen in a statement he wrote to Nicholas II in 1902.

> At the present troubled time, when from all sides perverted and mindless people are trying to engender depravity of thought in the *narod* and to develop in the ignorant mass dissatisfaction with the authorities, animosity, and the loss of its simple faith, the only reliable means for educating the new generation is precisely the parish school, which is inseparably bound to the Church, the school closest to the *narod* and most sympathetic to it. That is why from the very beginning both the Holy Synod and I have directed our most zealous concern toward these schools. And I can truly say that this school, with all its inevitable shortcomings, is growing and succeeding beyond [my] expectations, engendering among the *narod* the most tender sympathy.[24]

Pobedonostsev was amply satisfied with his work. He knew that much remained to be done, but he had seen his cherished parish schools grow into a school system that could challenge the schools of the Ministry of Education as the primary force in Russian elementary education. Millions of children had learned to read and write because of his efforts. In Russia in the nineteenth century, that was no small accomplishment.

The parish schools were the most significant result of Pobedonostsev's work as over-procurator. When he resigned his office in 1905, the 42,696 parish schools then in existence constituted 46.5 percent of all elementary schools in Russia.[25] They were the ultimate embodiment of Pobedonostsev's populist conservative ideology. They were based on his evaluation of the needs and desires of the *narod*, and were designed to appeal to and strengthen the *narod*'s attachment to the Orthodox Church. They represented a conscious rejection of Western models and modern pedagogical techniques in favor of an approach to elementary education that he considered more appropriate to conditions of the Russian countryside.

The claims Pobedonostsev made for the success of the schools and for the clergy's zeal in opening them were no doubt exaggerated. In fact, the clergy harbored a great deal of active and passive resistance to the new burden Pobedonostsev was trying to impose on them.[26] Pobedonostsev admitted that the material condition of most of the schools was pitiful; and the brief time a pupil attended the schools (a maximum of four years) must have meant that most children mastered only the basics of literacy at best. In evaluating the schools, however, we must remember that at the end of the nineteenth century Russia was still a poor country, economically and culturally backward by Western standards. Over 90 percent of the population was illiterate, and most of the peasants survived at a subsistence level.

Pobedonostsev understood these facts of Russian life very well. Like all other conservative reformers of his time, he faced the problem of reforming Russia into a society enjoying the benefits of industrialization without abolishing autocracy or the privileges that the Russian Orthodox Church enjoyed. While he understood a modern society's need for a literate population, he insisted that the *narod* learn to read and write without losing its traditional faith in God and the Orthodox Church. The parish schools were designed as a practical and realistic means of providing mass elementary education while retaining loyalty to Orthodoxy and autocracy. Much more than Pobedonostsev's efforts would have been required to achieve those goals, but his impact on education, ideas, and politics in late tsarist Russia was by no means insignificant.

CHAPTER 11

THE FRIENDS OF GOD:
NICHOLAS II AND ALEXANDRA AT
THE CANONIZATION OF SERAFIM OF SAROV, JULY 1903

Robert L. Nichols

On July 19, 1903, when the royal train from St. Petersburg carrying
Tsar Nicholas II, Tsarina Alexandra, and the imperial entourage arrived at
Arzamas in Russia's distant Nizhnii Novgorod province near the shrine of
Serafim of Sarov (1759-1833), it had reached an important joining point
between the capital of the empire and the vast interior of Russia's villages
and towns. The royal suite stepped off the train into the brouches drawn by
four horses especially relished by the empress and her maids of honor.
Plunging into a sea of pilgrims who had spent the night in the open fields
surrounding the Sarov monastery, the tsar greeted his subjects warmly and
they responded with enthusiasm, surging forward to get a closer look or
even touch a bit of his uniform. Slowly the imperial procession moved
away from the station toward the nearby hermitage.[1]

For a delightful and perilous moment the social and national divisions
segregating the classes and peoples of the empire broke down, carrying with
them for a time the warm breath of hope for a lost solidarity of tsar and
people. The precious resources of Serafim's holy relics made plain to those
present God's acceptance of the whole community; His mercy embraced all
its disparate members and reintegrated them, uniting high and low in a
shared community: "Bending the knee, eyes streaming with tears, the rich
and poor, well-born and commoners, widows and orphans, old and young,
prayed to God" before the sacred remains of God's chosen one.[2]
Numerous accounts of Serafim's glorification (the Orthodox term for
canonizing a saint), including official ones, later made a point of noting
how the saint's relics attracted all nationalities and united them into a single
family, healing their afflictions and giving them a moral rebirth and renewal
in the spirit. Typical of the hopes for future ethnic harmony that witnesses
invested in this event is the following account.

Here assembled representatives of nearly all of the nationalities settled in Great Russia. The majority of the pilgrims, of course, is formed of Great Russians and Little Russians; but there are among them many Belorussians, Mordvins, Karelians, Zyriane, and various other nationalities. All of these people, living in conditions that are far from similar to one another, here compose, as it were, one family inspired by a single thought--to bow before the relics of the righteous Serafim and before them find in simple-hearted but flaming prayer a joy and comfort for their souls.[3]

These accounts appeared at a time when national movements within the empire threatened to dissolve imperial bonds and as a wave of industrial strikes spread through southern Russia.

Newspapermen and other journalists produced dozens of accounts of the ceremony, sending back to the metropolitan centers daily dispatches to be read avidly by thousands curious to know the latest news, particularly about the royal couple Nicholas II and Alexandra.[4] Millions of Russians, including the royal family, saw the glorification of Serafim as a deeply satisfying demonstration of profound unity between the visible world of Russia's empire and God's invisible world of angels and saints. The event acted as a condenser for a number of strong atmospheric currents in the religious and political life of the late empire and crystallized Nicholas II's understanding of himself as a monarch, resolving him on a course of action ending in war with Japan in 1904.

For the royal couple and others, God's action in revealing the healing power of Serafim brought reassurance that those who struggled against a false enlightenment and revolutionary terror were not forgotten. Serafim had clearly understood the danger of Western rationalism. "In our days . . . ," he once declared, "we are completely estranged from life in Christ. We have lost the simplicity of the early Christians and with our so-called enlightenment we plunge ourselves into dark ignorance. . . ."[5] Were not these words of a penetrating and prophetic mind particularly relevant in 1903? By choosing "poor Serafim" to be numbered among the choir of saints, God was making His glory known to men and women, an auspicious sign of continuing care and concern for Russia. "In these holy relics--a new sign of God's mercy and grace toward the Russian people and the Orthodox church--as if heaven had opened up, there arose a new man of prayer for us unworthy ones, a new intercessor and intermediary at the throne of the Lord."[6] God's mysterious power found purposeful mediation through the sacred remains of Orthodoxy's saints. Through their relics the invisibly present saints, angels, the Mother of God, the apostles, and Christ himself brought divine power to earth, giving energy and purpose to a Christian people, refreshing them through a feast of communion and fulfilling God's promise for their deliverance.

For Nicholas one essential fact became increasingly clear. His rule was blessed by repeated discoveries and glorifications of saints, whose relics produced so much popular enthusiasm and so many miracles. The numerous canonizations, translations of relics, and reconsecrations of saints were important indications of God's immense mercy and providential concern, because the appearance of saints was not in the first instance a consequence of human action. God was the first giver, whose boundless grace made discovery possible and bestowed on the present generation a sense of protection and pardon, an amnesty from sin, and moods of public confidence in an unsteady world. The glorifications of Feodosii of Uglich, Serafim of Sarov, Metropolitan Pavel of Tobolsk, Pitirim of Tambov, Kuksha, apostle to the Viatichi, Patriarch Germogen, Evfrosiniia of Polotsk, Ioasaf of Belgorod, and Anna of Kashinsk were tangible means to perceive God's confidence in the Russian faithful. That Nicholas and the royal family very early understood the meaning of God's steady supply of remains of the holy dead was a mark of their piety, disturbing as the repeated acts of God's grace might be to timorous bishops of the Church's Most Holy Governing Synod. "I remember during a session of the Holy Synod," Metropolitan of Volynia Antonii (Khrapovitskii) later recalled, "how one of the hierarchs observed that they could not endlessly continue to glorify saints. The gaze of those present turned on me, and I replied: 'If we believe in God, then we must be joyous at the glorification of these holy ones pleasing to God.' From this one can see . . . how much greater was the piety of the Sovereign, who was almost the first to make up his mind in the matter."[7]

The hermitage of Sarov and its allied convent at Diveevo were placed in a setting of peace and beauty, with waters flowing in the small Sarovka River and trees rustling in the warm July days. For the imperial couple it was a definite break from the rigidities of the court and the capital; they could be engulfed in the vast tranquillity of the Sarov monks and nuns, who lived quiet lives of prayer and contemplation, doing simple agricultural work and icon painting to support themselves. One can understand how the beautiful shrine could encourage the empress in her hopes that God, through the prayers of Serafim, might heal her anxieties and aid her in becoming pregnant with a male heir to the throne. After giving birth to four girls--Olga, Tatiana, Maria, and Anastasia--and undergoing the humiliation of a "psychosomatic" pregnancy, the empress and her husband feared they could not produce a son.[8] It was a cause of constant worry and shame to a woman on whom such a solemn obligation had been placed; hers was a private guilt with public consequences, and she had come to Sarov to wrestle with it.

By the time the royal entourage arrived at Arzamas, nearly half a million pilgrims had already reached the monastery along roads clogged with the sick and poor coming to see the ceremony canonizing the saint, kiss the holy relics, perhaps experience a miracle of healing and forgiveness, and take advantage of the almsgiving that made a shrine enjoying imperial patronage an obvious place for the poor to congregate. For the empress gift-giving at the holy shrine seemed a natural extension of her usual public role in St. Petersburg, where she administered her orthopedic hospital for children at Tsarskoe Selo and directed a school for nurses modeled on the Princess Christian Home in England.

The long distance that the imperial pilgrims and others had to travel was a heightened reminder that by coming to Sarov, they were coming to a holy place, the residence of an invisible person present in the physical remains that had been so carefully washed and prepared for their repose in a new cypress-wood coffin. The mere act of journeying gave a precise gesture of goodwill and solidarity, and for that reason, when Nicholas and Alexandra, as ordinary pilgrims, took communion at the shrine without any attending suite, it produced a powerful and deep feeling of closeness between them and the congregation.[9] A still more affecting and moving intimacy came at Vespers on the day for the Solemnity of Glorification. At six o'clock that evening the deep-pitched cathedral bell sounded the "Blagovest" (Good News) calling the worshippers to the evening service. A hundred thousand pilgrims filled every corner of the monastery cathedrals and square for the most momentous occasion, when for the first time Serafim's relics would be opened as saintly remains ready for popular veneration.

Metropolitan of St. Petersburg Antonii led the royal family and other dignitaries and clergy in a procession into the Cathedral of the Assumption.[10] Inside the dark church candles burned in the hands of the Sarov monks, Diveevo nuns, and all the other worshippers, while the metropolitan's St. Petersburg choir, brought to Sarov for the occasion, sang hymns (*stikhera*) to Serafim and the clergy recited requiem prayers. Taking up the Cross, the metropolitan guided the procession out through the cathedral's western gates into the Church of Saints Zosima and Savvatii, where Serafim's holy remains reposed. Everyone bowed low and the metropolitan censed Serafim's coffin before it was lifted onto the shoulders of Nicholas II and the grand dukes to be carried out of the church.

The moment Serafim's coffin appeared in the open square, a deep silence fell on the crowd, broken only by the sounds of women weeping and lamenting. Peasants scattered bits of linen and skeins of thread along the path in front of the pallbearers, so that afterward they might gather up these precious tokens filled with the grace of the saint and take them home. Halting at the western gates of the Assumption Cathedral, the clergy delivered a prolonged and fervent prayer (*lite*), replicating at Sarov the same prayers as those that have been offered in Jerusalem since the fourth century to accompany processions to the holy places of Palestine. Eventually the procession entered the cathedral and the coffin was carefully placed on a special plinth, while the Bishop of Tambov Innokentii prepared to give a meditation.

What is the message of this grave? the bishop asked. Through God's mercy, he answered, it is the source of heavenly revelation, a witness to God's majestic power, a clear sign of heavenly reward for earthly righteousness, and the cause for the most elevated Christian feelings. Looking directly at Nicholas and Alexandra, he continued, "we all know

that [this coffin] conceals the worthy remains of a righteous one, one
pleasing to the Lord, a man of prayer and ascetic exploit, great in his
simplicity, crowned with modesty and humility, inflamed with Christ's love
for each person."[11] In Serafim's remains "we acknowledge the profound
truth of our holy Orthodoxy. . . . In the relics of this new man of prayer for
our Russian church we sense the pulse of life in our church. For it is not
dead, it has not grown cold or turned to stone; rather the church that is
adorned with new and righteous saints lives, grows ever younger, and
blossoms. . . . In these holy remains are a new sign of the mercy and grace
of God toward the Russian people and the Orthodox church, for in the
unfolding of the heavens a new man of prayer, a new intermediary and
intercessor for us unworthy ones, stands at the altar of the Lord . . . , and
in the tender joy of our faith, under the impress of his wondrous image, we
sing to him: 'we glorify thee, righteous father Serafim.' Amen."[12]

With Innokentii's sermon concluded, Metropolitan Antonii slowly lifted
the cover from the coffin. Everyone fell to their knees. This was the most
solemn moment. The fiery lights of the candles suddenly flickered at the
shock of deep sound coming from the great cathedral bells, producing an
intense feeling of spiritual triumph. Then all at once the entire church burst
out with the words of Serafim's magnification:

> We magnify
> We magnify thee
> Holy Blessed Serafim
> And we honor thy holy memory
> for you pray for us
> To Christ, our God.

The ceremony echoed throughout the empire, for the Holy Synod had
ordered a special liturgy for Serafim in all of Russia's Orthodox churches
on that same evening.[13]

The pilgrimage of the royal couple to Sarov climaxed a decade of
growing religious militancy and aroused mystical feeling that had inspired
patriotism and new directions for the monarchy. In the second half of the
nineteenth century Russia was a revisionist Great Power, trying to undo the

reduced role the West European nations had assigned it after the defeat in the Crimean War, and for complex reasons Nicholas II sought support and reassurance for the reign in traditional Orthodox values and Western pietist, mystical, and nationalist ideas, a combination very reminiscent of Alexander I's "spiritual mobilization" in the early part of the century. Nicholas's core beliefs deeply affected his rule, and they were far more militantly active ideas than has usually been recognized.[14]

Serafim's canonization concentrated in one event Nicholas and Alexandra's religious searchings during the first decade of the reign, expressing an outlook that combined a belief in the emperor's special place as head of a revitalized "holy Russia" and a divinely consecrated religious, cultural, and political mission to Asia. In this regard, it is important to notice the number of prominent personalities at Serafim's glorification who also played a major role in creating a new viceroyalty for the Far East, a step often seen as the most important cause for the outbreak of the Russo-Japanese War in January 1904. Nicholas's "mystical activism," which under other circumstances might have remained confined to his private life and worship, instead became the filter through which he viewed the world and how to deal with it. It defined his personal direction of the reign, giving it his own unique stamp, linking religion and politics in ways that directly affected imperial policies and the fate of the empire. For Nicholas, the glory of the reign and the glorification of the holy and humble man of God were somehow mysteriously connected.

The official inquiry into Serafim's sanctity first began in 1892, when a special commission appointed by the Holy Synod made an investigation into the holy elder's life and miracles. Three years later the bishop of Tambov reported to the Holy Synod that the commission had examined ninety-four cases of miracles performed with the aid of prayers for Serafim's intercession, and that these cases were only a fraction of the actual number of reported incidents. Nonetheless, the synod decided that more precise information should be gathered in these other cases and directed the abbot of Sarov to collect detailed evidence on the most remarkable ones and report on them to the bishop of Tambov. Twice in 1897 the Tambov bishop submitted copies of written statements of healings and miracles, but the synod found the moment not "timely" to proceed.[15] Still, it encouraged

the Sarov abbot to continue his efforts. In the meantime, the Sarov
hermitage reissued its official *Life of the Elder Serafim* (1893), and Father
Leonid Chichagov (later Bishop Serafim) published the memoirs and
testimony of Serafim's contemporaries, the monks of Sarov, the nuns of
Diveevo, and Serafim's friends, such as Mikhail Manturov and Nikolai
Motovilov.[16] Their stories and accounts form most of what is known about
the actual life and ministry of Serafim.

Leonid's work takes on new importance when one looks at the author's
somewhat surprising background as a young and vigorous officer in the
Russian army before he became an Orthodox priest. Leonid, the grandson
of the famous Admiral P. V. Chichagov, was born in 1856, the year the
Treaty of Paris concluded the Crimean War, a treaty that gave "little
gratification to Russian *amour propre.*"[17] He distinguished himself as an
officer in the Russo-Turkish War of 1877-78. His memoirs of the prowess
and courage of the Russian soldiers in the Danubian army pleased
Alexander II, who urged him to write more about the glories of the Russian
army in wartime. However, his experience in the Russo-Turkish War must
have shown him firsthand the army's technical and organizational
limitations, particularly when compared with the growing military might of
Germany, then already claiming military superiority over both Russia and
France. During the 1880s, he studied advanced military technology in
France (writing a manual on artillery that won him the Legion of Honor)
and then went to Bulgaria to reequip and modernize Prince Alexander's
army. It may be that in Bulgaria he consciously began to link Russia's
military and foreign policies with the Orthodox cause, a fairly common
sentiment in the Russian army in the Balkans and among the Russian public
at that time.

Suddenly in 1891, at age thirty-five, he retired from a successful army
career and, under the influence of Father John of Kronstadt's dynamic
ministry in St. Petersburg, he prepared for two years to become an
Orthodox priest. His new vocation, however, kept him in close contact
with military circles. He soon founded the Society of the White Cross for
the care of the children of army officers, and in 1895 he became the priest
of the military department of Moscow's military district.[18] As a widower,
Leonid took monastic vows in 1898, taking the name Serafim, inspired by

the elder of Sarov. During these years he collected and prepared the materials needed for a synodal investigation into Serafim's sanctity and for the subsequent canonization, if the synod approved. For his key role in the later ceremonies at Sarov, Nicholas II personally rewarded him with an expensive mitre. He became bishop of Sukhum in 1905.[19]

Leonid's background, career, and activities seem to have produced the same amalgam of military patriotism and piety that drew many contemporary French Catholics to the support of the royalist Action Française: maintenance of the national heritage, salvation of the Fatherland, and defense of monarchy. Coincidentally, perhaps, the founder of Action Française, Charles Maurras, a Catholic sympathizer, favored canonizing saints chosen "by the people," particularly Joan of Arc, whose canonization Maurras strongly supported at the same time Leonid was building the case for Serafim in Russia.[20] Joan of Arc had a high symbolic value to conservative French nationalists during the violent and protracted Dreyfus affair (1894-1906) and during the discussions leading to the disestablishment of the Church of France by the "Separation" of powers made law in December 1905. For many, Joan of Arc represented the native virtues that made France distinctive as a nation; her natural qualities also nostalgically recalled a lost paternalistic agricultural harmony and social hierarchy. For the enemies of Dreyfus, Joan symbolized the absolute authority of the state, as represented by the king, whom she so faithfully served, whatever his shortcomings. She upheld the idea of a fatherland defended by faith, military strength, and established order.

The movement to canonize Serafim did not depend on Leonid alone, and according to Sergei Witte, then minister of finance, decisive support in the matter came from Philippe Nizer-Vachot of Lyon ("Dr. Philippe"), who had gained a brief ascendancy over the tsar and tsarina because he claimed as a mesmerist and vitalist to be able to determine the sex of an unborn child. In a conversation with Father John of Kronstadt at the dacha of the Grand Duke Peter Nikolaevich near Peterhof, Philippe apparently urged a campaign for Serafim's canonization. In Lyon he had belonged to a circle of French nationalists who were outraged over the Dreyfus affair (a group which also included Count Valerian Murav'ev-Amurskii (b. 1861), a member of the Russian general staff and the younger brother of N. V.

Murav'ev, the Russian minister of justice).[21] Philippe saw in Serafim a
figure analogous to Joan of Arc, a woman whose pure and innocent life
challenged French secularity and revolutionary movements. He had
championed Joan's cause at a time when it was being pressed hard in
Rome.[22] The plan of Philippe and John of Kronstadt was well timed;
according to one report the empress had just been reading a biography of
Serafim. Over-procurator of the Holy Synod Pobedonostsev was invited to
breakfast at the palace, where Nicholas asked him to appoint a day for
celebrating Serafim as a saint.

According to Witte (who relates the episode as Pobedonostsev recounted
it to him), the over-procurator balked at the imperial intrusion into the
affairs of the Holy Synod, pointing out that saints are announced only after
a detailed investigation of a person, who by his holy life draws popular
attention to himself. The empress, listening to Pobedonostsev's objections,
pointedly observed, "the Sovereign can do anything." That evening
Nicholas sent the over-procurator a note agreeing that procedures must be
followed, and even though the matter could not be done immediately,
Serafim must be made a saint in the following year.[23] It is most unlikely
that Witte's (and Pobedonostsev's) account is entirely accurate in light of
the long delayed investigation in the Synod and the preparatory work
already done by Father Leonid. Moreover, Nicholas knew the procedures
by which saints are canonized in the Russian Orthodox Church. After all,
he had played some role in the canonizing of Saint Feodosii of Uglich in
1896.[24] Yet the story rightly emphasizes the strong personal interest the
emperor and empress took in the matter, an interest that moved them away
from Pobedonostsev's desire to keep religious matters safely within the
orderly flow of synodal business supervised by the over-procurator; and
their new interest also coincided with a departure from Witte's cautious
strategy for uniting economic development with an imperialist foreign
policy.

The religious outlook of Nicholas and Alexandra during the early years
of the century, particularly during the months before Serafim's
canonization, derived from both traditional Orthodoxy and from Western
mystical and pietist influences. As autocrat, Nicholas felt united with his
subjects through the Orthodox rite of his coronation in 1896. "You are

about to enter this ancient sanctuary to place upon your brow the Tsar's crown and to receive the holy oil," the metropolitan of Moscow had told Nicholas on that occasion, standing at the door of the Kremlin's Cathedral of the Assumption: "Your ancestral crown belongs to you alone, as Absolute Tsar, but all Orthodox Christians are worthy of the unction which is given but once. And should you be blessed through this sacrament to perceive a new life, the reason is this--that as there is no power higher, so there is no power on earth more arduous than the power of Tsar, no burden so wearisome as the duty of Tsar. Through this visible anointment, may the invisible might of heaven descend upon you to augment your prowess as Tsar and light the way for your autocratic pursuit of the welfare and happiness of your devoted subjects."[25] S. S. Oldenburg, who quotes this passage in his history of the reign, adds that "the coronation ceremony, so wondrous and yet so incomprehensible to most of Russia's intelligentsia, was a profoundly meaningful experience for him. He had been infused with the spirit of Russia since childhood, and this day was like being wed to her."[26]

To "sacrament" was added family example. At the turn of the century the imperial couple lived a life of aroused religious feeling nurtured by the Grand Duke Sergei, the tsar's favorite uncle and governor-general of Moscow, and the Grand Duchess Elizabeth, Sergei's wife and the empress's older sister. During Easter in 1900, both couples concentrated their devotions on the cathedrals and crypts of the Moscow Kremlin, which under the patronage of the Grand Duke and Grand Duchess flourished as a militant center of spiritual and contemplative asceticism. "What a joy it is to us, dear Mama, to prepare for Holy Communion here in the Kremlin, with all its various churches and chapels in the Palaces," Nicholas wrote to Maria Feodorovna that Easter. "We spend the best part of the day visiting them and deciding which church we shall attend for Morning Service or Mass or Evensong. . . . I never knew I was able to reach such heights of *religious* ecstacy as this Lent has brought me to. This feeling is now much stronger than it was in 1896, which is only natural. I am so calm and happy now, and everything here makes for prayer and peace of the spirit."[27]

Through Sergei and Elizabeth, the emperor was in touch with the cult of saints and piety of the Kremlin, a central repository radiating throughout the empire and even reaching the Holy Land. Sergei (he wore around his neck a small golden panagia holding a relic of Saint Arsenii, Russia's famous fourteenth-century ascetic and hesychast) kept contact with Russia's contemplative cloisters, and twice he traveled to the Holy Land to pray at the Tomb of Christ.[28] After taking the lead in forming the Russian Orthodox Palestine Society for promoting Russian pilgrimages to the holy shrines of the Near East, he and his wife personally dedicated the magnificent Church of Mary Magdalene in Gethsemane at the foot of the Mount of Olives. Elizabeth eventually became a nun in the Martha and Mary Convent of Love and Mercy she established in Moscow.

She greatly venerated the memory of Serafim of Sarov, and she and Sergei attended the saint's glorification in 1903. During the Russo-Japanese War she took relics of the reign's newly manifested saints to the sick and wounded in the hospital she founded in Moscow. Once each year she traveled to Russia's holy shrines as far away as Solovki in the far north and Siberia, where a *skete* built in 1914 was dedicated to Saint Elizabeth in her honor. The news of Russia's entry into the First World War reached her at the *skete* of Saints Serafim and Aleksei, a curiously appropriate place for a patriotic grand duchess inspired by the elder of Sarov and the crypt of Moscow's great saint.[29]

After the assassination of Sergei by revolutionary terrorists in 1905, Elizabeth gained Nicholas's permission to have her husband's remains interred in a crypt of the Chudov monastery in the Kremlin, where she later built a church in honor of Saint Sergii of Radonezh, Sergei's patron saint. Elizabeth often went there to pray during the years when Arsenii (Zhadanovskii, 1874-1968), the remarkable young prior of the Chudov monastery, encouraged Moscow's devotional and spiritual life.[30] As a young man, Arsenii had a vision of Saint Aleksei, one of Russia's greatest national saints, while standing at the crypt containing the saint's holy remains in the Chudov monastery.

While we do not know what transpired in the encounter, it reinforced the earlier advice given him by Father John of Kronstadt to pursue a monastic vocation of spiritual outreach to the people. He published *Spiritual Diaries*, a journal of religious direction for the pilgrims who flocked to the Chudov monastery. Tens of thousands of copies of his *Mite*

of the Hermitage of Saint Aleksei circulated throughout Russia, and he
gained a hearing among educated Russians through the journal *Voice of the
Church*, considered at the time to be one of Russia's liveliest theological
monthlies. Arsenii encouraged the Brotherhood of Moscow Saints,
organized to broadcast the miracles performed by the holy remains of saints
in the capital of Old Russia. He also gained fame as a spiritual director for
many admirers. Thus the Moscow Kremlin stimulated a certain religious
militancy and missionary fervor (Arsenii also opened a "branch" of the
Kamchatka Missionary Brotherhood there) dramatized by spectacular and
colorful processions through the city's streets carried out under the banners
of the Kremlin Society of Gonfaloniers dressed in special kaftans and
calling themselves the "Regiment of the Living Christ," as they sought to
lead the life of worship in Moscow's parishes.[31]

Nicholas and Alexandra drew on Western religious inspiration, too,
particularly the Protestantism of the courts of Hesse-Darmstadt and
England, where Alexandra had been raised. Her own strong religious
convictions ("She made her first [Lutheran] communion in the spirit of
absolute abandon to the will of God"),[32] which had obstructed Nicholas's
own ardent hopes of marrying her, were only set aside after Grand Duchess
Elizabeth "was able to assure Alix that the differences between Lutheran
and Orthodox doctrines were not so marked as the language and elaborate
ritual made them seem."[33] This remark stands fully in the mainline of
nearly two centuries of strong Protestant influence on Russian Orthodoxy,
and it also shows the pietism at court that could diminish the importance of
institutional creed and dogma, in favor of a mystical, emotional, and
universalizing religious faith. It is in this light that Alexandra's close
friend Anna Vyrubova needs to be understood when she writes that
Nicholas was a "born mystic," whose faith was "simply Christianity lived
and not merely subscribed to as a theory. They [Nicholas and Alexandra]
believed that prophecy, in the Biblical sense of the word, still existed in
certain highly gifted and spiritually minded persons. They believed that it
was possible outside the church and without the aid of regularly ordained
bishops and priests to hold communion with God and His spirit."[34]

In the winter of 1902-3 before Serafim's canonization, Nicholas and
Alexandra read widely in Western mystical and devotional literature.

Alexandra wrote to William Boyd Carpenter, the late Queen Victoria's court chaplain, that she now gave every spare moment to reading Jacob Boehme and many of the German and Dutch theosophists of the fifteenth and sixteenth centuries: "There are such splendors [in them] and they help one on in life, and make everything so much easier to bear."[35] Somewhat later the empress urged Anna Vyrubova to read *Les Amis des Dieu*, most likely August Jundt's account of the fourteenth-century mystics such as Suso, Ruysbroeck, Rulman Merswin, and the German Dominican Johannes Tauler.[36] In Jundt's presentation, the Friends of God--a select and restricted group of European medieval religious reformers, mostly monks and nuns--pursued a "divine mission" of popular social and spiritual renewal through education by those who believed deeply in the efficacious intercession of the Holy Virgin and saints venerated through their relics. The Friends of God developed an ascetical way of life mirroring the sufferings of the Savior and experienced mystical joy and visions. But Jundt pointed out that the prophetic Friends of God were not confined to the fourteenth century; true successors could be found in the canonizations of Saint John of the Cross, Saint Teresa of Avila, Saint Francis of Sales, Saint Jane Frances of Chantal, and others, indicating a continuing spiritual current.

The royal couple seem to have read Jundt's book as an invitation to surround the Russian throne with their own friends of God. By 1915 Alexandra had come to identify this insight only with Rasputin: "You remember," she told Nicholas, "dans *Les Amis des Dieu* it says, a country cannot be lost whose Sovereign is guided by a man of God's. Oh let Him guide you more."[37] But prior to the arrival of "Our Friend" (Rasputin), such a reading could have applied to several people, including Serafim of Sarov. To their eclectic reading of western Protestant and Catholic devotional writers they added Orthodox contemplative ascetics, Saint John of the Ladder and Ignatii Brianchaninov (1807-67), onetime abbot of the Sergiev hermitage near St. Petersburg, whose own writings about man and the universe were colored by Boehmist concepts.[38]

The Saxon visionary Jacob Boehme's writings about the saints contain language that could be read by the imperial couple as a summons to Christian battle for a religious victory over evil and disorder, a campaign

capable of rallying all--heathen, Jew, and gentile--to the banners of the
Godly marching forward on the way to Christ. His visions could also
provide each individual with a buckler and a shield in the struggle to cast
off the old earthly man tied to the corrupt world and, as a new spiritual
man, follow the inner light emanating directly from the divine substance. In
both instances, those who chose the "way to Christ" took part as Christian
soldiers in the cosmic drive toward universal integration, overcoming the
forces of disharmony. In Boehme, they could find a glimpse into the
mysteries of God, man, and the world. Thus, Boehme's mysticism could be
understood not as a summons to a life of quietism and withdrawal, but to a
dynamic interaction between the seekers of the Light and the world. This is
apparent as well in what Boehme says about the saints, those who have
constantly desired God and suffered for His truth, rejoicing in the future,
and praying, thinking, and working for their neighbors. One reaches the
saint through faith; faith, not the saint, works miracles. When we penetrate
to those resting in the bosom of Abraham, we do not obtain their
Petitioning of God on our behalf ("our salvation does not depend on their
begging"). They react upon the faith of the good and pure. "Thus some
wonderful works have been accomplished by invoking their [the saints']
memory." One faith grasps the other. The faith of the living catches that of
the saints, and the faith performs the miracle. "Faith can overcome
mountains. It could destroy the world if God were so to direct it."[39]

In this universal struggle with the horror of hell, the truly faithful,
regardless of sect or creed, race or confession, may count on not only the
divine principle of love, but also on Christ, the "warrior in battle," who has
the power to "bruise the head of the serpent," for God has made a covenant
with all mankind. "Only the children of wrath must be excepted, because in
them the incorporation of the name *Jesus* does not take place, but only the
incorporation of wrath. The latter, however, never extended over whole
races, but merely over such individuals among them as are like thistles
among the wheat."[40]

Combined with Tauler's constant comforting lament about the world's
wrongs inflicted upon the chosen lovers of God, Boehme could provide a
true and reassuring Christianity able to draw upon the spiritual resources of
Orthodoxy's saints for the spiritual development of the inner person,

preparing him or her for active battle with the world. "When the Lord
blamed Martha," Tauler told the nuns of the Dominican houses he
supervised in the Rhineland, "it was not because she was working. What he
blamed her for was over-anxiety." In an age of anxiety and rising danger
from enemies abroad and revolutionaries at home, such mystical reflection
lent a steadying confidence to Christian soldiers, guided by the "warrior in
battle." "What joy if in any small way we can help another wanderer bear
his heavy cross or give him courage to battle bravely on!" Alexandra wrote
Boyd Carpenter in January 1903: "My new country is so vast that there is
no lack of work to be done. Thank God the *people* are very religious,
simple-minded, childlike and with boundless love for their Sovereign and
faith in him; so that bad elements and influences take a time before rooting
amongst them. But much patience and energy are needed to fight against the
wave of discontent which has arisen and spreads itself all over the world--is
not the End soon coming?"[41]

Perhaps because Nicholas saw the vastness of his work as Alexandra
saw it, Serafim's glorification seemed still more justified and compelling as
it appeared more effective, particularly after that "great never-to-be-
forgotten day when the mercy of God" visited the royal family with a
son.[42] "As concerns the sanctity and miraculousness of Saint Serafim,"
Nicholas told Prince Obolenskii not long afterward, "in this I am already so
convinced that no one will ever shake my conviction. I have unarguable
proof for it."[43] The tsar hung a large portrait of Serafim on the wall of his
cabinet, and those among his officials who took part in the pilgrimage to
Sarov subsequently enjoyed the tsar's favor, particularly Witte's great rival
V. K. von Plehve, who now found himself the most powerful of Nicholas's
ministers supporting a policy that might lead to a "short victorious war" in
the Far East.[44] Prince Shirinskii-Shikhmatov, procurator of the Moscow
Synodal Office, who along with Father Leonid had been in charge of
preparing for the opening of Serafim's remains, became governor of Tver
and then briefly (for seventy-two days) over-procurator of the Holy Synod
during the Goremykin cabinet. Serafim (Fr. Leonid) became a bishop.

Nicholas's belief in the power of Serafim to unite tsar and people into
one purposeful whole seems to have given him the confidence and the

courage to carry forward "holy Russia's" religious and imperial mission in Asia. According to one recent historian of the "Far Eastern Question," it is clear that "the pilgrimage [to Sarov] was a profound experience for Nicholas II, and that it had repercussions which were political as well as religious. The tsar returned to Saint Petersburg determined, apparently, to move resolutely, and to take up the reins of government himself."[45] Following Serafim's glorification at Sarov in mid-July, Nicholas resisted the advice of Witte, A. N. Kuropatkin, Russia's war minister, and Count V. N. Lamsdorf, the foreign minister, who urged him to step back from a boldly assertive Far Eastern policy. Instead, on July 30 the government suddenly announced the formation of a "Viceroyalty of the Far East," including Port Arthur and northern Manchuria. Even Plehve apparently learned of the tsar's decision only two days earlier; Witte and Kuropatkin claimed they were caught completely unaware.

Serafim's canonization reassured the emperor that the burdens he had carried ever since the sacrament of his coronation anointment continued to be eased by God's divine support. Serafim became a kind of guardian saint for those who would protect the empire's eastern edge. Immediately after the outbreak of the Russo-Japanese War, Sarov became a place of special pilgrimage for soldiers, especially officers, setting out for the Far East. They came from all over European Russia, from Kursk and Moscow, from Tambov and the South, and from Warsaw and Lodz in Poland. Parents of soldiers in combat against Japan felt a duty to visit the hermitage to ask Serafim's protection for their sons.[46] This was the unofficial equivalent of the traditional visit by Russia's wartime military leaders to Saint Sergii of Radonezh's holy remains to pray for victory, just as Prince Dmitrii Donskoi had asked Sergii's blessing in 1380 on his way to defeat the Mongols. "From that time onward," Minister Kuropatkin was reminded when he journeyed to Sergii's crypt in February 1904, "our holy Orthodox Rus' has stood on sacred guard for the entire Christian world in the view of the pagan East, and Saint Sergii stands on guard for Rus' itself."[47] Significantly, Serafim's portrait was included along with those of Sergii and the Archangel Michael in the small silver triptych presented by the clergy to Kuropatkin for the protection of the Russian army. Nicholas and Alexandra regularly distributed icons of Serafim to the troops being sent to the front.

The tsar also subscribed to the prophecies attributed to Serafim that began to circulate after the canonization, claiming that Russia would soon go to war with Japan and that a victorious peace would be signed in Tokyo. Nicholas referred to the prophecy when he sent Admiral Rozhdestvenskii and the Baltic fleet to break the Japanese siege of Port Arthur in 1904, confident that he would be able to reverse the unfavorable course of the war. "After all," Witte records with sarcastic bitterness, "Serafim of Sarov had prophesied that peace would be concluded in Tokyo, which means only Jews [*Zhidy*] and the intelligentsia might think differently. . . ."[48]

Yet the religious elements in the decision to create a viceroyalty in the war-threatened Far East had additional underpinnings, and Nicholas's Sarov experience should not be seen in isolation from the militant religious and imperialist atmosphere in St. Petersburg and the Russian Far East around the turn of the century. For many years Nicholas had listened to clergy and other Orthodox spokesmen for Russia's "mission" in Asia. Several of the clergy who were later prominently visible at Serafim's glorification also advocated a Russian Orthodox role in the East. Archpriest Filosof Ornatskii, a member of metropolitan of St. Petersburg Antonii's delegation to Sarov, had once served in the Russian Orthodox mission to Japan. In 1889 he published a book about the mission, arguing that the Japanese, despite their "oldness" as a people, nonetheless mentally and physically preserved the "boldness and freshness" suited to future missionaries "for all Mongolian Asia, beginning with neighboring China and India."[49] To do so, however, they needed the saving faith of Orthodoxy. The Catholics, he felt, had shown they could not bring Christianity to the Japanese because they became entangled in Japanese politics, thereby drawing on Christianity the suspicion that it teaches opposition to authority and foments popular hostility to the government.[50] Those who took part in or supported the Orthodox mission did this great deed not only for the good of their souls but "for their entire motherland, a mighty deed for Orthodox Rus'.--From the Orient comes light! Holy Rus', the faithful and mighty repository of eastern Orthodoxy, must enlighten with the holy faith the still benighted peoples of the East." The Japanese, so well suited to receive the faith, could serve as Russia's best intermediary to the Far East, a role that deserved the support of both the Russian church and the Russian government.[51]

Later, as a very popular preacher in St. Petersburg, Ornatskii promoted such ideas through the Society for the Extension of Religious-Moral Enlightenment in the Spirit of the Orthodox Church. This was Russia's "first school of preaching," where young preachers, not as individual "soldiers," but in alliance with the entire Society, which had already "conquered the people's dispositions," entered into a living community with the national soul as its guide to the future."[52] Father Ianyshev, confessor of the royal family, served for many years as chairman of the Society, which drew its spiritual nourishment from the Valaamo monastery on Lake Ladoga. The Society's founder, M. I. Sokolov, referred to the first members as "Valaamo She-Asses," doing the donkey labor of carrying the Word into the world.[53] Valaamo had long been associated with the mission to the Far East, its monks being the first missionaries to Alaska at the end of the eighteenth century. Thus, it is significant, first, that Ornatskii gave his detailed report about the canonization at Sarov to this particular organization when he returned to the capital after the ceremony and, second, that he reminded the younger preachers of Serafim's words: "Sow in good soil, sow in sand, sow among the rocks, sow along the roads, sow among the tares. Everything will sprout somewhere and grow, and will bring forth fruit, although not quickly."[54] Bishop of Iamburg Sergii (Stragorodskii, the future patriarch of Russia during the Stalin years) also urged the members of the Society to be inspired by the Sarov events he had witnessed in the summer. Although in 1903 Sergii served as rector of the St. Petersburg Theological Academy, as a young man under the influence of the elders of Valaamo, he had become a monk and set off in 1890 to be a missionary to Japan. He briefly served as Nicholas's chaplain on board the ship *Memory of Azov* on the Asian leg of his round-the-world journey in 1891. When he later returned to St. Petersburg, he worked diligently for the Orthodox mission in the Far East, but by that time the focus had shifted from Japan to China.

Thus the spiritual currents of the nineteenth century, which gathered their energy from Russia's hermitages and holy shrines in order to reach out and heal the divisions in society, also nourished Orthodoxy's foreign missions. Preaching that drew on the spiritual resources of the cloisters and shrines--on Valaamo and Sarov, for example--attempted to reach beyond the disaffected (such as Russia's Old Believers, sectarians, and many workers of the empire's new industrial cities) to non-Christian Asia. It is instructive to realize that the first foreign language accounts of Serafim's life and glorification were written in Japanese by Akil Kadzim for distribution in Japan's Orthodox churches.[55] In any case, it is not surprising that just after the Japanese surprise attack on Port Arthur in January 1904, Ornatskii and several other prominent St. Petersburg preachers, including Father John of Kronstadt, sent a telegram to Nicholas praying for God's help for the emperor and for Russia in this difficult time and encouraging him with the news that they had just consecrated a new St. Petersburg chapel in honor of Serafim of Sarov.[56]

The connection between the ascetic cloister and the eastern mission found another advocate at court in the Buriat Mongol convert to Orthodoxy, Petr A. Badmaev, whose godfather had been Alexander III. Badmaev had attended the Irkutsk Theological Seminary, the center of the Orthodox mission in eastern Siberia, and the place where Nicholas, as heir apparent (*tsesarevich*) completing his Asian journey, had been told that 250 Buriats wished to accept holy baptism. Nicholas learned of this "desire" immediately after worshipping in the Voskresenskii monastery at the shrine of Saint Innokentii, the pioneer ascetic missionary to the Siberian lands. Allegedly, all the men among the converts wanted to take the name "Nikolai" in honor of the heir apparent's "unprecedented visit to the East."[57] In St. Petersburg, Badmaev later enjoyed the patronage of Sergei Witte for his efforts to promote Russia's expansion in Asia, a concern Badmaev combined with a growing experimentation in physical healing by the use of Tibetan herbs.[58] Thus one can see in Badmaev's background and skills some of the same features that were of interest to the royal family in the life and miracles of Serafim of Sarov. As recently noted, ". . . it was as de facto court physician that he made himself indispensable. His friendship with Nicholas lasted longer than that of any other court favorite, including Rasputin himself. . . ."[59]

Badmaev's writings on Orthodox Russia in Asia, scattered in various essays and letters published in the 1890s, were assembled in a single

pamphlet entitled *Russia and China*, and published in July 1900 at the
height of the Boxer Rebellion in China.[60] "From time immemorial," he
argued, "the people of Asia have sought protection, defense, friendship,
and subjugation by Russia. They have related with enthusiasm to the ruling
house in Russia, as they do today. Like Russian subjects, non-Russians and
foreigners in the East call the Russian tsar the White Tsar-knight." The
tsar's great authority, he said, for centuries was based on the evangelical
purity found in the lives and works of Russia's great Orthodox ascetics,
especially those associated with Moscow: Petr, Aleksei, and Sergii of
Radonezh. The Mongols were overcome by the Muscovite grand princes,
he explained, because they were armed with the higher religious-cultural
ideal provided by these ascetical saints. Russia subsequently succeeded in
extending its power and influence into Siberia, peacefully assimilating non-
Russian peoples because the natives of the region saw they could get justice
and protection from Russian rulers guided by such holy men, while
preserving their own customs, mores, and beliefs. Of course, Russia's
monarchs vigorously promoted Orthodoxy, but not by force.[61]

While Badmaev admitted that some Russian bureaucrats and
missionaries did not always understand Russia's selfless and nonexploitative
approach to the East, he explained that European prophets of national
separation among the peoples of the empire had misguided them. But those
same Europeans had never created anything but kingdoms of plunder in
Asia and could never stand as champions of "human rights" there, whereas
the "White Tsar" could do so by preparing the soil of the East for the
successful extension of Orthodoxy and the acquisition of Russian culture.
What was relevant for Muscovy in dealing with the Mongols in the
fourteenth century was just as pertinent for the Russian Empire confronted
by all of Mongolian Asia at the outset of the twentieth century.[62] Thus,
operating in the spirit of Orthodoxy and the evangelical truths embodied in
the lives of Russia's saints, Russian railroad developers and traders could
strengthen the empire's influence in the Far East. But without that true
Christian spirit, Russia would be unable to assimilate Mongolia, Tibet, and
China, even though those peoples were devoted to the ideal of paternal
autocracy and would submit to the autocrat's representatives, whom "*they
regard as elder sons and brothers, morally answerable for everything,*

*both before the father-monarch and before the younger brothers--his
subjects.*"[63]

Such thinking about Orthodoxy and Russia's Asian mission provides
some of the background for understanding Admiral Fedor Dubasov's
decision in 1898 to build a new Orthodox cathedral on the highest
promontory of Port Arthur immediately after Russia occupied the city. No
one could mistake the symbolism, for Dubasov was the commander of
Russia's Pacific Ocean naval squadron and chief director of the newly
annexed Kwantung Peninsula. His wife, Aleksandra Dubasova, undertook
the work of designing the cathedral's iconostasis. Empress Alexandra
quickly became the special patron of the project, which drew collaborators
from the army and navy. When her husband was transferred to St.
Petersburg, Aleksandra Dubasova also relocated the iconostasis work there
in a special room provided by the naval ministry in the Admiralty, where
the workers met on Tuesdays and Fridays during the winter of 1901-2. The
empress reviewed the ornamental gilding that had been done on the oaken
framework, and decided to work on three frames for the icons that would be
placed directly over the "Royal Doors" of the iconstasis. "Her August
Majesty," one journal of the time reported, "thus continues the custom
coming down from our ancient tsaritsas and grand princesses. Russia's
monasteries and cathedrals preserve in shrouds and icons numerous works
by royal hands. The Christian devotion of wives and daughters of our
sovereigns is incarnate in the holy succession from ancient days, and in the
Far East appears one of the examples of this spiritual continuity."[64] The
empress's decoration for the imposing cathedral in Russia's newest Far
Eastern military base can thus be seen as a symbol of the close relationship
between religion and politics during the period.

Saint Serafim's glorification and the royal couple's role in bringing it
about are best understood in the context of Russia's religious life at the
beginning of the twentieth century. That the crypt of Serafim of Sarov
could become a focus of public attention with implications for the domestic
and foreign policies of the empire is an indication of a resurgent and
revitalized Orthodoxy. As Bishop Innokentii of Tambov noted in his
meditation, in Serafim's holy remains one could sense the pulse of life in
the Russian church. That life found nourishment in a variety of sources,

including Russia's growing awareness of its particular place and lofty purpose in a modern world increasingly interconnected, homogenized, and impersonalized by the Great Powers. The question about what role Russia might play in this modern world found an answer in Orthodoxy's holy shrines and saintly relics that could promote a stronger sense of God's continuing mercy and providential concern. When people of all social classes and all ages dressed as pilgrims and tramped throughout Russia's own "northern Thebaid" or to the far-off holy land of Palestine, Egypt, and Mount Athos, as they did in rapidly growing numbers in the late nineteenth century, they could see themselves as part of some larger drama; they were conscious that in the core values of their faith they could find a resolution of the tension between themselves and Russia's two centuries of experience with a Western-oriented enlightenment.

For many Orthodox, that enlightenment left a haunting sense of the great distance between their world and God's heavenly kingdom. Modern Orthodoxy tried to shorten this distance by redoubling its concentration on the traditional intermediary points of contact. The relics of the saints and the sacred shrines--along with the intercession of the Holy Mother of God and the thaumaturgy of holy icons--served as bridges spanning the wide abyss separating God and humanity. Cloistered men and women, particularly the remarkable nineteenth-century Russian "elders" (*startsy*) like Serafim, who gave spiritual direction to thousands every day, provided by their lives of prayer a linking force that placed human beings into intimate contact with God. They were considered the majestic assertion of true order and righteousness in a divided and disorderly world. Through these intermediaries Orthodoxy could, in the religious view of that time, join high and low, Russian and non-Russian, town and country, young and old in a way that no other element in imperial society was capable of doing.

At the same time, as the religious views of Nicholas and Alexandra make clear, this renewing of the spirit had complex veins, even reaching into Western Protestant and Catholic mysticism and pietism. Consequently, the event at Sarov cannot be seen merely as a simple reproduction of a medieval drama or as the result of lingering medieval "survivals" that had no place in the modern world. Moreover, canonization of new saints was not confined to Russia, and the parallel example of Joan of Arc in France suggests the protean ways in which traditional religious elements can be adapted to new settings and requirements. The fine threads that interwove in popular and royal imaginations the numerous miraculous cures and healings at Serafim's shrine and the cures of such court healers as "Dr. Philippe" or the Buriat herbalist Badmaev also suggest a complex picture of modernity that has remained unexplored by those who study the rise of Russia's modern medicine.[65] That such "healers" appeared in many European countries at the same time requires a larger explanation than simply that of Russia's persisting medieval culture.

Serafim's glorification at a critical moment in Russia's national awakening and imperialist militancy cannot be considered a coincidence. The event projected a new solidarity that was as patriotic as it was spiritual. In the new community claimed by those who clustered around the Sarov shrine, there was ample room for both the modern soldiers of the spirit and modern soldiers of the empire. The impulses generated at the shrines found ready outlet in patriotic assemblies and military demonstrations.[66] This was the age, after all, when naval ships were named *The Twelve Apostles*, *Saint John Chrysostom*, and *Saint Theodore Strailite*.

It was at the christening of a battleship in the summer of 1903 that Nicholas decided to remove Witte's restraining influences in his Far Eastern policy. On that occasion Nicholas allegedly said, "the Lord put into my heart the thought that I must not delay that which I was already persuaded to do."[67] And it was also the age of religious missions fed by the great centers of monastic sanctity: Chudov, Holy Trinity-St. Sergii Lavra, Valaamo, and Sarov, among many others. Finally, it was for Tsar Nicholas II an age of convergence between his divinely inspired reign and the divinely discovered sanctity of Serafim of Sarov. In the words of the Psalmist (135), as read in the emperor's presence at Serafim's glorification: "Praise ye the Lord. . . . For the Lord hath chosen Jacob unto himself, *and* Israel for his peculiar treasure." Judging by Nicholas's subsequent behavior and actions following the pilgrimage to Sarov, the Psalmist's words carried a double meaning.

CHAPTER 12

THE DEBATE OVER INSTRUCTION OF MUSLIMS
IN POST-1905 RUSSIA: A LOCAL PERSPECTIVE

Edward J. Lazzerini

"No aspect of our domestic life is subject to so many complications
and all sorts of manipulations as is the question of public
education."
— V. D. Smirnov[1]

"It is first necessary to educate the people. Once educated, they will
find the path for themselves. . . ."
—Ismail Bey Gasprinskii[2]

"The goal of educating all the *inorodtsy* who inhabit the Russian
Empire is unquestionably their Russification and assimilation
[*sliianie*] with the Russian people."
— Council of the Ministry of Education[3]

For three days, from August 25 to 27, 1908, a group of forty-two men
gathered in Simferopol under the auspices of the Tavrida provincial zemstvo
board.[4] The board convened this conference as a result of meetings held in
the Evpatoriia, Perekop, Simferopol, and Yalta districts of the province.
Each of those gatherings had focused on one of the Russian Empire's most
divisive social issues: the education of ethnoreligious minorities.

In Tavrida province, despite the heterogeneity of its population and the
decades-long demographic shift favoring immigrant groups, a single people
garnered nearly all of the board's attention: the Crimean Tatars.
Turkic-speaking and Muslim, they had from the fourteenth century until
1783 dominated the region, shaping its political, social, economic, and
cultural character. Since the Russian conquest in 1783, the Tatars had
experienced profound changes in their traditional way of life and had seen

their number dwindle by half, to 190,514 according to the 1897 census.[5] Yet, notwithstanding diminished size and their reduction to the legal status of *inorodtsy* ("others") within an expanding Great Russian and Orthodox Christian empire, the Crimean Tatars continued to treat the peninsular portion of Tavrida province where almost all Tatars were clustered as rightfully theirs. For their publicly expressed complaints and aspirations, whose chorus was approaching a critical stage by the turn of the twentieth century, they received an attentive, respectful hearing from many local Russian compatriots, including some in positions of authority.

Of the many social issues confronting the Tatar community by 1908, education was most important. Part of the explanation for this can be found in the turn toward modernism that some of the native intelligentsia advocated. Since the early 1880s, Ismail Bey Gasprinskii, a local but widely influential proponent of syncretism between the modernist discourse shaping contemporary Western societies and the moral teachings and cultural heritage of Islam, had made educational reform central to a grand project that would, he hoped, ensure the future prosperity and dignity of his co-religionists everywhere.[6] By the time of the Simferopol conference, in which he participated, Gasprinskii had already dedicated nearly thirty years to matters of instruction and teacher training, having been moved to the challenge of educational reform by his experiences as a young man:

> For several years I was in the teaching profession, and [during that
> time] I became intimately acquainted with conditions in the Russian
> schools and Muslim *mektebs*. [In the latter] the poor students would
> rock at their reading desks for six or seven hours every day for five
> or six years. There were many nights when I was unable to sleep
> because of my bitterness and regret at seeing them deprived of the
> ability to write and of a knowledge of the catechism and other
> matters, and their failure to acquire, in the end, little more than a
> talent for repeating an Arabic phrase.[7]

For education alone, the results of his inspiration were dramatic, including: (1) creation of the first *jadid* (reformed, or "new method") *mekteb* (primary school) in Bakhchisarai in 1884, which spawned thousands of imitators across Muslim Russia by the second decade of the twentieth century; (2) establishment of reformed *medresses* (higher institutions for religious training) in such traditional Muslim cultural centers as Bakhchisarai, Kazan, and Ufa; (3) enrollment of growing numbers of Muslim youth in every type of Russian educational institution at every level; (4) increased willingness by Muslims to study the Russian language; and (5) encouragement of Muslim women in educational pursuits typically reserved for males.

In addition to such trends developing within the Tatar community, intermittent but often substantial government efforts to "improve" the organization and results of education involving minorities (especially Muslims) contributed no small portion to the public debate over educational matters. In 1870, for example, after several years of discussions involving numerous commissions, institutions, and experts in the provinces as well as the capital, the Ministry of Education issued new regulations that would remain official policy into the early twentieth century.[8] Along with other measures promulgated over the next several decades, these regulations made bluntly clear that the tsarist government's objectives in providing education to minority nationalities in the Russian Empire was to Russify them and, in consort with the Russian Orthodox Church, convert them to Orthodoxy. These policies, and the schools they spawned, justified the worst fears the Tatars and other minorities had for their cultural survival.

Once again, after the turn of the century, imperial interests stimulated another major outburst of attention to the subject, producing a new round of debates culminating in the Regulations of 1906-1907. Their conclusions reverberated in many of the "eastern" provinces, stimulating conferences like the one in Simferopol, whose deliberations and resolutions present the historian with a case study of the difficulties of introducing mass education without destroying cultural and spiritual values among peoples on the periphery of the Russian Empire.

The conference had as its principal goal the discussion of primary education for Tatars, although reference to more advanced learning was inevitable. Its agenda numbered twelve items, ranging from language of instruction to the place of religion in the curriculum, the preparation and distribution of textbooks, schooling for girls, teacher training, and the relationship between confessional and public schools. Several participants read reports during the conference, but Reshid Mediev delivered what amounted to a keynote address on the general topic of "The Contemporary Situation of Tatar Primary Schools."[9] It was hardly congratulatory or optimistic as it assessed the strengths and weaknesses of the various types of schools available to educate the province's native children: state-supervised institutions that were still administered essentially on the basis of the regulations of 1870; zemstvo-sponsored schools; and *mektebs*, *medresses*, and *mekteb-rushties* (the last of these were teacher-training institutions) that were supervised by the Tavrida Muslim Ecclesiastical Administration or private organizers.

Conditions appeared desperate, and not just to Mediev. All assembled seemed to agree that most schools were "deplorable" and "incompetent." To be sure, some were worse than others. The "old method" *mektebs*, for example, relying on a pedagogy that stressed rote memorization, staffed by ill-trained and narrow-minded mullahs, set within unhygienic surroundings, and saddled with an impractical curriculum, were justifiably condemned as unsuitable to "modern" conditions and as obstacles to progress (although many would argue elsewhere that "modern" conditions were irrelevant to the purposes of the *mektebs*). The schools that thrived most were the "new method" *mektebs*, which as if to contradict Gresham's law, were driving out their more tradition-spirited competitors. Employing modern methods of language instruction, encouraging the study of secular subjects, and advocating a commitment to the future more than to the past, they certainly were different. Yet they too were grossly underfunded, poorly organized, and inadequately staffed.

As for the so-called Russian-Tatar schools, Tatar attendance had always been paltry. Attendance varied, apparently, depending on whether these schools were administered by the Ministry of Education or the local zemstvos. Thus, while figures are scarce, scattered, and frequently contradictory, they suggest that the zemstvos opened more primary schools for the Crimean Tatars than did the state. Even so, the zemstvos opened significantly fewer schools in the five counties of Tavrida province where Tatars were heavily represented than in the three counties with little Tatar population. For 1898, the great chronicler of the zemstvos, B. B. Veselovskii, provides the following data: in Tatar counties the zemstvos built 82 primary schools; in non-Tatar counties, 329.[10]

Resources understandably were limited, and differences in population size may help explain some of this variation. Yet popular Tatar suspicion of the "Russian" spirit that they perceived imbued these institutions was clearly at the heart of the problem. The native Tatar language was ostensibly to be taught in these schools, but rarely was; instead Russian was the language of instruction, and most of the teachers were Russian. Still worse, the Islamic faith and its ethical principles had no chance of being taught at all. Not only did the uneducated, antirationalist masses, easily dismissed as "reactionary" by would-be modernizers, harbor this negative assessment of the Russian-Tatar schools; so too did eminently reasonable, enlightened, and progressive men like Gasprinskii and I. M. Mufti-zade (a member of the State Duma and a conference participant), who sympathized with the popular perceptions regarding schools that were "not ours," and admitted a personal concern for preserving the *mekteb* (albeit reformed) because they firmly believed that ethics and morality must be integral to education. "We owe our humanity and sense of decency to the *mektebs*," declared Mufti-zade. "These schools do not teach knowledge per se, but foster good breeding" (p. 17). That modern knowledge and character were not antithetical was unambiguously acknowledged when Mufti-zade subsequently charged: "I am not an opponent of science, but I have met many educated people who are ill-bred."

Here we have a hint of the most nettlesome dilemma facing the Tatar community in the early years of this century. One could, as did the participants at the Simferopol conference, discuss the innumerable issues relating to education, hoping to make headway with a subject possessing, as Smirnov reminds us, "so many complications." One also could, as Gasprinskii did during the final session (with frustration that virtually leaps off the page), argue that "if we can't teach them everything, at least give them some education"; another delegate, F. N. Andreevskii, made the same complaint: "We cannot wait for the masses who are always inert; we must push forward" (pp. 80, 81).

In the end, all of the issues and complications surrounding education resulted from a failure to find generally acceptable answers to harder questions. What is knowledge, after all, and what are the ends of education? Such questions, perhaps too philosophical for most, have to be answered first and at least by those with authority to influence the larger community, because responses to related matters--if for no other reason than consistency--should flow from their determination. Was education of Tatars primarily for their Russification, for fulfillment of their religious duties, or for their collective attainment of wealth and power?

Such a question is never easily resolved, especially during periods of major social change when consensus is increasingly vulnerable to assault. For Russia as a whole, the early twentieth century was such a period; for a minority like the Tatars, those years were perhaps even more disruptive given the added colonial dimension to their lives.

Thus, from at least two directions (the imperial center and the periphery), two cultural bases (the dominant Great Russian and the minority Tatar), two political positions (the colonial authority and colonized subject), and two discourses (the unassailable "we" and the unspeakable "other"), a small group of men assembled in an out-of-the-way place to uncover a problem, recognize their differences, and attempt to bridge them. To be sure, the record of their deliberations reveals divisions of opinion over the many issues on the agenda before them. On the other hand, that same record demonstrates several facets of the larger Russian context that suggest the different paths the country might have taken and that generally escape notice because emphasis is usually placed on St. Petersburg and Moscow, high politics, and the ultimate fate of the old regime. The conference record shows, among other possible observations, the enormous reservoir of good will that still existed. It shows the possibilities for change on the local level by uniting that good will with an already well-established zemstvo tradition. For the conference participants, the renewed vitality of the centrist position in the aftermath of the traumatic years 1904-07 represented an alternative to the extremism of the political left and right.

How vulnerable the center was, how quickly opportunities were lost (stolen?), how ephemeral the kind of rational discourse one heard at this gathering proved to be, events would shortly reveal. By 1910, the state was already reacting negatively (again) to new levels of Muslim cultural and political activity, seeking evidence of pan-Islamism and pan-Turkism to prove the disloyalty of at least some, and gaining the tacit, sometimes open support of Muslim defenders of the premodernist status quo. In late August 1908, however, for at least some in Simferopol, things were otherwise. If Russification, for example, existed "in ministerial plans," its pursuit by men responsible for local governance seemed decreasingly assured. If education was an overwhelmingly complex matter, those same men appeared willing to respect the complexities without being incapacitated, and likewise were willing to compromise in order to unravel some of its intricacies.

National and local affairs are, of course, often separated by an enormous gulf and frequently move in different directions, or at least are not synchronized. But the discrepancy between the whole and the parts deserves scrutiny so as to establish some of the latter's impact on the former, develop a sense of their interrelatedness, and understand some of the possibilities lost, rejected, ignored, or repressed.

TAVRIDA CONFERENCE ON TATAR EDUCATION
SIMFEROPOL, AUGUST 25-27, 1908

List of Participants

NAME	ETHNIC IDENTITY	RELEVANT BACKGROUND
Akhmetov, R.	Tatar	Teacher at Yalta Russian-Tatar school
Alibekov, A.	Tatar	Teacher at Evpatoriia Russian-Tatar school
Andreevskii, F. N.	?	
Beytullahoglu, Suleyman	Tatar	Member of Feodosiia zemstvo board
Biyarslanov, Mahmud Bey	Tatar	Teacher at Perekop Russian-Tatar school
Bosnyakov, S.	?	Teacher at Perekop Russian-Tatar school
Chelbashev, A.	Tatar	Teacher at Simferopol Russian-Tatar school
Chergeev, Hasan Bey	Tatar	Member of Perekop zemstvo board
Davidovich, M. M.	Tatar	Elder from Alushta

Dmitrevskii, A. M.	?	Member of Yalta zemstvo board
Dzhanklych, M. M.	Tatar	Teacher at Yalta Russian-Tatar school
Gasprinskii, Ismail Bey	Tatar	Publisher, educator
Isaev, Mulla Gani	Tatar	Teacher at Feodosiia Russian-Tatar school
Karashaiskii, Adil Mirza	Tatar	Mufti of Tavrida Muslim Ecclesiastical Assembly
Kazas, I. I.	Karaim (?)	Censor of Tatar publications
Khalitov, Hadzhi Kh.	Tatar	Member of Simferopol zemstvo board
Khasabov, R. G.	Tatar	Inspector of Simferopol district public schools
Kozlov, S. I.	?	Teacher at Yalta Russian-Tatar school
Krym, Sh. S.	Karaim (?)	Member of Feodosiia zemstvo board
Lemanov, A.	?	Teacher at Simferopol Russian-Tatar school

Lemanov, I.	?	
Levyi, A. D.	?	Teacher at Yalta Russian-Tatar school
Mansurskii, Ibrahim Mirza	Tatar	Teacher in Simferopol *mekteb-rushtie*
Margaritov, S. D.	?	Director of Tavrida public schools
Mediev, Reshid	Tatar	
Monastyrly, Kh. A.	?	Inspector of Simferopol Tatar Teachers' Seminary
Mufti-Zade, A. Ch.	Tatar	Teacher in Simferopol Tatar Teachers' Seminary
Mufti-Zade, A. M.	Tatar	
Mufti-Zade, I. M.	Tatar	Member of State Duma
Nalbandov, V. S.	Armenian	Chairman of Simferopol zemstvo board
Nechaev, O.	?	Teacher at Evpatoriia Russian-Tatar school
Neiman, Sh. I.	?	Member of Evpatoriia zemstvo board
Nogaev, A.	Tatar	Teacher at Simferopol Russian-Tatar school

Orazov, A.	?	Teacher at Simferopol Russian-Tatar school
Ozenbashly, I. I.	Tatar	Teacher at Yalta Russian-Tatar school
Serebriakov, M. E.	?	Member of Tavrida zemstvo board
Settarov, D.	Tatar	Teacher at Feodosiia Russian-Tatar school
Shirinskii, S. M.	Tatar	
Tayganskii, Ali Mirza	Tatar	
Tyncherov, M. Kh.	Tatar	Teacher at Yalta Russian-Tatar school
Ulanov, A. M.	Tatar	Secretary of Muslim charitable society
Vagin, L. S.	?	Head of department of public education of Tavrida zemstvo board

CHAPTER 13

CRIME, POLICE, AND MOB JUSTICE IN
PETROGRAD DURING THE RUSSIAN REVOLUTIONS OF 1917

Tsuyoshi Hasegawa

How did people live during the Russian revolutions of 1917? What
were their immediate concerns? What did they think and how did events
change their attitudes? Oddly, historians have rarely asked these questions.
For a long time the main focus of historical research on the revolutions of
1917 was the major characters in revolutionary politics. The ideologies,
organizations, strategies, and tactics of these elites were the dominant
topics. During the last decade or so, many Western historians have finally
begun to study mass movements. The result has been several excellent
monographs on workers, soldiers, sailors, and peasants, and on the
revolutionary process in provinces. Despite this shift of emphasis, these
historians have concentrated on the political implications of mass
movements; implicitly or explicitly, they seem to seek in the mass
movement the explanations for the October Revolution.[1]

The problem with this approach is that the complex social dimensions
of everyday life, considered politically unimportant, tend to be excluded
from analysis. The more immediate, direct changes in daily life during
1917 are not studied in their own right. The consequence of this rejection
of "social history with politics left out" is, ironically, the failure to
appreciate the real extent of the social polarization that developed within
spheres normally considered nonpolitical.[2]

This essay examines the relationship between crime and society in
Petrograd during the Russian revolutions of 1917 as the first step toward
broader issues in the social history of this period. Immediately after the
February Revolution, Petrograd was plagued with a phenomenal increase in
crime, not only numerically but in degree of violence. Since the newly
created law enforcement agencies could not cope with the rising crime rate,
the populace was forced to defend their security and property themselves--in
turn further contributing to the erosion of order and authority. Crime was
thus one of the most important causes for rapid disintegration of social

cohesion in Petrograd in 1917. But crime did not affect social classes equally. The well-to-do and the urban poor were the hardest hit, while the working class, which managed to maintain social cohesion, was least affected. The workers' militia proved to be more effective than the city militia in combating crime, and became an important basis on which the Bolshevik regime established the police system after the October Revolution.

This essay presents a picture of city life increasingly threatened by crime, and citizens and various organizations attempting to cope with it. While it cannot contain all elements of the mosaic, it conveys a part of the reality of life in Petrograd in 1917, and may serve as a starting point to further our understanding of social disintegration in urban centers in Russia in 1917.[3]

On the whole, Russian cities, and Petrograd in particular, were free from violent crimes during World War I. As Table 1 (appended to this essay) shows, the most common crimes committed in Russian cities during the war were thefts, followed by such economic crimes as embezzlement, extortion, and swindling. Murder, armed robbery, and arson ranked only ninth, tenth, and fifteenth in nineteen types of crime. As the largest economic and population center in the empire, Petrograd led all other cities in number of people arrested and number of thefts and other economic crimes. But when the number of arrests is considered in proportion to the population, Petrograd ranked only eighth (see Tables 2 and 3 in appendix). In the rank order of violent crimes in different cities, Petrograd was low in murders, armed robberies, and attempted murders (Table 4). The number of murders in Petrograd in 1914 was fourteen, and only nineteen in 1915. Armed robberies were almost nonexistent, with only three cases in 1915. Unarmed robberies even decreased, from 207 in 1914 and 60 in 1915. These figures reveal an extremely low crime rate in a city of more than two million people.[4]

All this was changed by the February Revolution of 1917, which contributed in three fundamental ways to a rise in crime. First, all prisoners formerly incarcerated in Petrograd's prisons were freed during the insurrection. Soviet archives indicate that as of February 26 the city's prisons held 7,652 prisoners.[5] The records do not indicate how many of these were political prisoners, but we can assume that a large majority were common criminals. Second, a large number of weapons were given out in great quantities to the insurgents, and presumably some of them fell into the hands of criminals as well. Easy access to weapons after the revolution led to crime more violent and easier to commit.[6] Third, the tsarist police force was annihilated during the February Revolution, and the newly created militia was ineffective.

Thefts and Robberies. Despite expectations by the new government and citizens alike that increased crime was merely a by-product of confusion arising from the revolution, crimes did not subside even after the new political system was established under the Provisional Government. Robberies, in the guise of searches allegedly authorized by the militia or the military authority, took place so frequently that newly installed Mayor (*gradonachal'nik*) Iurevich felt compelled to issue an order strictly forbidding illegal searches. But it was relatively easy to forge documents.[7] In some cases, soldiers' uniforms or militiamen's arm bands were enough to silence the frightened property owners. Often illegal searches were committed by professional criminals.[8] The number of illegal searches reported in newspapers suddenly decreased after April, but this did not mean that order was gradually restored in Petrograd. On the contrary, by then criminals had learned how to get what they wanted without bothering to disguise themselves as militiamen.

In late April and early May, the number of thefts and robberies showed a sharp increase. Several spectacular bank robberies were committed.[9] Newspapers did not even bother to report petty thefts. But major thefts and robberies were so frequent that *Petrogradskii listok* began a special column called "Thefts in the Capital" (*Stolichnye khishchniki*), in which it listed several major thefts and repeated at the end, like a ritual, "And many more were also reported." On June 16 it reported that in the previous twenty-four hours more than forty cases of theft and robbery had been filed. With a sense of alarm the press complained that this was unprecedented anarchy.[10] But this was merely the beginning.

The political crisis of the July Days was fully exploited by criminals to conduct illegal searches. It is estimated that at least fifty stores were attacked by robbers and two to three million rubles worth of goods were stolen during the crisis.[11] On July 15, ten reports of theft were filed, including six major ones ranging from 15,000 to 100,000 rubles in value of stolen property.[12] On July 27, about twenty soldiers in uniform arrived at the Chernigov Refrigeration Company in an official vehicle and executed with military precision a heist worth 230,000 rubles.[13] On August 15, a major theft was committed at the Historical Museum of property worth five million rubles.[14] On August 29, more than thirty thefts and robberies were reported.[15]

In the last two months before the October Revolution the crime rate rose so high that Petrograd was on the verge of collapse. Statistics of thefts and robberies showed an exponential leap. On September 13, twenty thefts were registered.[16] But on October 4 the total rose to 250, and on October 7 to 310. On October 14 *Petrogradskii listok* reported that in the previous forty-eight hours more than 800 thefts and robberies had been registered.[17] We should remember that only five months earlier, the press had been alarmed by the sharp increase in thefts and robberies to forty per day. Nothing remained sacred. Thefts took place in Spasskaia Church in Sennaia Square, Volkov Cemetery, the Museum of Jewelry, and even in the Petrograd Soviet in Smol'nyi Institute. The apartment of Vera Figner, the legendary populist revolutionary, was burglarized. At least one professional thief was robbed.[18]

Armed Robberies. The numbers of armed robberies reported in the papers show that Petrograd was becoming extremely violent. Compared to 1915 when only three armed robberies were reported, eighty-seven cases were reported in Petrograd newspapers from March through October in 1917 (see Table 5). Even this figure is extremely conservative, since almost certainly an equal number of cases were simply not sufficiently newsworthy to be printed in newspapers or were not even reported to police. In response to the increase in armed robberies, citizens began to arm themselves for protection.

One interesting twist was that in numerous incidents, particularly in May and June, self-proclaimed anarchists attempted to "expropriate the expropriators." They raided the apartments and villas of property owners, and robbed them under the banner of anarchism. The anarchists' occupation of the dacha owned by the family of the late P. N. Durnovo, formerly minister of interior, and the Provisional Government's attempt to reconquer it are too well known to be repeated here.[19] The Durnovo case was merely one of many attempts by genuine or pseudo-anarchists to dispossess the privileged. On April 28, the palace of the duke of Likhtenberg was expropriated by eighteen "anarchists" armed to the teeth, some of whom turned out to be professional criminals with prison records.

On May 7 "anarchists" raided the apartment of a former high tsarist government official, and stole all his valuables. The same day the home of Count Ruge was attacked by armed anarchists who took away 5,000 rubles' worth of property. On May 18, three men in soldiers' uniforms calling themselves anarchists and communists--they later turned out to be ex-convicts--broke into the home of K. K. Grigoriev on Kalinin Square, and shot the owner and a servant. On May 21, two well-dressed men and a young woman attacked a house in Soldatskii Lane. After seriously wounding a doorman, they ransacked the apartment and made off with all the valuables.[20] We do not know how many such incidents were carried out by politically committed anarchists as opposed to criminals who wrapped the anarchist banner around themselves. But clearly "anarchism" was becoming a favored "political doctrine" for criminals. A cartoon published in *Petrogradskaia gazeta* on April 23 shows a militiaman approaching the scene of a crime where a thief is about to run off with a big sack of loot. The militiaman says to the thief: "I think you are a thief." To this the thief replies: "What a reactionary you are, comrade. The tsarist police thought the same."[21]

Arsons. In July and August, newspapers reported several fires, some of mysterious origin. On July 21, sabotage was suspected in an explosion at the "Dinamo" factory. Four days later the factory "Respirator" was burned. Donetsko-Iurievsky factory caught fire under suspicious circumstances on July 30. A week later Electric Station No. 76 was burned to the ground. On August 16 a large portion of the Westinghouse complex was destroyed by fire; a week later another fire burned one of the buildings at the Putilov factory.[22] By far the largest fire in 1917 was the spectacular one on August 11 that raged for more than ten hours burning four factories in Okhta, destroying some barges on the Neva River, and claiming twenty lives. The fire was so intense that it spread to the other side of the Neva. Immediately after the fire started, pillaging and looting began in the evacuated apartment buildings, and more than fifty looters were arrested.[23]

Undoubtedly, declining worker discipline and inadequate security measures at factories contributed to some of these fires. But arsons and alleged arsons might also have been the result of rapidly deteriorating labor relations. When industrialists began a militant counteroffensive against the workers' demands after the July Days, the workers became more combative.[24] Although arson was not a standard weapon in the labor movement, the increased number of arsons might be a sign of workers' growing radicalism. Or, considered from the opposite angle, these boulevard newspapers, which took a strong stand against the workers' movement, might have used the fires to cast a negative image on the labor movement.

Murders. The most important feature of crime in Petrograd after the February Revolution was the frightening increase in the murders. Table 5 shows monthly statistics for murders from March through October as reported in the newspapers. During that period, at least ninety murder cases were reported. Compared with the prewar statistics, this number may not seem significant, but compared with fourteen murders in 1914 and nineteen in 1915 during the war, this was an alarming increase.[25] In addition, this number is definitely conservative. First, deaths caused by mob justice are excluded, since the number of victims is unknown. Second, I was unable to read all the newspapers, and for a total of twenty-nine days between March and October 10, I could not use even one newspaper. But even with these incomplete data, we see the rise in daily average number of murders as follows: .038 for 1914, .052 for 1915, but 0.448 from March 5 through October 10, 1917. This means an average of one murder every two or three days in 1917. Table 5 shows that during the same period, the murder rate per day also increased: 0.24 in March-April, 0.45 in May-June, 0.55 in July-August, and 0.58 in September-October.

Two types of newspaper murder reporting can be contrasted: for the Schlossberg murder and the Sezakh-Kulero case. On March 10, a barrister named Schlossberg was attacked on Kazan Street by three men, wearing sailors' uniforms, who had just left a house of prostitution. The innocent victim offered everything he owned, but the attackers stabbed him with knives several times, continuing to attack him even after he had fallen to the ground. Militiamen rushed to the scene, but by the time the assailants were subdued and arrested, Schlossberg had died.[26]

The second type is represented by the most sensational murder of the period, on April 16. Two men in officers' uniforms escorted a French singer, Margarette Sezakh-Kulero, and her live-in friend, Mariia Popova, to their apartment on Kamenoostrovskii Prospekt in a plush residential area in the Petrograd District. After they were properly entertained with sumptuous dinner and wine, the guests suddenly attacked the hostess, brutally cutting her head with their sabers, and proceeded to hack to death Mariia Popova and the servant who came to rescue her mistress. The assailants ransacked the apartment and stole valuables worth 30,000 rubles. One turned out to be none other than Baron von Schrippen, who in 1916 had pulled off a daring illegal search of the apartment belonging to the wealthy industrialist Zhitovskii. For this crime he had been serving a term in a Petrograd prison until he escaped amid the confusion of the February Revolution. After gaining unexpected freedom, he had openly joined the circles of money and pleasure which the French night club singer and her friend frequented.[27]

The tone of the reporting on the Schlossberg murder was indignation at the senselessness of the violence and fear that such a fate could befall anyone. The report on the Sezakh-Kulero case demonstrated the typical sensationalism of these boulevard papers, appealing to the readers' appetite for details of violent acts. This sensationalism, reminiscent of the coverage of some murder cases and famous trials prior to the February Revolution, was a departure from the norm in reporting violent crimes in 1917. Two factors explain the difference. First, this case dealt with a crime in which both the victims and the assailants belonged to a small circle of pleasure seekers, far removed from the common readers of these newspapers. The existence of such circles was indicative of the chaos of the times in which people of privilege were driven into the world of decadence. The newspapers reported widespread use of cocaine among members of these circles and the presence of high-class prostitutes. Unlike the Schlossberg murder, which was frightening to the general readers because anyone could be a potential victim, the premeditated murder in the Sezakh-Kulero case was far removed from the general reader's experience. Second, this incident aroused the curiosity of the general reader because the main culprit, von Schrippen, had acquired notoriety by raiding Zhitovskii's apartment. Although newspaper reports of the raid had a tone of admiration for his daring and precise execution, the reports also had a note of apprehension and confusion about the violence committed by this counterculture former hero.

The boulevard papers, of course, continued to report grisly details of murder cases to satisfy their readers. For instance, they reported that on May 18 a woman's dead body was found in Ekaterinogofki River with her hands tied at the back and a deep wound in her head.[28] On May 24, a young Chinese woman, an apparent rape victim, was found dead. Her eyes were cut out, her throat slit open, and many knife wounds were on her breast and other parts of her body.[29] Boulevard papers did not forget to include, amid the news of the Kornilov affair, the discovery of a headless torso with severed legs and arms wrapped in three separate packages and found in different parts of the city.[30] In August they reported news of a psychopath in Lesnoi. In grisly detail, sometimes accompanied by illustrations (no photographs were printed in newspapers in those days and even illustrations were rare), they described how authorities dug up body after body in his backyard.[31]

One senses, however, that the general tone of even these usually sensational boulevard papers was gradually becoming one of fear and anger at extreme violence grown out of control, particularly regarding murders committed against common people. Two such murders occurred in Lesnoi. Once a quiet residential suburb of Petrograd, Lesnoi became the site of several nightmarish murders. The fact that violent crimes had spread to previously quiet residential districts was another frightening aspect of 1917. For instance, on May 2, two deserters broke into a house in Lesnoi, strangled to death a servant, beat a thirteen-year-old boy into unconsciousness, and stole money and valuables worth approximately 20,000 rubles.[32] An even more frightening murder was committed in Lesnoi on October 1. A father and his three small children were brutally murdered in the very building that housed the Lesnoi militia headquarters.

Out of anger and frustration, irate Lesnoi residents sacked the militia headquarters.[33]

Two additional comments should be made with regard to murders in 1917. First, after the July Days an increasing number of murders occurred as a result of political arguments. This reflected the temper of the times, when the means to settle political differences were rapidly shifting from persuasion and compromise to physical violence. The civil-war mentality has its origin in this period.[34]

Second, the Chinese ethnic question became enmeshed with the question of crime in Petrograd in 1917. At least five Chinese were murdered during July and August, and the murder suspect arrested for the Lesnoi family murder was also Chinese. During the war, Russian industrialists had brought Chinese laborers to Petrograd to combat the serious labor shortage.[35] It is estimated that by 1917 more than 10,000 Chinese had arrived in Petrograd, where they worked primarily on construction projects and as unskilled laborers in factories. Working virtually as slave laborers, and unable to speak the language, they were usually the first to be thrown into the streets when recession hit the economy. Unemployment became a serious problem among the Chinese. They formed segregated communities in Novaia Derevnia and Peski in the Rozhdestvenskii district of Petrograd, where they lived in crowded, unsanitary hovels. They practiced the habits they brought with them of opium-smoking and gambling.[36] In the summer, with no work available and no possibility of returning home, some of them formed into gangs of robbers. Presumably the murdered Chinese were victims of infighting among various gangs. But there were disturbing signs that Chinese gangs were beginning to commit crimes in Russian communities. Although Chinese crimes were no more vicious than the norm for Petrograd, outraged residents of Novaia Derevnia demanded their deportation from Petrograd.[37]

The February Revolution opened the floodgate of crime in Petrograd. Extremely safe during the war, Petrograd increasingly became a dangerous place to live after February. The crime rate rose sharply as social disintegration continued, and the increase in crime, in turn, contributed to further social disintegration. It would not be an exaggeration to say that on the eve of the October Revolution, Petrograd was on the verge of collapse, threatened by waves of crime. This opinion was expressed vividly by former Petrograd Okhrana Chief K. I. Globachev, who had been arrested after the February Revolution and released from prison at the end of August:

> In the entire month of September and October, anarchy essentially ruled over Petrograd. Criminals multiplied to an unimaginable extent. Every day robberies and murders were committed not only at night, but also in broad daylight. Residents could not but be disturbed for the safety of their own lives. The populace, seeing that it would be impossible to expect any help from the nominally existing authority, began to organize themselves and form house guards or take other security measures in case of attack by robbers. In every residential house armed guards were posted every night. But this did not help and robberies did not decline.[38]

Criminals and deserters. The most alarming source of lawlessness in Petrograd was the presence of numerous criminals and deserters. The Provisional Government passed decrees favorable to criminals, such as the abolition of the death penalty on March 12.[39] On March 17, it decreed a reduction and cancellation of the penalties for those who had committed criminal offenses under the old regime. According to this decree, death sentences were commuted to hard labor in exile not exceeding fifteen years. Those who had been sentenced to hard labor in exile had their term reduced by half, with a maximum of twelve years. All sentences of exile were reduced to three years. Prisoners who were serving their terms in prison were freed. Those who were supposed to be in prison but had been freed during the February Revolution were ordered to turn themselves in by May 1, 1917. They would be rewarded for such good behavior by having their sentences cut in half.[40] Needless to say, few prisoners responded to the new government's offer to return to prison. In an additional appeal to former prisoners, Kerensky issued another decree shortly after Easter freeing criminals who were willing to serve at the front.

According to Globachev, who shared prison experience with criminals in the Kresty Prison, almost all criminals volunteered to go to the front.

They openly admitted: "You think we are fools to fight in war? We will be clothed and fed, and at the first railway stop, we will disappear."[41] To paraphrase Lenin's famous expression, Russia had suddenly become the freest country in the world for criminals, and they certainly took full advantage of that freedom. *Petrogradskii listok* attributed the sharply rising crime rate to the presence of criminals. In a tone of alarm, it editorialized:

> If Petrograd is now being robbed and plundered, it should not surprise us, since as many as 20,000 thieves were let go from various prisons. Robbers, enjoying full civil rights, are now freely walking the streets of Petrograd. Officers of the Criminal Militia often encounter thieves in the streets, but there is nothing they can do. Among them there are many who were deprived of their rights by the previous courts, but they now ignore such decisions.[42]

Deserters presented another problem. Some insurgent soldiers who had left their barracks during the February Revolution never returned. They were soon joined by deserters from the front who arrived in the capital looking for better opportunities. Brutalized by the war, these armed deserters contributed significantly to the rising crime rate in Petrograd. With no attachment to an official institution, the *sine qua non* for getting food rations, they had only crime as a means of survival. It was estimated that some 50,000 to 60,000 deserters were in Petrograd in July.[43]

Gradually, criminals and deserters formed their own colonies into which not even a militiaman dared set foot. Such colonies existed around the Olympia amusement park on Zabalkanskii Prospekt; in Village Volkovo in the Narva District; Galernaia Gavan; Gavanskoe Pole, and Golodai on Vasilevskii Island, Ligovki, Peski, and Poliustrovo.

During March and April the militia conducted periodic raids on cafes, restaurants, and cheap hotels in these colonies. Among those apprehended were well-known ex-convicts, who had fled jail during the February Revolution.[44] Such raids, however, did not prevent a frightening increase in the criminal population in Petrograd, for the new criminal system contained a fatal weaknesses, which will be explained below. Against this tidal wave--swollen daily by newly arriving professional criminals, deserters from the front, and restless urban youths--sporadic raids by the militia could hardly be effective.

By summer, criminals and deserters no longer meekly surrendered to the militia. In several instances they actively counterattacked. In fact, some of the militia's raids can better be described as military operations, sometimes assisted by military detachments. Such operations occurred, for example, against the robbers' colony in Volkovo at the end of July. In response to the militia detachment's first raid, the criminals defended themselves by firing back. In a crossfire that lasted more than half an hour, one militiaman was seriously wounded. All but three criminals escaped. It was not until the end of August that the militia, this time joined by a few detachments of the Izmailovskii Regiment and the Fourth Don Cossack Regiment, carefully laid siege to Volkovo and arrested 150 deserters and criminals. Such incidents were by no means isolated. Of twenty-four raids reported in July and August, the militia were attacked in at least eight instances.[45]

On occasion, residents in these colonies rioted when the militia arrested one of their comrades. One such riot took place in Olympia amusement park. Arrests of several hooligans and suspicious characters in the park occasioned a group of deserters, criminals, hooligans, and others to gather in protest. Shouting "Pharaohs! Oppressors!"--reminiscent of shouts heard during the February Revolution among demonstrators against the tsarist police--they attacked the militia headquarters. Several militiamen were caught and brutally beaten, and one was thrown from the third floor to the ground, where a mob lynched him.[46]

The New Criminal Justice System. As Leonard Schapiro has observed, the men in the Provisional Government were motivated by "innocent faith in the perfectibility of man" and "detestation of violence and coercion."[47] This was particularly true of the two ministers who were directly responsible for the criminal justice system: Minister of Internal Affairs Prince G. E. L'vov and Minister of Justice Alexander Kerensky. These predilections explain the abolition of the death penalty and the decree on March 17 granting amnesty to criminals. Moreover, the Provisional Statute on the Militia, issued by the Provisional Government on April 17, imposed heavy restrictions on the militia's treatment of persons arrested. For instance, Article 28 stipulated that the militia had no right to detain the arrested for more than twenty-four hours without specific criminal charges. Thus the majority of those apprehended in periodic raids of criminal colonies were back on the street the following day.[48]

Furthermore, the newly created Temporary Court (*Vremennyi sud*), presided over by a justice of the peace assisted by two mandatory assistant justices (representing the soldiers and the workers), was far from effective in instilling a sense of justice among the populace. Originally designed as an emergency measure to "remove misunderstandings" between the insurgents and the privileged class during the February Revolution, when the tsarist legal and court system ceased to function, the Temporary Court became virtually the only court in Petrograd handling both criminal and civil cases.[49] Arbitrariness was one of its distinct characteristics. V. Menshutkin, who wrote a valuable, sympathetic record of this court, states that it was allowed to impose a wide variety of punishments for theft ranging from a warning to a maximum fine of 10,000 rubles. He admitted that in general the Temporary Court was lenient in punishing thieves. On the other hand, apartment-house owners were often found guilty for not keeping sanitary conditions, and had to pay the maximum fine. Despite its original intention to remove misunderstandings between the privileged and those who had participated in the February Revolution, this court system probably contributed to intensifying antagonism between the two classes. Furthermore, the new court, which handled cases ranging from wives' complaints about their husbands' extramarital affairs and illegal brewing of alcoholic beverages to serious murder cases, could not possibly handle the deluge of criminal cases. In March alone the Petrograd Temporary Court dealt with 5,237 cases, but the astonishing increase in the rate of crime surely precluded the court from rendering justice even for crimes where the perpetrators were apprehended and brought before the court.[50]

The destruction of the old police system paralyzed one important prerevolutionary crime-prevention device. Although not formally integrated into the police system, the doormen (*dvorniki*)--those men who guarded virtually every public building, kept watch over those who came and went, and maintained close contact with the police--performed an essential security function before the February Revolution. But resenting the allegation that they were a part of the tsarist police, the doormen organized themselves into a trade union and refused to perform security duties.[51] On May 9, in the face of a sharp rise in crime, Mayor Iurevich ordered obligatory night duty for doormen under penalty of law. The offended doormen declared that they would not obey an order issued without prior consultation with them, and on May 16 Iurevich was forced to rescind the decree. In return, the doormen agreed to do the night watch on a voluntary basis.[52] Consequently, most of Petrograd's buildings were left without guards.

Finally, even if thieves and robbers were caught, tried, and sent to prison, there was no guarantee that they would stay there. The February Revolution caused a serious breakdown in security at prisons as well. The Provisional Government carried out a prison reform, the first step of which was to fire prison wardens and guards.[53] They were replaced by untrained former soldiers and other volunteers hired on the spot. Globachev described the condition of the Kresty Prison, which was ostensibly one of the tightest security prisons in Petrograd: guards often fell asleep, abandoned their posts, or left their rifles behind within easy reach of prisoners, and they often left prisoners totally unguarded during the periods they were allowed to walk in the yard. Of course, many prisoners escaped. The only reason Globachev did not escape was that he felt safer behind bars than in the street, given his former status as Okhrana chief.[54] Prison security became particularly lax in the summer. During the July Days, many political prisoners were incarcerated, but after the Kornilov affair they were either freed or escaped, often with the connivance of prison guards. On August 30, for instance, 208 prisoners ran away from the Kresty Prison, and 150 prisoners fled the Peterhof Commissariat.[55] Not all of these were political prisoners; common criminals also took advantage of the opportunity. Only thirty of those who broke from Kresty on August 30 were political prisoners.

The new criminal justice system, created by Kerensky with so much goodwill and idealism, simply did not work. On the contrary, criminals fully exploited it, crime spread rapidly, and the criminal population swelled. Threatened by crime, people surely felt frustrated, powerless, and frightened.

Ineffectiveness of the militia. A major reason that crime increased was the ineffectiveness of the newly created militia. It was divided into a dual power structure composed of the city militia and the workers' militia.[56] Organized by the Petrograd City Duma, the city militia was based on democratic principles in the sense that the organization was to include all classes and serve the entire population, transcending class differences. Its function was to ensure security of life, property, and public order. In contrast, the workers' militia was a class organization, serving only the working class, and composed only of members of that class. Its primary function was the political task of protecting the gains of the revolution from anticipated counterrevolutionary actions by its class enemies.[57] If combating crime became also a function of the workers' militia, it resulted from necessity.

Although the authority of the city militia was nominally recognized by the workers' militia, the latter maintained itself as an autonomous organization. On the whole, the workers' militia exerted exclusive control in the outlying workers' districts, while the city militia was predominant in the center of the city. But as Rex Wade points out:

This neat dichotomy . . . breaks down on close examination. Some factory-based workers' militia units accepted directions from and subordinated themselves to the City Militia authorities, although they retained varying degrees of autonomy. Others rejected all subordination. Within the City Militia there were units made up largely of workers but operating strictly within the City Militia framework. Many districts were divided between workers' militia and City Militia commissariats by subdistricts. In some subdistricts even further division took place as certain streets, buildings, and areas were patrolled by autonomous workers' militia units while other streets and buildings were guarded by the City Militia. In such areas there were parallel militia structures, with an ad hoc territorial division of the subdistrict. Finally, though these lines of division and authority generally followed those established during the February Revolution, there was some shifting and reorganizing, as well as recurring efforts by city officials to close down or more tightly control worker units.[58]

The basic principle on which both the city militia and the workers' militia functioned was that of local self-determination.[59] Specifically, they insisted on local autonomy and election of their chiefs. Neither the Provisional Government's Ministry of Justice nor the City Administration controlled the local militia organizations, and their attempts to reorganize them on the principle of centralization met effective resistance by both the city militia organizations and the workers' militia.[60]

Another reason the militia was so ineffective was the poor quality of militiamen, particularly in the city militia. In the beginning, the city militiamen were volunteers, predominantly students and others from the middle class--including, at the very beginning, boy scouts.[61] Later, each district militia head, called commissar, became more selective in hiring militiamen, but the new men also usually lacked basic training as police officers. The condition was not much better for the workers' militia, since turnover was extremely high. Faced with rising crime and the ineffectiveness of the militia, the City Administration and the Ministry of Justice recognized the need to establish a criminal division by recruiting former tsarist police officers. The problem was that almost all veteran police officers of the criminal division had been arrested and locked up in the city's prisons. After the Petrograd mayor created the Criminal Investigation Division on March 9, two who had been agents of the former tsarist Criminal Police (*syskaia politsiia*) were released from prison to serve in the new institution. But Kirpichnikov, the former head of the Criminal Police, remained under arrest for a while longer before he was made head of the new institution. Eventually, all the members of the former Criminal Police joined the Criminal Militia, which was directly subordinated to the Ministry of Justice.

Among all other amateur militiamen, these experienced investigators were the only effective agents in dealing with hard-core criminals. However, they had to work against tremendous odds; they were poorly paid (mostly 100 to 200 rubles a month), understaffed, and overworked.

The Criminal Police was headed by a chief, and staffed by two assistant chiefs, ten inspectors, and 200 junior inspectors. It was hamstrung by the Supervisory Commission, which included representatives from the Petrograd Soviet, the City Duma, and the military authorities.[62] The stigma of having served in the former tsarist police also hampered their effectiveness.

Another weakness was lack of financial support for militia organizations and militiamen. The city militia was financed by the City Administration, whose financial base rapidly deteriorated. The workers' militiamen received their wages from the factory management, but as antagonism between labor and management intensified, the issue of the factory managers' obligation to finance the workers' militia became contentious. The City Administration's failure to provide financial support for the city militia had dire consequences for its effectiveness. First of all, it resulted in a lack of firearms. Amazingly, not all city militiamen were armed. The shortage of weapons posed a serious threat to the militiamen on duty, who were often attacked by criminals and hooligans. In one instance a militiaman was seized by a gang of young hooligans and forced at gunpoint to crawl on all fours and bark like a dog.[63] The insufficient funds for the militia also caused a shortage of boots and uniforms. But most important, it necessitated low wages, and significantly contributed to gradual demoralization.

This situation led the city militiamen to organize their own trade union, and through it they, ironically, requested official affiliation with the Petrograd Soviet. Their major complaints focused on the shortage of uniforms, boots, and weapons and the low wages. Their demand for a wage increase was supported by the conservative Criminal Militia, which sent a petition to the Ministry of Justice, complaining that they had received no salary since July. One can imagine their frustrations, knowing that well-armed thieves and robbers were living in expensive apartments, keeping permanent rooms in luxury hotels, and being served by their own entourage and chauffeurs. Having received no satisfactory answer to their demands from the City Administration, the militiamen held a general conference in which they decided to go on strike unless they received satisfactory settlement to their wage demands from the City Administration by

October 11. Frustrated by the City Administration's inaction on their demands, some of the city militiamen brought their complaints to the district soviets and sometimes to the factory committees.[64] The City Administration was still negotiating with the militia representatives to avert a strike, and was simultaneously beginning to plan a sweeping reorganization of the militia forces, when the October Revolution began.[65]

The alarming increase in the crime rate led the public to criticize the ineffectiveness of the militia. Already in the spring, newspapers had begun criticizing the militia, and carried articles exposing militiamen engaged in criminal acts. These criticisms also found an echo in the City Duma.[66] Whereas the spring newspaper articles had focused on isolated cases of militiamen committing disgraceful acts or former criminals infiltrating the militia organizations, by fall the tone had shifted to a complete denunciation of the militia organization itself.[67] The changing attitude of the press toward the militia was vividly illustrated in a cartoon in *Petrogradskii listok* on October 20. A couple walking on a deserted street are about to be attacked by a mugger from behind, and in front of them a militiaman is patrolling at the corner. The caption reads: "How horrible! A robber behind, and a militiaman in front!"[68]

Mob Justice (Samosudy). Threatened by sharply increasing crimes, and deserted by doormen to protect their buildings, the city's residents began to organize themselves to protect their homes from criminals. As early as April, residents had already organized many apartment house committees (*domovye komitety*) in residential buildings. Some of these committees decided to lock all the gates day and night, issue a pass to all residents, and organize compulsory guard duty for residents. Others went a step farther by creating a private apartment house (*domovaia*) militia.[69] By autumn, when it had become clear that residents could not rely on the city militia, many apartment house committees began hiring military guards and soldiers from nearby barracks. The City Administration, which was reluctant to give weapons to its own militia, handed out weapons to such vigilance groups organized by apartment house committees![70]

It is against the background of increasing lawlessness and a sense of powerlessness that acts of mob justice (*samosudy*, literally "self-made trials")--one of the most frightening practices of 1917--became commonplace in the city's major streets.[71] On May 13, *Petrogradskii listok* reported: "Incidents of minor mob justice against thieves have been observed earlier, but yesterday they took a sharp turn." It then described three incidents of mob justice in graphic detail.[72] From then on, such incidents began to fill the pages of the boulevard newspapers. In broad daylight at the busiest intersection of the city, Sadovaia and Nevskii streets, two pickpockets were lynched. An angry crowd broke into a store and beat the shop clerks suspected of hoarding goods. Whenever a crowd gathered, it was enough for someone to shout "Beat him! I know he did it!" to turn the angry mob against the accused. No evidence was necessary; a voice counseling moderation was invariably drowned out, and often the person objecting was himself attacked by the angry mob.[73] Incidents of mob justice were so numerous that *Gazeta-Kopeika* began to carry a column called "Today's mob trials [*samosudy*]."

During May and June a total of twelve acts of mob justice were reported. In July and August the number rose to twenty-three, and in September and October to thirty-three. The average number of acts of mob justice reported daily in newspapers shows clearly a sharp increase from March to October: 0.02 in March-April, 0.26 in May-June, 0.53 in July-August, and 0.82 in September-October. (See Table 5.) A typical case transpired on August 19 at the intersection of Smolenskaia and Lubenskaia streets. A group of people caught a thief. A crowd gathered. Not wishing to turn him over to the militia, they decided to hold a public trial on the spot. "A people's court is the most just and quickest!" someone shouted. "Thieves will run away from the militia!" others responded. Discussions were brief, and the unanimous verdict was the death sentence. Immediately, they began beating him with shoes, sticks, fists, and stones. When militiamen arrived to rescue him, the crowd reacted with hostility, and threw stones at them. The thief, bleeding heavily and already unconscious, was brought to a hospital, where his condition was pronounced hopeless.[74] In another instance, three unknown men fired shots from a moving automobile at soldiers standing at the entrance of the People's House near Aleksandr Garden, killing a bystander and wounding two soldiers. The snipers were caught by angry soldiers, and literally torn limb from limb. The militiamen, who came to the scene too late, had to pick up pieces of their bodies.[75]

Where in the previous months acts of mob justice had been directed mainly against thieves, during the summer such acts began to be reported more frequently against merchants. Often these mob actions bore a character of anti-Semitism. A Jewish leather merchant, who was pulling his cart on Sennaia Square, was attacked by the angry crowd that suspected him of hoarding goods. Despite intervention by a militiaman and despite the merchant's innocence, the crowd of over a thousand discussed what to do with him. Some suggested killing him on the spot, while others recommended drowning. But "more reasonable" elements prevailed and the crowd decided to tie him to the cart and deliver him to the Petrograd Soviet. They pushed the cart all around the city, beating him constantly on the way. The innocent victim was in a state of delirium when he was finally freed from the ordeal at the Smol'nyi Institute.[76] At the end of August and the beginning of September, a sudden upsurge of food riots began in various parts of the city. Particularly in the Kolomenskii District, several food riots were accompanied by pogroms against Jewish merchants.[77]

The ugly specter of mob justice raged violently as the October Revolution approached. An inmate of a mental institution escaped into the streets on September 14, claiming that he had been beaten by nurses. An outraged crowd attacked the hospital and subjected the administrator to a mob trial. A week later a crowd brought about swift justice by beating to death a thief who stole an apple on Sennaia Square.[78] On October 15 two shoplifters were caught in a store at the corner of Sadovaia and Apraksin streets--one in a soldier's uniform and another an elegantly dressed woman. Such a huge crowd gathered at the corner that it halted all streetcar traffic. A militia detachment rushed to the scene, but confronted by the extremely hostile crowd demanding that the shoplifters be handed over for a mob trial, the militia had to request assistance from soldiers stationed nearby at the state bank. The soldiers arrived at the scene and cordoned off the store, separating the criminals from the crowd. The angry crowd shouted at the soldiers: "You are like militia, hiding the thieves!" Some, pushing their way, broke into the store and dragged the male shoplifter out into the streets. Immediately the crowd began pounding him. The frightened female accomplice escaped into a telephone booth in the store. One militiaman stood on a table in front of the telephone booth with a revolver in his hand to protect the woman. The mob pulled him off the table and began beating him also. The mob then pulled the young woman out of the telephone booth and beat her severely. One person in the crowd shouted: "What are we waiting for?" Pulling a revolver, he fired two shots into the male shoplifter, killing him instantly. A few minutes later, the mob executed the woman also.[79]

Alarmed by a sudden upsurge in mob justice, criminals sent out an ultimatum, declaring that they would "kill anybody we meet at the dark corner of streets. . . . Breaking into a house, we will not simply loot, but will murder everyone, even children, and won't stop our bloody revenge until acts of mob justice are stopped."[80] It seemed as though another "class struggle" was in progress in Petrograd--between criminals and the public.

Nothing indicates more clearly the ugly mood of the citizens than these instances of mob justice. Citizens were angered and frustrated by creeping lawlessness, the inability of the militia to prevent crime, and the uselessness of the criminal justice system. Every day, insolent crimes were committed directly under the nose of the militia, sometimes with the complicity of the militiamen themselves. Even if burglars and robbers were caught, they either received lenient sentences in the Temporary Court or escaped from jail. Mob trials were thus the public's attempt to bring swift justice. By inflicting the death penalty even for a minor offense, they were also venting their frustration and anger. Renderings of mob justice were visible expressions of the general social breakdown, but they contributed to the further erosion of order and authority.

Sociology of crimes. Who were the victims of crime? Should crime be considered in the context of the deepening social chasm between the wealthy and the poor, and interpreted as an act of revolt by the downtrodden against their oppressors? Or, did crime affect all segments of the population indiscriminately? Who committed crime? Was it committed mostly by criminals and deserters, or were other segments of the population drawn into the criminal population? Can regional differentiations be discerned in the crime rate?

Reading the boulevard newspapers, one immediately notices the heavy concentration of reported crimes and acts of mob justice in the center of the city, in such districts as Kazan, Kolomenskii, Moscow, Narva, Rozhdestvenskii, and Aleksandr-Nevskii. These districts were characterized by a mixed population consisting of the privileged and the urban poor and by the absence of large contingents of factory workers. Partly, the concentration of reported crimes in these districts can be explained by the bias of the boulevard papers, which drew the majority of their reader from the lower class outside the organized proletariat. It is possible, therefore, that crimes committed in the outskirts of the city, where the factory workers were heavily concentrated, were simply not reported.

Nevertheless, the concentration of reported crimes in the center of the city cannot be explained only by the bias of the newspapers. It was also the result of the sociology of crime during this period of revolution. Two segments of the population were most deeply affected by crime. First was the propertied class--the class that owned something worth stealing. They were the first to desert the city. According to reports, some 6,000 Petrograders had arrived in the Crimea in July, far more than the usual summer vacationers.[81] For some, émigré life started long before the Bolshevik seizure of power. Obviously, crime was not the only cause for the mass exodus of the privileged and the middle class, but no doubt it provided a powerful motivation.

Second, crime deeply affected the lower classes. They included those who belonged, at least in consciousness if not income, to the lower middle class, such as civil servants at the lowest ranks, small merchants, pharmacists, and owners of small restaurants, taverns, and tearooms. A segment of the working class not included in the organized working class movement--such as workers in small factories and workshops, carpenters, street sweepers, plumbers--were also in this group. Also affected were the artisans (remeslenniki), including shoemakers, watchmakers, locksmiths, carpenters, painters, and others; and the servants and service employees (sluzhashchie), including house servants, doormen, porters, butlers, shop clerks, waiters and waitresses, laundresses, office workers, and others. We must also consider their wives, who had to shop in the crime-ridden streets. These urban poor bore the brunt of economic and social dislocation.

Mostly uneducated, disoriented by changing values, not united by a class-consciousness, and unorganized by any class-based organizations, they were deeply affected by crime. The boulevard papers expressed, above all, the fear and anger felt by these people. Those who participated in acts of mob justice came from these urban poor. They represented simultaneously ideologically reactionary and revolutionary elements. On the one hand, they expressed strong anti-Semitic sentiments, and engaged in anti-Jewish pogroms. On the other hand, some of the groups affiliated themselves with the Petrograd Soviet, and showed intense class hatred of the privileged. Probably the urban youths coming from the urban poor were drawn into the city's criminal element.

The attitudes of soldiers toward crime varied. Some were active participants in crimes; others were the ultimate authority to be relied on to combat crime. After the Kornilov affair, demoralization and disintegration took root in the reserve forces in the city. With the exception of a few reserve units that maintained political cohesion, the masses of soldiers were probably turning into potential criminals.

Compared with all other classes in Petrograd, the working class alone maintained social and political cohesion. More important, it maintained coherent, effective organizations through which it could enforce discipline and combat the spread of crime into the working-class districts. No doubt, crimes did take place in the working-class districts as well, but the crime rate in these districts was markedly lower than in the center of the city. Among the workers' organizations that played an important role in preventing and combating crime were the factory committees, the district soviets, and especially the workers' militia and the Red Guards. The main purpose of the workers' militia and the Red Guards was political, and aimed at organizing the workers militarily to prepare for expected counterrevolutionary attacks against the working class. But in the absence of an effective police force in the working class districts, the workers' militia had to assume the task of security duties as a matter of necessity. For instance, the Militia Commission of the Vasilevskii district soviet included, among the tasks assigned to the workers' militia, security of life and property as well as investigation of murders, robberies, and thefts.[82] While it is true, as Rex Wade argues, that the Red Guards were to arm the workers to combat counterrevolution, it is also interesting that the draft statutes of the "Workers' Guards," adopted by the Vasilevskii district soviet, included as one of their tasks "security of life [and] property of all citizens without regard to sex, age, and nationality."[83]

After the July Days, the Provisional Government attempted to abolish the workers' militia by issuing the new statutes on the militia, which aimed to create a centralized militia organization. But this attempt did not succeed. Although weakened in strength, the workers' militia continued to exist.[84] This was partly because it functioned as the most effective, and in some districts the sole, instrument to maintain order. For instance, despite the Provisional Government's directive, the managers of the Pipe Factory refused to discontinue paying salaries to the workers' militia on the grounds that its abolition would endanger the security and discipline of the factory.[85]

As the city militia became ineffective and demoralized, the workers' militia and the Red Guards served an increasingly important security function, not only in the working-class districts but also in the center of the city. The First City District Soviet, which included the most crime-ridden former Liteinyi, Rozhdestvenskii, Aleksandr-Nevskii, and Moscow districts and also including Ligovki and the Olympia amusement park, had to be concerned with crimes in the district. In August, the soviet decided to close down the Olympia, to increase the patrol duties of the workers' militia in Ligovki and other troubled areas, and in general to assume increased responsibility for security duties in the district.[86]

As the October Revolution approached, the conflict between political struggle against counterrevolution and security duty became a subject of intense discussion among the activists of the district soviets and the factory committees. Generally, the Vyborg, Vasilevskii, and Peterhof district soviets took the stand that the workers' militia and the Red Guards were an instrument of class struggle, and should not waste time in doing security duties. This position coincided with the policy of the Bolshevik Party. On the other hand, the Petrograd, Rozhdestvenskii, and First City district committees (where crime rates were higher) tended to accept security duties as a necessary part of their functions.[87] Despite these differences, the workers' militia and the Red Guards fulfilled the function of security duty even in those districts where the district soviet leaders rejected it as a proper function of the workers' armed organizations.

Conclusion. Crime contributed to disintegration of society in Petrograd in 1917. A society that is reduced to anomie cannot exist for long, and such a situation dictates the emergence of a strong power that can restore order, even if it must use an iron fist. In 1917 only the working class possessed the social cohesion and effective instruments needed to restore order. And only the Bolsheviks, who were riding the crest of working-class support, had the will to exercise violence to impose order. Crime did not stop suddenly when the Bolsheviks seized power. On the contrary, violent crimes and acts of mob justice even increased after October. The Bolsheviks, who had stood aloof from the problem of crime throughout 1917 until their seizure of power, declared that crimes were instigations by the bourgeoisie to overthrow the proletarian regime. The Bolsheviks used the presence of crime as justification to create a repressive police system.

Increase in crime resulted from more than the causes discussed in this essay. A profound change in people's consciousness was also a cause. The old regime was gone, and with it many of the values of the old world. Everything was questioned, and much was rejected. Old notions of right and wrong were reversed, and the line that separated criminal acts from legality became blurred. The notion of inviolability of property and life came under assault. The political ideology that was gaining popularity among the masses further contributed to undermining this concept. Moreover, the downtrodden and the oppressed had gained a sense of self-respect--a consciousness that they had now become the master. At the same time, this sense of self-respect was closely mixed with a sense of revenge against the privileged. It might be said, therefore, that revolution conceals within itself an element of criminality.

Table 1

CRIMES IN RUSSIAN CITIES: 1914-1915

	1914		1915	
Crime	Cases	Solved	Cases	Solved
Theft, less than 300 rubles	41,946	21,043	34,093	16,537
Theft, forced entry	8,521	3,537	7,678	3,124
Theft, more than 300 rubles	4,284	2,132	5,037	2,323
Embezzlement	2,446	2,015	1,548	1,238
Swindling, extortion	1,889	1,521	1,569	1,221
Unarmed robbery	1,667	1,024	734	453
Horse theft	1,228	589	1,367	516
Railway theft	955	286	603	199
Murder	504	405	473	371
Armed robbery	334	211	275	190
Attempted murder	261	201	251	211
Theft of weapons from military units	239	115	225	211

Forgery of documents	189	185	191	169
Counterfeiting	145	100	101	77
Arson	125	73	97	52
Theft in post office, banks	59	54	30	25
Thefts in church	45	35	40	19
Trade in humans	37	34	21	21
Evasion of military service	31	30	220	210

Source: "Gorodskiia prestupleniia za 1915 god," *Vestnik politsii*, 1916, no. 39:940-41.

Table 2

CRIMES IN RUSSIAN CITIES: NUMBER OF ARRESTS

City	1914			1915		
	Men	Women	Total	Men	Women	Total
Petrograd	10,341	612	10,953	9,438	962	10,400
Odessa	8,100	1,097	9,197	6,938	1,079	8,017
Ekaterinoslav	2,819	308	3,127	1,283	161	1,299

Rostov-on-Don	2,789	131	2,920	660	65	725
Samara	2,165	316	2,481	1,804	309	2,113
Moscow	1,494	243	1,737	1,245	176	1,421
Kharkov	1,420	224	1,444	1,765	167	1,932
Riga	1,403	32	1,435	1,289	61	1,350
Astrakhan	1,231	47	1,278	1,337	77	1,414
Tashkent	1,148	46	1,194	852	42	894
Saratov	969	154	1,123	819	20	839
Baku	995	18	1,013	888	33	921

Source: "Gorodskiia prestupleniia za 1915 god--prodolzhenie," *Vestnik politsii*, 1916, no. 40:958.

Table 3

NUMBER OF ARRESTS IN RELATION TO POPULATION
IN 1914

City	Population (in 1000)	Number Arrested	Ratio
Odessa	499.5	9,197	18.4
Samara	143.8	2,481	17.3
Rostov-on-Don	172.3	2,920	17.0
Ekaterinoslav	211.1	3,127	14.8
Astrakhan	151.5	1,278	8.4
Saratov	235.7	1,444	5.9
Kharkov	2,244.7	1,444	5.9
Petrograd	2,118.5	10,953	5.2
Baku	232.2	1,013	4.4
Riga	558.0	1,435	2.6
Moscow	1,762.7	1,737	1.0

Sources: "Gorodskiia prestupleniia za 1915 god--prodolzhenie," *Vestnik politsii*, 1916, no. 40:958; A. Rashin, *Naselenie Rossii za 100 let* (Moscow, 1956), 93.

Table 4

CRIME IN PETROGRAD, 1914-1915

Crime	Rank among Cities	1914	1915
Theft, less than 300 rubles	1	3,710	3,657
Theft, forced entry	1	1,125	1,050
Theft, more than 300 rubles	1	1,002	1,369
Swindling, extortion	1	94	153
Embezzlement	1	388	496
Horse theft	2	68	62
Unarmed robbery	1	207	60
Murder	4	14	19
Armed robbery	24		3
Attempted murder	3		11

Sources: "Gorodskiia prestupleniia za 1915 god," *Vestnik politsii*, 1916, no. 39:941-42; "Gorodskiia prestupleniia za 1915 god-- prodolzhenie," *Vestnik politsii*, 1916, no. 40:957-58.

Table 5

CRIMES IN PETROGRAD

Crime	1914	1915	March-October 1917				
			Mar.-Apr.	May-June	July-Aug.	Sept.-Oct.	Total
Murder cases	14	19	13	21	30	26	90
per day*	0.038	0.052	0.24	0.45	0.55	0.58	0.448
Armed robberies	0	3	23	26	24	14	87
Samosudy cases			1	12	29	33	75
per day**			0.02	0.26	0.53	0.82	
Missing days			2	15	7	5	29

*The murder rate per day = (Number of murder cases) / {(Number of days of the month) - (Number of missing days)}.

**The rate of mob acts per day = (Number of mob acts) / {(Number of days of the month) - (Number of missing days)}.

CHAPTER 14

DONALD WARREN TREADGOLD,
HISTORIAN IN OUR MIDST: A BRIEF APPRECIATION

Nicholas V. Riasanovsky

I have known Donald Warren Treadgold for a long time and I have
known him well. We first met in 1939 or 1940. I am proud of the fact that
my mother and I taught him Russian--may all teaching bear such fruit! Don
and I proceeded to go together through three universities: the University of
Oregon in our hometown of Eugene; Harvard, where we roomed in the
same house; and Oxford, where both of us were Rhodes scholars
representing the state of Oregon, and where we completed the work for our
doctorates in 1949. Between the University of Oregon and Harvard, each
of us spent approximately three years in the army, much of that time in the
European theater of operations.

After Oxford our paths diverged only geographically, for we joined
much the same American academic community of historians and Russian
"specialists." We continued to see each other with some regularity, at
various conferences, when visiting our respective universities, or at such
outlying points as Paris and Moscow. I have read most of Donald
Treadgold's writings, commenting on many of them, informally or
formally.[1] Don has been kind enough to pay similar attention to my work.

His central, perhaps the defining, trait as a historian, intellectual, and
human being is his magnificent curiosity. To be sure, all of us possess
curiosity or we would not be in our present occupations. Yet, even in this
milieu, Don's is outstanding, both because of its scope and because of the
intense delight he takes in discovering words, phrases, sentences,
languages, and also buildings and works of art, events, circumstances,
people, almost everything. All these items have their own special life for
him, often a fascinating one. My college reminiscences are full of little
incidents connected with Donald Treadgold and all kinds of minor
occurrences and details, especially with words in half a dozen languages.
This trait is all the more noteworthy, because, as we all know, and as will
become clear even in this brief appreciation, Donald Treadgold is anything

but simply an antiquarian, a student of railroad schedules for their own sake, or a collector of meaningless trivia.

Endowed with such a curiosity, he naturally became a many-sided historian. Powerfully attracted by numerous aspects of intellectual and cultural history, deeply concerned with politics, whether those of the Russian imperial government or of the Communist Party of the Soviet Union, determined to establish the main lines of economic and social development following Alexander II's "Great Reforms," on the eve of the revolutions of 1917, or in the course of Stalin's collectivization and industrialization, inevitably preoccupied with international relations, Don Treadgold has written significantly and at length on these and many other topics. One should also bear in mind his treatment of religious history, central to his recent scholarly work, which often distinguishes him very favorably from other scholars specializing in Russian and Soviet history, both inside and outside the Soviet Union.

Yet, despite Don Treadgold's encyclopedic interests, his writings are almost never vague, confused, or out of focus. In fact, characteristically he writes *à thèse*, and he argues his theses hard. His doctoral dissertation, later published as a book, *Lenin and His Rivals: The Struggle for Russia's Future, 1898-1906* (1955), is, as the title suggests, a refusal to accept the closed Soviet view of Russia becoming inevitably Leninist, and an argument for other possibilities. *The Great Siberian Migration* (1957) is an application of Frederick Jackson Turner's hypothesis to Russian history, in particular to Siberia, as still another alternative in the Russian past (Don Treadgold has an excellent knowledge of United States history and began graduate studies with that history as his main field). His widely read *Twentieth Century Russia*, first published in 1959 (I am at the moment looking at the fifth edition, and I understand the sixth will soon come out), is again a strongly argued and hard-hitting book, which has produced considerable controversy. I am not, however, in a good position to criticize it, because I agree with most of the opinions expressed in it.

Donald Treadgold's proclivity to write *à thèse* is perhaps best developed in his notable two volumes entitled *The West in Russia and China* (1973)-- of which volumes, I have some competence to comment on the first. There, in a rich and learned manner, valuable especially for the earlier period of contact, Treadgold argues that there were three main Russian reactions to the West: a blind rejection, a blind acceptance, and a desirable and difficult selective and integrative acceptance.

Don Treadgold's approach, or approaches, can, of course, be criticized. I, for one, am no admirer of Stolypin and his determined attempt, in effect, to save the Russian monarchy, and I am not much impressed by the positive and integrative approach to Westernization, especially as embodied in such figures as Tsarevich Alexis. Our field produces many grimmer visions than Treadgold's; perhaps equally compelling, for instance, is that of Theodore Von Laue. Many of us are not sufficiently well organized intellectually to suggest any consistent pattern at all. But it must be stated that Don Treadgold presents his arguments not only ardently but well. And it bears reminding that not only history, but also historiography, is generally made, not by doubters and shilly-shallyers, but by people who drive toward clear answers and successful solutions.

Donald Treadgold, then, is obviously not the proverbial ivory tower academician, although I must state that I know few, if any, individuals whose ability to appreciate true ivory tower scholars is equal to Don's. After choosing history over law, Don has developed into as practical and as active a historian as I can name in the profession. Very appropriately, Professor Byrnes's contribution, following mine in this volume, deals with that major aspect of his activity. I have to mention here, however, that he served for many years as the editor of our leading journal, *Slavic Review*, translating into English for that journal contributions in various languages, in addition to performing more usual editorial tasks.

Don Treadgold's volumes on the West in Russia and China were accompanied by at least one major conference and by Don's argumentation that in addition to knowing Russia or China well, specialists should acquire at least some knowledge of the language, culture, and history of the other country, to help advance our study of both. Although how much knowledge is "some knowledge" is difficult to establish, I am not proud of the majority's solution--myself prominently included--of learning no Chinese at all. And, yes, it was most appropriate indeed that it was Donald W. Treadgold more than anyone else who organized and staged the Third

World Congress for Soviet and East European Studies (October 30 to November 4, 1985) in Washington, D.C.

What will be the subject of his next book, and the ones after that? Will they include a fast-paced study of Ethiopia, based, of course, on materials in Amharic, integrating religious history with other aspects, exposing tyranny, and at least hinting at a possible successful development for the third world? Or will they deal with more mundane topics? Will Don pursue further his religious studies? Whatever the answers will be, may Donald W. Treadgold live and labor for many more years!

CHAPTER 15

DON TREADGOLD: A BUILDER OF SLAVIC STUDIES

Robert F. Byrnes

We all assume that the institutions and values that sustain our lives and work grow by themselves in some quiet and mysterious way. Even those presumably informed because of their age and engagement often fail to appreciate, or even to remember, those whose devotion and energy created the conditions and spirit from which they benefit. I therefore welcome with special warmth this opportunity to recall briefly, especially for those scholar-teachers not active in the three or four decades after the Second World War, the fundamental role that Don Treadgold has already played in making Slavic studies in the United States a solid and lively intellectual enterprise and in helping American specialists become active participants in the international community of Slavicists. If it were not for Don, the basic instruments of this important field, the American Association for the Advancement of Slavic Studies (AAASS) and its journal, *Slavic Review*, would be only pale imitations of these now vigorous institutions, and the field would not enjoy harmonious interaction among its separate disciplines and friendly spirit among its competing academic institutions and points of view. Those who understand the stormy history of Asian studies since 1945 will especially value the quiet, sane contributions Don has made to a field of study that could also have suffered tempestuous intrigues and feuds.

The records or *curricula vitae* of most men and women in the academic community demonstrate that they have served on large numbers of committees and boards and have been active, or at least visible, members of the common instruments that make our work easy. Don's papers in some ways resemble all those records, except that he has been *the* editor, chairman, director, or president and, above all, that he has invariably been *the* responsible person. He has been and remains a *builder*. He has the magic touch: those many programs to which he has devoted his attention have bloomed and prospered, establishing roots and a vitality that indicate their continued success.

For those distant from Seattle and the Northwest, Don's achievements in the Slavic field have been national and international. However, Don has always recognized that we live within a series of concentric circles, with the base the local institution in which one lives and works. Since 1949, Don has been a significant contributor to the growth in quality and stature of the University of Washington. His career there as a renowned scholar and teacher (he received the national E. Harris Harbison Award for Distinguished Teaching in 1968 and was named University of Washington Distinguished Faculty Lecturer in 1980) has been his first priority. He has helped make the Department of History a distinguished one, serving as chairman for ten consecutive years (imagine!) while remaining a productive scholar, helping to make Washington's programs in the Russian and East European area and in international politics respected in the Pacific Northwest as well as recognized nationally and internationally, engaging in a most energetic and constructive way in a number of national and international enterprises.

More than twenty-five years ago, by ensuring that East Central Europe receive proper attention, he was responsible for the University of Washington's avoiding an issue that has plagued many institutions and deeply divided the Slavic field. In fact, the multi-volume *History of East Central Europe*, which he and Peter Sugar planned as early as 1961, serves as visible evidence of this wisdom. The attention the University of Washington has given to the Soviet Union's neighbors, those in the West as well as the People's Republic of China, Japan, and Taiwan in the East, reflects the framework of Russian studies that Don has helped give to the national instruments of Slavic studies. This spirit and broad perception have been enormously important, not only in avoiding overconcentration on Russia and on the twentieth century in particular, but in creating the worldwide framework in which most of us view the Slavic world.

Finally, in Seattle as in every place in which he has worked, Don early recognized that the responsibility of those who "would gladly learn, and gladly teach" extends far beyond the walls of one's university. He quickly and continually penetrated "the sheepskin curtain" that separates our schools from our colleges and universities, and he has injected that understanding and commitment into our national organizations and instruments. In the

same way, his lectures to public service organizations and to other
institutions throughout the Northwest and the nation have helped break the
old definition of the scholar-teacher's obligations and have given a national
and international spirit to Slavic studies as a whole.

Advancing from this solid local and regional base, Don has been
imaginative and constructive in every aspect of the growth of Slavic studies.
Some of these actions have been invisible; I am sure that even those who
have worked most closely with him are not aware of many of his services.
Thus, he led the campaign that dissuaded the Director of the New York
Public Library in 1965 from moving the Slavic collection from the main
building and the central research sources at Fifth Avenue and 42nd Street.
He served for years as a consultant to the Ford Foundation when the
Foundation's service as an intellectual clearing house and as a source for
fellowships and research funds made it a critical contributor to the survival
and progress of Slavic studies. He served in the same way for IREX, the
International Research and Exchanges Board, that since 1968 has sponsored
and administered the exchange of research opportunities between American
and Soviet and East European academic institutions. He was one of those
who established the framework and basic policies for the two main supports
of research in Slavic studies in this country in the past decade. He was a
member of the Board of Trustees of the National Council for Soviet and
East European Research from its founding in 1978 until 1984. He was a
member of the Academic Council of the Kennan Institute for Advanced
Russian Studies from 1977 through 1981 and became Chairman of the
Council in 1986.

However, Don's major contributions as a builder of Slavic studies are
his sterling services to its professional association and its journal. Both of
these would without doubt exist, but their role and their quality would be
far less central but for Don Treadgold. For a number of curious reasons,
in part the supervisory role that the Ford Foundation, the American Council
of Learned Societies, and the Social Sciences Research Council had played
in promoting Slavic studies after the Second World War, in part because
the field so quickly became national, in part because some from the
established centers on the two coasts resented the rapid rise of new
programs in other parts of the country, American scholars in the Slavic

field were remarkably tardy in creating a national membership organization. Indeed, this organization even now is less than thirty years old.

The Joint Committee on Slavic Studies, a committee of scholars from several disciplines and institutions whom the presidents of the ACLS and the SSRC appointed, served most effectively from 1940 until late in the 1960s as a guiding instrument for the field, analyzing national needs, educating college and university presidents and deans concerning the need to include these studies as a part of the educational process, and obtaining and dispersing research funds. That committee, after a thorough analysis in which Don played a critical role in 1957-59, decided that the United States possessed enough men and women Slavic specialists to justify and support a national organization. The two years, 1962-64, in which Don served as chairman of the Joint Committee, were important in ensuring a healthy start for the AAASS.

The AAASS's contributions to the progress of the field are a tribute to the foresight and leadership Don especially showed. His colleagues recognized this by awarding him the Association's Distinguished Service Award in 1975 and electing him president in 1977-78: Don is the only member who has received both of these tributes. That last honor proved an act of great foresight, for the Association in 1977 was in deep crisis--organizationally, financially, and philosophically. When Don left office, it had recovered its unity, financial equilibrium, and spirit, a remarkable but back-breaking achievement in just one year. His services and recognitions did not end there; the AAASS chose him to organize the program of the Third World Congress for Soviet and East European Studies in the fall of 1985 in Washington, D.C., a responsibility which he carried out so well that this complicated and delicate international conference was a resounding success. Indeed, Don's achievement in 1985 was a replicate of another signal contribution he had made ten years earlier, when he served as the chairman of the Organizing Committee of the International Congress of the Historical Sciences in San Francisco, an even larger and more difficult assignment.

Mention of the San Francisco congress recalls that Don is first and foremost a historian. His work on the Executive Council of the American Historical Association and in the association's Pacific Coast Branch has shown the same quality and, above all, has helped educate his colleagues in other more established fields of history concerning the intellectual quality and respectability of this new and somewhat suspect field.

But the clearest illustration of all Don's achievements as a builder are his two constructive terms as editor of the *Slavic Review*. On the first occasion, 1961-65, he took over what had been the *American Slavic and East European Review* and, with the support of the new membership organization, greatly expanded and improved the contents, circulation, and finances of the journal, which was renamed *Slavic Review*. He accomplished this achievement, at the expense of his scholarly work (as a builder always does) by developing new editorial policies and procedures for the journal, marshaling the support of a board of editors whom he inspired to work, and attracting articles and reviews of high quality that interested scholar-teachers in all disciplines. Other ideas he injected to make the review attractive and successful were equally impressive: he introduced in each number the section entitled "Discussion," which was composed of a special, brief article on a fundamental issue, with two or more comments by other specialists on that topic. He encouraged review articles and much more critical and lively book reviews. He made the *Slavic Review* an essential bibliographic tool for everyone interested in the profession.

Above all, he gave the *Slavic Review* the constant and confident direction and intellectual quality that have made it one of the premier American scholarly journals. Don quickly made the journal an intellectual magnet and dynamo for Slavic studies and a business success. Indeed, circulation doubled by the end of Don's first year as editor. Retiring from these responsibilities once he had placed the *Slavic Review* on a firm foundation, he accepted an urgent call to return in 1968, when the journal had fallen so far behind in its publication schedule that it had begun to lose the confidence of those whom it was designed to serve and to weaken the national spirit of American Slavic specialists. Don reestablished his earlier principles and formulas, so that when he retired a second time in 1975, to the applause of everyone, the review truly was well established.

The principles behind Don's work at the *Slavic Review* illustrate the many ways in which he has helped give Slavic studies their high qualities.

First, he has excited all by his willingness to sacrifice his personal interests as a scholar to a large national and international concern. He has helped create a genuine intellectual community of a far-flung, many-disciplined, somewhat ill-defined area of studies by giving sympathetic and full attention to all disciplines and interests, making certain that East Central Europe received appropriate recognition, and placing Slavic studies in an international framework, with attention to its near neighbors, other communist systems, and the larger world in which Russia and Eastern Europe exist. He has successfully encouraged participation by scholars in other countries, including those ruled by communists, so that the *Slavic Review* has helped break the parochialism of the American community and has itself become a part of the international community.

Those interested in Slavic studies in the United States need only to look at the AAASS and the *Slavic Review* to understand Don Treadgold's achievements as a builder. He has not accomplished this by himself, because others have contributed, often because he has persuaded them. But he has undertaken the primary responsibility, and he has helped increase the contributions of others by the way in which he has inspired, induced, and cajoled them. He has emphasized the highest quality in everything he has done, from rewriting book reviews, to proofreading, to selecting colleagues. He has been the embodiment of candor and integrity. He has been selfless and the ultimate in fairness and evenhandedness. In a field that has an increasing political flavor, he has been completely nonpartisan. He has shown imagination, insight, and above all courage. One must always remember, though, that his principal contributions have been of the spiritual kind, almost invisible, but as important for the survival and progress of this field of studies as the will to win is for an army or a basketball team.

Somehow, Don has been the consummate builder while at the same time serving as a teacher of most impressive abilities and a scholar whose works in quality, quantity, and above all range match those of even the most cloistered and dedicated scholar. Moreover, he has completed these achievements in a cool, relaxed way, with no haste and frenzy, with little show of emotion. He is a most straightforward and candid colleague. However, his standards are so high, his integrity so visible, and his tact so genuine that his frankness has won him increased respect and affection. His only flaw, at least to those of us who benefit from his work, is that he has concealed the secrets of his success. Many others have intellectual abilities, but his additional talents for organizing and directing his energies, and for administration and diplomacy, as well as his attractive personal qualities and an interest in the general welfare, set him apart. In American slang, he is a "triple threat." He is truly one of the great builders of Slavic studies. Long may he reign!

NOTES

CHAPTER 1
INTRODUCTION

1. Gerhard Simon, "Church, State and Society," in George Katkov, Erwin Oberländer, Nikolaus Poppe, and Georg von Rauch, eds., *Russia Enters the Twentieth Century, 1894-1917* (London: Temple Smith, 1971), 216. For a pre-*perestroika* type of study emphasizing the church-state alliance, see P. N. Zyrianov, *Pravoslavnaia tserkov' v bor'be s revoliutsiei 1905-1907 gg.* (Moscow: Nauka, 1984). While the Holy Synod and others at the pinnacle of the Russian Orthodox Church administration sought from above to find remedies in such measures as reforming the curriculum in Russian Orthodox seminaries, parish priests were more likely to be advocates for social, political, and economic reform of society and for reform of Church administration itself. Especially, they wanted to strengthen their church by emancipating it from government control. For a discussion of attitudes toward Church reform in the nineteenth and early twentieth centuries, see chapters 7 and 10 of Gregory Freeze, *The Parish Clergy in Nineteenth-Century Russia: Crisis, Reform, Counter-Reform* (Princeton: Princeton University Press, 1983).

2. Priscilla Roosevelt's *Apostle of Russian Liberalism: Timofei Granovsky* (Newtonville, Mass.: Oriental Research Partners, 1986) is a good case study of the transmission of ideas from Germany into the University of Moscow and the intellectual ferment of the 1840s and 1850s. Daniel R. Brower, *Training the Nihilists: Education and Radicalism in Tsarist Russia* (Ithaca: Cornell University Press, 1975) tells the story for the 1860s and 1870s. The essay by Alan Kimball in this volume expands the literature on this topic.

3. See Russell Zguta, "Peter I's 'Most Drunken Synod of Fools and Jesters,'" *Jahrbücher für Geschichte Osteuropas* 21(1973): 18-28 for a discussion of the origin and activities of this body.

4. Freeze, *Parish Clergy*, 12-22; also by the same author: "Handmaiden of the State? The Church in Imperial Russia Reconsidered," *Journal of Ecclesiastical History* 36(1985): 82-102.

5. For a short sketch of the events surrounding the second and third partitions of Poland, see Michael T. Florinsky, *Russia: A History and an Interpretation*, 2 vols. (New York: Macmillan Company, 1953), 1:538-41. For numbers of Jews added to the empire and the areas of Jewish settlement, see John Klier, *Russia Gathers Her Jews: The Origins of the "Jewish Question" in Russia, 1772-1825* (Dekalb: Northern Illinois University Press, 1986).

6. In addition to sources William James cites in the notes of his essay, a useful short sketch of the history of the Jesuit presence in Poland prior to Russian annexation and in the Russian Empire afterward is Daniel L. Schlafly, Jr., "Jesuits in Russia," in *The Modern Encyclopedia of Russian and Soviet History* (hereafter *MERSH*) 15(Gulf Breeze, Florida: Academic International Press, 1978): 128-36. See also James T. Flynn, "The Role of the Jesuits in the Politics of Russian Education, 1801-1820," *Catholic Historical Review* 56(July 1970): 249-65. For Jesuit activities beyond their role in education during the reign of Paul I, see William James, "Paul I and the Jesuits in Russia" (Ph.D. diss., University of Washington, 1977).

7. See Florinsky, *Russia*, 1:528-29, for the annexation of the Crimean Tatars and 2:979-86 for Russian expansion into Central Asia in the 1860s and 1870s.

8. The most concise and easily accessible general explanation of the types and categories of national minorities within the Russian Empire is Richard Pipes, *The Formation of the Soviet Union: Communism and Nationalism, 1917-1923* (Cambridge: Harvard University Press, 1955), 2-21. For the best readily accessible definition listing all the groups under this rubric, see "Inorodtsy," *Entsiklopedicheskii slovar* 25(St. Petersburg: Brokgauz-Efron, 1894): 224-25.

9. Hugh Seton-Watson, *The Russian Empire, 1801-1917* (Oxford: Clarendon Press, 1967), 215.

10. Information in this paragraph is a synthesis of information from the following works: Simon, "Church, State and Society"; Violet Conolly, "The 'Nationalities Question' in the Last Phase of Tsardom," in Katkov et al., eds., *Russia Enters the Twentieth Century*, 152-81; John Shelton Curtiss, *Church and State in Russia: The Last Years of the Empire, 1900-1917* (New York: Columbia University Press, 1940), 35-86; Marc Szeftel, "Church and State in Imperial Russia," in Robert L. Nichols and Theofanis G. Stavrou, eds., *Russian Orthodoxy under the Old Regime* (Minneapolis: University of Minnesota Press, 1978), 127-41; and Donald W. Treadgold, "Russian Orthodoxy and Society," ibid., 21-43. These works are mentioned in subsequent footnotes only to indicate page numbers for specific information or quotations.

11. Conolly, "Nationalities Question," 170.

12. N. Barsov, "Zakon Bozhii," *Entsiklopedicheskii slovar* 24(St. Petersburg, 1894): 174-77; B. Titlinov, "Zakon Bozhii," *Novyi entsiklopedicheskii slovar* 18(St. Petersburg, 1910?): 166-69. See Baron N. A. Korf's recommendations to teachers in zemstvo schools for "Moral-religious discussions between teacher and pupils," teaching "Zakon Bozhii," and "Church Singing" in his *Russkaia nachal'naia shkola: Rukovodstvo dlia zemskikh glasnykh i uchitelei zemskikh shkol*, 2d ed. (St. Petersburg, 1870),

296-309. A major textbook for this course for older children was Priest M. Sokolov, *Zakon Bozhii dlia detei mladshago vozrasta* (St. Petersburg, 1876). See Paul Miliukov's list of course requirements in Russian universities in his "Universitety v Rossii," *Entsiklopedicheskii slovar* 68(St. Petersburg, 1902): 800.

13. Simon, "Church, State and Society," 200.

14. Ibid. Curtiss, *Church and State in Russia*, 35.

15. Szeftel, "Church and State," 137-38.

16. "Dukhovno-uchebnyia zavedeniia," *Entsiklopedicheskii slovar* 21 (St. Petersburg, 1890): 268-69.

17. "Akademii dukhovnyia pravoslavnyia," *Entsiklopedicheskii slovar* 1 (St. Petersburg, 1890): 254-57.

18. "Dukhovno-uchebnyia zavedeniia," 269.

19. Schlafly, "Jesuits in Russia," 128-36; also by the same author, "Golitsyn, Alexander Nikolaevich (1773-1844)," *MERSH* 12(1979): 238-240. Dmitrii Tolstoi, future minister of education, published a book in French on the harmful effects of Roman Catholicism and Judaism in the Russian Empire: Dmitrii Andreevich Tolstoi, *Romanism in Russia: An Historical Study*, translated from the French by Mrs. M'Kibbin (New York: AMS Press, 1974; reprint of the 1874 edition).

20. "Vilenskii universitet," *Entsiklopedicheskii slovar* 11 (St. Petersburg, 1892): 328-329 and "Akademiia dukhovnaia rimsko-katolicheskaia," ibid., 1 (St. Petersburg, 1890): 257-59.

21. Conolly, "Nationalities Question," 156.

22. "Akademiia dukhovnaia rimsko-katolicheskaia," 257-58; "Vilenskii universitet," 328. D. Margolin, *Spravochnik po vysshemy obrazovaniiu,* 3d ed. (Petrograd and Kiev, 1915), 81-82. John McErlean, "Catholicism in Russia," *MERSH*, 6:132-39; Schlafly, "Jesuits in Russia," 128-36.

23. Conolly, "Nationalities Question," 173.

24. "Akademiia dukhovnaia rimsko-katolicheskaia," 259.

25. Margolin, *Spravochnik*, 69-73; "Varshavskii universitet," *Entsiklopedicheskii slovar* 10(St. Petersburg, 1892): 563-65.

26. Charles E. Timberlake, "Higher Learning, the State, and the Professions in Russia," in Konrad H. Jarausch, ed., *The Transformation of Higher Learning, 1860-1930: Expansion, Diversification, Social Opening, and Professionalization in England, Germany, Russia, and the United States* (copublished in Germany in 1982 as volume 13 of *Historisch-Sozialwissenschaftlichte Forschungen,* by Klett-Cotta, Stuttgart, and in the United States in 1983 by University of Chicago Press), 321-44; Donald W. Treadgold, "Protestantism in Russia," *MERSH*, 30:36-39; Daniel Rowland,

"Lutherans in Russia and the Soviet Union," *MERSH*, 20:199-204; "Gel'singforskii universitet," *Entsiklopedicheskii slovar* 15(St. Petersburg, 1892): 291.

27. "Iur'evskii universitet," *Entsiklopedicheskii slovar* 81(St. Petersburg, 1904): 437.

28. Conolly, "Nationalities Question," 170; Michael H. Haltzel, "Religious Turmoil," in Edward Thaden et al., *Russification in the Baltic Provinces and Finland, 1855-1914* (Princeton: Princeton University Press, 1981), 161-67.

29. "Iur'evskii universitet," 437.

30. "Akademiia dukhovnaia rimsko-katolicheskaia," 269-70; Leon Arpee, *A History of Armenian Christianity from the Beginning to Our Own Time* (Princeton: Armenian Missionary Association of America, 1946), 247.29. "Iur'evskii universitet," 437.

31. Ibid., 270; Margolin, *Spravochnik*, 81.

32. Conolly, "Nationalities Question," 178; Seton-Watson, *Russian Empire*, 216.

33. Seton-Watson, *Russian Empire*, 216.

34. Patrick L. Alston, *Education and the State in Tsarist Russia* (Stanford: Stanford University Press, 1969), 121; Klier, *Russia Gathers Her Jews*, chapter 1.

35. George Kline, *Religious and Anti-Religious Thought in Russia* (Chicago and London: University of Chicago Press, 1968).

36. Edmund Heier, *Religious Schism in the Russian Aristocracy, 1860-1900: Radstockism and Pashkovism* (The Hague: Martinus Nijhoff, 1970), 31.

37. Ibid., xv.

38. Ibid., 138.

39. "Iur'evskii universitet," 437; Miliukov, "Universitety v Rossii," 800ff.

40. Conolly, "Nationalities Question." 170.

41. *Uspenski Cathedral*, text by Irinja Nikkanen (Finland: Varisuomi Oy, 1980), 4.

42. Alston, *Education and the State*, 130.

43. Conolly, "Nationalities Question," 179.

44. Alston, *Education and the State*, 120.

45. Arpee, *Armenian Christianity*, 298.

46. Conolly, "Nationalities Question," 157.

47. Heier, *Religious Schism*, 138.

48. Ben Eklof, *Russian Peasant Schools: Officialdom, Village Culture, and Popular Pedagogy, 1861-1914* (Berkeley and Los Angeles: University of California Press, 1986), 171.

49. Theofanis G. Stavrou, *Russian Interests in Palestine, 1882-1914: A Study of Religious and Educational Enterprise* (Thessaloniki: Institute for Balkan Studies, 1963), 110-14; 151-57.

50. The main provisions of this act are available in English translation in *A Source Book for Russian History from Early Times to 1917*, edited by George Vernadsky, Ralph T. Fisher, Jr., Alan D. Ferguson, Andrew Lossky, compiled by Sergei Pushkarev, 3 vols. (New Haven and London: Yale University Press, 1972), 3:766.

51. For debate over implementation of the act of toleration, see Alfred Levin, "Toward the End of the Old Regime: The State, Church, and Duma," in Dennis Dunn, ed., *Religion and Modernization in the Soviet Union* (Boulder: Westview Press, 1977), 23-59, p. 30 for the quotation of Stolypin's position.

52. Levin, "Toward the End," 34; Conolly, "Nationalities Question," 157, 172.

53. Quoted in Levin, "Toward the End," 51-53.

54. Sidney Monas' "Religion and the Intelligentsia," in Dunn, *Religion and Modernization*, 105-35, is one of the most reasoned presentations of this line of thought.

55. Treadgold, "Russian Orthodoxy and Society," in Nichols and Stavrou, *Russian Orthodoxy*, 39-41, on the Marxists' return. S. D. Cioran, "The Dialogue Between Church and Intelligentsia: The Petersburg Religio-Philosophical Gatherings of 1901-03," in S. D. Cioran, S. W. Smyrniw, and G. Thomas, eds., *Studies in Honour of Louis Shein* (Hamilton, Ontario: McMaster University Press, 1983), 15-20.

56. Quoted in Sergei Pushkarev, *The Emergence of Modern Russia, 1801-1917* (New York: Holt, Rinehart, and Winston, 1963), 298.

CHAPTER 2
RUSSIA'S EARLY INQUISITIONS

1. Cf. Max Weber's definition of a "Church" in *Economy and Society*, translated and edited by Guenter Roth, Claus Wittich, et al., 2 vols. (Berkeley: University of California Press, 1978), 56, 1163-76. Clearly, any ideological movement/party of this kind must have a purging apparatus.

2. Joseph Lecler, S.J., *Histoire de la Tolérance au siècle de la Réforme*, 2 vols. (Paris: Aubier, 1955), 1:133-37.

3. Thomas Aquinas, *Summa theologica*, translated by the Fathers of the English Dominican Province (New York: Benziger Brothers, 1947), 1218-19 (II-II, question 10, article 8).

4. Jean Bodin, *The Six Bookes of a Commonweale*, edited by Kenneth Douglas McRae (Cambridge, Mass., 1962; facsimile of the London, 1606, translation of Richard Knolles), 536-37, 648-49. Bodin appears to approve of the alleged practice of the crowned heads in Asia, Africa, and Spain (but not the rest of "Europe") of prohibiting religious disputes.

5. According to a Hindu acquaintance of Donald Treadgold's, "all truly Orthodox religions are inherently tolerant" (pers. comm.). If so, *religion* must be separate from *church*.

6. See Donald W. Treadgold, *The West in Russia and China*, 2 vols. (Cambridge: Cambridge University Press, 1973), vol. 1, chaps. 1 and 2. Since that book was completed, an important new source has been published: N. N. Pokrovskii, ed., *Sudnye spiski Maksima Greka i Isaaka Sobaki* (Hereafter *SSMGIS*) (Moscow, 1971). Among the most important new works are a set of new studies concerning Maksim, especially N. A. Sinitsyna, *Maksim Grek v Rossii* (Moscow, 1977), Edgar Hösch's comprehensive and judicious *Orthodoxie und Häresie im alten Russland* (Wiesbaden: Harrassowitz, 1975), with a superb bibliography, and his "Orthodoxie und 'Rechtgläubigkeit' im Moskauer Russland," in Uwe Halbach, Hans Heckler, and Andreas Kappeler, eds., *Geschichte Altrusslands in der Begriffswelt ihrer Quellen: Festschrift zum 70. Geburtstag von Günther Stökl* (Stuttgart: Steiner Verlag, 1986), 50-68.

7. In addition to the sources noted in Iosif Volotskii, *Prosvetitel' ili oblichenie eresi zhidovstvuiushchikh*, 4th ed. (Kazan, 1903), see Hösch, *Orthodoxie und Häresie*, 106-7, and notes 894, 897.

8. See, for example, E. E. Golubinskii, *Istoriia Russkoi tserkvi*, 2 vols. in 4 (Moscow, 1901-11), 1.2:791-95. "Andrian the castrate and heretic," the "evil heretic Dmitrii," and the "heretic Seit" are first noted in the (Iosifite) *Nikon Chronicle* under 1004, 1123, and 1326 respectively and are thus suspect from the outset. "Zosima," whom Iosif Volotskii called Russia's "initial heretic," was first mentioned in the *Sofiia I Chronicle* in a fashion that is clearly dependent on the tale of the monk Zosima, who apostatized to Islam and extorted money in Iaroslavl for the Mongols, a story originally in the more reliable *Laurentian Chronicle*. The "heretic," who is allied to an (anachronistic) adherent of the "paradise perished" doctrine, and against whom Metropolitan Petr allegedly held a *sobor* in Pereiaslavl in 1313, first appeared in Tatishchev, is called "Vavil" in a second manuscript, and seems to be a transfiguration of "Seit" and ultimately of the *Sofiia* "Zosima." "Martin," whom E. F. Grekulov as late as 1964 saw as a popular heretic of 1157 (*Pravoslavnaia inkvizitsiia v Rossii* [Moscow, 1964], 11), has been known to derive from a spurious early

eighteenth-century source for more than a century. None are found in the
Laurentian, Hypatian, or *Novgorod I Chronicle.* See *Polnoe sobranie
russkikh letopisei* (hereafter *PSRL*), 2d ed. (St. Petersburg-Leningrad and
Moscow, 1846---), 1:476; 5:190; 9:68, 152, 190; 10:192; S. Tatishchev,
Istoriia rossiiskaia, ed. A. N. Andreev, S. N. Valk, and M. N.
Tikhomirov, 7 vols. (Moscow and Leningrad, 1962-68), 5:72 and var. 45;
Hösch, *Orthodoxie und Häresie,* 53, 176, 191. Also suspect is the validity
of the report from the mid-sixteenth-century *Life of Bishop Iakov of Rostov*
(1386-89) concerning a local *sobor* under the prince against an "Armenian"
heretic, who sounds more like a 1470-1555 dissident, but is accepted as real
by A. I. Klibanov in *Reformatsionnye dvizheniia v Rossii v XIV-pervoi
polovine XVI v.v.* (Moscow, 1960), 164-66. Among contemporary scholars,
B. M. Kloss has raised the question of the authenticity of the Andrian and
Dmitrii tales: "'Nikonovskaia letopis''i Maksim Grek," *Trudy Otdela
drevnerusskoi literatury* (hereafter *TODRL*), 30(1976): 128-29.

9. *PSRL* 1:355-57, 2:552-53; A. N. Nasonov, *Novgorodskaia pervaia
letopis'* (hereafter *NPL*) (Moscow and Leningrad, 1950), 63, 182-83.

10. The basic source for these dissidents remains the sermon of Stefan
of Perm: N. A. Kazakova and Ia. S. Lur'e, *Anti-feodal'nye ereticheskie
dvizheniia na Rusi XIV-nachala XVI veka* (Moscow and Leningrad, 1955),
234-42; hereafter *AfED.*

11. This information, though not found in the "Extended" *NPL,* goes
back to the pre-Iosifite "common Russian" *svod* of 1448 as reflected in the
Novgorod IV and *Sofia I* chronicles: *PSRL* 4:72, 5:275, 11:24, 23:120,
24:123, 25:192. The verb *pobiti* employed in the earliest versions (as
opposed to *ubiti* in the later ones) does not seem to have been used in the
more officious sense of "execute." I. I. Sreznevskii, *Materialy dlia
slovaria drevnerusskago iazyka,* 3 vols. (St. Petersburg, 1893-1906), 2:985-
86; 3:1109-11.

12. *AfED,* 230-43.

13. Ibid., 242-53.

14. The earliest sources for the heretics from Novgorod are in *AfED,*
309-20. Recent attempts to determine the original heresy as a quarrel over
certain icons only show how problematic these dissidents are and how rich
the state of inquiry concerning them remains. Jana R. Howlett, "The
Heresy of the Judaisers and the Problem of the Russian Reformation"
(Ph.D. diss., Oxford University, 1976); Fairy von Lilienfeld, "Das
Problem der Ikonographie, der Ikonentheologie und der Ikonenverehrung
bei Erzbischof Gennadij von Novgorod und Joseph von Volokolamsk vor
1490: Ein Beitrag zur Entwirrung des Rätsels um die sogennante Häresie
der 'Judaisierenden,'" *Forschungen zur osteuropäischen Geschichte*
38(1981): 110-129.

15. Iu. K. Begunov, "Kormchaia Ivana Volka Kuritsyna," *TODRL* 12:141-59. The accusation of astrology and other parascientific interests was made by Volotskii: *AfED*, 471. Fedor's few original writings are found in *AfED*, 256-76. Cf. Thomas M. Seebohm, *Ratio und Charisma: Ansätze und Ausbildung eines philosophischen und wissenschaftlichen Weltverständnisses im Moskauer Russland* (*Mainzer philosophische Forschungen*, vol. 17; Bonn: Bouvier, 1977). An explicated publication of the Old Russian *kormchie* has yet to appear.

16. This is clear from his very frustrated February 1489 missive to former Archbishop Ioasaf of Rostov: *AfED*, 315-20.

17. For the course of events and Gennadii's propaganda techniques, see the documents in *AfED*, 309-19, 373-79; for the turn to the West, Treadgold, *The West in Russia and China*, 1:7-12.

18. *AfED*, 373-79.

19. Ibid., 378, 381.

20. The report was published by A. D. Sedel'nikov, "Rasskaz 1490 g. ob inkvizitsii," *Trudy Komissii po drevnerusskoi literature* 1(1934): 49-50. Gennadii's memorandum considered the two chief inquisitors to have been papal bishop-legates, while they were actually all Spanish Dominicans. *Pace* Gennadii, the king's two leading "boyars" played no role as they did in the Novgorod inquests. The number of executed mentioned, however, may have been only a 100 percent exaggeration, since Queen Isabella's secretary, Pulgar, estimated a total of 1,000 for 1480-1504. Thousands more were subjected to tribunals and may have been tortured to obtain evidence, but such treatment was not considered punishment: those who repented after they had been sentenced to death (for obduracy or relapsing) were, as a humanitarian measure, strangled before they were burned. None were subject to the "gruesome" punishments Gennadii related. See the sympathetic(!) treatment of the Spanish Inquisition from its origin through 1490 in William Thomas Walsh, *Characters of the Inquisition* (New York, 1940/1969), 151-75.

21. *AfED*, 482. (For an authenticated example of such punishment, see below, note 46.)

22. Ibid., 384-86.

23. Ibid., 482. Volotskii's detailed description of the materials used to costume the victims betrays an eyewitness report. The Western influence is obvious, as Jan Hus had a conical hat with the inscription "This is the Heresiarch," corresponding to a similar hat of the Novgorodians inscribed with "This is Satan's Army." An Eastern model for parading heretics on animals, as found in the Life of Amphilocus of Iconium and reported by none other than Vassian Patrikeev, is also possible: Henry Charles Lea, *A History of the Inquisition in the Middle Ages*, 3 vols. (New York,

1888/1955), 2:491; N. A. Kazakova, *Vassian Patrikeev i ego sochineniia* (hereafter *VPS*) (Moscow and Leningrad, 1960), 270; J.-P. Migne, *Patrologiae cursus completus*, Series Graeca (161 vols., Paris, 1857-66; hereafter *PG*), 39:26.

24. Cf. David Goldfrank, "Old and New Perspectives on Iosif Volotsky's Monastic Rules," *Slavic Review* 34(June 1975): 279-301; and "Pre-Enlightenment Utopianism in Russian History," *Russian History/Histoire russe* 11(Summer-Fall 1984): 129-30.

25. Ia. S. Lur'e and A. A. Zimin, *Poslaniia Iosifa Volotskogo* (Moscow and Leningrad, 1959), 160-78; hereafter *PIV*.

26. These were the secularizing lay canonist Volk Kuritsyn; the archpriest Ivan Maksimov, who had influenced Ivan III's daughter-in-law; and Archimandrite Kassian and his brother Samo Cherny, who apparently obstructed Gennadii's policies in Novgorod. The tradition that Vasilii III also presided is found in the "common Russian" 1518 chronicle *svod*. The later Iosifite *Nikon Chronicle* has Vasilii also presiding in 1490: *PSRL* 12:224-27, 258; 28:337.

27. *PIV*, 64; *AfED*, 490. Inherited Eastern Church traditions, as transmitted by Nikon "Of the Black Mountain," follow Chrysostom's insistence that condemning under certain conditions is licit, but not as Iosif so liberally interpreted. Nikon Chernogorets, *Pandekty* (Vologda, 1670/Pochaev, 1795), "*Slovo*" 39:288-90; cf. *PG* 57:307-9. Note that on the basis of handwriting samples, Ia. S. Lur'e (Luria) has even suggested that the presumed founder of the "Nonpossessors," Nil Sorskii, actively collaborated with efforts against inquisitorial proceedings, including smearing the heretics with the charge of Judaism. "The Ideological Movements of the Late Fifteenth Century," *Medieval Russian Culture*, ed. Henrik Birnbaum and Michael S. Flier, *California Slavic Studies* 12(1984): 163-71. In addition, Donald Ostrowski has recently tried to demonstrate that there was no grouping of genuine "Nonpossessors"--that is, a faction committed to the secularization of monastic lands. "Church Polemics and Monastic Land Acquisition in Sixteenth-Century Moscovy," *Slavonic and East European Review* 64(July 1986): 355-79.

28. *AfED*, 490.

29. Ibid., 510-13; *VPS*, 250-53.

30. *AfED*, 503-10.

31. *PIV*, 227-28, 367; *VPS*, 176; *Velikiia Minei chetii, sobrannye vserossiiskim Mitropolitom Makariem* (hereafter *VMch*), 22 vols. (St. Petersburg, 1868-1917), September, 474-75. Vassian's source for Novatianism is, as he states, Nikon Chernogorets, *Pandekty*, "*Slovo*," 51:414 ob.

32. *VPS*, 270, from Nikon Chernogorets, *Pandekty*, *"Slovo"* 25:183 ob. Cf. Aquinas, as in note 3 above.

33. *Prosvetitel'*, *"Slovo"* 16:526-41.

34. Ibid., 14:503-08. A source for positive as well as negative strategems is Nikon Chernogorets, *Pandekty*, *"Slovo"* 16:123 ob.

35. Hence the titles of the last five chapters of *Prosvetitel'* which begin, as do ten of the first eleven: *Slovo protiv eres' novgorodskikh eretikov....*

36. *PIV*, 367-68. The source, *"Pis'mo o neliubkakh,"* is not to be fully trusted, but Vassian's willingness to terrorize opponents is corroborated by Mikhail Medotvartsov's testimony at Maksim Grek's second trial. *SSMGIS*, 103.

37. *PIV*, 368; *VMch*, September, 475.

38. *PIV*, 178-79.

39. A. A. Zimin, *Ivan S. Peresvetov i ego sovremmeniki* (Moscow, 1958), 173.

40. Daniil's views are discussed in detail by V. Zhmakin in "Vzgliad mitropolita Daniila na otnoshenie k eretikam," *Zhurnal Ministerstva narodnago prosveshcheniia* 203(1879): 1-51, and *Mitropolit Daniil i ego sochineniia* (Moscow, 1881) also in *Chteniia v Imperatorskom Obshchestve istorii i drevnostei rossiiskikh* (hereafter *ChOIDR*), 1881, vols. 1-2:397-420. Daniil's literary corpus still awaits publication more than a century after Zhmakin's seminal study.

41. The *sobor* against "Isaak the Jew," claimed by Ikonnikov to have occurred in 1520, may be pure myth. Maksim did write a brief essay with the caption *Inoka Maksima sovet k soboru pravoslavnomu na Isaka zhidovina, volkva i charodeia i prelestnika*, but with no internal indication that it was anything but an abstract statement about dangerous heretics. Found first as "Glava 45" in a mid-sixteenth century *sbornik* of Maksim's protector, ex-Metropolitan Ioasaf, this work merely repeated some of Iosif's arguments in defense of icons and called for capital punishment. Intended, perhaps, to clear Maksim's name before Tsar Ivan IV, it cannot be taken as evidence that such a *sobor* was held between 1517, when Maksim arrived, and 1521, when Daniil, who certainly was unlikely to have requested Maksim's advice concerning heretics or sorcerers, became metropolitan. Ikonnikov seems to have accepted on face value the testimony of Zinovii Otenskii in the late 1560s that after Iosif's death "many magnates," who were secret Judaizers, revealed themselves. *Maksim Grek i ego vremia* (Kiev, 1915), 208-10; also Golubinskii, *Istoriia*, 2.1:235; A. I. Ivanov, *Literaturnoe nasledie Maksima Greka* (Leningrad, 1969), 106-7; Sinitsyna, *Maksim Grek*, 223-35, 329-34. The text is found in *Sochineniia prepodobnago Maksima Greka*, 3 vols. (Kazan, 1859-62), 1:51-55.

42. N. A. Kazakova, "Vopros o prichinakh osuzhdenii Maksima Greka," *Vizantiiskii vremennik* 28(1968): 109-26.

43. *SSMGIS*, 90.

44. *Akty sobrannye v bibliotekakh i arkhivakh Rossiiskoi imperii Arkheograficheskoi komissieiu* (hereafter *AAE*), 3 vols. (St. Petersburg, 1836), 1, no. 152.

45. "Novyi pamiatnik politicheskoi literatury XVI v.," *Moskovskii krai v ego proshlom*, pt. 2 (Moscow, 1930), 112.

46. *SSMGIS*, 121-25.

47. According to "*Pis'mo o neliubkakh*," Vasilii III "became angry with him [Vassian] and sent him to Iosifov Monastery"; there is no mention of any church trial, just an allusion to "God's judgment" of Vassian's vendetta with the Iosifites: *PIV*, 369.

48. *SSMGIS*, 96-120.

49. Ibid., 114. Curiously, in this instance Maksim claimed lack of memory for such details of his past. Just as in 1490 when reverberations from the Spanish Inquisition in a sense affected those Novgorodians who read Maimonides (*Logika*), so in 1531 the tentacles of the Papal Inquisition reached Moscow and stung a former devotee of some of the ideas of Ficino, Pico, and Savonarola! Is it possible that agents from Moscow actually checked into Maksim's Italian career?

50. *SSMGIS*, 118-19. Here too, the text begs a question. Maksim was accused as well for upbraiding the Russians for not respecting Isidor, the last Byzantine-appointed metropolitan, who had accepted Union with Rome in 1439. Maksim is not reported to have replied to this charge, which itself indicates that his accusers drew pro-papal, as well as pro-Ottoman conclusions from his loyalty to the Greek Church. According to the Muscovite thinking of the time, favoring the Union was itself actionable as heresy. In fact, one could argue that the initial set of writings from the Moscovite metropolitanate that threatened death for heresy or apostasy was the cycle of Metropolitan Iona's missives to Western Rus, especially his circular of 1460. These were copied around 1500 in the same manuscripts as the writings against the *strigolniki*. See L. V. Cherepnin, *Russkie feodal'nye arkhivy*, 2 vols. (Moscow, 1948-51), 2:20-23; *AfED*, 230-32; *Russkaia istoricheskaia biblioteka* (hereafter *RIB*), 39 vols. (St. Petersburg-Petrograd-Leningrad, 1872-1927), 6, no. 87.

51. Aphtharodocetism was one of the doctrines of the Monophysites, who claimed that Christ's divine nature completely sublated his human nature, hence his flesh was incorruptible.

52. *VPS*, 285-318.

53. Vassian's inquisitional views, which are close to those of Nikon of the Black Mountain, are found in *VPS*, 270-79; cf. *Pandekty*, "*Slovo*" 25:183-86 ob.; 51-52:405 ob-416; 65:550-61 ob.

54. *SSMGIS*, 120.

55. Ibid.

56. Sinitsyna, *Maksim Grek*, 65-66.

57. Golubinskii, *Istoriia*, 2.1:719; J. L. I. Fennell, *Prince A. M. Kurbsky's History of Ivan IV* (Cambridge: Cambridge University Press, 1965), 82-83.

58. *SSMGIS*, 80. M. N. Pokrovskii, editor of the *Sudnyi spisok*, or trial record, assumes that the information in the *spisok* is reliable. Whether Sobaka actually obtained this post is questionable. Archimandrite Filofei appears directly in documents of Simonov Monastery as late as 7050 (a period extending from September 1541 to August 1542), and "Simonova arkhrimandrita Filofev prikashchik Korobovskogo sel'tsa Ivashko Kubyshka" took part in a land suit in August 1543, after Makarii was ordained metropolitan (March 16, 1542). Sobaka's name is never mentioned in these documents. See L. I. Ivina, ed., *Akty feodal'nogo zemlevladeniia i khoziaistva: Akty moskovskogo Simonova monastyria (1506-1613)* 67(Leningrad, 1983): 67, 72; *PSRL* 13, no. 1:142.

59. Pokrovskii believes that this occurred sometime during 1545-48. Stroev, however, having reviewed the Chudov archives, listed Mikhail, who became bishop of Riazan in April 1548, under 1545 and Vassian Glazatyi under 1549. If the Sobaka documents are correct about the Chudov post, the appointment must have come in 1548 between late April and early November, when his case opened up. Again, whether he actually officiated as archimandrite is another matter. See *SSMGIS*, 80, 125; P. M. Stroev, *Spiski ierarkhov i nastoiatelei monastyri Rossiiskiia tserkvii* (St. Petersburg, 1877), 163.

60. Sinitsyna, *Maksim Grek*, 148-60.

61. On Silvestr, see Zimin, *Peresvetov*, 43-70.

62. *PSRL* 13, no. 2:524, depicts him as an unofficial grand vizier.

63. This "system" is revealed in the surviving documents from the Viskovatii and Artemii cases: *AAE* 1, no. 238-39.

64. *SSMGIS*, 138. Brother of Maksim's Iosifov jailer Tikhon and Vassian's Iosifov warden Feognost, and soon to become one of Matvei Bashkin's inquisitors, Gerasim Lenkov may have had a hand in the composition of the trial record: why else would his role have been singled out?

65. *PSRL* 13, no. 2:524-26.

66. O. M. Bodianskii, ed., "Rozysk ili spisok o bogokhul'nykh strokakh i somnenii chestnykh ikon d'iaka Ivana Mikhailova syna Viskovatogo v leto 7062," *ChOIDR* 1858, vol. 2, otd. 2:1-42.

67. *AAE* 1, No. 238:1-2.

68. Golubinskii, *Istoriia*, 2.1:843-44. Cf. David B. Miller, "The Viskovaty Affair of 1553-53: Official Art, the Emergence of Autocracy, and the Disintegration of Medieval Russian Culture," *Russian History* 8(1981): 293-323.

69. Zimin, *Peresvetov*, 170.

70. *AAE* 1, no. 238:3-4, 239.

71. Ibid. 1, no. 238:3-4.

72. Ibid., no. 239:249-51; *PSRL* 13, no. 1:232-33; O. Bodianskii, "Moskovskie sobory na eretikov XVI-go veka," *ChOIDR* 1847, vol. 3, otd. 2:1-2. The chronicle account reveals a more credible flow of events than does Makarii's report at the beginning of his instructions to the Solovetskii authorities concerning Artemii.

73. *AAE* 1, no. 239:253.

74. Ibid., no. 289, "box" 229.

75. The sources indicated above are somewhat corroborated by Kurbskii. Fennell, *Kurbsky's History*, 266-73. The Orthodox Kurbskii, like Vassian Patrikeev, believed in the judiciousness of inquisitorial proceedings against genuine heretics such as Lutherans. Zimin's observation that Artemii's trial was lawless, even on the basis of the norms of ecclesiastical justice of the time, seems to miss the point that heresy trials in Russia after 1488 were generally mixtures of Russia's Orthodox "legality" and political justice (*Peresvetov*, 162).

76. Starets Artemii, *Poslaniia*. *RIB* 4:1213, 1366.

77. The depiction of full sectarian tendencies is found in the reported demand that people "give" to them, the heresiarchs, rather than to the regular church in pseudo-Zinovii's *Poslanie mnogoslovnoe: sochinenie inoka Zinoviia*, ed. A. Popov (Moscow, 1880); also in *ChOIDR* 1880, vol. 2, *Slovo'* 4:143-220. Feodosii's career in Lithuania suggests that he may have been less of an anarcho-sectarian and more an establishment Protestant than is generally recognized in Soviet historiography. If this is the case, then Zinovii (author of *Istiny pokazanie*) and pseudo-Zinovii were really attacking genuine and somewhat heretical Russian sectarians, who had probably been developing in the shadows since the late fourteenth century and whom the "Muscovite Inquisition" could not reach.

78. Bodianskii, "Moskovskie sobory," 1-2.

79. Golubinskii, *Istoriia*, 859-60; Fennell, *Kurbsky's History*, 262-85. Kurbskii's reliability here rests in part on the verification from other sources of his information concerning the persecution of Artemii and Savva Shakh.

80. It is actually possible that Bodin's observation at the beginning of this chapter holds the key to the apparent disappearance of the Iosifites, Nonpossessors, and prominent heretics in the latter part of Ivan IV's reign. A despotic state that forbids religious disputes does not care what people really believe, so long as they keep quiet in public and make no disturbances. Such a state needs no religious inquisition--only a political one. This may be why religious/intellectual disputes did not flare up again in Russia until the Troubles and post-Troubles reconstruction, when the state lacked cohesion at the top: cf. Treadgold, *The West in Russia and China*, 1:46.

81. Ikonnikov, *Maksim Grek*, 266-67.

82. On Zinovii's social criticism and attitude toward heretics, see F. Kalugin, *Zinovii, inok Otenskii i ego bogoslovsko-polemicheskiia i tserkovono-uchitel'niia proizvedeniia* (St. Petersburg, 1894), 231-34, 345-52; A. I. Klibanov and V. I. Koretskii, "Poslanie Zinoviia Otenskogo d'iaku Ia. V. Shishkinu," *TODRL* 17(1961):201-24; Pseudo-Zinovii, *Poslanie mnogoslovnoe*, 256-300. Pseudo-Zinovii was strictly Iosifite concerning the inquisition, while Zinovii was careful to base his arguments on the New Testament and Basil the Great and thus was reduced to emphasizing the Church's teaching role and simply praising Ivan III and Vasilii III for their zeal. Zinovii was also honest enough to link the spread of heresy to social and economic problems and administrative abuses.

83. A. Popov, *Bibliograficheskie materialy*, vol. 8: *Kniga Erazma o Sviatoi Troitse*, in *ChOIDR* 1880, 4:1-124; V. Rzhiga, *Literaturnaia deiatel'nost' Ermolaia-Erazma* (Leningrad, 1926), "Prilozhenie," 192-94. A. I. Klibanov, "Sbornik sochinenii Ermolaia-Erazma," *TODRL* 16(1960): 178-207. Without challenging directly ecclesiastical power or touching upon the inquisition per se, Erazm preached love and moderation to all authorities.

84. On Maksim's reformist views, note the classic V. Rzhiga, "Opyty po istorii russkoi publitsistiki XVI veka: Maksim Grek kak publitsist," *TODRL* 1(1934): 5-120; the more recent N. A. Kazakova, "Maksim Grek kak nestiazhatel'," *Istoriia SSSR*, 1967, no. 2:82-95; and Sinitsyna, *Maksim Grek*, 148-60. On the inquisition in theory, see above, note 41. After his release, Maksim stuck to his views, but declined to follow Ivan IV's request to participate in the prosecution of Bashkin: *Akty istoricheskie*, 5 vols. (St. Petersburg, 1841-42), 1, no. 161.

85. See the very suggestive work by A. I. Klibanov, "'Pravda' Fedora Karpova," *Obshchestvo i gosudarstvo feodal'noi Rossii (Sbornik statei posviashchennykh 70-letiiu akademika L'va Vladimirovicha Cherepnina)*, edited by V. T. Pashuto (Moscow, 1975), 142-58.

86. Goldfrank, "Pre-Enlightenment Utopianism," 133.

87. Zimin, *Peresvetov*, 389-90, and A. A. Klibanov, *Narodnaia sotsial'naia utopiia v Rossii: period feodalizma* (Moscow, 1977), 16.

88. Peresvetov also was a utopian, but a "hard" one, giving instruction on what was Caesar's and not paying any attention to what was God's. His basic program is in D. L. Likhachev and A. A. Zimin, eds., *Sochineniia I. Peresvetova* (Moscow and Leningrad, 1956), 123-84.

89. Ibid., 182.

90. *RIB* 4:1418, 1438.

CHAPTER 3

THE JESUITS' ROLE IN FOUNDING SCHOOLS

1. This prayer, from Luke 12:49, is quoted from *The Roman Missal: The Sacramentary* (New York, 1974), 676.

2. St. Ignatius of Loyola, *The Constitutions of the Society of Jesus*, translated by George E. Ganss, S.J. (St. Louis: The Institute of Jesuit Sources, 1970), 171-72. John W. Donohue, S.J., *Jesuit Education: An Essay on the Foundations of Its Idea* (New York: Fordham University Press, 1963), 139-40.

3. Ignatius, *Constitutions*, 224; Donohue, *Jesuit Education*, 171.

4. Michael T. Florinsky, *Russia: A History and an Interpretation*, 2 vols. (New York: Macmillan, 1953), 1:592-96.

5. Ibid., 592.

6. Christopher Hollis, *The Jesuits: A History* (New York: Macmillan, 1968), 169.

7. Cited in "Memoirs of the Jesuits in White Russia Taken from Thence" (hereafter "Memoirs"), manuscript in the archives of Stonyhurst College, England, copied by Ann Hippisly, 8-9. Plowden gave a similar account of Paul's visit to Polotsk, with some additional details, in "Account," 6:287 (Charles Plowden, S.J., "Account of the Preservation and Actual State of the Society of Jesus in the Russian Dominions, 1783-4," manuscript in the archives of Stonyhurst college, serialized in vols. 6 and 7 of *Letters and Notices*, a journal published by the English Province of the Society of Jesus). The Jesuits treated Prince Potemkin to an extensive ceremony during his visit to Polotsk in June 1782 ("Memoirs," 19).

8. Paul Pierling, *La Russie et le Saint-Siège* (Paris, 1912), 5:114-15. Plowden also provides some information about a drama "exhibited before the Empress in the College at Micislaw." "Account," 7:159.

9. M. J. Rouët de Journel, *Un Collège de Jésuites à Saint-Pétersbourg, 1800-1816* (Paris, 1922), 27-28.

10. M. Moroshkin, *Iezuity v Rossii s Tsarstvovaniia Ekateriny II-i do nashego vremeni*, 2 vols. (St. Petersburg, 1867), 1:244.

11. Plowden, "Account," 7:223-24.

12. TsGIA, fond 822, opis' 1, delo 492, listy 574, 578. The Jesuits opened their schools at Mogilev and Mstislavl during Catherine II's reign. Besides these, the Jesuits maintained two other schools in Belorussia: one at Chechersk and one at Slutsk. Neither seems, however, to have enjoyed the status of the other Jesuit colleges. On the school at Chechersk, see Jan Marek Gizycki, ed., *Materyały do dziejów Akademii Połockiej i szkół od niej zależnych* (Krakow: W. L. Anczyca, 1905), 196-98. A copy of this work is available in the Bibliothèque slave in Paris.

13. Donohue, *Jesuit Education*, 35-36.

14. The range of ages in each class in the Jesuit school in Vitebsk, for example, was seven to twenty in the first class; twelve to sixteen in the second; ten to fifteen in the third; fifteen to eighteen in the fourth; and fifteen to twenty-two in the fifth. TsGIA, fond 822, listy 450-51.

15. Jan Marek Gizycki, ed. *Materyały do dziejów Akademii Połockiej i szkół od niej zależnych* (Krakow: W.L. Anczyca, 1905), 2.

16. Donohue, *Jesuit Education*, 64.

17. Gizycki, *Materyały*, 2-3.

18. Donohue, *Jesuit Education*, 37-38.

19. TsGIA, fond 822, list 50.

20. Student enrollment in the Jesuit schools was as follows: Vitebsk, 64; Mstislavl, 126; Dunaburg, 96; Mogilev, 190, Chechersk, 33; Orsha, 61; Polotsk, 376; Slutsk, 44. Because the school at Slutsk was located in the Diocese of Minsk, its students were not included in the total given in the text. Ibid., 574, 578. For more information on Chechersk (Czeczersk), consult Gizycki, *Materyały*, 196-98.

21. See ibid., 262-68, 494-95, and 507-10, for a description of the Piarist and Dominican curricula.

22. Ibid., 450-51, 473-91. The most easily accessible explanation of the Jesuits' curriculum and school organization in Russia is found in Rouët de Journel, *Un Collège*, 55-64. However, this work gives the impression that all Jesuit schools in the empire had eight grades as did the school at Polotsk. In fact, most Jesuit schools maintained only a Faculty of Letters

with a curriculum identical to the one in Polotsk. Special arrangements had to be made before a student could enter the Faculty of Liberal Arts. In Vitebsk in 1801, for example, one student was in the sixth grade. TsGIA, fond 822, list 35.

23. Donohue, *Jesuit Education*, 35.

24. Gizycki, *Materyały*, 20.

25. Ibid., 4.

26. Allan P. Farrell, S.J., *The Jesuit Code of Liberal Education* (Milwaukee: Bruce, 1938), 342-48; TsGIA, fond 822, listy 473-91.

27. TsGIA, fond 822, list 473.

28. Farrell, *Jesuit Code*, 342-48; TsGIA, fond 822, list 461. See Max J. Okenfuss, "The Jesuit Origins of Petrine Education," in J. G. Garrard, ed., *The Eighteenth Century in Russia* (Oxford: Clarendon Press, 1973), 118-19.

29. Gizycki, *Materyały*, 21-23.

30. Rouët de Journel, *Un Collège*, 62-64.

31. Farrell, *Jesuit Code*, 292.

32. Gizycki, *Materyały*, 22-23.

33. Archivum Romanum Societatis Iesu (ARSI), Russia, 7-II-3; Moroshkin, *Iezuity*, 245; Plowden, "Account," 7:227.

34. Gizycki, *Materyały*, 20-21.

35. Plowden, "Account," 6:282.

36. Gizycki, *Materyały*, 23.

37. TsGIA, fond 822, listy 450-51, 473-91.

38. Gizycki, *Materyały*, 22-23. The school register for Polotsk recorded the school's financial arrangements with students. In 1802, for instance, the Jesuits paid the educational expenses of twenty-four students, at 100 silver rubles per student.

39. Plowden, "Account," 6:279. They were, of course, ex-Jesuits in the sense that the order had been dissolved in 1773 by the pope. Catherine II refused to promulgate the papal brief in Russia and the pope allowed the activities of the Jesuits to continue there.

40. Gizycki, *Materyały*, 17-19.

41. Cited in Plowden, "Account," 6:281.

42. The details concerning Gruber's biography are from Paul Pierling's manuscript on Gruber in the Bibliothèque slave in Paris. (Because this manuscript lacks consecutive pagination, it will be cited hereafter as "Gruber" without page reference. The manuscript is based on the Jean Rozaven manuscript, "Histoire de la Compagnie de Jésus conservee en Russie," also in the Bibliothèque slave.) All data cited in this essay are

from the two sections devoted to Gruber's life. I have presented the dates in Gruber's biography according to the New Style, or Gregorian, calendar. For published accounts of Gruber's life and works, see Ludwig Koch, *Jesuiten-Lexikon* (Paderborn, 1934; Belgium, 1962), 1:738-39; Moroshkin, *Iezuity*, 366-67; Pierling, *La Russie*, 290-91; and Rouët de Journel, *Un Collège*, 13-14.

43. Cited in "Memoirs," 68-69. See also Plowden, "Account," 7:225.

44. Gizycki, *Materyaly*, 3.

45. Pierling, "Gruber."

46. Cited in John W. Padberg, "The General Congregations of the Society of Jesus: A Brief Survey of Their History," *Studies in the Spirituality of Jesuits* 6(January and March 1974): 38.

47. Thomas J. Campbell, S.J., *The Jesuits, 1534-1921* (New York, 1921; repub. Boston: Milford House, 1971), 658. For a description of the commission's work, see Nicholas Hans, *History of Russian Educational Policy (1701-1917)* (New York: Rusell and Russell, 1964), 23-30.

48. Pierling, "Gruber"; Pierling, *La Russie*, 291; Gruber's ambitious architectural plans for Polotsk are in the Jesuit archives in Rome: ARSI, Russia, 3-VIII-14; 3-VIII-15.

49. Campbell, *The Jesuits, 1534-1921*, 659-60.

50. ARSI, Russia, 7-IV-1; *Historia domus Collegii Polocencis*, 2.

51. Cited in Pierling, *La Russie*, 294.

52. Ibid., 294-95; Cf. Rozaven, "Histoire," 102-5. Although Pierling's account of Paul's visit to Orsha is based on the Rozaven manuscript housed in Bibliothèque slave, Pierling omitted some colorful details evidencing Paul's considerable familiarity with Gruber.

53. *Polnoe sobranie zakonov rossiiskoi imperii*, 26(St. Petersburg, 1830), no. 19,597:339.

54. Stanislas Zalenski, *Les Jésuites de la Russie-Blanche*, translated by A. Vivier, 2 vols. (Paris, 1886), 2:89-90.

55. Quoted in J. Gagarin, "L'empéreur Paul et le P. Gruber," *Etudes* 34(January 1879): 46 (hereafter cited as Gagarin, "Gruber").

56. Rouët de Journel, *Un Collège*, 35; Gagarin, "Gruber," 45.

57. Rozaven, "Histoire," 127.

58. TsGIA, f. 822, op. 11, d. 911: "Dnevnik nastavnika seminarii pri Peterburgskoi kollegii sv. Pavla Obshchestva iezuitov za 1801-1804 gg.," 3. This diary of the Jesuit college in St. Petersburg exists in at least three forms. What appears to be the original manuscript is in TsGIA in Leningrad. This curious document is handwritten to the beginning of 1801 and typed thereafter. Although it has detailed entries for November and

December 1800, it is blank for January and February 1801. A second version, in the Jesuit archives in Rome, is a copy prepared in Russia just prior to World War I by Father François Gaillard. This version contains entries for January and February 1801. It can be found in "The Gaillard Collection," filza 31. Finally, the Bibliothèque slave in Paris has one page of the diary for November-December 1800. It is apparently a typed, abridged version of the document in TsGIA.

59. Moroshkin, *Iezuity*, 427; Rozaven, "Histoire," 130.

60. Moroshkin, *Iezuity*, 427.

61. Donald W. Treadgold, *The West in Russia and China*, 2 vols. (Cambridge: Cambridge University Press, 1973), 1:135; TsGIA, f. 1003, op. 1, d. 3: "Pis'ma Ek Iv. Neilidovoi imp. Marii Fedorovne," pis'mo 9. A former favorite of Paul I's, Catherine Nelidov wrote of her visit to the church in the spring of 1801: "I was well pleased with the music there, . . . it was the first time I have seen [anything like it] and I am told this chapel has never before been as noble in style as it is today and that it is all Fr. Gruber's doing."

62. Moroshkin, *Iezuity*, 442.

63. Zalenski, *Les Jésuites*, 2:93-94.

64. Gagarin, "Gruber," 48-49.

65. "Dnevnik," 4. Gruber also met the duke of Glouchester (Rozaven, "Histoire," 134).

66. Pierling, "Gruber," "Fr. Gruber," 2 min. 21.

67. ARSI, 4-I-5, January 9, 1801.

68. See Gruber's correspondence in the Jesuit archives in Rome (Russia: 4A) or the more legible copies, apparently transcribed around 1912 from the originals for Pierling's work on his unpublished biography of Gruber, in the Bibliothèque slave in Paris. Topics mentioned above are in numbers 63 and 64 of the Paris collection, which contains both the Pierling manuscript and the Rozaven manuscript as well as additional letters and papers.

69. Rozaven, "Histoire," 131.

70. Ibid., 132.

71. For a Marxist interpretation of the Jesuits as a politically counterrevolutionary force, see Eduard Winter, "Die Jesuiten in Russland (1772 bis 1820)," *Forschen und Wirken*, 3 vols. (Berlin, 1960), 3:175-79.

CHAPTER 4

DIPLOMAT PRINCE P. B. KOZLOVSKII

1. The standard account is Gleb Struve's *Russkii evropeets* (San Francisco, 1950). This pioneering work, on which all succeeding studies

depend, is strong on the literary side of Kozlovskii's activities. Struve also wrote a number of articles, including "Towards a Biography of Prince Peter Kozlovsky," *California Slavic Studies* 11(1980): 1-24, and "Un russe européen," *Revue de littérature comparée* 24(1950): 522-46. Viktor Frenkel', *Petr Borisovich Kozlovskii* (Leningrad, 1978), adds unpublished letters from Soviet literary archives and gives the best account of Kozlovskii as a popularizer of science. George F. Kennan discussed Kozlovskii in *The Marquis de Custine and His 'Russia in 1839'* (Princeton, 1971), drawing on the study of M. Cadot, *La Russie dans la vie intellectuelle française, 1839-1856* (Paris, 1967). An extremely valuable article which reviews the literature available on all aspects of Kozlovskii, as well as drawing on archives in the USSR, is V. V. Pugachev, "Kniaz' P. B. Kozlovskii i Dekabristy," *Uchenye zapiski gor'kovskogo gosudarstvennogo universiteta* (Seriia Istoriko-Filologicheskaia), 1963, vyp. 58. In 1985 there appeared the massive work by Julien-Frédéric Tarn, *Le Marquis de Custine* (Paris). Elements of Kozlovskii's diplomatic activities have been investigated by Léonce Pingaud, "Un diplomate russe il y a cent ans en Italie, le prince Kosloffsky," *Revue d'histoire diplomatique*, 1917; G. Berti, *Rossiia i italianskie gosudarstva v period Risordzhimento* (Moscow, 1959); Robert Triomphe, *Joseph de Maistre* (Geneva, 1968); and Marianna Koval'skaia, *Dvizhenie karbonariev v Italii* (Moscow, 1971). And other studies have drawn upon his dispatches in the archives in Moscow. Some of Kozlovskii's literary activities are discussed in *Literaturnoe nasledstvo* 91(1982). The earliest long account of Kozlovskii is that of Wilhelm Dorow, *Fürst Kosloffsky* (Leipzig, 1846), still useful because he published some of the prince's writings and the account of him at the Congress of Vienna by La Garde. N. I. Turgenev's assessment of Kozlovskii is in a letter to P. A. Viazemskii, in Frenkel', *Kozlovskii*, 130. References by friends to Kozlovskii's bulk are by General A. I. Chernyshev in F. Ley, *La Russie, Paul de Krüdener et les soulèvements nationaux, 1814-1858* (Paris: Hachette, 1971), 45, and A. Ia. Bulgakov, in Frenkel', *Kozlovskii*, 37. Kozlovskii's activities in Italy at the end of 1811 were closely monitored by agents: Archives Nationales, F^7 6552, d. 2174 sér. 2, f. 156. Varnhagen, cited by Frenkel', *Kozlovskii*, 44. The first caricature was made in Rome in 1811 (Frenkel', 32), but the best known ones were English, discussed by Struve, *Russkii evropeets*, and in *California Slavic Studies* 11. He published some of them. Many of the sources utilized here were first cited by Struve, but I do not cite his use of them nor the occasions on which I add to, reinforce, or differ from his account. In limited space it is not possible to be exhaustive. Priority has been given to information not available to earlier writers.

2. On this development see D. W. Treadgold, *The West in Russia and China*, 2 vols. (Cambridge: Cambridge University Press, 1973), vol.1, chap. 5, and on Chaadaev, passim. Some aspects of the Russian Orthodoxy

which they abandoned are discussed by D. W. Treadgold and R. L. Nichols in R. L. Nichols and T. G. Stavrou, eds., *Russian Orthodoxy under the Old Regime* (Minneapolis: University of Minnesota Press, 1978).

3. J. Gagarin, S.J., "Tendances Catholiques dans la Société Russe," *Le Correspondant* 50(1860): 310, 318. The Decembrist Mikhail S. Lunin had in common with Kozlovskii some years spent in France and in Poland, where the former was converted.

4. M. Pekelis, *Aleksandr Sergeevich Dargomyzhskii i ego okruzhenie* (Moscow, 1966), 1:49.

5. Kozlovskii's comments on his education are in an undated letter to his son, postmarked 1834, in the Gleb Struve Collection, Hoover Institution Archives. On Lunin's education, see G. Barratt, *M. S. Lunin: Catholic Decembrist* (The Hague: Mouton, 1976), 2-3.

6. *Henry V*, act 4, sc. 3, line 60.

7. Details from Pingaud, "Un diplomate russe," 39-40; Frenkel', *Kozlovskii*, 14-22, 44.

8. The exact date is established by a reference in *Vneshnaia politika Rossii* (hereafter *VPR*), ser. 1, 1:407. His departure was noted in a letter of April 16 of Iakov I. Bulgakov to his son Aleksandr, "Poet . . . arkhivskii iunker," *Russkii arkhiv* (hereafter *RA*), 36(1898), pt. 3, no. 3:368.

9. Kozlovskii mentioned his conversations with Chateaubriand to Aleksandr Bulgakov, Letter to his brother Konstantin, *RA* 37(1899), no. 5: 25-26.

10. Pingaud, "Un diplomate russe," 40-44; Frenkel', *Kozlovskii*, 23-26; She referred to Kozlovskii on May 1, 1805, "Lettres inédites de Mme de Staël à Vincenzo Monti," *Giornale Storico della Letteratura Italiana* 46(1905): 21-22; Simone Balayé, *Les carnets de voyage de Madame de Staël* (Geneva, 1971), 219, 468.

11. Frenkel', *Kozlovskii*, 26.

12. Pingaud, "Un diplomate russe," 44-46; Public Record Office, FO 67/37. William Hill to George Canning, Cagliari, October 16, 1808, explains Lizakevich's shortage of money; October 30, he explains that this is not mentioned publicly to save appearances. In a letter to Marquis Wellesley, May 5, 1810, FO 67/40, Hill said he had heard that Lizakevich was being given a pension and allowed to retire. Because of their anti-French views, Vorontsov, Razumovskii, Pozzo di Borgo et al. retired from active Russian service after the treaty of Tilsit.

13. AN, F^7 8823, d. 3635. In a letter of August 15, 1810, Kozlovskii wrote that in one year he ransomed and sent home 117 people at his personal expense.

14. Archives du Ministère des Affaires Etrangères, Corr. Pol. Sardaigne 281, ff. 569-70; hereafter AMAE, CP. These files also contain intercepted correspondence.

15. AN, F^7 6552, d. 2174. sér. 2, ff. 159, 164, June 1811.

16. Published by Pingaud, and discussed by Struve.

17. Hill to Canning, September 4, 1809, FO 67/39, refers to Kozlovskii's "constant correspondence with Gl. Morand," his "having become the Chief of the Jacobins," and reports that the king has had him told that Count de Maistre in Petersburg will settle questions between the two governments.

18. Frenkel', *Kozlovskii*, 28-29. More details of Kozlovskii's activities in Sardinia will appear in an article currently in preparation.

19. J. de Maistre, *Mémoires politiques et correspondance diplomatique*, ed. A. Blanc (Paris, 1858), 331, 335. Maistre also mentions this in his *Correspondance diplomatique*, ed. A. Blanc, 2 vols. (Paris, 1860), 1:190-91.

20. Intercepted letter, AN, F^7 6520, d. 1245, sér. 2, f. 38.

21. *VPR*, ser. 1, 6:21-4, February 1811; J. de Maistre, *Oeuvres complètes* (Lyon, 1887), 11:507-508; hereafter *OC*.

22. Hill to Wellesley, September 20, 1810, FO 67/40, enclosing two of Kozlovskii's intercepted letters (one to Rumiantsev), a proof of intrigue.

23. AN, F^7 8828, d. 8644, December 27, 1811, and F^7 6552, d. 2174, f.156, December 19, 1811; Napoleon to Count de Lacépède, November 12, 1811, *Correspondance de Napoléon* (Paris, 1868), 23:12, no. 18256.

24. *Dekabrist N. I. Turgenev: pis'ma k bratu S. I. Turgenevu* (Moscow and Leningrad, 1936), 107; N. N. Varvartsev, *Ukraina v Rossiisko-Ital'ianskikh obshchestvennykh i kul'turnykh sviaziakh* (Kiev, 1986), 21.

25. Maistre, *OC*, 12:113-14; Vyderzhki iz zapisok A. Ia. Bulgakova, *RA*, 1867, col. 1368; Letter of A. Bulgakov to his brother, *RA*, 38(1900), no. 5:15; A. A. Zherve, "Biograficheskii ocherk," *Russkaia starina* 92(1897), no. 4:108; hereafter *RS*.

26. La Garde, version published by Dorow, *Fürst Kosloffsky*, 109.

27. *VPR.*, ser. 1, 6:471-72; Maistre, OC, 12:254-55; *Correspondance diplomatique*, 1:187-93, 215-17; M. A. Dodolev, *Rossiia i Ispaniia, 1808-1823 gg.* (Moscow, 1984), 27.

28. P. A. Viazemskii, *Polnoe sobranie sochinenii* (St. Petersburg, 1882), 7:244; hereafter *PSS*.

29. Frenkel', *Kozlovskii*, 36-8.

30. Kozlovskii to Count Lieven, Wergo (Sweden), November 28, 1812, British Library. Additional Manuscripts (hereafter BL. Add. MSS) 47287A, f. 132; Frenkel', *Kozlovskii*, 38; Kozlovskii to Rumiantsev, November 12, 1812, in *Rossiia i Shvetsiia: dokumenty i materialy, 1809-1818* (Moscow, 1985), 234ff. (In this letter he mentions Bardaxi.) V. V. Roginskii, *Shvetsiia i Rossiia: soiuz 1812 goda* (Moscow, 1978), 145, 149.

31. George Gordon, Lord Byron, *Letters and Journals* (London, 1973), 3:45, 50, 69, 76, and 83; 4:45; *Correspondence of Sarah Spencer, Lady Lyttelton* (London, 1912), 141-42; I am indebted to J.S.G. Simmons, of All Souls College, for a correction to his reference to Kozlovskii in "Turgenev at Oxford," *Oxoniensia* 31(1968): 146; *The Bath Archives: Diaries and letters of Sir George Jackson, 1809-1816* (London, 1873), 2:6-7, 139; Maistre, *Correspondance diplomatique*, 1:340.

32. *Letters of Harriet Countess Granville, 1810-1845*, 2d ed. (London, 1894), 1:32-33. The beautiful girl in question was Mrs. Tom Sheridan's youngest daughter.

33. C. Quenet, *Tchaadaev et les Lettres Philosophiques* (Paris, 1931), 76-78.

34. *Mémoires de la Comtesse Rosalie Rzewuska* (Rome, 1939), 2:149.

35. West Yorkshire Archive Service, Leeds, George Canning, Bundle 9.

36. Kozlovskii to Custine in Custine, *The Empire of the Czar* (London, 1843), 1:72. A few of his dispatches from early 1814 are in *VPR*, ser. 1, vol. 7.

37. I am most grateful to the staff at the Royal Archives in Windsor Castle for this information.

38. "Predstaviteli Rossii na Venskom Kongresse v 1815 godu (iz vospominanii A. I. Mikhailovskogo-Danilevskogo)," *RS* 89(1899): 649.

39. Some of his dispatches are in *VPR*, ser. 1, vol. 8. One is in Berti, *Rossiia i italianskie gosudarstva*, 292-94.

40. The comte de La Garde-Chambonas met Kozlovskii at the congress. In his account he presents himself as a frequent companion of the prince. Dorow reproduces the relevant sections. The best edition of La Garde is that edited by the Comte Fleury, *Souvenirs du Congrès de Vienne, 1814-1815* (Paris, 1901). There are differences from the version given by Dorow. Police reports on Kozlovskii are in M. H. Weil, *Les dessous du Congrès de Vienne* (Paris, 1917). Some other references are in Niels Rosenkrantz, *Journal du Congrès de Vienne* (Copenhagen, 1953), 60, 124, 208. "Iz pisem K. Ia. Bulgakova k ego bratu" for 1814 and 1815 has some references to Kozlovskii, *RA* 42(1904), pt. 3:189, 199, 350-51.

41. Struve, "Who Was Pushkin's 'Polonophil'?" *Slavonic and East European Review* 29(1950-51): 451-52; A. S. Pushkin, "Table-talk," *Polnoe sobranie sochinenii* (Moscow and Leningrad, 1949), 12:156.

42. Kozlovskii to Pozzo di Borgo, Turin, August 18/30, 1814, Archives Pozzo di Borgo. I am greatly indebted to Madame la Duchesse Pozzo di Borgo for her kind permission to consult her family papers. Subsequent references to Pozzo di Borgo correspondence are all from this archive unless otherwise noted.

43. E. Pictet, *Biographie, travaux et correspondance diplomatique de C. Pictet de Rochemont* (Geneva, 1892), 353; Paul Waeber, *La formation du Canton de Genève, 1814-1816* (Geneva, 1974), 345-50; *VPR*, ser. 2; Lucien Cramer, ed., *Genève et les Traités de 1815: Correspondance diplomatique de Pictet de Rochemont* (Geneva, 1914), 2 passim.

44. Maistre, *OC*, 12:396, to Vallaise, July 15, 1816.

45. Nesselrode to Kozlovskii, February 25, 1816, in *VPR*, ser. 2, 1:82-83.

46. Kozlovskii's correspondence with Nesselrode on this issue is published in *Literaturnoe nasledstvo* 29-30(1937): 652-76, and discussed by Triomphe, *Joseph de Maistre*, 317-23, and Berti, *Rossiia i italianskie gosudarstva*, 300-302. Kozlovskii's role in this affair is discussed in the letter of the Comte de Gabriac to the Duc de Richelieu, Turin, June 10, 1816, reproduced in *Les carnets du Comte Joseph de Maistre* (Lyon and Paris, 1923), 232-34.

47. Kozlovskii gave some account of this in 1820: *Souvenirs de la Baronne du Montet, 1785-1866* (Paris, 1914), 196.

48. Archives Pozzo di Borgo.

49. Archives Pozzo di Borgo; "Pismo Grafa Iosifa de Mestra k Kn. P. B. Kozlovskomu," *RA*, 1866:1493-98. The same letter is in Maistre, *OC*, 13:168-73. Another letter of February 1816 (pp. 249-53) also discusses the study of law. The comments in these two letters might be considered a miniature precursor of those later made by Custine. In letters to other correspondents he mentioned further discussions on law with the prince.

50. Starhemberg to Metternich, October 5, 1815: Kozlovskii "is busy only with his pleasures, that he seeks amongst the lowest classes," *Le relazioni diplomatiche fra l'Austria e il Regno di Sardegna*, ser. 1: 1814-30, vol. 1, ed. Narciso Nada (Rome, 1964), 141; hereafter cited as Nada. Rosalie Rzewuska was bemused that Kozlovskii frequented "mediocre" men, *Mémoires*, 2:148. Mary Berry attended a fête given by Kozlovskii which she found extremely vulgar. BL. Add. MS. 37726, f. 361.

51. No precise date has been fixed for this event, but it must have been in this period, rather than 1809, since Iohanna Rebora was born in 1802, according to N. Arseniev, quoted in N. Ikonnikov, *La noblesse de Russie* (Paris, 1959; 2d ed.), vol. H.1 (entry p.h. 397 3 166). See Pingaud, "Un diplomate russe," 72-73, where the matter is discussed in the light of dispatches of Pictet and Gabriac in 1816. Her correspondence in the Bibliothèque Nationale shows that she was usually known as Madame Rebora. Gabriac's comment to Richelieu, August 19, 1816, may be apposite here: "Prince Kosloffsky, bored by Turin and who is happy in Milan, scarcely thinks of returning." AMAE., CP. Sardaigne 284, f.81.

52. Not all accounts agree on the dates of Kozlovskii's trip to Paris. See, for example, comments of N. I. Turgenev, cited by Pugachev, "Kniaz' Kozlovskii," 490. Confirmation of his presence in Paris in February 1817 is in a letter of February 22, 1817, *Epistolario di Vincenzo Monti*, ed. Alfonso Bertoldi, 6 vols. (Florence, 1929), 4:376. Dalberg reported to Richelieu his departure on September 25, 1816, and his return on February 9, 1817, AMAE, CP. Sardaigne 284/5.

53. See S. Durylin, "G-zha de Stal' i ee Russkie otnosheniia," *Literaturnoe nasledstvo* 33-34(1939): 310ff. A duplicate letter was also sent to de Maistre, who comments on it in a letter to Kozlovskii.

54. Starhemberg to Metternich, May 29, 1816 (Nada, 212). Dalberg to Richelieu, September 26, 1816, CP. Sardaigne 284 f. 190.

55. AMAE, CP. Sardaigne, 284, f. 94, Gabriac to Richelieu, May 22, 1816. Kozlovskii's dispatches went first to the Emperor Alexander, who then passed them to the ministers. Starhemberg to Metternich, May 10, 1816, "He writes perfectly, easily and his views are in general equitable and sound," and February 15, 1817, "He writes with staggering assurance to his master whatever passes through his head; this is not resented because he is nonetheless ready to obey." Nada, 210, 275.

56. AMAE, CP. Sardaigne, 284, f. 129, July 16, 1816, confidential.

57. Kozlovskii to Pozzo, Milan, April 1/11, 1819: "I had one foot in my grave."

58. Kozlovskii to Pozzo, Rivoli, December 7/19, 1818: "I was so badly treated in that Aix-la-Chapelle"; Stuttgart, March 28, 1820.

59. *VPR*, ser. 2, 3:810, n. 302.

60. Grand Duke Nikolai Mikhailovich, *Les rapports diplomatiques de Lebzeltern (1816-1826)* (St. Petersburg, 1913), 324, 338; *Lettres du Prince de Metternich à la comtesse de Lieven, 1818-1819*, ed. J. Hanoteau (Paris, 1905), 11-13.

61. Notably Pozzo di Borgo. See P. K. Grimsted, *The Foreign Ministers of Alexander I* (Berkeley, 1969), 282.

62. Metternich to Starhemberg, January 28, 1819 (Nada, 408). But as the letter was designed to be shown to Kozlovskii, perhaps it should be treated with caution.

63. FO 67/57, June 25, 1818. "There was no abuse which the former did not bestow on the latter."

64. FO 67/55, W. Hill to Lord Castlereagh, October 9, 1817; FO 67/57, June 25, 1818; M. Koval'skaia, *Dvizhenie*, 182-85; Berti, *Rossiia i italianskie gosudarstva*, 304.

65. Koval'skaia, *Dvizhenie*, 185.

66. FO 67/57. Hill to Castlereagh, December 22, 1818. See also, Koval'skaia, *Dvizhenie*, 5, 87, 182-85; Berti, *Rossiia i italianskie gosudarstva*, 303ff., and particularly 380; Dodolev, "Zapiski russkogo diplomata ob Italii," *Istoriia SSSR*, 1976, no. 5:159; Franco Venturi, "Italo-Russkie otnosheniia c 1750 do 1825 g.," *Rossiia i Italiia* (Moscow, 1968), 45-6.

67. FO 67/57. Hill to Castlereagh, Secret, June 19, 1818; FO 67/ 55, October 9, 1817; Koval'skaia, *Dvizhenie*, 184.

68. See note 66 above.

69. Kozlovskii to Pozzo, Stuttgart, March 28, 1820: Berti, *Rossiia i italianskie gosudarstva*, 392. Bardaxi had been in Russia in 1812, representing the Cortes. Balbo became minister of the interior in 1819 and was the father of the future prime minister, Cesare Balbo.

70. M. A. Dodolev, "Rossiia i ispanskaia revoliutsiia 1820-1832 gg.," *Istoriia SSSR*, 1969, no. 1:114.

71. To Pozzo di Borgo, Stuttgart, March 28, 1820. See also M. A. Dodolev, *Rossiia i Ispaniia 1808-1823 gg.* (Moscow, 1984), 139 and passim.

72. Koval'skaia, "Revoliutsionnoe dvizhenie v Italii i oppozitsionnye krugi Russkogo dvorianstva (1818-1821 gg.)," in *Rossiia i Italiia*, 134. Pingaud, in 1917, had made this claim.

73. FO 66/55, October 9, 1817; FO 66/59, Secret, May 1, 1819; Secret, August 1, 1819.

74. June 21, 1819 (Nada, 420).

75. FO 67/59, Secret, August l; Secret, May l; Secret, July 4, 1819.

76. *Literaturnoe nasledstvo*, 29-30:667-68, and discussed by Triomphe, *Joseph de Maistre*, 321-22.

77. *Aus dem Nachlass Varnhagen's von Ense: Briefwechsel zwischen Varnhagen und Rahel* (Leipzig, 1875), 6:19-20, 142-47, 300-303; *Denkwürdigkeiten und vermische Schriften von K. A. Varnhagen von Ense*, Neue Folge (Leipzig, 1859), 5:602 ff.; Hereafter *Denkwürdigkeiten*.

78. *Aus dem Nachlass Varnhagen's von Ense. Tagebücher* (Bern, 1972, reprint), 4:131; 5:197, 344; 7:197-201; 9:211, 380; 11:360; 13:160; 14:324.

79. R. A. F. Varnhagen von Ense, *Rahel: Ein Buch des Andenkens für ihre Freunde*, 3 vols. (Berlin, 1834), 3:179.

80. A recent short account is Terry H. Pickett, *The Unseasonable Democrat: K. A. Varnhagen von Ense (1785-1858)* (Bonn, 1985).

81. FO 82/13 Alex Cockburn to Castlereagh, December 26, 1820.

82. AMAE, CP. Bade, 17, f. 29. Montlezun to Pasquier, March 28, 1820 (in cypher) refers to Kozlovskii's very liberal principles and his recall at the request of the king of Württemberg. CP. Württemberg, 51, f. 174, de la Moussaye to Pasquier, October 1, 1820, writes about Kozlovskii's complete disgrace.

83. Paris, April 11, 1820, *Carteggio del Conte Federico Confalonieri*, ed. Giuseppe Gallavresi (Milan, 1911), 2:255.

84. The letter was sent by a private messenger, but might still have fallen into undesirable hands. Kozlovskii asked a second time in May for confirmation it had been delivered safely.

85. "Prince Kosloffsky flatters himself that he is to replace Tatishcheff in Madrid." H. de la Moussaye to Pasquier, Stuttgart, July 12, 1820, in AMAE, CP. Württemberg, 51, f. 142.

86. There is an interesting echo of these complaints in Kozlovskii's fragmentary memoirs (Dorow, *Fürst Kosloffsky*, 72-73), where a conversation with a Scottish doctor in Russian service made "the accents of liberty ... refresh my heart" and then note: "Yet how badly informed are these princes, filled with aversion to men accused of English liberalism!"

87. Archives Pozzo di Borgo (in Italian). Kozlovskii flattered his correspondents by supposing them as multilingual as himself and switching from language to language, sometimes more than once in the same letter.

88. There is a discussion of the relations between Varnhagen and Kozlovskii in G. Wiegand, *Zum deutschen Russlandinteresse im 19. Jahrhundert* (Stuttgart: Klett, 1967), 221-23; Varnhagen, *Denkwürdigkeiten*, 5:606.

89. April 30/May 17, 1820, copy sent to Pozzo. This may be the same Denkschrift mentioned by Varnhagen, *Denkwürdigkeiten*, 608.

90. In a letter dated March 8, Kozlovskii made no mention of resignation nor of Spain, but rather defended the parliamentary proceedings in Württemberg: to Count Lieven, BL. Add. MSS. 47290. Some of Nesselrode's circulars to Russian diplomats in Germany for early 1820 are in *VPR*, ser. 2, vol. 3, but none of Kozlovskii's dispatches. On the constitutional questions, see Ulrike Eich, *Russland und Europa: Studien zur*

russischen Deutschlandpolitik in der Zeit des Wiener Kongresses (Cologne, 1986), 409-11.

91. AMAE, CP. Württemberg, 51, Ségur to Pasquier, January 23, March 10, 29, 1820 (all in cypher).

92. Same source, March 1. To Varnhagen Kozlovskii spoke of the tsar as he was five years before and of his speech in Poland about constitutions, *Denkwürdigkeiten*, 606-8.

93. AMAE, CP. Württemberg 51, f. 173, de la Moussaye to Pasquier, September 20, 1820.

94. See Pingaud, "Un diplomate russe"; Berti, *Rossiia i italianskie gosudarstva*, 382-3; Grimsted, *Foreign Ministers*, 246-7.

95. Details of the salary are in K. Bulgakov's letter to his brother, October 28, 1820, *RA* 40(1902), no. 11:383.

96. O. V. Orlik, *Dekabristy i Evropeiskoe osvoboditel'noe dvizhenie* (Moscow, 1975), 51.

97. Koval'skaia, in *Rossiia i Italiia*, 134.

98. Heine, quoted by Struve, "Un russe européen," 542-43.

99. S. S. Prawer, *Frankenstein's Island: England and the English in the Writings of Heinrich Heine* (Cambridge: Cambridge University Press, 1986), 8-11, 21-22, 79-82.

100. A. A. Balmain describes his and Kozlovskii's involvement in the changes in a letter to Prince Lieven, January 5/17, 1827, BL. Add. MSS. 47272.

101. Many references to meetings and discussions with Kozlovskii are in *Pis'ma Aleksandra Ivanovicha Turgeneva k Nikolaiu Ivanovichu Turgenevu* (Leipzig, 1872). The best treatment of Alexander Turgenev is an unpublished five-volume thesis by Michel Thiery, *Le cosmopolitisme russe* (Paris, 1982). Consulted too late to cite in this essay, it has significant references to Kozlovskii. There is a recent discussion of Nicholas Turgenev in Martin A. Miller, *The Russian Revolutionary Emigrés, 1825-1870* (Baltimore: Johns Hopkins University Press, 1986), 32-49.

102. Struve, *Russkii evropeets*, chapter entitled "Dekabrist bez dekabria."

103. V. V. Pugachev, "Kniaz' P. B. Kozlovskii i Dekabristy," already cited. A recent helpful study is *Le 14 décembre 1825*, ed. Alexandre Bourmeyster (Paris: Institut d'études slaves, 1980).

104. Pugachev, "Kniaz' Kozlovskii," 500. Kozlovskii drafted a memorial in favor of Nikolai Turgenev, discussed by Thiery.

105. J. F. Cooper, *Gleanings in Europe: France* (Albany: State University of New York Press, 1983), 235.

106. Rzewuska, *Mémoires*, 2:148.

107. Pugachev, "Kniaz' Kozlovskii," 487.

108. E. Pictet, *Biographie*, 355.

109. Lady Granville, *Letters*, 1:32-33.

110. N. N. Bolkhovitinov, *Russko-Amerikanskie otnosheniia 1815-1832 gg.* (Moscow, 1975), 555ff.

111. This identification was discussed at the October 1986 meeting of the Central Slavic Association, in Kansas City, and I am glad to acknowledge the helpful suggestions made on that occasion.

112. Some details about Kozlovskii's family are in the anonymous *Balzac mis à nu* (Paris, 1928), 163ff. This curious publication seems well informed about Kozlovskii. Its claim that the Grand Duchess Helen gave Kozlovskii's daughter Sophie a pension (queried by Struve) seems borne out by V. A. Mukhanov, "Iz drevnykh zapisok," *RA* 35(1897), nos. 1-6:276.

113. Madame Swetchine to Countess Nesselrode, December 12, 1829, in Comte de Falloux, ed., *Lettres de Madame Swetchine* (Paris, 1901), 1:396-97.

114. To his brother, October 18, 1833, *RA* 42(1904), pt. 12, no. 2:273.

115. J. W. Rooney, *Revolt in the Netherlands: Brussels, 1830* (Lawrence, Kans: Coronado Press, 1982), 149; A. S. Namazova, *Bel'giiskaia Revoliutsiia 1830 goda* (Moscow, 1979), 10, 119-20. This episode seems to explain the allegation in *Balzac mis à nu* that Kozlovskii was anxious to sell his services.

116. L. Hastier, "Le Prince et la Princesse Bagration," *Revue des Deux Mondes*, October 1962, no. 19:420.

117. Pekelis, *A. S. Dargomyzhskii*, 1:39.

118. Correspondence in the Pozzo di Borgo archives, some between Nesselrode and Pozzo.

119. Kozlovskii to Nesselrode, Paris, January 13, 1833, in Gleb Struve Collection.

120. M.-J. Rouët de Journel, *Une Russe Catholique: La vie de madame Swetchine* (Paris, 1953), 273-85. She had been very much influenced by J. de Maistre in person at the time of her conversion. I hope to be able to discuss these incidents more fully elsewhere.

121. P. A. Viazemskii, *PSS*, 2:289; K. Bulgakov to his brother, *RA* 42(1904), pt. l, no. 3:440.

122. Viazemskii, *PSS*, 7:236

123. Since Kozlovskii's literary activities with Pushkin and Polonophile influences on Paskevich have been extensively discussed by Struve, there is little point in discussing them further. His publications of these years, especially scientific, are discussed by Frenkel', *Kozlovskii*, 49-112. See

Struve, "Who Was Pushkin's 'Polonophil'?" already cited and "Kto byl pushkinskii 'polonofil'?" *Novyi zhurnal* 103(1971). Some of Struve's claims were disputed by W. Lednicki, whose most recent contribution to their running debate was in *Russia, Poland and the West* (New York, 1954), 96-104.

124. V. I. Kuleshov, *Literaturnye sviazi Rossii i zapadnoi Evropy v XIX veke* (Moscow, 1965), 392. Pugachev states that there is a chapter on Kozlovskii (87-191) in a study by Erofeev, but criticizes certain interpretations. I have not succeeded in consulting V. V. Erofeev, *Zhurnal Pushkina "Sovremennik" (1836 god) v sviazi s zhurnal'no-literaturnym dvizheniem 30-x godov XIX veka*, Avtoref. diss., Leningrad, 1952.

125. Viazemskii, *PSS*, 2:288.

126. There is an enormous literature on this. See Raymond T. McNally, *Chaadayev and His Friends* (Tallahassee: Diplomatic Press, 1971), and many other works of the same author.

127. Kozlovskii is mentioned in Pushkin's letter to Chaadaev, discussing the letter in the *Teleskop*, but not in that context, Pushkin, *PSS*, 16:173.

128. In conversation with Gabriac, reported to Richelieu, CP. Sardaigne 284, f. 129, July 1816, and discussed below. Probably he wrote at this time saying much the same to Maistre.

129. Kozlovskii had received Grand Duke Michael, the youngest son of Paul I, in Turin, in December 1818, and had been Russian minister to Württemberg.

130. Varnhagen, *Tagebücher*, 2:197-98; Rzewuska, *Mémoires*, 2:150. He had met Grand Duchess Helen in Germany.

131. See "Memoirs," in Dorow, *Fürst Kosloffsky*, for Kozlovskii's account.

132. Viazemskii, *PSS*, 7:254. Hertzen refers also to this incident, in "Plach," A. I. Gertsen, *Sobranie sochinenii*, 30 vols. (Moscow, 1954-65), 17:69. Both draw on Dorow.

133. His appointment was announced on June 22, *Journal de St. Pétersbourg*, 1836, no. 75:307, but he did not leave at once.

134. Lord Durham to Lord Palmerston, St. Petersburg, June 11, 1836, FO 67/224. Stuart J. Reid, *Life and Letters of the First Earl Durham* (London, 1906), 2:49-51; Chester W. New, *Lord Durham* (Oxford, 1929), 296.

135. Austrian Ambassador Ficquelmont to Metternich, November 7/19, 1836, cited by M. Cadot, "Chaadaev en France: quelques remarques préliminaires," *Revue des Etudes Slaves* 55(1983), no. 2:268.

136. Rzewuska, *Mémoires*, 2:148-51; A. Shcherbatov, *Le Feld-Maréchal Prince Paskevitsch*, 7 vols. (St. Petersburg, 1896), 5:126-28.

137. The most convenient account of Custine and his relations with Kozlovskii is that of Geroge Kennan, who quotes extensively from Kozlovskii's purported conversations with Custine, gives summaries of what he does not quote, and discusses the whole.

138. The place and date of their meeting is discussed by Cadot, *La Russie*, 187. For second thoughts, see Tarn, *Custine*, 772, n. 104.

139. On this incident see Kennan, *Custine*, 49-50. In a way, Custine's book might be considered a counterblast to Grech's *Putevyia pis'ma iz Anglii, Germanii, Frantsii,* 3 vols. (St. Petersburg, 1839).

140. Kennan makes this suggestion (*Custine*, 60), on the basis of a passage in *Empire of the Czar*, 1:294 (chap. 14), describing Custine's visit to a prince in the capital.

141. On this mystification see especially Tarn, *Custine*, the chapter titled "Les mystères de *la Russie en 1839.*"

142. Cadot, *La Russie*, 189.

143. Charles Corbet, *L'opinion française face à l'inconnue russe (1799-1894)* (Paris, 1967), 219.

144. See Henry Gifford, *Times Literary Supplement*, December 10, 1982: 1368.

145. On this see V. Lednicki, *Pouchkine et la Pologne* (Paris, 1928), and *Russia, Poland and the West: Bits of Table Talk About Pushkin . . .* (The Hague, 1956). Struve, *Russkii evropeets*, discusses Balzac. Pozzo di Borgo's correspondence shows Kozlovskii to have been in Versailles. Other materials, consulted too late for discussion here, suggest strongly that he knew Balzac.

146. Maistre, *OC*, 13:251. Cf. Maistre to Kozlovskii, note 49 above, where he points to the interest of studying Russia.

147. Viazemskii, *PSS*, 2:286, 293.

148. Pugachev, "Kniaz' Kozlovskii," 486. It was to this that he referred in his memoirs, Dorow, *Fürst Kosloffsky*, 62.

149. Cadot, *La Russie*, 209.

150. Custine, *Empire*, 1:69. In general, reference is made to this edition of 1843, because it is much more complete than the condensed version given by Phyllis Penn Kohler, *Journey for Our Time* (London, 1953/1980), but when possible the quotations are taken from the Kohler version, much superior as a modern translation.

151. Custine, *Empire*, 1:110.

152. Gabriac to Richelieu, July 16, 1816, CP. Sardaigne 284, f. 129.

153. Custine, *Empire*, 1:74; Kozlovskii to Pozzo di Borgo, Milan, April 12, 1819.

154. Custine, *Empire*, 1:103-4; Pushkin had called Kozlovskii "friend of the English bards" and "admirer of Byron" in 1836, *PSS*, 3, pt. 2:1037. The prince's role as friend of the English poets is discussed in *Literaturnoe nasledstvo*, 91, chapter 5:452, which refers to this very discussion with Custine.

155. Custine, *Empire*, 1:105; Kozlovskii to Pozzo, Turin, March 20 (1817). To Canning in 1813 he had lauded the British jury.

156. Custine, *Empire*, 1:105ff.; Kozlovskii to Pozzo, Stuttgart, May 16 (1820). He compares the first Russian emperor with Pope Gregory VII.

157. For Peter see Dorow, *Fürst Kosloffsky*, 53. He claims that he intends to write on Russian history (i.e., "Essai sur l'histoire de la Russie") at a future date and denounces the Russian court and the physical and moral atmosphere of Russia.

158. Custine, *Empire*, 1:79. The novel was recited, not written down (Struve, "Un russe," 545). For other examples of Kozlovskii's views on serfdom, slavery, and the oppression of the Greeks, see Pugachev, "Kniaz' Kozlovskii."

159. Pekelis, *Dargomuzhskii*, 1:47.

160. A. I. Gertsen, *Sobranie sochinenii*, 7:287, cites Haxthausen, who was in Russia in 1843. A. von Haxthausen, *Studien uber ... Russlands*, 3 vols. (Hannover, 1847-52), 1:104-5 gives no date for the liberation nor any identification of "Furst Kosslowski."

161. Custine, *Empire*, 1:78; to Pozzo, Turin, December 12, 1815.

162. These remarks come at the end of Kozlovskii's memoirs (Dorow, *Fürst Kosloffsky*, 73-74).

163. Custine, *Empire*, 1:76.

164. Ibid., 79.

165. This passage is not in *The Empire of the Czar*, vol. 1 (it should be on page 79). It is, however, in *La Russie en 1839* (Brussels, 1843), 1:87 and is also in *Journey for Our Time*, 32.

166. Cadot, "Chaadaev en France," 268.

167. Letter published by Pingaud. This part of the letter is written in Italian; later he switches to French, and quotes an English poet!

168. Quoted by Frenkel', *Kozlovskii*, 31, from *Arkhiv brat'ev Turgenevykh*.

169. *Arkhiv Kniazia Vorontsova*, 36:444-45. Karamzin's book was one of Custine's sources.

170. Gabriac to Richelieu, July 16, 1816, already cited.

171. So he claimed of himself, as reported in *Balzac mis à nu*. But was this one of his jokes?

172. Gagarin, "Tendances catholiques," 310.

173. Pingaud published a letter of the comte de Gabriac to Richelieu, Turin, January 25, 1818, to this effect. Kozlovskii's letter to Dalberg defending the pope was given to the duc de Richelieu, in whose papers at the Bibliothèque Victor Cousin it has not survived. Dalberg's reply to Kozlovskii was sent by the latter to Pozzo di Borgo, who kept it.

174. "Lettre d'un Protestant d'Allemagne à Monseigneur l'évêque de Chester" (1825), published in Dorow, *Fürst Kosloffsky*, 22-44. The first edition is in the Bibliothèque Nationale.

175. A. Turgenev to Viazemskii, cited by Frenkel', *Kozlovskii*, 15. See page 35 for details of the settlement of the estate. Miss Berry records an extravagant fête he gave in Italy, BL. Add. MSS. 377746.

176. N. I. Turgenev to P. A. Viazemskii, 1869, in Frenkel', *Kozlovskii*, 130-31.

177. But at the Congress of Vienna in conversation with La Garde, he referred to his first lesson in liberalism, when on his first journey from Russia his coachman had applied the whip to him. See Dorow, *Fürst Kosloffsky*, 110-11.

178. Published by Pingaud.

179. BL. Add. MSS. 37746. Compare this and the letter to Cavour with Custine, *Empire,* 1:78-80.

180. *Mémoires*, 2:149.

181. Mme Swetchine, Countess Rzewuska, and Miss Berry were all sympathetic but perplexed: Falloux, *Lettres*, 1:396-97; Rzewuska, *Mémoires*, 2:150; *Journals and correspondence of Miss Berry*, ed. Lady T. Lewis (London 1865), 3:164. See also Maistre, *Correspondance diplomatique*, 1:198; *OC*, 12:113-14; A. Bulgakov, *RA*, 37(1899), no. 5:21, no. 8:497.

182. *Arkhiv Kniazia Vorontsova*, 36:444-45.

183. *Mémoires*, 2:150.

184. See the contributions by Messrs. Wittfogel, Riasanovsky, Spuler, Roberts, Raeff, and Szeftel, in D. W. Treadgold, ed., *The Development of the USSR: An Exchange of Views* (Seattle: University of Washington Press, 1964).

185. Varnhagen, *Tagebücher*, 10:210.

186. Viazemskii, *PSS*, 2:286.

CHAPTER 5

THEOLOGICAL ACADEMIES AND OLD CATHOLICS

1. Döllinger discussed his views with visitors from the East even before
the Munich meeting. Wilhelm Kahle, *Westliche Orthodoxie: Leben und
Ziele Julian Joseph Overbecks* (Leiden, 1968), 129. He also tried to attract
Orthodox attention by sending an open letter to Russia that was published in
early 1871 in *Pravoslavnoe obozrenie*. A most striking example of his
interest in Orthodoxy can be found in his lectures: The Eastern Church
"has clung tenaciously to all that had been established at the time of the
great movements and definitions of the fourth and fifth centuries." J. von
Döllinger, *Ueber die Wiedervereinigung der christlichen Kirchen*
(Nordlingen, 1888), 38-39.

The Munich Congress was attended by I. T. Osinin, a professor from
the St. Petersburg Theological Academy, and A. Dimitrapulos, the learned
Greek theologian resident in Leipzig. Both men expressed interest and
sympathetic feelings to the newly formed group. I. Osinin, "Staro-
katolicheskoe dvizhenie i miunkhenskii tserkovnyi kongress," *Khristianskoe
chtenie* 11(November 1871): 777.

2. *Izvlechenie iz vsepoddanneishago otcheta ober-prokurora
Sviateishago Sinoda Grafa D. Tolstago po vedomstvu pravoslavnago
ispovedaniia za 1872 g.* (St. Petersburg, 1873), 231.

3. In 1873 the Old Catholics created a committee composed of three
professors from the University at Bonn to work with the St. Petersburg
branch of the Friends of Spiritual Enlightenment. Theodorus, *The New
Reformation: A Narrative of the Old Catholic Movement from 1870 to the
Present Time* (London, 1875), 205, and "Otsutsvie u starokatolikov
opredelitel'nago ispovedaniia very," *Tserkovnyi vestnik* 10(March 1875).

The official reports of the Bonn conferences were written by Heinrich
Reusch, a professor of theology at the Bonn University. Written in a dry
and impersonal manner, they reveal little about the personalities of these
who attended or spoke at the sessions. *Report of the Proceedings at the
Reunion Conference Held at Bonn on September 14, 15, and 16, 1874*,
translated from the German of Professor Reusch with a preface by H. P.
Liddon (London, 1875), *Report of the Union Conferences held from August
10-16, 1875, at Bonn, under the Presidence of Dr. Von Döllinger*, ed.
Heinrich Reusch, trans. Samuel Buel, with a preface by Robert J. Nevin
(New York, 1876). A Russian perspective on the Bonn conference of 1875
was published during the month of August in *Tserkovnyi vestnik*.

4. It was well known in Europe at the time that the German imperial government was giving aid to the Old Catholics, but the government's hope to use them as obedient crown servants in the struggle against the truculent Ultramontanes, gathering strength behind the leadership of Ludwig Windhorst, was not fulfilled. "Old Catholics," *The Times*, August 14, 1875, p.10. Lillian Parker Wallace, *The Papacy and European Diplomacy 1869-1878* (Chapel Hill: University of North Carolina Press, 1948), 216.

5. Juergen Doerr, "Germany, Russia and the Kulturkampf, 1870-1875," *Canadian Journal of History* 10(April 1975): 57-62, and Francis A. Arlinghaus, "The Kulturkampf and European Diplomacy, 1871-1875," *Catholic Historical Review* 28 (October 1942): 349, 355, 362. The Russian ambassador to Berlin at this time was Pavel Ubri, a Roman Catholic. This unusual warming of relations between St. Petersburg and the Vatican can be easily explained from the perspective of Pius IX, who wanted to prevent Bismarck from enlisting international aid in his attack against the Roman Church in Germany. According to Eduard Winter, however, it was the Russian imperial government's fear of the sudden appearance of independent Catholic and Orthodox churches, a new Hussitism, that inspired Alexander II to seek closer ties with Rome. Winter, *Russland und das Papsttum*, 2 vols. (Berlin: Akademie-Verlag, 1960-61), 2:346-47.

6. Some Anglican clergy and some Old Catholic leaders blamed Julian Joseph Overbeck, German theologian, former Catholic priest, and, by the 1870s, zealous Orthodox believer, for turning the Russians against the Old Catholic movement. According to Döllinger, Overbeck deliberately wrecked good relations between the Old Catholics and the Russians because a union of the two parties would have displaced Overbeck's plan to establish a Western Orthodox Church. *Deutscher Merkur* 50(September 12, 1876): 429-30. Among the Anglicans, it was Frederick Meyrick who saw Overbeck as a stumbling block to union, especially in his June 16, 1876, speech to the Anglo-Continental Society. On the other hand, the Russians scoffed at suggestions that they were swayed by the intrigues of Overbeck; see "Po povodu otmeny bonskoi konferentsii v nastoiashchem godu," *Tserkovnyi vestnik* 26(June 1876). In fact, they had grown cool toward Overbeck by 1875 (perhaps even earlier, depending on how one interprets the Grand Duke Constantine's meeting with Overbeck in Paris in 1874). It should also be noted that some of Overbeck's reservations about the Old Catholics, on dogmatic grounds, had been raised by some Russians as early as 1872; see "Inostrannoe obozrenie," *Khristianskoe chtenie* 9(September 1872): 172. At that time Overbeck was still an enthusiastic supporter of the Old Catholic cause in Russia. Kahle, *Westliche Orthodoxie*, 132.

7. This second phase of Old Catholic activity was further removed from Rome than the first phase had been. When Döllinger died in 1890, with him went the restrictions against a married clergy and lay control of

ecclesiastical affairs. The decrees of the Council of Trent were rejected in the Declaration of Utrecht (the German Old Catholics had cut this tie with Rome at its Heidelberg meeting in 1888), and alterations were made in the Roman liturgical service. Although it was not noticeable at Utrecht, an internal shift was also taking place among Old Catholics that would soon bring many of them into sympathy with so-called liberal scholarship on questions of church history and then to a relativist stand on questions of dogma. The Old Catholic activity in the 1890s was also international in scope. The Swiss and Austrian influence was pronounced, and in the early twentieth century the Polish Mariavitians accepted an invitation to join the sect. In the earlier period, the chief Old Catholic newspaper was *Deutscher Merkur*, with its focus on Catholic activity in the Rhineland and Munich, but after 1893 the official Old Catholic publication was the multilingual *Revue Internationale de Théologie*. It was edited by the French former Catholic priest, E. Michaud. The appearance of the Dutch Old Catholics introduced yet another dimension. The Dutch Little Catholic Church did not break away from Rome as a result of conclusions reached by the Vatican Council in 1870, but had been in schism since the eighteenth century. Its presence at the international congresses now tied the anti-infallibility Catholics in Germany and Switzerland to theological positions taken by the Dutch 150 years earlier. All these new developments made Old Catholicism a far more complicated and divided phenomenon than it had been when Döllinger and his colleagues founded the sect in 1871.

    8. *Collected Works of Georges Florovsky*, vol. 2: *Christianity and Culture* (Belmont, Mass.: Nordland, 1974), 221.

    9. Vladimir Kerenskii, *Starokatolitsizm: ego istoriia i vnutrennee razvitie* (Kazan, 1894), 3-8, 36, 136-37.

    10. N. Ia. Beliaev, *Proiskhozhdenie starokatolichestva* (Moscow, 1892), 17-20, 24-25.

    11. J. Janyschew, *Ueber das Verhältniss der Altkatholiken zur Orthodoxie* (Wiesbaden, 1891), 5. Ianyshev wrote his first scholarly work on the history of papal power. I. P. Sokolov, "Protopresviter I. L. Ianyshev, kak deiatel' po starokatolicheskomu voprosu," *Khristianskoe chtenie* 2(February 1911): 230-31.

    12. A. A. Kireev, *Sochineniia*, 2 vols. (St. Petersburg, 1912), 2:97.

    13. Ibid., 1:7, 118.

    14. Ibid., 1:336-42, 2:117.

    15. Ibid., 1:60-61.

    16. Ibid., 1:27, 29, 83.

17. A. Katanskii, "Starokatolicheskii vopros dlia pravolsavnago vostoka," *Tserkovnyi vestnik* 46(November 1892): 723.

18. It should be pointed out, however, that the idea of encouraging the growth of independent Slavic Catholic churches was not new to the Russian clergy. Winter, *Russland*, 2:343-45.

19. A typical expression of this view can be found in "K voprosu o starokatolitsizm," *Tserkovnyi vestnik* 24(June 1896): 772-73.

20. Küppers's conclusion that Russian sympathy for Old Catholicism represented an "ecumenical outward looking spirit" seems in need of some qualification. Werner Küppers, "Die russische orthodoxe Kirche und die Kirchen des Westens," in Robert Stupperich, ed., *Die Russische Orthodoxe Kirche in Lehre und Leben* (Witten, 1967), 246.

21. It is not true that the criticism of Old Catholicism began in Athens and then spread to Russia. Rejection of Döllinger and doubts about the movement had appeared in the Russian press in the 1870s long before it became an issue in Greece. "Otsutsvie" (see note 3), 7-10, and "Prichiny malouspeshnosti starokatolicheskago dvizheniia v germanii," *Tserkovnyi vestnik* 30(August 1875): 2-4.

22. Propst v. Maltseiv, "Altkatholicizmus und Orthodoxie," *Germania*, nos. 180 and 182 (August 10 and 12, 1898).

23. Part of the long history of the *filioque* controversy has been described by John Meyendorff, *Byzantine Theology: Historical Trends and Doctrinal Themes* (New York: Fordham University Press, 1974), but a complete explanation of this topic remains to be written. The word itself was probably first introduced into the creed in Spain in the sixth century as a defensive measure against the Arians, although the theological concept is much older. By the ninth century it had become a major source of friction between the Eastern and Western churches, but Rome did not finally affirm the addition until the Council of Bari in 1098 and it was not actually defended as doctrine until 1274 at the second council of Lyon.

24. *Deutscher Merkur* 34(August 21, 1875): 295, reported Döllinger as having said: "Die Confessio orthodoxa hat ihrerseits willkürlich den Zusatz μόνον ins Glaubensbekenntnitz gebracht, wie die Abendländer das Filioque." However, John Meyendorff interprets this evidence as Döllinger's reference to "a *general meaning* of Orthodox consciousness, . . . and not to the text of the creed." Meyendorff strongly states that "nobody [in the East] ever interpolated the creed itself with the word μόνον. . . ." Meyendorff in a letter to John Basil, October 3, 1986.

25. Three of the strongest contributions to the *filioque* literature in the 1870s were: E. B. Pusey, *On the Clause 'And the Son' in Regard to the Eastern Church and the Bonn Conference: A Letter to the Rev. H. P. Liddon* (New York, 1876); Joseph Langen, *Die Trinitarische Lehrdifferenz*

zwischen der abendländischen und der morgenländischen Kirche (Bonn, 1876), and H. B. Swete, *On the History of the Doctrine of the Procession of the Holy Spirit: From the Apostolic Age to the Death of Charlemagne* (Cambridge, 1876).

26. Döllinger made regular references to the *filioque* controversy. "Reden Döllinger's auf der II Unions-Conferenz," *Deutscher Merkur* 34(August 21, 1875): 295. He was inclined to dismiss the importance of the question and was heard to refer to it as logomachy.

27. The Russian literature on the *filioque* controversy that appeared during the episode with the Old Catholics was considerable. Some of it was summarized by A. Brilliantov, "Trudy prof. V. V. Bolotova po voprosu o Filioque i polemika o ego 'Tezisakh o filioque' v russkoi literature," *Khristianskoe chtenie* 4(April 1913): 431-57.

28. A. Gusev, "Iezuitskiia apologiia, filiokvisticheskago ucheniia," *Vera i tserkov* 4 and 5(April and May 1900): 522-53, 659-79.

29. V. Kerenskii, *Chto razdelialo i razdeliaet vostochno- pravoslavnuiu i zapadnuiu staro-katolicheskuiu tserkvi?* (Kharkov, 1910), 39-41; A. P. Mal'tsev, "Starokatolitsizm i pravoslavie," *Vera i tserkov* 4:5(1902): 704; A. Gusev, *Vers i tserkov* (April 1900): 527; A. Gusev, *Starokatolicheskii otvet na nashi tezisy po voprosu o Filioque i presushchestvlenii: polemiko-apologeticheskii etiud* (Kazan, 1903). The official Old Catholic argument on the *filioque* was to agree that it was incorrectly included in the creed, but to deny that its exclusion was demanded for dogmatic belief. "Is the doctrine of the filioque dogma? No. Was it correct to introduce the *filioque* into the creed? No." "Russische Stimmen über den Altkatholizismus--Erklärungen des Herrn Bischof Weber--Simples remarques de la Direction," *Revue Internationale de Théologie* 5(July-September 1897): 554.

30. "Thesen über das 'Filioque': von einem russischen Theologen," *Revue Internationale de Théologie* 6(October-December 1898): 681-712.

31. Vladimir Lossky, "The Procession of the Holy Spirit in the Orthodox Triadology," *The Eastern Churches Quarterly* (Supplementary Issue: *Concerning the Holy Spirit*) 7(1948): 33.

32. Johannes O. Kalogiru, "Die orthodoxe Kirche des Ostens und der Altkatholizismus," *Evangelische Theologie*, 1949-50:514-15.

33. Lossky, "Procession of the Holy Spirit," 33.

34. "Starokatolicheskii vopros v Athinakh," *Russkoe obozrenie* (October 1896): 920-22.

35. A. P. Mal'tsev, "Starokatolichestvo i pravoslavie," *Tserkovnyia vedomosti* 42(1898): 1564-65.

36. Sergii, Episkop Iamburgskii, "Chto nas razdeliaet so starokatolikami?" *Tserkovnyi vestnik* 45(November 7, 1902): 1411-15.

37. Reinhard Slenczka, *Ostkirche und Ökumene: Die Einheit der Kirchen als dogmatisches Problem in der neueren ostkirchlichen Theologie* (Göttingen, 1962), 199-201.

38. E. Michaud, "Erreurs de quelques théologiens orientaux sur l'Eglise d'Occident," *Revue Internationale de Théologie* 11(April-June 1903): 357-66.

39. D. Kyriakos, "Professor Kyriakos über den Altkatholizismus," *Revue Internationale de Théologie* 4(April-June 1896): 321-32.

40. P. Ia. Svetlov, "Starokatolicheskii vopros v ego novom fazise," *Bogoslovskii vestnik* 2(1904): 283, 287-308.

CHAPTER 6

ALEXANDER HERZEN

1. As visitors approach the exit of the Moscow State Historical Museum, they confront a quotation from the Program of the Communist Party of the Soviet Union, spelled out in tall white letters on the wall: "At the beginning of the 20th century the center of the international revolutionary movement transferred itself to Russia. Under the leadership of the Bolshevik Party, led by Vladimir Il'ich Lenin, the heroic working class of Russia became the vanguard of this movement." It is disheartening to learn after arduous passage through three dozen halls of the museum that the origin of it all lies elsewhere. What place can there be in the previous halls of the museum for an Hegelian revolutionary tornado that "transfers" itself suddenly from West to East and puts itself at the disposal of the Bolsheviks?

2. In English, the classic text in the "internationalist" tradition is Edmund Wilson's *To the Finland Station: A Study in the Writing and Acting of History* (London and New York, 1940). An early effort to shift attention to the fuller domestic political scene was Donald W. Treadgold's *Lenin and His Rivals: The Struggle for Russia's Future, 1898-1906* (New York: Praeger, 1955); another was Jacob Walkin's *The Rise of Democracy in Pre-Revolutionary Russia: Political and Social Institutions Under the Last Three Czars* (New York: Praeger, 1962); and more recently Terrence Emmons's *The Formation of Political Parties and the First National Elections in Russia* (Cambridge: Harvard University Press, 1983). At this juncture I am not concerned with the rich bibliography on political movements among peasants, workers, and soldiers, but with the literature on the political activism of the intelligentsia. A full accounting of the

Russian political tradition awaits a time when we can deal uniformly with all social strata involved in it.

3. G. G. Vodolazov, *Ot Chernyshevskogo k Plekhanovu: ob osobennostiakh razvitiia sotsialisticheskoi mysli v Rossii* (Moscow, 1969); "Obshchina i revoliutsiia u Chernyshevskogo," *Vestnik Moskovskogo universiteta*, 1966, no. 3:35-46, and *Osobennosti razvitiia sotsialisticheskoi mysli v Rossii v otrazhenii russkoi zhurnalistiki 60-70 godov XIX v.: Avtoreferat ... kandidata istoricheskikh nauk* (Moscow, 1967).

4. *Rabota aktera nad soboi* (Moscow, 1938) [translated as *An Actor Prepares*], 521-22.

5. Alan Kimball, "Revolutionary Situation in Russia (1859- 1862)," *The Modern Encyclopedia of Russian and Soviet History* 31(1983): 54-57; and "I. I. Mints and the Representation of Reality in History," *Slavic Review* 35(December 1976): 715-23.

6. See, for example, N. Ia. Eidel'man, *Gertsen protiv samoderzhaviia: sekretnaia politicheskaia istoriia Rossii XVIII- XIX vekov i Vol'naia pechat'* (Moscow, 1973).

7. The classic study is Boris Koz'min, "'Raskol v nigilistakh' . . . ," in *Iz istorii revoliutsionnoi mysli v Rossii: izbrannye trudy* (Moscow, 1961), 20-67.

8. A sort of bureaucratic charade, pretending that responsible authorities had never before independently read Herzen's subversive publications, was played out May 9, 1862, when Alexander II approved a plan to allow A. A. Suvorov, governor-general of St. Petersburg, and I. V. Annenkov, city police chief, to subscribe to Herzen's dreaded *Kolokol*. S. D. Gurvich-Lishchiner, B. F. Egorov, K. N. Lomunov, and I. G. Ptushkina, eds., *Letopis' zhizni i tvorchestva A. I. Gertsena, 1812-1870*, vol. 3: *1859-iiun' 1864* (Moscow, 1983), 310.

9. Karl Mannheim made Alfred Weber's concept of the *freischwebende Intelligenz* famous in *Ideology and Utopia: An Introduction to the Sociology of Knowledge* (New York, 1936); see especially pages 155-61, where he treats what he calls the "socially unattached intelligentsia."

10. Daniel Brower decided on "the complete abandonment of the 'intelligentsia' as a tool for scholarly analysis." *Training the Nihilists: Education and Radicalism in Tsarist Russia* (Ithaca: Cornell University Press, 1975), 35.

11. Martin Malia's intellectual biography, *Alexander Herzen and the Birth of Russian Socialism, 1812-1855* (Cambridge: Harvard University Press, 1961), may still be the best work on Herzen. See also Edward Acton, *Alexander Herzen and the Role of the Intellectual Revolutionary* (Cambridge: Cambridge University Press, 1979).

12. Nicholas Riasanovsky, *A Parting of Ways: Government and the Educated Public in Russia, 1801-1855* (Oxford: Clarendon Press, 1976).

13. One discovers here a surprising parallel between Herzen's and Weidlé's visions: two émigrés, two epochs, two quite different political sensibilities, but the *skvoznaia liniia* shines through. See Wladimir Weidlé, *La Russie absente et présente* (Paris, 1949), translated as *Russia: Absent and Present* (London and New York, 1952).

14. One of the first users of the term was an officer active in support of the student demonstrations at St. Petersburg University in October 1861. Boris Chicherin's brother wrote him, quoting a friend who overheard the following remark: "We are letting the students move ahead, as they are representatives of the young generation and of the intelligentsia, but if they do not get the job done, we will move in." Boris N. Chicherin, *Vospominaniia Borisa Nikolaevicha Chicherina*, vol. 3: *Moskovskii universitet* (Moscow, 1934), 20-21.

15. Alexander Herzen, *My Past and Thoughts: The Memoirs of Alexander Herzen*, translated by Constance Garnett, revised by Humphrey Higgins, introduced by Isaiah Berlin, and abridged, with a preface and notes, by Dwight MacDonald (New York, 1973), 82; *Poliarnaia zvezda*, 1856, no. 2:127; Aleksandr Gertsen [Herzen], *Sobranie sochinenii*, 30 vols. (Moscow, 1954-65), 8:107. The translations here are from the MacDonald edition, adjusted in accordance with *Sobranie sochinenii*. All passages quoted here from Herzen's *Past and Thoughts* are footnoted with reference to the MacDonald edition, then to the first appearance in the original, and finally to *Sobranie sochinenii*, the most authoritative scholarly edition of Herzen's works.

16. The most comprehensive brief history of *chin* is L. E. Shepelev, *Otmenennye istoriei: chiny, zvaniia i tituly v rossiiskoi imperii* (Leningrad, 1977). Historically, the wide and decisive use of *chin*--a system of rank and titles--is unparalleled in the experience of other European peoples. The Table of Ranks set out to measure and define a person's place in the civil, military, and court hierarchy, and quickly became one of the essential pathways to aristocracy. See also V. A. Evreinov, *Grazhdanskoe chinoproizvodstvo v Rossii: istoricheskii ocherk*, which is an appendix to *Istoricheskii vestnik* (St. Petersburg) for 1887; and P. A. Zaionchkovskii, "Vysshaia biurokratiia nakanune Krymskoi voiny," *Istoriia SSSR*, 1974, no. 4:154-64. As Shepelev slyly observes (p. 47), even Lenin could say, of the civil service, "the real work of governing rested in the hands of the giant army of chinovniks." Shepelev believes, as did Lenin, that the state is the committee of the economically ruling "class."

Gregory Freeze attempts an ambitious summary of the development of the *sosloviia* in "The *Soslovie* (Estate) Paradigm and Russian Social History," *American Historical Review* 91(February 1986): 11-36.

17. Shepelev, *Otmenennye*, 77.

18. M. G. Sedov, *Revoliutsionnaia situatsiia v Rossii v 1859-1861 godov: Materialy k lektsii, posviashchennoi 100-letiiu padeniia krepostnogo prava* (Moscow, 1961), 9; quoting N. Rubakin, *Rossiia v tsifrakh* (St. Petersburg, 1912), 136. See also A. P. Korelin, *Dvorianstvo v poreformennoi Rossii 1861-1905 gg.: sostav, chislennost', korporativnaia organizatsiia* (Moscow, 1979), esp. 124ff.

In compensation for the emancipation of serfs, the nobility received about 500 million rubles. One-half of that went immediately to cover prior indebtedness. A large part of the compensation came in the form of bonds which depreciated immediately by 30 percent and had to be cashed to cut losses still further. There was no bank to aid the nobles until 1885, and over this period the international value of grain declined by one-half. See Roberta Thompson Manning, *The Crisis of the Old Order in Russia: Gentry and Government* (Princeton: Princeton University Press, 1982), chapter 1.

19. Iu. B. Solov'ev, *Samoderzhavie i dvorianstvo v kontse XIX veka* (Leningrad, 1973), 135ff., ascribes "Asiatic" characteristics to the tsarist state for its independence from "social roots," but he notes the peculiar historical pressures that forced the state to favor the *dvorianstvo*, especially those who managed their own landed estates.

20. Shepelev, *Otmenennye*, 55, 100.

21. Alfred J. Rieber, *Merchants and Entrepreneurs in Imperial Russia* (Chapel Hill: University of North Carolina Press, 1982), 3-39. See especially p. 23: "By any criteria, the merchantry must be ranked as the most passive soslovie in Russian society."

22. Gregory Guroff and Fred V. Carstensen, eds., *Entrepreneurship in Imperial Russia and the Soviet Union* (Princeton: Princeton University Press, 1983), 63-65. See also Thomas C. Owen, *Capitalism and Politics in Russia: A Social History of the Moscow Merchants, 1855-1905* (Cambridge: Cambridge University Press, 1981); L. E. Shepelev, *Tsarizm i burzhuaziia vo vtoroi polovine XIX veka: problemy torgovo-promyshlennoi politiki* (Leningrad, 1981); and V. Ia. Laverychev, *Krupnaia burzhuaziia v poreformennoi Rossii (1861-1900 gg.)* (Moscow, 1974).

23. K. S. Kuibysheva, "Krupnaia moskovskaia burzhuaziia v period revoliutsionnoi situatsii v 1859-1861 gg.,"in *Revoliutsionnaia situatsiia v Rossii v 1859-1861 gg.*, 4(Moscow, 1965): 318.

24. Flerov, *Dukh khristianina*, February 1863: 85-90.

25. Gregory L. Freeze, *The Parish Clergy in Nineteenth-Century Russia: Crisis, Reform, Counter-Reform* (Princeton: Princeton University Press, 1983), xxvi. See also, by the same author, "Revolt from Below: A Priest's Manifesto on the Crisis in Russian Orthodoxy," in Robert L. Nichols and

Theofanis G. Stavrou, eds., *Russian Orthodoxy under the Old Regime* (Minneapolis: University of Minnesota Press, 1978), 90-124.

26. A recent study of the status of the clergy in late tsarist Russia is Gregory L. Freeze, "Between Estate and Profession: The Clergy in Imperial Russia," in Michael L. Bush, ed., *Social Orders and Social Classes in Europe since 1500: Studies in Social Stratification* (London and New York: Longman, 1992), 47-65.

27. For instance, the nobleman-poet and later very successful gentleman farmer Afanasii Shensin [Fet]. See his "Iz derevni," *Russkii vestnik*, 1863, no. 1:438-70.

28. A. M. Unkovskii, *Aleksei Mikhailovich Unkovskii (1818-1893)* (Moscow, 1979).

29. For a discussion of the tsarist government's use of *chin* to reward specialists and members of the emerging professions in late tsarist Russia, see Charles E. Timberlake, "The Middle Classes in Late Tsarist Russia," in Bush, *Social Orders and Social Classes*, 86-113.

30. For a detailed exposition of this point, see Alan Kimball, "Who Were the Petrashevtsy?" *Mentalities/mentalités* 2(1988): 1-12.

31. Charles E. Timberlake, "Higher Learning, the State, and the Professions in Russia," in Konrad H. Jarausch, ed., *The Transformation of Higher Learning, 1860-1930: Expansion, Diversification, Social Opening, and Professionalization in England, Germany, Russia, and the United States* (Chicago: University of Chicago Press, 1983), 321-44. Copublished as volume 13 of *Historisch-Sozialwissenschaftliche Forschungen* (Stuttgart: Klett-Cotta, 1983).

32. *Byloe i dumy*, in *Poliarnaia zvezda*, 1855, no. 1: 163-68; *Sobranie sochinenii*, 9: 147-51.

33. In 1828 A. Kh. Benkendorf, first head of the notorious tsarist secret police, the Third Section, reported to Nicholas I: "Young folks from 17 to 25 years old are, taken as a group, the most dangerous part of the empire. Among these extravagant youths [*sumasbrodov*] we see the embryos of Jacobinism and the revolutionary and reformist spirit expressing themselves in a variety of forms but most often hidden beneath the mask of Russian patriotism." Benkendorf perceived that the fundamental question was "whose patriotism?" The students were beginning to lay hold on their own, not the state's, vision of the nation's future. T. G. Snytko, "Studencheskoe dvizhenie v russkikh universitetakh v nachale 60-kh godov i vosstanie 1863 g.," in V. D. Koroliuka and I. S. Miller, eds., *Vosstanie 1863 g. i russko-pol'skie revoliutsionnye sviazi 60-kh godov: sbornik statei i materialov* (Moscow, 1960), 183-84.

34. Even the antiprogressivist publicist Mikhail Katkov kept to the recognized contour of the *skvoznaia liniia* when, thirty years after Herzen's *kruzhok* was crushed, he generalized on this process: "The characteristic feature of our environment is that it stifles the organizing forces which bind people together who have a common interest, which flows throughout them and lives in them.... Such is the historical fate of our civilization. History has smashed all of our social ovaries, and given a negative direction to our artificial civilization...."

Katkov continued around the same curve of thought: "People thus live a double life--an external one, in which they do not take an intellectual and moral part [official public life], and an internal one, which enters more into the world of dreams than reality." See Katkov, "O nashem nigilizme po povodu romana Turgeneva," *Russkii vestnik* 1862, no. 7 (July): 411-12; See also Martin Katz, *Mikhail N. Katkov, 1818-1887: A Political Biography* (The Hague, 1966), 76.

Katkov said "environment" and "history" where Herzen might more explicitly have said "the state," but otherwise Herzen could have penned these lines himself. The *skvoznaia liniia* was not partisan.

35. *Past and Thoughts*, MacDonald edition, 114-16; *Poliarnaia zvezda*, 1856, no:2:164-66; *Sobranie sochinenii*, 8:162-63.

36. An excellent capsulation of Saint-Simon's revolutionary implications is given by J. H. Billington, *Fire in the Minds of Men: Origins of the Revolutionary Faith* (New York: Basic Books, 1980), 208-18. But Billington's imbalanced emphasis on fires in the mind not only contributes to his misdating the actual fires in St. Petersburg at one point (they were in 1862, not 1861, p. 5), it also encourages implausible assertions like this: "Thus the revolutionary label that now controls the destiny of more than one billion people in the contemporary world sprang from the erotic imagination of an eccentric writer." Billington is speaking here of Restif de la Bretonne, in Paris, before the French Revolution. Billington's lively book traces an external, spiritual *skvoznaia liniia*, what he calls the "signs along the path from Restif to Lenin" (p. 7).

37. *Past and Thoughts*, MacDonald edition, 230-31; *Poliarnaia zvezda*, 1855, no. 1:82; *Sobranie sochinenii*, 9:11, 17.

38. *Sobranie sochinenii*, 9:17.

39. A budding entrepreneurial class was attracted to Saint-Simon's vision of a future in which economics (i.e., public organization of daily life) rules over politics, rather than the other way around. See the enthusiastic article about joint stock companies in *Severnaia pchela* 25(1862): 97.

40. I expand on this argument more fully in "Student Interests and Student Politics: Kazan University Before the Crisis of 1862," *Acta Slavica Iaponica* (Sapporo) 6(1988): 1-15. A conspectus of this argument may be

found in *Referativnyi zhurnal: obshchestvennye nauki za rubezhom*, ser. 5 (Moscow, 1988): 46-49.

41. *Past and Thoughts*, MacDonald edition, 104; *Sobranie sochinenii*, 8:144.

42. *Past and Thoughts*, MacDonald edition, 246-49; *Poliarnaia zvezda*, 1862, no. 7:112-17; *Sobranie sochinenii*, 9:35-39.

43. See Brower, *Training the Nihilists*.

44. When members of a Moscow University student circle, led by Perikl Argiropulo and Petr Zaichenevskii, were arrested in 1861, they were found to have in their possession the poems of Shevchenko, Herzen's articles from *Poliarnaia zvezda* (apparently the chapter from "Past and Thoughts" titled "Zapad i vostok Evropy" (1855, no. 1:148-68), along with a portrait of Herzen, photographs of Decembrists, and of Polish radicals. The main activity of the circle had been to create a secret printing press, employing wooden type, to reprint Herzen and Ogarev's *Razbor knigi Korfa*. See Iu. V. Kulikov, "Voprosy revoliutsionnoi programmy i taktiki v proklamatsii 'Molodaia Rossiia' (1862 g.)," in *Revoliutsionnaia situatsiia v Rossii v 1859-1861 gg.*, 2(1962): 241-62.

45. The great public debate in response to a one-half page interview with Anatolii Logunov, who was then rector of Moscow State University and vice-president of the Academy of Sciences of the USSR, illustrates the influence these larger Saint-Simonian ideals have even in the era of *perestroika*. See "Intelligentsiia--poniatie russkoe," *Pravda*, August 7, 1989, p. 3.

CHAPTER 7

TVER ZEMSTVO'S TECHNICAL SCHOOL AT RZHEV

1. "Tekhnicheskoe obrazovanie," *Entsiklopedicheskii slovar* (Brokgauz-Efron) 65(1901): 127-28.

2. "Real'nyia uchilishcha," ibid., 51(1899): 411.

3. "Professional'noe obrazovanie," ibid., 25(1898): 569.

4. "Tekhnicheskiia obshchestva," ibid., 65(1899): 122-23. In the 1880s, the Technical Society's Permanent Commission on Technical Education published an annual list of schools it maintained. See, for instance, *Uchilishcha Imperatorskago Russkago Tekhnicheskago Obshchestva: adres, lichnyi sostav i rospisanie urokov v 1888/9 uchebnom godu: spravochnaia kniga* (St. Petersburg, 1889).

5. *Polnoe sobranie zakonov Rossiiskoi imperii* (2d series) 44, pt. 2 (St. Petersburg, 1873): 44-47. See also *Entsiklopedicheskii slovar* 25(1898): 568-69.

6. A. V. Dubrovskii, *Svedenie po statistike narodnago obrazovaniia v Evropeiskoi Rossii, 1872-1874* (St. Petersburg, 1879), 129-35.

7. *Protokoly zasedanii ocherednago Tverskogo zemskago sobraniia 1869 goda* (Tver, 1870), 45-47; hereafter Tver *Protokoly*, plus year and page number.

8. "Rzhev," *Entsiklopedicheskii slovar* 52(1899): 672.

9. Tver *Protokoly, 1869*, 47.

10. TsGIA, f. 1282, op. 2, d. 1822 ("Delo o zemskikh uchrezhdeniiakh po Tverskoi gubernii 8 Dekabria 1865 goda do 22 Fevralia 1879 goda"), 35.

11. B. B. Veselovskii, *Istoricheskii ocherk deiatel'nosti zemskikh uchrezhdenii Tverskoi gubernii, 1864-1913* (Tver, 1914), 287.

12. *Trudy Vol'nago ekonomicheskago obshchestva*, 1870, 4, no. 1:44-45.

13. Tver *Protokoly, 1870*, in *Materialy dlia istorii Tverskago gubernskago zemstva, 1866-1908 g.g.*, 10 vols. (Tver, 1894-1912), 8:380.

14. TsGIA, f. 1282, op. 2, d. 1822:34-36.

15. Tver *Protokoly, 1871*, 75-77.

16. TsGIA f. 1282, op. 2, d. 1822:43-43 ob.

17. Ibid., 36-37.

18. Ibid., 43.

19. Tver *Protokoly, 1871*, 75-76.

20. Ibid.

21. TsGIA, f. 1282, op. 2, d. 1822:61-62. On April 22, the minister of the interior passed this information on to the governor of Tver province.

22. *Trudy*, 1872, 1, no. 2:221.

23. Report by the board, in Tver *Protokoly, 1873*, 65.

24. Tver *Protokoly, 1872*, 17-18.

25. Report by the board, Tver *Protokoly, 1873*, 63-65.

26. *Protokoly, 1873*, regular session, 66-67.

27. Ibid.

28. TsGIA, d. 1822:73-74.

29. Tver *Protokoly, 1873*, 67.

30. TsGIA, d. 1822:69-70.

31. Ibid., 70.

32. Ibid., 71-73.

33. Ibid., 71.

34. Ibid., 72.

35. Ibid., 73-74.

36. Ibid., 83-84.

37. Ibid., 84-86.

38. Ibid., 86-87.

39. Ibid., 87-87 ob.

40. Ibid., 87 ob.

41. Ibid., 87 ob-88.

42. Ibid., 93-94 ob.

43. Report by the board, in Tver *Protokoly, 1873,* 72.

44. TsGIA, d. 1822:98-110.

45. Veselovskii, *Istoricheskii ocherk,* 289.

CHAPTER 8

MARXISM AND AZIATCHINA

1. Paul Miliukov's much-used concept has been expanded at length by Karl A. Wittfogel, *Oriental Despotism: A Comparative Study of Total Power* (New Haven: Yale University Press, 1959), esp. chapter 3.

2. Ibid., esp. chapter 4.

3. Cf. Donald M. Lowe, *The Function of "China" in Marx, Lenin, and Mao* (Berkeley and Los Angeles: University of California Press, 1966), 25; Hélène Carrère d'Encausse and Stuart R. Schram, *Marxism and Asia* (London: Allen Lane, 1969), 10-11; see also J. A. Doerig, ed., *Marx vs. Russia* (New York: Frederick Ungar, 1962), esp. the afterword by Hans Kohn.

4. Karl Marx, "The British Rule in India," in Karl Marx and Frederick Engels, *Selected Works in Two Volumes* (Moscow, 1958), 1:347. Marx wrote this article in English, which explains its grammatical idiosyncrasies

5. Ibid., 346.

6. Ibid., 350.

7. See Karl A. Wittfogel, "The Marxist View of China," *China Quarterly, no. 11* (July-September 1962): 1-20, and no. 12 (October-December 1962): 154-69; Dona Torr, ed., *Marx on China, 1853-1860: Articles from the New York Daily Tribune* (London, 1951), among others.

8. Marx followed Engels, "Deutschland und der Panslawismus," *Marx-Engels Werke* (Berlin, 1956-68), 11:197.

9. Karl Marx, *Secret Diplomatic History of the Eighteenth Century and The Story of the Life of Lord Palmerston,* edited by Lester Hutchinson (New York: International Publishers, 1969), 121, 123, 125.

10. Karl Marx, Letter to the Editors of *Otechestvennye zapiski* (November 1877) in *Marx-Engels Werke*, 19:107.

11. G. V. Plekhanov, "Chto takoe sotsializm?" in D. L. Deich, ed., *Sbornik No. 3, Gruppa Osvobozhdenie Truda* (Moscow and Leningrad, 1925), 7-20.

12. G. V. Plekhanov, "Nashi raznoglasiia," *Izbrannye filosofskie proizvedeniia* (Moscow: Gosudarstvennoe izdatel'stvo politicheskoi literatury, 1956), 1:258; See also G. V. Plekhanov, "Sotsializm i politicheskaia bor'ba," ibid., 2:70-71.

13. Plekhanov, "Sotsializm i politicheskaia bor'ba," 65.

14. Ibid., 67; see also Plekhanov, "Nashi raznoglasiia," 208.

15. Plekhanov, "Nashi raznoglasiia," 321ff.

16. V. N. Alekseev, "Ot izdanii," *Sotsial-Demokrat*, book 1 (London, February 1890), I-II; Paul Axelrod, "Das politische Erwachen der russischen Arbeiter und ihre Maifeier von 1891," *Die Neue Zeit*, 10:2(1891-92): 37.

17. Vera Zasulich, "Revolutsionnery iz burzhuaznoi sredy," *Sotsial-Demokrat*, book 1 (February 1890): 69.

18. G. V. Plekhanov, "Die sozial-politischen Zustände Russlands im Jahre 1890," *Die Neue Zeit*, IX-2/48-52, 832-33.

19. G. V. Plekhanov, "Vnutrennee obozrenie," *Sotsial-Demokrat*, book 2 (Geneva, August 1890), 61-81. Boris Krichevskii thought this statement significant enough to quote in his own appraisal. See "Die russische revolutionäre Bewegung einst und jetzt," *Die Neue Zeit* IX-1/22 (1890-91): 708.

20. A. Voden, "Talks with Engels," *Reminiscences of Marx and Engels* (Moscow: Foreign Languages Publishing House, undated), 328-33.

21. V. I. Lenin, "Chto Takoe 'Druz'ia Naroda' i kak oni voiuiut protiv sotsial-demokratov?" *Polnoe sobranie sochinenii*, 5th ed., 55 vols. (Moscow: Gosudarstvennoe izdatel'stvo politicheskoi literatury, 1958-65), 1:240-41; hereafter *PSS*. (Italics are Lenin's in all quotations.)

22. V. I. Lenin, "Zadachi russkikh sotsial-demokratov," *PSS*, 2:455f.

23. Ibid., 459, quoting P. L. Lavrov.

24. Lenin, "Ot kakogo nasledstva my otkazyvaemsia?" *PSS*, 2:549.

25. Lenin, "Razvitie kapitalizma v Rossii," in *PSS*, 3:381.

26. Lenin, "Nekriticheskaia kritika," *PSS*, 3:624.

27. Lenin, "Proekt programmy nashei partii," *PSS*, 4:220.

28. Ibid., 227-30.

29. Lenin, "Protest rossiiskikh sotsial-demokratov," *PSS*, 4:175f.

30. Lenin, "Nasha programma," *PSS*, 4:185.

31. Lenin, "Kiraiskaia voina," *PSS*, 4:383.

32. Lenin, "Otdacha v soldaty 183-kh studentov," *PSS*, 4:393.

33. Lenin, "Rabochaia partiia i krest'ianstvo," *PSS*, 4:432.

34. Lenin, "Tsennoe priznanie," *PSS*, 5:77.

35. Lenin, *Chto delat'? PSS*, 6:112.

36. Ibid., 28.

37. Lenin, "Dve taktiki sotsial-demokratii v demokraticheskoi revoliutsii," *PSS*, 11:35.

38. G. V. Plekhanov, "K agrarnomu voprosu v Rossii," *Dnevnik sotsial-demokrata* 5 (March 1906): 11.

39. Ibid., 12.

40. Ibid., 15-16.

41. Ibid., 17.

42. W. I. Lenin, "Eine Revolution vom Typus des Jahres 1789 oder vom Typus des Jahres 1848," in W. I. Lenin, *Sämtliche Werke* (Vienna and Berlin: Verlag für Literatur und Politik, 1929), 7:249.

43. Lenin, *PSS*, 10:58, 75.

44. *Protokoly Ob"edinitel'nogo S"ezda Rossiiskoi Sotsial-Demokraticheskoi Rabochei Partii* (Moscow, 1907), 44.

45. Ibid., 103-4.

46. Ibid., 115.

47. Ibid., 86.

48. Lenin, "Agrarnaia programma sotsial-demokratii v pervoi russkoi revoliutsii 1905-1907 godov," *PSS*, 16:260-61.

49. Ibid., 306.

50. Ibid., 307.

51. Ibid., 311n.

52. Ibid., 405-6.

53. Ibid., 409.

54. Ibid., 329.

55. See the elaboration of this point in Karl A. Wittfogel, "The Marxist View of Russian Society and Revolution," *World Politics* 12 (July 1960): 503-4.

CHAPTER 9

MIKHAIL GERSHENZON'S "SECRET VOICE"

1. Renato Poggioli, *The Phoenix and the Spider: A Book of Essays About Some Russian Writers and Their View of the Self* (Cambridge: Harvard University Press, 1957), 212. Arthur A. Levin provides the most complete biographical account of Gershenzon in "The Life and Works of Mikhail Osipovich Gershenzon, 1869-1926" (Ph.D. diss., University of California, Berkeley, 1968). See also James P. Scanlan's excellent introduction to his translation of Gershenzon's *Istoriia molodoi Rossii* in *Russian History* 1(1974): 46-64; and Georges Florovsky's perceptive analysis, "Michael Gerschensohn," in *Slavonic Review* 5(1926): 315-31.

2. M. 0. Gershenzon, "Tvorcheskoe samosoznanie," in *Vekhi: sbornik statei o russkoi intelligentsii,* 5th ed. (Moscow, 1910), 70-96. This essay has been translated by Marshall S. Shatz and Judith Zimmerman, "Creative Self-Consciousness," in *Canadian Slavic Studies* 3(1969): 1-21. The polemical and scholarly literature on *Vekhi* is voluminous. The best account of Gershenzon's role is Arthur A. Levin, "M. 0. Gershenzon and *Vekhi,*" *Canadian Slavic Studies* 4(1970): 60-73. See also Leonard Schapiro, "The *Vekhi* Group and the Mystique of Revolution," *Slavonic and East European Review* 34(1955): 56-76.

3. V. I. Ivanov and M. 0. Gershenzon, *Perepiska iz dvukh uglov* (Petrograd, 1921). Two English translations have appeared: "A Corner-to-Corner Correspondence" in Marc Raeff, ed., *Russian Intellectual History: An Anthology* (New York: Harcourt, Brace and World, 1966), 373-401; and Lisa Sergio, trans., *Correspondence Across a Room* (Marlboro, Vermont: The Marlboro Press, 1984). For commentary see Poggioli, *The Phoenix and the Spider,* 208-28; Boris Thomson, *Lot's Wife and the Venus of Milo: Conflicting Attitudes to the Cultural Heritage in Modern Russia* (Cambridge: Cambridge University Press, 1978), 22-28; Robert Louis Jackson, "Ivanov's Humanism: *A Correspondence from Two Corners,*" in *Vyacheslav Ivanov: Poet, Critic and Philosopher* (New Haven: Yale Center for International and Area Studies, 1986), 346-57; Donald W. Treadgold, *The West in Russia and China,* 2 vols. (Cambridge: Cambridge University Press, 1973), 1:235-36.

4. *Perepiska iz dvukh uglov,* 60-61.

5. M. 0. Gershenzon, "Pis'ma k bratu," *Russkaia mysl',* 1907, no. 5 (May): 86-96. Compare Ivan's statement in Dostoevsky's novel ("Why have you been looking at me in expectation for the last three months? To ask me 'what do you believe or don't you believe at all?'") with the beginning of Gershenzon's letters ("Isn't it strange that for all these years

neither one of us thought it necessary to peer deeply into the eyes of the other and ask: 'Brother, are you happy? What do you believe in?'").

6. In his writings, Gershenzon also employed the adjectives "internal" (*vnutrennee*), "external" (*vneshnee*), and "real" or "authentic" *(podlinnoe)* when referring to the self.

7. Florovsky points out, however, that there is no necessary connection between what Gershenzon called "cosmic feeling" and "religious consciousness" ("Michael Gerschensohn," 320).

8. Because he was Jewish, Gershenzon was prevented from pursuing an academic career despite his outstanding record as a student in the Historical Faculty at Moscow University.

9. M. 0. Gershenzon, *Istoricheskie zapiski* (Moscow, 1910), 45.

10. Morse Peckham, *The Triumph of Romanticism* (Columbia: University of South Carolina Press, 1970), 31-44; *Romanticism and Behavior* (Columbia: University of South Carolina Press, 1976), 55-58.

11. *Istoricheskie zapiski,* 201-2.

12. While this assertion remains controversial, subsequent studies have also argued that the post-Napoleonic period witnessed the emergence of the problem of personal identity in sharper forms than previously. See Lionel Trilling, *The Opposing Self* (New York: Viking, 1955), x-xi. Quentin Anderson, *The Imperial Self* (New York: Knopf, 1971), treats this issue in America in the same period and ventures that "it was in the great provincial societies, the United States and Russia, that the presumptions on which Western society had been built began to die out" (p. 3).

13. A joke circulated in Moscow at the time that "only one Slavophile remains in Russia, and *that* one is a Jew." V. A. Maklakov, *Iz vospominanii* (New York, 1954), 205.

14. *Istoricheskie zapiski,* 215.

15. Ibid., 13-14.

16. Russian symbolist poetry in this period also shared these underlying assumptions. Romantic influences were apparent in many--though certainly not all--of the features of modernism at the beginning of the twentieth century. There has been considerable scholarly debate over the extent to which modernism represented a revolt against romanticism as opposed to an extension of some of its aspects. For a summary see Monroe K. Spears, *Dionysus and the City* (New York: Oxford University Press, 1970), 13-20.

17. Gershenzon attributes the following view to Iurii Samarin and adds his own approval: " . . . all real knowledge is based on personal experience [and thus] the content of our cognition is entirely determined by the character of those organs of perception to which a person is disposed" *Istoricheskie zapiski,* 125.

18. Henri F. Ellenberger, *The Discovery of the Unconscious* (New York: Basic Books, 1970), 209-10. Ellenberger's portrayal of Romantic ideas about the unconscious should be quoted at length because of their close similarity to Gershenzon's: "Another basic concept of Romantic philosophy was that of primordial phenomena. . . . No less basic . . . was the notion of the unconscious. This word no longer meant St. Augustine's forgotten memories or Leibniz's 'unclear perceptions' but was the very fundament of the human being as rooted in the invisible life of the universe and therefore the true bond linking man to nature. Closely related to the notion of the unconscious was that of the 'inner' or 'universal sense' (*All-Sinn*) by which man, before the fall, was able to cognicize nature. Imperfect though this sense had become, it still enabled us, said the romantics, to gain some direct understanding of the universe, be it in mystical ecstasy, poetic and artistic inspiration . . . or dreams" (Ellenberger, 203-4).

19. The nomenclature referring to these states differed with each psychologist, and the term "unconscious" is used here generically. "Dissociation" is the accepted English translation for Janet's French term, *désagrégation.* Myers used the word "subliminal." Somewhat related is Morton Prince's idea of "co-consciousness" and William James's "psychic fringe." In his *Psychology: The Briefer Course* (1892), James wrote: "It is . . . the reinstatement of the vague and inarticulate to its proper place in our mental life which I am so anxious to press on the attention. . . . What must be admitted is that the definite images of traditional psychology form but the very smallest part of our minds as they actually live. . . . Every definite image in the mind is steeped and dyed in the free water that flows around it" (p. 32).

20. See Ernest R. Hilgard, "Dissociation Revisited," in Mary Henle, Julian Jaynes, and John J. Sullivan, eds., *Historical Conceptions of Psychology* (New York, 1973), 205-19. See also Kenneth S. Bowers and Donald Meichenbaum, eds., *The Unconscious Reconsidered* (New York, 1984). Freudian categories have monopolized the application of psychology to the study of history (as well as to literary criticism), excluding other possible connections between the two disciplines. Virtually all the contributions relating psychology and history over the past seventeen years in the *Journal of Interdisciplinary History* have taken Freudian approaches. Indeed, "psychohistory" is a term that means psychoanalysis and history combined.

21. Ellenberger, *Discovery of the Unconscious,* 173, 314.

22. *Istoricheskie zapiski,* 42-43.

23. Ibid., 115-16.

24. Ibid., 24.

25. Gershenzon, *Vekhi,* 70.

26. Ibid., 71.

27. Ibid., 77-78. These views anticipated some of the concerns later developed by Michael Polanyi, who also rejects the ideal of scientific detachment and passive experience in favor of an alternative ideal of the "personal participation of the knower in all acts of understanding." Michael Polanyi, *Personal Knowledge: Towards a Post-Critical Philosophy* (Chicago: University of Chicago Press, 1958), vii.

28. In Gershenzon's letters to his brother, he wrote: "I don't need to know . . . the meaning of life but . . . to return to the condition of a wild man or animal, which is the course of universal life [and] to be carried along its unknown channel" ("Pis'ma k bratu," 94). This statement again invites comparison with Ivan Karamazov's comment to Alyosha about "loving life more than the meaning of it"; or Dostoevsky's point, at the end of "The Dream of a Ridiculous Man," against the idea that "consciousness of life is higher than life."

29. Gershenzon, *Epokha Nikolaia Pervogo* (Moscow, 1911), 3.

30. Poggioli, *The Phoenix and the Spider*, 220.

31. *Istoricheskie zapiski*, 26.

32. *Perepiska iz dvukh uglov*, 38.

33. Ibid., 62.

34. *Vekhi*, 84.

35. Gershenzon, *Mechta i mysl' I. S. Turgeneva* (Moscow, 1919), 55.

36. See Arthur A. Levin, "Andrey Bely, M. 0. Gershenzon and *Vekhi*," in Gerald Janecek, ed., *Andrey Bely: A Critical Review* (Lexington: University Press of Kentucky, 1978), 169-80.

37. Gershenzon, *Vestnik Evropy*, 1908:408.

38. A. A. Blok, *Sobranie sochinenii*, 8 vols. (Moscow and Leningrad, 1963), 7:139.

39. M. 0. Gershenzon, *Kliuch very* (Moscow, 1922). This quotation is taken from the English translation by Herman Frank, *The Key to Faith* (New York, 1925), 155-56.

40. According to Gorky, Blok said: "If only we could stop thinking completely for ten years. Simply switch off this deceitful will-o'-the-wisp that is leading us deeper and deeper into the night of the world and listen in our hearts to the harmony of the universe. The brain, the brain . . . . It is not a reliable organ, it is monstrously large, monstrously developed." Avril Pyman, *The Life of Aleksandr Blok*, 2 vols. (Oxford: Oxford University Press, 1979-80), 2:343.

41. Ivan Turgenev, *Turgenev's Literary Reminiscences*, translated by
David Magarshack (London, 1958), 246. Turgenev continues: "All
these--sometimes radiant, sometimes stern, living, dead, triumphant,
perishing figures, these intertwining, scaly, serpentine coils . . . these
bodies, the most beautiful human bodies in every kind of position,
incredibly brave, melodiously shapely--all these most diverse expressions of
faces, supreme movements of limbs, this triumph of malice, and despair,
and divine gaiety and divine cruelty--why, it is a world, a whole world, and
its revelation sends a cold shiver of delight and passionate reverence
through one's veins. And one thing more: at the sight of all these
irrepressibly fine wonders, what becomes of all our accepted ideas about
Greek sculpture, its severity, serenity, about its confinement within the
borders of its particular art, of its classicism--all those ideas which have
been inculcated in us as indubitable truths by our instructors, theoreticians,
aesthetes, by the whole of our training and scholarship?"

42. Leopold Haimson has argued that Bolshevism originated out of an
intellectual milieu in which the categories of "consciousness"
(soznatel'nost') and "elemental spontaneity" *(stikhiinost')* framed much of
the debate. Both Lenin's personal life and his politics put a great premium
on "consciousness" perhaps precisely because he glimpsed the immense
eruptive powers of spontaneous forces lurking below. Haimson draws
considerably on Gershenzon's formulations in this book. Leopold H.
Haimson, *The Russian Marxists and the Origins of Bolshevism* (Cambridge:
Harvard University Press, 1955), 6-8, 132-41.

CHAPTER 10

POBEDONOSTSEV'S PARISH SCHOOLS

1. *Pis'ma o puteshestvii Gosudaria Naslednika Tsesarevicha po Rossii
ot Peterburga do Kryma* (Moscow: Tipografiiia Gracheva i komp., 1864),
90.

2. G. Fal'bork and V. Charnolusskii, "Narodnoe nachal'noe
obrazovanie," *Entsiklopedicheskii slovar* 40(St. Petersburg and Leipzig:
Brokgauz-Efron, 1897): 753-59.

3. Ibid., 759.

4. Allen Sinel, *The Classroom and the Chancellery: State Educational
Reform in Russia under Count Dmitry Tolstoy* (Cambridge: Harvard
University Press, 1973), 227.

5. Ibid., 235.

6. Ibid., 251-52.

7. "Narodnoe nachal'noe obrazovanie," 759.

8. K. P. Pobedonostsev, *Izvlechenie iz vsepoddanneishago otcheta ober-prokurora Sviateishago Sinoda K. Pobedonostsev po vedomstvu pravoslavnago ispovedaniia za 1880 g.* (St. Petersburg, 1882), 109. Although the Holy Synod published only an abstract (*izvlechenie*) of Pobedonostsev's full, annual report on the status of the Russian Orthodox Church for the years 1880, 1881, 1882, and 1883, these are major works and closely resemble the full reports published for later years. (Hereafter, these abstracts will be cited as *Izvlechenie za* plus the year covered by the report).

9. *Izvlechenie za 1881 g.*, 92; *Izvlechenie za 1882 g.*, 86.

10. *Izvlechenie za 1883 g.*, 55-60.

11. K. P. Pobedonostsev, *Vsepoddanneishii otchet ober-prokurora Sviateishago Sinoda K. Pobedonostseva po vedomstvu pravoslavnago ispovedaniia za 1884 g.* (St. Petersburg: Sinodal'naia tipografiia, 1886), 23 (further page numbers are included in the text). These full, published annual reports exist for 1884 through 1905. Hereafter they will be cited as *Vsepoddanneishii otchet za ...* [plus the year].

12. Pobedonostsev to Il'minskii, June 13, 1884. TsGIA, f. 1574, op. 1, ed. khr. 146.

13. Pobedonostsev to Il'minskii, May 24, 1884. Ibid.

14. *Vsepoddanneishii otchet za 1884 g.*, 114-17.

15. *Vsepoddanneishii otchet za 1885 g.*, 178.

16. TsGIA, f. 1151, op. 10, ed. khr. 666. Zapiska no. 13,441, November 21, 1885: "Ob otpuske iz summ Gosudarstvennago kaznacheistva c 1886 g. po 120,000 r. na tserkovno-prikhodskiia shkoly."

17. *Vsepoddanneishii otchet za 1886 g.*, 181-82.

18. *Vsepoddanneishii otchet za 1890-1891 gg.*, 342.

19. *Vsepoddanneishii otchet za 1888-1889 gg.*, 342.

20. TsGIA, f. 1152, 1895 g., ed. khr. 213. "Zapiska no. 360, April 23, 1895. "Ob ezhegodnom assignovanii iz sredstv Gosudarstvennago kaznacheistva 3,279,205 rublei na soderzhanie tserkovno-prikhodskikh shkol i shkol gramoty i na inspektsiiu za simi shkolami."

21. Ibid., listy 36-41. Zapiska no. 1476, March 23, 1895.

22. *Vsepoddanneishii otchet za 1899 g.*, 225-27.

23. *Vsepoddanneishii otchet za 1905-07 gg.*, 293. The author of this report was probably Pobedonostsev's successor, V. K. Sabler, but certainly was not Pobedonostsev.

24. TsGIA, f. 1574, op. 1, ed. khr. 16, listy 41-42. Pobedonostsev to Nicholas II, November 9, 1902.

25. *Bol'shaia sovetskaia entsiklopediia* (Moscow and Leningrad: Izdatel'stvo "Sovetskaia entsiklopediia"), 46:576.

26. A good example of a report of such resistance is S. A. Rachinskii's letter to Pobedonostsev of December 23, 1885 (in Otdel rukopisei, Gosudarstvennaia biblioteka imeni Lenina, f. 230, m. 4412, ed. khr. 2), asserting that the parish schools failed in the dioceses of Smolensk and Tver because the bishops were ignorant and incompetent.

CHAPTER 11
CANONIZATION OF SERAFIM OF SAROV

1. A draft of this essay was presented at the Third World Congress of Soviet and East European Studies in Washington, D.C., October 30–November 4, 1985. The author would like to thank those who read and criticized the paper then: Father John Meyendorff, Dimitry Pospielovsky, Stephen K. Batalden, John Basil, and Alan Kimball. Since that time the author has benefited from the help of many others: Edward Kasinec, Leonard N. Beck, Elizabeth H. Cuthbert, George Tokmakoff, Robert D. Warth, William Woehrlin, Theofanis G. Stavrou, and most particularly Hugh Olmsted, Irene Hay, and Gregory L. Freeze. Finally, the author wishes to acknowledge his gratitude to Father Panteleimon and Father Nicholas of the Holy Transfiguration Monastery for their kindness and generosity.

Note: Since this essay was written, Gregory Freeze has included some archival information on this canonization in an unpublished paper ("Tserkov', religiia, i politicheskaia kultura na zakate starogo rezhima v Rossii") he presented at the Institute of History in St. Petersburg in 1990. This information shows that the canonization had less public impact than the royal couple wished because a rumor spread that Serafim's relics were found "corrupted" when the casket was opened for inspection.

2. The quotation is the inscription on the gravestone of the popularly venerated Archbishop Antonii (Smirnitskii); see *Pravoslavnaia bogoslovskaia entsiklopediia* (St. Petersburg, 1904-10), 1:805.

3. P. G., "Sarovskiia torzhestva," *Pribavleniia k tserkovnym vedomostiam* (hereafter *PTV*), 1903, no. 30:1127, col. 1. Archbishop of Kazan Dmitrii, in his sermon at Serafim's glorification, noted: "[Serafim] has already long ago blessed and glorified with profound tenderness and reverence all the peoples of the Russian land." *PTV*, 1903, no. 30:1126, col. 1.

4. The following is only a small sampling of the periodical press and books concerning the glorification of Serafim: Mikhail Chubov, "V Sarove: iz dnevnika palomnika," *Poltavskie eparkhial'nye vedomosti*, 1904, no. 20/21:821-29; N. Lender, "Poezdka v sarovskuiu pustyn'," *Russkii*

vestnik 285(June 1903): 575-92; 286(July 1903): 234-67; M. Makarevskii, *Na prazdnike u prepodobnago Serafima, sarovskago chudotvortsa: vospominaniia i vpechatleniia ochevidtsa* (St. Petersburg, 1904); "Moshchi prepodobnago Serafima sarovskago," *Russkii vestnik* 286(July 1903): 388-89; N. N., "Puteshestvie v Sarov: iz vospominanii sarovskago palomnika," *Dushepoleznoe chtenie*, 1904, 1:103-13; Arkhimandrit Nikon, "Sarovskaia 'Paskha'," *Dushepoleznoe chtenie*, 1903, 8:154-66; "Po puti v Sarov," *PTV*, 1903, no. 30:1142-46; E. Poselianin [pseud.], *Prepodobnyi Serafim, sarovskii chudotvorets* (St. Petersburg, 1904); A. Predmestin, "K proslavleniiu prepodobnago Serafima sarovskago chudotvortsa," *PTV*, 1903, no. 24:910-11; P. I. Preobrazhenskii, *Otkrytie sviatykh moshchei prepodobnago Serafima, sarovskago chudotvortsa* (St. Petersburg, 1904); "Proslavlenie prepodobnago Serafima, startsa sarovskago," *Russkii vestnik* 284(March 1903): 431-32; A. S--ii, "U raki prepodobnago Serafima sarovskago," *PTV*, 1904, no. 40:1525-28; Sergii [Tikhomirov], *Pis'ma iz Sarova, 13-22 Iulia 1903 goda* (St. Petersburg, 1903); Tikhon Skvortsov, "Chuvsta i vpechatleniia sel'skago iereia ot sarovskikh torzhestv," *Missionerskoe obozrenie* 8(1903): 291-96; A Speranskii, "Iz Sarova: vpechatleniia palomnika," *PTV*, 1903, no. 33:1259-62; Aleksei A. Tsarevskii, *Sarovskaia pustyn': ko dniiu proslavleniia sarovskago ottsa Serafima* (Kazan, 1903); "Tsar v Sarove," *Russkii vestnik* 286(August 1903): 758-59.

The most extensive newspaper coverage was in *Novoe vremia* for the dates July 15-24.

5. Valentine Zander, *St. Serafim of Sarov*, translated by Sister Gabriel Anne with an introduction by Fr. Boris Bobrinskoi (Crestwood, N.Y.: St. Vladimir Seminary Press, 1975), xiv.

6. "Slovo preosviashchennago Innokentiia, episkopa tambovskago i shatskago," *PTV*, 1903, no. 30:1125.

7. As quoted in Kirill I. Zaitsev, *Pamiati posledniago tsaria; Rossiia i tsar. Taina lichnosti tsaria. Katastrofa* (Shanghai, 1948), 46.

8. Professor John F. Hutchinson, a historian of medicine, in a private letter to the author dated January 16, 1984, writes: "[Dr.] Ott received no thanks at all from the Tsar when he exposed 'Dr. Philippe' as a fraud by establishing that Alexandra's supposed pregnancy was purely psychosomatic." Professor Hutchinson states that there is no discussion of Serafim in the medical literature for that period.

Recently, Robert D. Warth, "Before Rasputin: Piety and the Occult at the Court of Nicholas II," *The Historian* 47(May 1985): 329, has suggested that perhaps the empress "simply had a miscarriage and that the story of the false pregnancy was a widespread but vicious rumor."

9. Andrei Elchaninov, *The Tsar and His People*, translated by A.P.W. (London, n.d.), 670.

10. The description of the service of glorification is based on the official documents published in *PTV*, 1903, no. 30:1119-36.

11. Ibid., 1124, col. 1.

12. Ibid., 1124, col. 2.

13. I have used with slight modification the translation of the words for the Magnification by Natalia Challis, "Glorification of Saints in the Orthodox Church," *Russian History/Histoire russe* 7, pts. 1-2 (1980): 46.

14. I discussed the content of Nicholas's religious views and their role in the tsar's efforts to define his reign in new ways in "The Religious Views of Nicholas II," an unpublished paper presented at the Southern Conference on Slavic Studies in Savannah, Georgia, March 21-23, 1991.

15. An official statement about the synod's inquiry is found in "Deianiia sviateishago sinoda 29 ianvaria 1903 goda," *Tserkovnyia vedomosti* (hereafter *TV*), 1903, no. 5:29-34, and in a slightly abbreviated form in *Vsepoddanneishii otchet oberprokurora Sviateishago Sinoda po vedomstvu pravoslavnago ispovedaniia za 1903-1904 gody* (St. Petersburg: Sinodal'naia tipografiia, 1909), 1-13. Without knowing the evidence to be found in the archives of the Holy Synod, one might speculate that the "untimeliness" of Serafim's case resulted from its close proximity in time to the canonization of Saint Feodosii of Uglich in 1896.

16. Sarov's official "life" is *Zhitie startsa Serafima* (St. Petersburg, 1863; 4th ed., 1893). Leonid's book is entitled *Letopis' serafimo-diveevskago monastyria* (Moscow, 1896; 2d ed., St. Petersburg, 1903).

17. Michael T. Florinsky, *Russia: A History and an Interpretation*, 2 vols. (New York: Macmillan, 1953), 2:950.

18. Russia's military clergy were created by Paul I in 1800 as a separate division of the clergy with its own administration. By 1900, eighteen cathedrals, several hundred regimental churches, and more than six hundred clergy belonged to the military clergy. Among other duties, the military clergy supervised military cemeteries, organized philanthropic societies, educational brotherhoods, church libraries, and extraliturgical religious and moral "conversations" with enlisted men. See A. Bogoliubov, *Ocherki iz istorii upravleniia voennym i morskim dukhovenstvom v biografiiakh glavnykh sviashchennikov ego za vremia s 1800 po 1901 god* (St. Petersburg, 1901).

19. Very little information is available about Father Leonid. I have relied largely on *Polnyi pravoslavnyi bogoslovskii entsiklopedicheskii slovar* (London: Variorum Reprints, 1971), vol. 1, cols. 1322 and 2041.

20. On the Action Français and Joan of Arc, see Marian Warner, *Joan of Arc: The Image of Female Heroism* (New York: Knopf, 1981), 260-65.

21. S. Iu. Vitte, *Vospominaniia tsarstvovaniia Nikolaia II* (Berlin, 1922), 1:236.

22. Martin Kilcoyne, "The Political Influence of Rasputin" (Ph.D. diss., University of Washington, 1961), 101.

23. Vitte, *Vospominaniia*, 1:242-43.

24. For Feodosii's canonization, see N. N. Esipov, *Sviatitel' i chudotvorets arkhiepiskop chernigovskii Feodosii uglitskii* (St. Petersburg, 1897).

25. As quoted in S. S. Oldenburg, *Last Tsar: Nicholas II, His Reign and His Russia*, translated by Patrick J. Rollins (Gulf Breeze, Florida: Academic International Press, 1975), 1:59.

26. Ibid., 60.

28. The panagia was given him by Archbishop Leonid (Krasnopevkov), who had a close friendship with the Grand Duke, when Sergei was a boy. See Archbishop Savva, *Vospominaniia o vysokopreosviashchennom Leonide, arkhiepiskope iaroslavskom i rostovskom* (Kharkov, 1877), esp. "Poezdka," 35-42. Sergei's activity in the Holy Land is studied in Theofanis G. Stavrou, *Russian Interests in Palestine, 1882-1914* (Thessaloniki: Institute for Balkan Studies, 1963).

29. Father Demetrios Serfes, compiler, *The Royal Martyr Sisters: Empress Alexandra and Grand Duchess Elizabeth* (n.p., n.d.), passim.

29. *The Secret Letters of the Last Tsar*, edited by Edward J. Bing (New York: Longmans, Green, 1938), 137.

30. For Arsenii, see the valuable but brief information found in Lev Regel'son, *Tragediia russkoi tserkvi, 1917-1945* (Paris: YMCA-Press, 1977), 560-65.

31. E. F. Grekulov, *Tserkov', samoderzhavie, narod (2-ia polovina XIX-nachalo XX v.* (Moscow: Nauka, 1969), 88. A description of the Chudov monastery is *Moskovskii kafedral'nyi chudovskii monastyr'* (Sergieva Lavra, 1896).

32. E. M. Almedingen, *The Empress Alexandra, 1872-1918: A Study* (London: Hutchinson, 1961), 12.

33. Antony Bird, *Empress Alexandra of Russia* (distributed by Heron Books, n.p., n.d.), 41. Bird's account is marred by many fanciful remarks, such as the suggestion that Alexandra's mysticism derived from her being conceived when her mother was undergoing a mental struggle over religion (p. 33).

34. Anna Viroubova, *Memories of the Russian Court* (New York, 1923), 151.

35. Henry D. A. Major, *The Life and Letters of William Boyd Carpenter . . . Bishop of Ripon, Chaplain to Queen Victoria and Clerk of the Closet to Edward VII and George V* (London, 1923), 262. I have also consulted the unpublished letters of Empress Alexandra to William Boyd Carpenter on deposit in the British Library's Department of Manuscripts. His Additional Manuscripts 4671 (ff. 227-48) contain the empress's letters for the period 1894-1915. The author thanks Dr. Dorothea McEwan in London for typing a transcript of the letters for him.

36. Jundt's book is *Les Amis de Dieu au Quatorzième siècle* (Paris, 1879). See especially the conclusions, pp. 343-66.

37. *The Letters of the Tsaritsa to the Tsar, 1914-16* (Stanford: Hoover Institution Press, 1973), 100.

38. For a survey of Boehme's influence in Russia, see Zdenek V. David, "The Influence of Jacob Boehme on Russian Religious Thought," *Slavic Review* 21(March 1962): 43-64; for a list of Alexandra's books dated from those years, see Aleksandr Kiselev, *Pamiat' ikh v rod i rod: to chto nado znat', sokhranit', donesti* (New York: Put' zhizni, 1981), 28-29.

39. *Personal Christianity: The Doctrines of Jacob Boehme*, with an introduction and notes by Franz Hartmann (New York: Frederick Ungar, 1958), 303-4.

40. Ibid., 221.

41. Major, *Life and Letters of Carpenter*, 262.

42. Robert K. Massie, *Nicholas and Alexandra* (New York: Atheneum, 1967), 105.

43. Vitte, *Vospominaniia*, 1:243.

44. The struggle between Witte and Plehve is meticulously studied in Edward H. Judge, *Plehve: Repression and Reform in Imperial Russia, 1902-1904* (Syracuse: Syracuse University Press, 1983), 150-74.

45. Ibid., 166.

46. *PTV*, 1904, no. 8:286.

47. Ibid., no. 10:361-62. Sarov did more than most other monasteries in supporting the subsequent war effort, giving 5,000 rubles for "strengthening the fleet" in the fall of 1904 (*TV*, 1904, no. 40:430); Bishop Innokentii of Tambov sent Nicholas II a portable cathedral pavilion for use by the Russian army operating in the field in the Far East. The cathedral was consecrated in the name of Saint Serafim: "In the coming days of great Christian recollections [i.e., Easter], may it be a source of comfort and joy about Christ the Savior for our Christ-loving army" (*TV*, 1905, no. 13:540).

48. Vitte, *Vospominaniia*, 1:345.

49. *Russkaia pravoslavnaia missiia i pravoslvnaia tserkov' v Iaponii* (St. Petersburg, 1889), 6.

50. Ibid., 7.

51. Ibid., 21-22.

52. "Dvadtsatipiatiletie deiatel'nost' 'Obshchestva rasprostraneniia religiozno-nravstvennago prosveshcheniia v dukhe pravoslavnoi tserkvi,'" *Tserkovnyi golos* 1(1906), no. 16:466.

53. Ibid., 469.

54. *PTV*, 1903, no. 42:1625.

55. I have not been able to identify Akil Kadzim or locate the Japanese copies of his books. The Russian titles were *Novoproslavlennyi sviatoi, prepodobnyi Serafim* and *Prepodobnyi otets nash Serafim, sarovskii chudotvorets.*

56. *TV*, 1904, no. 7:67-68.

57. Ivan Popov, *Poseshchenie goroda Irkutska . . . velikim kniazem Nikolaem Aleksandrovichem* (Irkutsk, 1891), 18-19.

58. Warth, "Before Rasputin," 334-36. See also V. P. Semennikov, ed., *Za kulisami tsarizma (Arkhiv tibetskogo vracha Badmaeva)* (Leningrad, 1925), and R. Edward Glatfelter, "Badmaev," in *The Modern Encyclopedia of Russian and Soviet History*, 2:234-37.

59. Warth, "Before Rasputin," 334.

60. *Rossiia i Kitai* (St. Petersburg: G. P. Pazharov, 1900).

61. Ibid., 16.

62. Ibid., 21.

63. Ibid., 34. Italics in original.

64. *PTV*, 1902, no. 12:426-27.

65. Bishop Serafim (Leonid Chichagov), who organized the canonization ceremony for Serafim of Sarov, also wrote a book on religion and medicine entitled *Chto sluzhit osnovaniem kazhdoi nauki* (Moscow, 1890).

66. See, for example, the solemn meeting of veterans of the Russo-Turkish War, officers still on active duty, sisters of the Red Cross and diplomats from Serbia, Bulgaria, and Romania held in St. Petersburg's SS. Peter and Paul Fortress on April 17, 1902. Nicholas's confessor Father Ianyshev, the military clergy of the capital, and court archpriests performed a special liturgy at the coffin of Tsar Alexander II. *TV*, 1902, no. 17:538.

67. Judge, *Plehve*, 167.

CHAPTER 12

INSTRUCTION OF MUSLIMS

1. V. D. Smirnov, "Po voprosu o shkol'nom obrazovanii inorodtsev-musul'man," *Zhurnal Ministerstva narodnago prosveshcheniia* 222(July 1882): 1.

2. O. Akcokrakli, "Kart Muallim ve Yazicilarimizdan Ismail Gasprinski," *Oku Isleri* 2(June 1925): 7, citing Gasprinskii from an unidentified source.

3. From a meeting of the council, March 26, 1870.

4. The record of this gathering, which is the primary source for this paper, is *Zhurnal soveshchaniia pri Tavricheskoi gubernskoi zemskoi uprave po voprosam obucheniia tatar* (Simferopol: Simferop. tip. Tavr. Gubernsk. Zemstva, 1908; hereafter *Zhurnal*).

5. Tsentral'nyi statisticheskii komitet ministerstva vnutrennykh del, *Raspredelenie naseleniia imperii po glavnym veroispovedaniiam (Po dannym pervoi vseobshchei perepisi 1897 g.)* (St. Petersburg, 1901), 22-23. In the Crimean Peninsula proper, the number of Tatars was 188,576.

6. On Gasprinskii, see the following works by Edward J. Lazzerini: "Ismail Bey Gasprinskii and Muslim Modernism in Russia, 1878-1914" (Ph.D. diss., University of Washington, 1973); "*Gadidism* at the Turn of the Twentieth Century: A View from Within," *Cahiers du monde russe et soviétique* 16(April-June 1975): 245-77; "From Bakhchisarai to Bukhara in 1893: Ismail Bey Gasprinskii's Journey to Central Asia," *Central Asian Survey* 3(1984): 77-88; and "Ismail Bey Gasprinskii, the Discourse of Modernism, and the Russians," in Edward Allworth, ed., *Tatars of the Crimea: Their Struggle for Survival* (Durham: Duke University Press, 1988), 149-69.

7. Ismail Bey Gasprinskii, *Mebadi-yi Temeddu"n-i Islamiyan-i Rus* (Bakhchisarai: Tipografiia Perevodchika, 1901), 4.

8. The fullest discussion in English of these regulations is found in Isabelle Kreindler, "Educational Policies Toward the Eastern Nationalities in Tsarist Russia: A Study of Il'minskii's System" (Ph.D. diss., Columbia University, 1969), 78-88.

9. *Zhurnal*, 3-9 (further page references are in the text).

10. B. B. Veselovskii, *Istoriia zemstva za sorok let*, 4 vols. (St. Petersburg, 1909-11), 1:718, 723.

CHAPTER 13

CRIME, POLICE & MOB JUSTICE IN PETROGRAD

1. For the recent monographs on social aspects of the October Revolution, see Ronald Grigor Suny, "Toward a Social History of the October Revolution," *American Historical Review* 88 (1983): 31-52. In his provocative article, Suny argues that the social history of the October Revolution cannot exist independently of political history. In his opinion, the social history of the revolution "has been more concerned with the movement and movements of social groups and classes than with patterns of fertility or mortality." The task of social historians, he declares, is to examine the deepening social polarization between those at the top (*verkhi*) and those at the bottom (*nizy*) of society, with sufficient attention paid to the political implications.

2. A good example is Rex A. Wade's, *Red Guards and Workers' Militias in the Russian Revolution* (Stanford: Stanford University Press, 1984). This excellent study examines the conflict between the workers' militia and the city militia in Petrograd and the growing radicalization of the working class, accompanied by the rapid development of the Red Guards. Wade's primary approach is precisely what Suny proposes as the only method applicable for social historians of the Russian revolutions: to examine the militia organizations from the point of view of deepening social polarization. In this it is exceptionally successful. But since crime is a nonpolitical issue not directly related to the main focus of social history, it is excluded from Wade's study. This omission is serious in two respects. First, the militia organizations' effectiveness in dealing with crime had an important bearing on the relationship between the workers' militia and the city militia. Second, as I will show in this article, politics had a tendency to be enmeshed with the question of crime. By excluding crime from his range of analysis, therefore, Wade fails to see the extent of politicization of society that affected even what was considered to be nonpolitical areas.

3. In dealing with this question, one is faced with a serious problem of sources. As society began to break down in 1917, the systematic collection of criminal records was seriously disrupted. The highly meticulous statistical data compiled by the Ministry of Justice ceased to be published in 1917. There must be a wealth of material in Soviet archives, but it has not been examined systematically. My request to use archival material was rejected during my stay in the Soviet Union in the early 1980s. We do not have to wait, however, until the Soviet archives become open to have a general picture of crime in Petrograd during the revolution. One source that gives us a clue to the relationship between crime and society is contemporary newspapers, particularly the boulevard newspapers.

Historians have ignored these papers as a serious source of evidence until recently. The boulevard newspapers contain a wealth of information on daily life in Petrograd during these turbulent days in 1917, particularly with regard to crime. Recent works that have imaginatively used these newspapers include: Jeffrey Brooks, *When Russia Learned to Read: Literacy and Popular Literature, 1861-1917* (Princeton: Princeton University Press, 1985); Louise McReynolds, "Images of Crime in the City: Crime Reporting in the St. Petersburg Tabloid *Gazeta-Kopeika*," a paper presented at the AAASS Convention, November 1984, Washington, D.C.; Joan Neuberger, "Hooliganism and the *Mirovoi Sud* in St. Petersburg, 1900-1914" (Ph.D. diss., Stanford University, 1985).

4. In mid-1914, the population of Petrograd and its suburbs was 2,103,000; by the end of 1915 it had risen to 2,347,850. By the beginning of 1917 it was 2,420,000, but after the February Revolution it began to decline. By autumn 1917 it had diminished to 2,300,000. But the most drastic decline occurred only after the October Revolution. By June 1918, it had shrunk to 1,468,000. See Z. G. Frenkel', *Petrograd perioda voiny i revoliutsii: sanitarnye usloviia i kommunal'noe blagoustroistvo* (Petrograd, 1923), 9-13.

Actually, the crime rate, which sharply declined at the outbreak of World War I, began to increase in the second half of 1916. Particularly important was the increase in juvenile crimes. See E. N. Tarnovskii, "Voina i dvizhenie prestupnosti v 1911-1916 gg.," *Sbornik statei po proletarskoi revoliutsii i pravu* (Petrograd, 1918), 100-104; M. N. Garnet, *Revoliutsiia, rost prestupnosti i smertnaia kazn'* (Moscow, 1917), 2.

5. TsGAOR, f. DPOO, d. 341, ch. 57/1917, listy 24, 29; Tsuyoshi Hasegawa, *The February Revolution: Petrograd, 1917* (Seattle: University of Washington Press, 1981), 289.

6. Hasegawa, *The February Revolution*, 287-88.

7. For Iurevich's order, see *Petrogradskaia gazeta* (hereafter *PG*), March 5, 1917. Robberies in the guise of searches were reported in *Petrogradskii listok* (hereafter *PL*), March 5, 16, 17, 21, 26, and 28, April 28, 1917; *PG*, March 8, 19, 1917.

8. *PL*, March 16, 1917.

9. *PL*, April 7, 20, 23, and 25, May 9, 17, 1917.

10. *PL*, April 27, 29, May 10, 17, 18, 19, and 21, June 8, 9, and 17, 1917. "Stolichnye khishchniki," first appeared in *PL* on April 26. According to *Gazeta-Kopeika* (hereafter *GK*), the number of reported thefts and robberies on June 15 was 60.

11. *PL*, July 7, 1917; *GK*, July 6, 11, 1917.

12. *PL*, July 16, 1917; *PG*, July 16, 1917.

13. *PL*, July 28, 1917.

14. *PL*, August 17, 1917; *GK*, August 15, 1917.

15. *GK*, August 30, 1917.

16. For thefts in September see, *GK*, September 2, 6, 7, and 9, 1917; *PL*, September 12, 14, 1917.

17. *PL*, October 1, 14, and 18, 1917; *GK*, October 3, 4, and 8, 1917.

18. *PL*, September 12, 14, 17, 19, 20, and 11; October 4, 1917.

19. Alexander Rabinowitch, *Prelude to Revolution: The Petrograd Bolsheviks and the July Uprising* (Bloomington: Indiana University Press, 1968), 64-66; Michael M. Boll, *The Petrograd Armed Workers' Movement in the February Revolution* (Washington, D.C.: University Press of America, 1979), 146-52.

20. *PL*, April 29, May 7, 20, 21, and 30, 1917.

21. *PG*, April 23, 1917.

22. *PL*, July 20, 21, and 25, August 30, 1917; *PG*, August 6, 17, 1917.

23. *PL*, August 12, 13, 1917.

24. S. A. Smith, *Red Petrograd: Revolution in the Factories, 1917-1918* (Cambridge: Cambridge University Press, 1983), 168-71; David Mandel, *The Petrograd Workers and the Soviet Seizure of Power: From the July Days 1917 to July 1918* (London: Macmillan, 1984), 264-86.

25. Murder statistics reported in *Ves' Peterburg* are as follows:

Year	St. Petersburg	Suburbs
1896	117	10
1899	127	17
1900	178	11
1902	156	16
1903	206	24

These figures were given to the author by Joan Neuberger.

26. *PL*, March 11, 1917; *Rech'*, March 11, 1917.

27. *PL*, April 17, 20, 1917; *PG*, April 18, 1917. Von Schrippen's raid on Zhitovskii's apartment was reported in *GK*, November 4, 16, and 20, 1916.

28. *PL*, May 19, 1917.

29. *PL*, May 25, 1917.

30. *PL*, August 29, 1917.

31. *PL*, August 12, 13, 1917.

32. *PL*, May 3, 1917.

33. *PL*, October 2, 4, 1917.

34. *PL*, July 13, 1917.

35. See Lewis Siegelbaum, "Another Yellow Peril? Chinese Migrants in the Russian Far East and the Russian Reaction before 1917," *Modern Asian Studies* 12 (1978): 307-30; *Vestnik gorodskogo samoupravleniia*, July 4, 1917.

36. *PL*, April 25, May 2, 1917; *PG*, July 26, 1917.

37. *PL*, September 23, 1917.

38. K. I. Globachev, "Pravda russkoi revoliutsii: vospominaniia byvshego nachal'nika Petrogradskogo okhrannogo otdeleniia," manuscript, Bakhmeteff Archives, Columbia University, 131-32.

39. Robert P. Browder and Alexander F. Kerensky, *The Russian Provisional Government 1917: Documents*, 3 vols. (Stanford: Stanford University Press, 1961), 1:199-200.

40. *PL*, March 18, 1917.

41. Globachev, "Pravda russkoi revoliutsii," 117-18.

42. *PL*, April 24, 1917.

43. *PL*, July 28, 1917.

44. *PL*, March 10, 16, 22, and 30, 1917.

45. *PL*, July 26, August 24, 1917; *PG*, July 26, 27, 29, and 31, August 24, 1917; *PG*, July 26, 1917; *GK*, August 5, 8, and 20, 1917.

46. *PL*, July 25, 1917; *GK*, July 25, 1917.

47. Leonard Schapiro, "The Political Thought of the First Russian Provisional Government," in Richard Pipes, ed., *Revolutionary Russia* (Cambridge: Harvard University Press, 1968), 113.

48. Browder and Kerensky, *Provisional Government*, 1:220.

49. For the Temporary Court in Petrograd, see V. Mantushkin, "Vremennye sudy v Petrograde," *Zhurnal Ministerstva iustitsii*, 1917, no. 4:184-92. For the Statutes of the Temporary Court, see ibid., 190-92. For a reaction to the Temporary Court, see *PL*, August 8, 1917.

50. Mantushkin, "Vremennye sudy," 189.

51. *PL*, May 22, 1917.

52. *PL*, May 9, 16, 17, 1917.

53. Browder and Kerensky, *Provisional Government*, 1:205-06.

54. Globachev, "Pravda russkoi revoliutsii," 124.

55. *GK*, August 31, 1917; *PL*, August 31, 1917. For other prison escapes see, *PL*, July 2, August 2, 9, 1917; *GK*, July 27, 1917.

56. See Tsuyoshi Hasegawa, "The Formation of the Militia in the February Revolution: An Aspect of the Origins of Dual Power," *Slavic Review* 32(June 1973): 303-22; Wade, *Red Guards and Workers' Militias*, chaps. 2 and 3.

57. The existence of two competing political principles--the democratic principle and the class principle--and the eventual triumph of the latter are important aspects of the October Revolution not thoroughly examined at either the national or the local level. Valuable suggestions are made, however, in monographs by Rosenberg, Startsev, Raleigh, and Wade. Particularly, Wade describes the contradiction of the working class demand. While insisting on democracy, the workers rejected any all-people body or solution that might result in a nonworking class or nonsocialist majority. This contradiction, Wade insists, presaged a civil war *(Red Guards and Workers' Militias*, 64-65).

58. Ibid., 68.

59. The principle of local self-determination is one of the important aspects of the October Revolution often ignored by historians. This aspect has recently been emphasized by Donald J. Raleigh, *Revolution on the Volga: 1917 in Saratov* (Ithaca: Cornell University Press, 1986).

60. Wade describes the workers' protest against I. G. Tseretelli's attempt to centralize the militia structures *(Red Guards and Workers' Militias*, 124-26). But Tseretelli's attempt provoked equally vigorous protests among the district militia organization under the city militia. On this topic, see *Vestnik gorodskogo samoupravleniia*, July 19, 20, 21, 25, 29, and 30, August 2, 4, 8, 11, and 22, 1917.

61. Z. Kel'son, "Militsiia fevral'skoi revoliutsii," *Byloe* 29 (1925): 163.

62. *PL*, April 1, 7, 1917; *PG*, April 13, 1917.

63. *PL*, October 19, 1917.

64. The city militiamen's demands were discussed in some district soviets and factory committees. See *Raionnye sovety v Petrograde v 1917 godu: protokoly, rezoliutsii, postanaovleniia obshchikh sobranii i zasedanii ispolnitel'nykh komitetov* (hereafter *RSP*), 3 vols. (Moscow and Leningrad, 1964), 2:278; *Fabrichnozavodskie komitety Petrograda v 1917 godu: protokoly* (Moscow, 1917), 456-59, 605.

65. *GK*, September 28, October 5, 7, 1917.

66. *PL*, May 14, 19, 29, and 30, June 2, 1917. For the City Duma's discussion on the city militia, see *PL*, May 11, 1917.

67. *PL*, September 12, 14, 17, 19, 20, and 22, October 4, 1917.

68. *PL*, October 20, 1917.

69. *PL*, April 28, 1917.

70. *PL*, October 19, 1917.

71. Mob justice, or trial by the mob (*samosud*, plural is *samosudy*), was rooted in the Russian criminal tradition. For some examples of *samosudy* in villages, see Valerii Chalidze, *Ugolovnaia Rossiia* (New York: Khronika, 1977), 23-32.

72. *PL*, May 13, 1917.

73. *GK*, June 25, 1917. Also see Garnet, *Revoliutsiia, rost prestupnosti i smertnaia kazn'*, 27-30; A. Askii, "Samosud: Pis'mo ochevidtsa," *Vestnik gorodskogo samoupravleniia*, August 6, 1917.

74. *PL*, August 20, 1917.

75. *GK*, July 9, 1917. Other cases of trials by the mob were reported in *PL*, July 20, 26, August 2, 3, and 10, 1917; *GK*, July 9, August 3, 19, 1917.

76. *PL*, July 16, 1917; *GK*, July 16, 1917.

77. *PG*, July 16, 29, 1917; *PL*, July 16, 1917; *GK*, July 16, 1917.

78. *PL*, October 2, 4, 5, 7, 8, 10, 11, 12, and 17, 1917.

79. *GK*, October 16, 1917.

80. *PL*, July 9, 1917.

81. *GK*, July 14, 1917. Those who left the city were not merely the well-to-do. By fall of 1917 approximately 120,000 had left Petrograd. Frenkel', *Petrograd perioda voiny i revoliutsii*, 13.

82. *RSP*, 1:72; 3:186, 189.

83. Ibid., 1:135.

84. Wade, *Red Guards and Workers' Militias*, 121-32. For the new militia statutes issued by Tseretelli, see *Vestnik gorodskogo samoupravleniia*, July 19, 1917.

85. Wade, *Red Guards and Workers' Militias*, 126-27.

86. *RSP*, 1:225-26.

87. See *RSP*, 1:234-36; 3:120, 338; *Fabrichno-zavodskie komitety Petrograda v 1917 godu* (Moscow, 1979), 390, 450, 491.

CHAPTER 14

DONALD W. TREADGOLD: AN APPRECIATION

1. Nicholas V. Riasanovsky, review of Donald W. Treadgold, *The Great Siberian Migration: Government and Peasant in Resettlement from Emancipation to the First World War*, in *Journal of Central European*

Affairs 18(January 1959): 434-35, and review of *The West in Russia and China: Religious and Secular Thought in Modern Times*, vol. 1: *Russia, 1472-1917*, in *American Historical Review* 79 (February 1974): 192-93.

Encyclopedias. The best place to begin searching for materials on topics discussed in this book is in specialized encyclopedias. Traditionally, encyclopedias list short bibliographies at the end of each article. In English, the most useful are *The Modern Encyclopedia of Russian and Soviet History* (Gulf Breeze: Academic International Press, 1968-), with some fifty-eight volumes already published, and others being published each year; *The Great Soviet Encyclopedia*, which is a translation by Macmillan of the third edition of *Bolshaia sovetskaia entsiklopediia.* See also specialized encyclopedias on Catholicism, Judaism, religion, philosophy, and literature for other useful references.

In Russian, the most useful encyclopedias are *Entsiklopedicheskii slovar* 88 vols. (St. Petersburg and Leipzig, 1890-1906) and its sequel *Novyi entsiklopedicheskii slovar* by the same company, 1906-17. Its last volume had reached the word *Otto* when the Bolshevik Revolution abolished the company. The Granat Brothers publishing company was also publishing an *Entsiklopedicheskii slovar* at the time of the Bolshevik Revolution, but that company survived by hiring V. I. Lenin and others of the new government to write articles on their favorite topics. Although less useful than the other encyclopedias mentioned here, it is worth while. *Sovetskaia istoricheskaia entsiklopediia* is also very useful for bibliographies and, occasionally, maps.

General histories. Full, detailed histories of the period of approximately 1801 to 1917, written in English, are still small in number, despite a prolific annual outpouring of works on the history of Russia and the former Soviet Union. The most monumental studies, which serve well as permanent additions to a personal reference library, are Hugh Seton-Watson, *The Russian Empire, 1801-1917* (Oxford: Clarendon Press, 1967) and Michael T. Florinsky, *Russia: A History and an Interpretation* 2 vols. (New York: Macmillan, 1953). More readable is Sergei Pushkarev, *The Emergence of Modern Russia, 1801-1917*, translated by Robert H. McNeal and Tova Yedlin (Holt, Rinehart, and Winston, 1963). A work now out of print, but available in most academic libraries, that begins with events in 1801 but covers events to 1970, is Edward C. Thaden, *Russia Since 1801:*

The Making of a New Society (New York, London, Sydney, and Toronto: Wiley, 1971).

Longman (London and New York) has virtually completed publication of a series of volumes commissioned in the early 1980s, collectively called The Longman History of Russia, concentrating on designated periods of Russian history. Two volumes cover the period 1801 to 1917: David Saunders, *Russia in the Age of Reaction and Reform, 1801-1881*, and Hans Rogger, *Russia in the Age of Modernisation and Revolution, 1881-1917*.

Sets of documents in English. The largest set of translated documents on topics covered in this book is: George Vernadsky, Ralph T. Fisher, Jr., et al., eds., *A Source Book for Russian History from Early Times to 1917*, 3 vols. (New Haven and London: Yale University Press, 1972).

Collections of essays on the most salient topics of this period are useful. Particularly well researched and presented are: George Katkov, Erwin Oberländer, Nikolaus Poppe and Georg von Rauch, eds., *Russia Enters the Twentieth Century, 1894-1917* (London: Temple Smith, 1971); Robert Nichols and Theofanis Stavrou, eds., *Russia under the last Tsar* (Minneapolis: University of Minnesota Press, 1974); and Cyril E. Black, ed., *The Transformation of Russian Society* (Cambridge: Harvard University Press, 1960), which is still useful though dated.

Religion in Russia. Only within the past two decades has Western scholarship turned away from studying figures of the revolutionary movement to study other topics such as the Russian Orthodox Church. The one exception for many years was John S. Curtiss, *Church and State in Russia: The Last Years of the Empire, 1900-1917* (New York: Columbia University Press, 1940). A recent, useful collection of essays is Robert L. Nichols and Theofanis Stavrou, eds., *Russian Orthodoxy under the Old Regime* (Minneapolis: University of Minnesota Press, 1978).

Gregory Freeze has published two major books and several articles on the Russian Orthodox Church and clergy. The most useful for our purposes here are: *The Parish Clergy in Nineteenth-Century Russia: Crisis, Reform, Counter-Reform* (Princeton: Princeton University Press, 1983); "Handmaiden of the State? The Church in Imperial Russia Reconsidered," *Journal of Ecclesiastical History* 36(1985): 82-102; and "Between Estate and Profession: The Clergy in Imperial Russia," in Michael L. Bush, ed.,

Social Orders and Social Classes in Europe since 1500: Studies in Social Stratification (London and New York: Longman, 1992), 47-65. Theofanis Stavrou's *Russian Interests in Palestine, 1882-1914: A Study of Religious and Educational Enterprise* (Thessaloniki: Institute for Balkan Studies, 1963) is an excellent work on a little known aspect of Russian state and Orthodox Church activities near the end of the tsarist regime.

On other religions, and questions on religion in general in Russia and the Soviet Union, see Donald W. Treadgold, *The West in Russia and China*, 2 vols. (Cambridge: Cambridge University Press, 1973) and Dennis Dunn, ed., *Religion and Modernization in the Soviet Union* (Boulder: Westview Press, 1977).

Leon Arpee, *A History of Armenian Christianity from the Beginning to Our Own Time* (Princeton: The Armenian Missionary Association of America, 1946) is one of the few studies of a non-Orthodox religion in Russia. George Kline, *Religious and Anti-Religious Thought in Russia* (Chicago and London: University of Chicago Press, 1969) and Edmund Heier, *Religious Schism in the Russian Aristocracy, 1860-1900: Radstockism and Pashkovism* (The Hague: Martinus Nijhoff, 1970) are two studies of challenges to Russian Orthodox thought--the first from secularism, the second from Protestantism.

Many major topics on religion in Russia remain unexplored in English. Among these are monasteries, ecclesiastical education, missionary work, and the role of the clergy among the urban poor during the period of rapid industrialization and urbanization.

Educational institutions as disseminators of secular and revolutionary ideas. The following are a sampling of some standard or recent works: Daniel Brower, *Training the Nihilists: Education and Radicalism in Tsarist Russia* (Ithaca: Cornell University Press, 1975); Patrick L. Alston, *Education and the State in Tsarist Russia* (Stanford: Stanford University Press, 1969); Samuel Kassow, *Students, Professors, and the State in Tsarist Russia* (Berkeley and Los Angeles: University of California Press, 1989); James T. Flynn, *The University Reform of Tsar Alexander I, 1802-1835* (Washington, D.C.: Catholic University of America Press, 1988); Priscilla Roosevelt, *Apostle of Liberalism: Timofei Granovsky* (Newtonville, Mass.: Oriental Research Partners, 1986); Ben Eklof, *Russian Peasant Schools: Officialdom, Village Culture, and Popular Pedagogy, 1861-1914* (Berkeley and Los Angeles: University of

California Press, 1986);   Konrad H. Jarausch, ed. *The Transformation of Higher Learning, 1860-1930: Expansion, Diversification, Social Opening, and Professionalization in England, Germany, Russia and the United States* (Chicago: University of Chicago Press, 1983).

Among several books on Russification of the borderlands, the following are especially noteworthy: Edward C. Thaden, ed., *Russification in the Baltic Provinces and Finland, 1855-1914* (Princeton: Princeton University Press, 1981) and Richard Pipes, *The Formation of the Soviet Union: Communism and Nationalism, 1917-1923* (Cambridge: Harvard University Press, 1955).

John Basil is Professor of History at the University of South Carolina in Columbia.

Robert Byrnes is Distinguished Professor of History at Indiana University in Bloomington.

David Davies is Professor of History at the University of Waterloo in Waterloo, Ontario, Canada.

David Goldfrank is Associate Professor of History at Georgetown University in Washington, D.C.

Tsuyoshi Hasegawa is Professor of History at the University of California at Santa Barbara.

William James is Academic Adviser at the U.S. Information Agency in Washington, D.C.

Alan Kimball is Professor of History at the University of Oregon in Eugene.

Edward Lazzerini is Professor of History at the University of New Orleans, Louisiana.

John McErlean is Associate Professor of History at York University in Ontario, Canada.

Robert Nichols is Professor of History at St. Olaf College in Northfield, Minnesota.

Nicholas Riasanovsky is Sidney Hellman Ehrman Professor of European History at the University of California-Berkeley.

Joseph Schiebel was Associate Professor of History and Director of Russian Area Studies at Georgetown University, Washington, D.C., at the time of his death in 1976.

Thomas Sorenson is an attorney in Seattle, Washington.

Charles Timberlake is Professor of History at the University of Missouri in Columbia.

Gary Ulmen is an independent researcher and author in New York City.

INDEX